The Emergence
of Western Political
Thought in the
Latin Middle Ages

The Emergence of Western Political Thought in the Latin Middle Ages

———◦———

VOLUME ONE

*Empty Bottles of Gentilism:
Kingship and the Divine in
Late Antiquity and
the Early Middle Ages
(to 1050)*

VOLUME TWO

*The Mortgage of the Past:
Reshaping the Ancient Political
Inheritance
(1050–1300)*

VOLUME THREE

*The Watershed of Modern Politics:
Law, Virtue, Kingship,
and Consent
(1300–1650)*

Empty Bottles of Gentilism

Kingship and the Divine in Late Antiquity and the Early Middle Ages (to 1050)

FRANCIS OAKLEY

Yale UNIVERSITY PRESS
New Haven and London

Published with assistance from the foundation established in memory of
Calvin Chapin of the Class of 1788, Yale College.

Copyright © 2010 by Francis Oakley.
All rights reserved.
This book may not be reproduced, in whole or in part, including
illustrations, in any form (beyond that copying permitted by
Sections 107 and 108 of the U.S. Copyright Law and except
by reviewers for the public press), without written
permission from the publishers.

Designed by Sonia Shannon.
Set in Filosofia type by Integrated Publishing Solutions.
Printed in the United States of America.

Library of Congress Cataloging-in-Publication Data
Oakley, Francis.
Empty bottles of gentilism : kingship and the divine in late antiquity and the
early Middle Ages (to 1050) / Francis Oakley.
p. cm. — (The emergence of Western political thought in the Latin Middle Ages ; 1)
Includes bibliographical references and index.
ISBN 978-0-300-15538-9 (cloth : alk.paper)
1. Kings and rulers—Europe—History—To 1500. 2. Church and state—
Europe—History—To 1500. 3. Middle Ages. I. Title.
JC375.O34 2010   321'.6—dc22   2009032624

A catalogue record for this book is available from the British Library.

This paper meets the requirements of ANSI/NISO Z39.48–1992
(Permanence of Paper).

10 9 8 7 6 5 4 3 2 1

To
Corpus Christi College
Oxford

If a man could well observe that which is delivered in the histories, concerning the religious rites of the Greeks and Romans, I doubt not but he might find many . . . [of those] . . . old empty bottles of Gentilism, which the doctors of the Roman Church, either by negligence or ambition, have filled up again with the new wine of Christianity, that will not fail in time to break them.

THOMAS HOBBES, *Leviathan,* pt. 4, ch. 45

Contents

General Introduction	ix
Acknowledgments	xiv
Prologue: Kingship and the Long Shadow of the Archaic Past	1

I Prolegomenon: The Cosmic Kingship in Mediterranean Antiquity

1. Historical Orientation:
   Hellenic, Hellenistic, Hebraic, and Roman Antiquity — 13

2. Ancient Affections:
   The Archaic Pattern of Royal Sacrality and the Hellenistic Legacy — 18

3. Abrahamic Departures:
   The Hebraic and Christian Contribution — 40

II The Long Twilight of the Sacral Kingship in Greek and Latin Christendom (c. 300–c. 1050)

4. Historical Orientation:
   The Heirs of Rome — 67

5. Patristic Affirmation:
   The Greek Fathers and the Eusebian Tradition in Christian Rome, Byzantium, and Russia — 79

6. Patristic Reservation:
   The Latin Fathers from Tertullian to Augustine — 111

7. The Early Medieval West (i):
   Sacral Kingship in the Germanic Successor Kingdoms   143
8. The Early Medieval West (ii):
   Fidelity, Consent, and the Emergence of "Feudal" Institutions   177
9. The Early Medieval West (iii):
   The Clerical Order and the Rise of the Papal Monarchy   200

Epilogue   220
Notes   225
Bibliography   265
Index   287

General Introduction

IN THE THREE VOLUMES I plan for this series it is my ambition, let it be confessed, not simply to address, and in adequate depth, the political thinking of the centuries labeled by stubborn historiographical convention as "medieval" but also to effect something of a shift in the perspective from which we characteristically view that body of thought.[1] And, beyond that, to engineer, if I at all can, a modest measure of reshaping in the constitutive narrative that has long served to frame the way in which we understand the full course of Western political thought. No more than implicit, that narrative has served nonetheless to determine the periods to which most attention has usually been paid (classical Greece—or, more accurately, Athens—of the fifth and fourth centuries BCE and western Europe of the sixteenth to the twentieth centuries), to foreground the texts on which students have habitually been encouraged to focus (Plato and Aristotle, Machiavelli, the great contract theorists from Hobbes to Kant, the nineteenth-century Utilitarians, and so on), and to frame the interpretative perspective from which those texts have usually been approached. In that formative narrative, it is fair to say, the medieval contribution has never bulked all that large. Certainly it has never succeeded in finding a place under the bright lights of center stage. Instead, the Middle Ages have characteristically been seen as standing out in the long history of Western political thinking as something of an aberration, as a deviation from the norm, as a period in which the "natural" categories of political thinking were pushed to one side by religious motifs of supernatural bent.

Thus despite a century and more of cumulative endeavor in the fields of cultural anthropology and comparative religion, we continue to hear about "the essentially *secular* unity of life in the classical age" and about the Hellenistic propensity for *introducing* the supernatural into politics. We are still reminded that Christianity made "*purely political* thought impossible," that "the peculiar problem of Church and State," which Christianity introduced, involved "the greatest perturbation which has ever drawn men's thoughts about the state *out of their properly political orbit*," that "Medieval Europe offers *for the first time in history* the paradoxical spectacle of a society trying to organize itself politically on the basis of a spiritual framework," and that it was only with the collapse of the medieval ideal of a Christian commonwealth" that there occurred "*a return to a more purely political* conception of the State."[2] Such was the perspective embedded also in Walter Ullmann's many learned contributions to our understanding of medieval political thinking.[3] Implicit in this view is the assumption that despite all surface differences there is a fundamental continuity between modern political thought and that of the classical world, both periods being committed, presumably, to the "natural" and "secular" modes of analysis proper to "purely political thought."

I would venture to suggest, however, that that way of looking at things is destined to change if one makes the bracing effort to approach and judge the European and Western political experience from the outside as well as the inside and to see it, especially, from the broader perspective afforded by a reflective engagement with the millennial unfolding of universal or world history. In this work, then, it is my endeavor to do precisely that.

Adopt that perspective, of course, and the transition from the archaic and classical (or, indeed, from the world of Celtic and Germanic paganism) to the Christian outlook emerges as a shift, not so much from a secular to a religious viewpoint, as from one ancient and widespread mode of religious consciousness to another and radically different one. In effect, the historical "rhythm" that one finds emerging from the ebb and flow of ideas is not a secular–religious–secular one, but rather, religious–religious–secular. Adopt that perspective, too, and one's attention is inevitably drawn not simply to the marked secularity characteristic of political thinking in the modern era but also to some other of its features that are, historically speaking, really quite singular—namely, its preoccupation with the nation-state and the emphasis it tends to place on the limited, instrumental, "artificial" nature of that state; the intensity of its focus on the problem of political obligation; its reliance on the notion of consent as the principal route to a resolution of that problem; its specific understanding of consent not in collective terms but as a concatenation of individual acts of willing, and, presupposed by that, its bone-deep commitment to the notion of autonomous individuality, and, with it, its marked preoccupation with the vindication of the subjective rights of individuals.[4] These dominant characteristics of modern political thinking are so familiar to us, so much part of the inherited furniture of our minds, that we are habitually tempted, sometimes at the expense of rampant anachronism, to take them utterly for granted as something *natural* to humankind. Seen from world-historical perspective, however, those characteristics stand out instead (and in comparison no less with what we identify as our own ancient past than with the cultural heritage of civilizations other than our own) as marked by great singularity and as calling, accordingly, for a strenuous effort at explanation. Embark upon such an effort, moreover, or so I will be arguing, and one is led ineluctably to focus on the Latin Middle Ages as the intellectual seedbed, in political thinking as in so much else besides, of Western cultural singularity. For it was "the Middle Ages," as Umberto Eco once memorably put it, that "turned us into Western animals."[5]

Hence the overall title of this series, obviously and by intention tendentious. That duly acknowledged, I should concede that it is also inadequately descriptive because in order to achieve my purpose, I have had to transgress, and at both ends, the confines of the period traditionally designated as "medieval." Thus at one end I have been led to reach deep into the ancient past, and at the other to extend my story well into the centuries we are now accustomed to labeling as "early modern." Though it remains immovably embedded in the chronological vocabulary we are forced, willy-nilly, to deploy, the traditional periodization of European history into ancient, medieval, and modern (essentially a Renaissance humanist contrivance) is as much a hindrance as a help when it comes to understanding the course of European and Western intellectual history. It has come across time, indeed, to take on the attributes of a cumbersomely Ptolemaic system, calling for an ever-increasing number of enabling epicycles to remain at all functional. If we must operate within that system, it should be recognized that we do so, perforce, uneasily.

Those to whom it is anathema for a historian to seek from the past answers to questions generated by "presentist concerns" rather than chastely restricting himself to the questions that people in the particular period under scrutiny themselves generated, or who are prone to insisting that the historian *must* derive his notions of what is significant from those of people living in the particular historical period under discussion, may doubtless be inclined to label my admittedly present-oriented approach to the medieval phase in the history of political thought as crassly "presentist" or as mired in some sort of "mythology of prolepsis."[6] While doubtless useful for frightening the children, the charge, however, carries no real intellectual force. Any intellectual history, certainly, that was written in strict conformity with such strictures would be a very odd history indeed. Most such histories, accordingly, will be found to combine, albeit in differing measure, the historian's traditional focus on the historicity of past texts with some orientation also to the concerns and questions generated by the era and circumstances in which the historian is himself doing his writing.[7] And properly so. To attempt to preclude such an approach on the grounds of some forlorn quest for a species of historical "purism" reflects, I believe, a confusion of concerns pertaining to the genuine historicity of the *meanings* we wrest from the documents of the past with those very different concerns that pertain to the *significance* that we ourselves, anchored in the present, attach to such meanings.[8] As Quentin Skinner has properly acknowledged, there is nothing illegitimate about a historian's being "more interested in the retrospective significance of a given historical work or action than in its meaning for the agent himself"—always assuming, of course, that that historian is not tempted to turn judgments about such a work's significance into affirmations about its contents.[9]

In this work, then, my choice of perspective notwithstanding, it is my hope that medieval specialists will find that the texts discussed have been handled with due attention paid to their embedment in the historically specific conditions and circumstances of the era and society in which they were produced. It being my hope, too, that my overall interpretation may conceivably have something useful to say to nonmedievalists whose concerns have focused on the modern phase in the history of political thought, I have attempted to encourage an appreciation of the conditioning specificities of time and place by prefacing each part with brief "Historical Orientations." Their aim is to provide at least the general coordinates needed if the evolving argument is to be situated on the historical map. Readers for whom such historiographic props are redundant need not hesitate to skip those chapters and to move on without delay to engage the unfolding argument in the more substantive chapters that follow them.

In this first volume, which takes the story down to the mid-eleventh century and the run-up to the historic assertion of papal monarchical independence associated with the pontificate of Gregory VII, I focus most intently upon the theme of kingship that was central to the first millennium of the Christian or Common era—its ubiquity worldwide, its rootage in the archaic past, its fundamentally sacred character, and the complex transpositions its supportive ideology underwent at the hands of Jewish, Muslim, and Christian writers, Greek as well as Latin. In 1046, the German emperor Henry III, vindicating his intitulation as vicar of Christ and the supremacy he and his Saxon and Salian predecessors had wielded in matters ecclesiastical, summarily deposed three rival claimants to the papal office and, in subsequent years, went on to appoint three successive popes, all of them German and the last of them, Leo IX, a relative of his. By so doing, he brought the burgeoning movement of ecclesiastical reform to Rome itself. And by so doing he also set in motion, unwittingly and ironically, the forces that were to issue in a frontal challenge to the established regime of "emperor-pontiffs" (of which he himself was so outstanding a representative) and to usher in the markedly different phase in the development of Western political thinking to which I propose to devote the second volume in the series. If in this volume we will see Hobbes's "old empty bottles of Gentilism" being refilled with the new wine of Christianity, in that second volume we will witness the inception of the process that was to lead (as he had predicted) to their eventual breakage.

Acknowledgments

MY ENGAGEMENT as both teacher and scholar with the issues addressed in these volumes is of such long standing that my indebtednesses exceed my ability to remember, let alone acknowledge, all of them. But some debts stand out and call for recognition. For the sabbatical support and research awards or appointments that afforded me the opportunity over the years to spend much-needed time in a whole series of European and American research libraries and rare-book rooms, I must thank the President and Trustees of Williams College, the Social Science Research Council, the American Council of Learned Societies, the National Endowment for the Humanities, the Institute for Advanced Studies, Princeton, the National Humanities Center, North Carolina, the Woodrow Wilson International Center for Scholars and the Folger Shakespeare Library, both in Washington, D.C. For the timely award of the Mellon Emeritus Research Fellowship that encouraged and enabled me to commit in my retirement years to a project of these dimensions I owe a particular debt of gratitude to the Andrew W. Mellon Foundation, New York. For their imagination, insight, tenacity and general good cheer as they wrestled with the challenges posed by such as Eusebius, Augustine, the canonists, Aquinas, John of Paris, Marsiglio of Padua, Locke, Rousseau and the like, I must thank the generations of fine students it was my privilege to teach here at Williams College in my seminars and tutorials in the history of political thought. For his careful reading of the latter chapters of this first volume, I must thank Eric Goldberg, colleague and friend in the Williams History Department. I must also thank my colleagues in the weekly fellows' seminars at the Oakley Center for the Humanities and Social Sciences with whom I was able to share several other chapters and who aided me with their criticism and advice. For her characteristic promptness, accuracy and efficiency in preparing the manuscript for the press, it gives me pleasure to thank once more Donna Chenail, Coordinator of our Faculty Secretarial Office. For permission to incorporate in revised and extended form material drawn from my *Kingship: The Politics of Enchantment* (2006), I must thank Wiley-Blackwell. This volume, the first of a projected series of three, I have taken the liberty of dedicating to the fine, old college which nurtured me as an undergraduate and which has properly retained an abiding purchase on my affections. In so doing, I wish to convey the deep gratitude I feel to my tutors there and at Merton : T. H. Aston, Max Beloff, J. R. L. Highfield, C. H. Wilson and, especially, Michael Brock, whose stimulating teaching and kindly encouragement I have never forgotten.

Williamstown, Massachusetts, October 2009   F.O.

Prologue

Kingship and the Long Shadow of the Archaic Past

IF THE ARCHAIC PAST did indeed cast a long shadow down through the European centuries, it was a shadow cast first across the classical era of the Greek polis and the Roman res publica. For it was a millennial past that stretched back long before that era. So far as what we call the "political" is concerned and if we take within our purview the whole global history of humankind, what I have in mind is a fundamental fact, simple enough in itself but commonly overlooked—namely, that the institution of kingship emerges, in terms no less of its antiquity than of its quasi-ubiquity and wholly extraordinary staying power, as the most common form of government known, worldwide, to man.[1] Similarly long-lived was the ideological pattern that in one form or another had for long millennia sustained that monarchical institution. Characterized by a rich variety of subpatterns woven intricately around some resilient central threads, that ideology can lay strong claim, in terms certainly of its ubiquity and longevity, to having been nothing other than the political *commonsense* of humankind. And, like the institution of kingship itself, that commonsense turns out to have been deeply embedded in the sacred. For "that kings are sacred," it has well been said, is "an anthropological and historical truism."[2]

The roots of kingship and of regal sacrality reach so deeply into the past that they are lost to us in the shadows of prehistory. Some of their seeds have continued to germinate in the stonily disenchanted political soil of the twentieth and twenty-first centuries. But the institution clearly enjoyed its heyday across the world during the extended period stretching from the "Neolithic Revolution" and the spread of agrarian modes of subsistence around the eastern Mediterranean (c. 7500–c. 5000 BCE) down to the early nineteenth century. At that time it came under challenge in the wake of both the French and the Industrial revolutions, the rise to prominence of forms of government based on consent, and the accelerating shift of a growing segment of the world's population from the land and into essentially urbanized modes of occupation. Thus by the beginning of the third millennium BCE when, with the invention of writing, the historiographic shadows begin finally to lift, we find that kingship had long since established itself in the ancient Near East. It had done so in the Nile Valley in Egypt and in the Tigris and Euphrates basin in Mesopotamia, as well as in the flatlands that stretched between them. If in Egypt society appears always to have been organized along monarchical lines, in Mesopotamia the Sumerian kingship had been preceded by more broadly participatory forms of governance centered on temples and sanctuaries. But there, too, kingship was to become the universally dominant system of government. As such it was to leave its imprint also on the modes of rulership characteristic elsewhere of the ancient Near East and, more broadly, on the lands bordering on the eastern Mediterranean—on the Hittite, Syrian, Canaanite, and Minoan kingship of the mid-third to mid-second millennium BCE, as well as on the types of kingship found in Crete and Greece during the Mycenaean era (c. 1600–1100 BCE), in the realms of Israel and Judah during the first half of the following millennium, and in the great Persian empire that occupied a position of hegemony in the Near East between the sixth and fourth centuries BCE.

By the Mycenaean era, altogether independently and at the other end of the world, kingship had already made its appearance on the Chinese mainland. It had done so with the establishment of the Shang dynasty (c. 1500–1027 BCE), and it was destined to attain its classic form a millennium later during the Ch'in and Han periods (225 BCE–222 CE). The following centuries witnessed its appearance or consolidation also in Central Asia, Japan, and Korea, as well as in South and Southeast Asia and Polynesia, in most of which regions it was destined to persist into the nineteenth and even twentieth centuries. During the early medieval centuries, the same was to be true of the Christian kings of western, central, and eastern Europe, successors alike of the Roman emperors and the Celtic and Germanic kings of the pre-Christian era as well as of those kingly rulers who rose to prominence right across the vast reaches of the Muslim world.

Meanwhile, on the other side of the Atlantic, during the centuries labeled in Eurocentric historiography as late antique, medieval, and early modern, the lands of Mesoamerica and South America witnessed the wholly independent emergence of the Olmec, Maya, Toltec, Aztec, and Inca monarchies. Similarly, in sub-Saharan Africa, the "medieval" and subsequent centuries down to the twentieth were punctuated by the rise, persistence, or fall of a myriad of kingdoms, great and small, from that of the Shilluk in the north to that of Swaziland (still extant) in the south, or those of Benin, Kuba, and Yorubaland in the west to those that flourished in Tanzania and Uganda to the east.

The career of kingship as a form of government having been characterized, then, by a wholly singular degree of longevity and ubiquity on the world-historical stage, it is tempting to consign to merely *provincial* status (again, world-historically speaking) the consensual, representative, republican, or democratic forms that bulk so large on our contemporary political landscape, and to which those of us who are concerned with political thought and its history have tended to devote by far the greater part of our attention. Certainly it is hard not to be struck by the fact that the era of the Greek polis and the Roman republic, when seen from this perspective, stands out in bold relief as something of a fleeting episode, a beleaguered island lapped by the waves of an engulfing monarchical sea.[3] And, seen in this way, it is even harder to miss the fact that the *direct* political legacy of Greece to the Roman world and of Rome to the European centuries that followed was in both cases a predominantly monarchical one.

Moved, however, by the long love affair of medieval and Renaissance intellectuals with the classical Greek past as they themselves in their own ages intuited it, the intense preoccupation with that Greek (or, more accurately, *Athenian*) legacy of those who came after was less with the actual practices or conditions of life in the polis (the impact of which on later centuries was, in fact, negligible) than with the exceptional and in some ways unrepresentative views of Plato and Aristotle, philosophers who did their teaching and writing at a time when the great age of the polis was already reaching its term. And, even then, what those great, classical philosophers actually had to say was destined to be refracted for later, modern thinkers by its passage through two successive sets of conceptual lenses. The first, that interposed by the thinking of the Roman (or Romanized) commentators of late antiquity—not least among them Polybius, Plutarch, and (quintessentially) Cicero. The second, that interposed more immediately for us by the highly individualistic political commonsense of West European and North American modernity and by the way in which that affects the very process of translating into our modern languages what it was that Plato and Aristotle had to say.

It is true that the Greeks of the classical era were the first to elaborate what Michael Oakeshott once referred to as "a fully-considered politics," and that in our very political vocabulary and in so many phases of our modern Western political thinking our indebtedness to them is obvious and profound. So obvious, indeed, and so profound that it would be difficult to overstress the degree to which our political thinking is in continuity with theirs. Difficult it may well be, but by no means impossible. On this, as on other matters, our inherited sense of the magnitude of the debt we owe to the Greeks often gets in the way of our seeing them clearly and disposes us to a persistent anachronism in our attempts to understand them. Noting that in "the great days of Victorian scholarship ... when the Classics were recognized as furnishing models for English gentlemen to follow, there was perhaps a tendency to overemphasize similarities and lose sight of differences," and acknowledging the vivifying impact upon classical scholarship made since then by the findings of the anthropologists, W. K. C. Guthrie has warned, "For all the immense debt which Europe ... owe[s] to Greek culture, the Greeks remain in many respects a remarkably *foreign* people, and to get inside their heads requires a real effort, for it means rethinking much that has become part and parcel of our mental equipment so that we carry it about with us unquestioningly and for the most part unconsciously."[4]

Testimony to the latter fact is the continuing willingness of some commentators, moved still by a stubborn sense that "the outlook of the Greeks, particularly of archaic and fifth-century Greeks is nearer to our own than is often thought,"[5] to dispute the comparative "strangeness" of Homer's world.[6] To adopt such a stance is, of course, to challenge the (by now) common set of claims to the effect that "Homer's man experiences himself as a plurality, rather than a unity, with an indistinct boundary,"[7] reflecting, it may be, the survival in the Homeric psychology of an archaic pattern of thought to which a clearly differentiated concept of individual identity was foreign, one that saw, in effect, no strongly defined boundaries between the self and the collectivity to which it belonged.[8] To adopt such a stance is also to brush to one side related but broader claims to the effect that the later world of the Greek polis was still something of a shame culture,[9] one that predicated its moral judgments on conformity with the external norms of behavior embedded in the existing mores of society. A culture, in effect, that lacked a sense of what Charles Taylor has called "reflexive inwardness" and of the notion of the individual will that is presupposed by the modern emphasis in the judgment of action on inward intention and moral responsibility.[10]

I do not believe, however, that such claims can so readily be dismissed. Nor do I believe that we would be wise to resonate to Nietzschian frequencies, with their projection back onto the archaic past of a version of nineteenth-century individualism.[11] Far better to take our stand behind the Hegelian intuition that "the principle of the self-subsistent inherently infinite personality of the individual, the principle of subjective freedom" (which he viewed as "the pivot and center of the difference between antiquity and modern times"), was "historically subsequent to the Greek world."[12]

Few today, I suspect, would wish to deny that the average inhabitant of the Greek polis was conceived (and, like his archaic forebears, somehow intuited himself) less as an individual possessed of a personal history unique to him and standing ultimately alone than as an integral part of the society to which he belonged, deriving therefrom his identity and whatever value he possessed.[13] So far as participation in public life was concerned, and if we take as an illustration Athens, about which we are comparatively well informed, even the members of the small and exclusively male minority that enjoyed the privilege of citizenship did not do so by virtue of their status as individuals. The political society to which they belonged was constituted not by a body or community of individual citizens but by a collection of genes and phratries, groupings based on blood or tribal relationships, whether real or fictitious—or, from the time (507 BCE) of the reforms of Kleisthenes onward, composed of territorial groupings known as *demes*. Those who enjoyed the privilege of citizenship, then, did so not by virtue of any individual status but because of their membership in a demos to which their ancestors had belonged and which was possessed, like the earlier genes or phratries, of its own ancestor or hero cult and of the priesthood that went with it.[14]

But, all of that duly acknowledged, some would still bridle at Hegel's implication that not even the Plato of the *Republic* had succeeded in breaking through to a sense of "reflexive inwardness" or come truly to embrace "the principle of the self-subsistent, inherently infinite personality of the individual." And understandably so. No less than Aristotle, Plato may have been circumscribed in his thinking by the deeply embedded notions of order characteristic of the Greek society of his day, what Voegelin has called "the mortgage" of the polis.[15] But there is still present in the political thinking of both philosophers an element that has no roots in the inherited archaic norms. That element is alien to the theory of the political implicit in the life of the Greek polis, and its *historical* significance is as difficult as it is important to evaluate. For us it is perhaps the most sympathetic strand in the thinking of these men, the strand in which we most readily recognize our own, modern commitments. That being so, we obviously run the risk—in this like the pioneering Hellenists of the late eighteenth and nineteenth centuries[16]—of overemphasizing both its role in the thinking of the two philosophers themselves, as also the extent of its immediate impact on the thinking of those who came after them. Writing well before the emergence of anthropology and comparative religion as distinct academic disciplines, the French historian Fustel de Coulanges was precocious enough to warn his contemporaries about the danger of historical narcissism and had admitted that the Greek philosophers could not easily disengage themselves from the trammels of the archaic way of thinking about matters political. But even he insisted, nonetheless, that "in the midst of all this the new ideas appear. Plato proclaims, with Socrates and the Sophists, that the moral and political guide is in ourselves; that tradition is nothing, that reason must be consulted, and that laws are just only when they conform to human nature." Aristotle, he added, went still further. So, too, did the Cynics and Epicureans, until with the Stoics the individual and the individual conscience were finally emancipated. For as Stoicism "rejects the religion of the city, it rejects also the servitude of the citizen. It no longer desires that the individual man shall be sacrificed to the state. It distinguishes and separates what ought to remain free in man, and frees at last the conscience."[17]

Fustel is probably guilty here of transposing Stoic ideas into a more accommodating modern key.[18] But bracketing that issue and limiting the focus to what he says about Plato, I would insist that what he, like many another, misses is the fact that the moral responsibility and freedom, which in his rendering seems to be ascribed to the individual as such, Plato himself, to whose thinking anything like the Stoic notion of the equality of man was foreign, ascribed to the philosopher alone. And for him, the philosopher was an exceedingly rare figure, the happy coincidence in a single person of innate "virtue" and the right type of education. Having, unlike other men, been able to traverse by the power of reason "the ascent which is rough and steep" and which leads up from the darkness of the cave into the illumination of "the intelligible region," the philosopher will indeed be able to grasp the objective and rational norms or laws in accordance with which men ought to govern themselves and be governed. However corrupt the polis into which he was born, he will also retain within his soul, as an eternal standard after which he can frame his own morality, the beckoning vision of "the city whose home is in the ideal," a pattern of which is "laid up in heaven" but which "can be found nowhere on earth."[19] We have to remember, however, that this does not alter the stubborn fact that for the vast majority of human beings the tissue of laws and customs (*nomoi*) attaching to their own particular political community, however inferior or corrupt it may be, still remains, even for Plato, the moral standard in terms of which they must shape their lives. And it is a sole standard from which there can be no appeal to any higher norm.

The same limitation is even more clearly evident in Aristotle. Nowhere in his *Politics* do we encounter a hint that even the philosopher, not to mention any other citizen, possesses that freedom from the *nomos* of his particular polis which philosophical insight might be expected to confer. Only in the *Nichomachean Ethics* does he teach that for his own fullest spiritual development the philosopher must extricate himself from active involvement in the affairs of the polis—the setting in which alone the majority of men can attain to a good quality of life—and turn to that solitary life of contemplation which is better than the political.[20] Again, only in the *Rhetoric* do we find adumbrated something akin to a doctrine of natural law, an objective moral norm that can afford, though only to the philosopher, some superior "standard of speculative judgment" by which the *nomos* of a political community can be judged.[21]

Ironically enough, then, Fustel's treatment of Plato and Aristotle serves itself to underline the pertinence of his own earlier warning that "we rarely fail to deceive ourselves regarding [the Greeks and Romans] . . . when we see them through the opinions and facts of our own time."[22] And the point can be driven home by way of conclusion via the simple juxtaposition, say, of John Locke's *Second Treatise of Government* even with so "scientific" and seemingly "secular" a work as Aristotle's *Politics*. For the fundamental political vision that informs the latter is vastly different from that presupposed by Locke. Basic to this difference is the fact that Locke's state possesses in its own right no religious or moral dimension. Its very existence, moreover, and the demands it makes on the loyalty of its citizens present for him (as for other modern political philosophers) something of a problem. He begins his political thinking from the standpoint of the autonomous praeter-political individual, free to choose whether or not to engage himself in political life. Only insofar as the state restricts itself to the task of meeting certain limited and specific needs of that individual is the oppressive weight of political authority legitimated.[23]

For Aristotle, on the other hand, this problem of political obligation—the very focal point of early modern and much of modern political philosophizing—simply does not arise. For him, Locke's autonomous individual existing in a pre- or praeter-political state would be "in the position of a solitary advanced piece in a game of draughts," "a poor sort of being, or a being higher than man,"—in effect, "a beast or a god," perhaps, but certainly not truly a man.[24] Only by membership in political society can one become truly human. A political society as restricted in purpose as that envisaged by Locke would not in Aristotelian terms be a true polis at all. For the polis is not simply "an association for residence on a common site, or for the sake of preventing mutual injustice and easing exchange." Its end, instead, is something far nobler than that. It "is not mere life" but "a good quality of life," and "any polis which is truly so called, and is not merely one in name, must devote itself to the end of encouraging goodness."[25] And to say that is to say also that the very purpose of political association is to make possible not only man's physical survival but also his moral and spiritual perfection. Hence the amount of time devoted in the *Politics* to matters "educational" and to the training of the citizen in "virtue." Hence, too, Aristotle's treatment of the priesthood as an integral part of the system of magistracies in the polis and his willingness to discuss in a "political" treatise matters pertaining to the proper disposition of the civic cult. For he acknowledges no real distinction between what we would call the "religious" and the "political."[26]

The note that Aristotle strikes here was characteristic of classical

Greece. And while it has not been altogether without its harmonics in modern political thinking,[27] in that connection the impact of the changed attitudes and conditions of life characteristic of the medieval centuries proved transformative. During these centuries a great ideological gulf opened up between the political views native to the world of the polis and those that, finally and in bold relief, were to rise to prominence in the early modern era. In this respect it is Locke and not Aristotle who informs our modern political thinking. While our political vocabulary continues in large degree to be Hellenic in its provenance, we ascribe to words like "polity," "politics," "political," and so on a far narrower meaning than that possessed by their Greek originals. It is that very fact, indeed, that helps explain the oddly anachronistic accusations of "totalitarianism" levied periodically against the ideal commonwealth whose lineaments Plato evokes in the *Republic,* and even more vehemently against that quasi-theocratic "second-best" commonwealth which he describes in the *Laws.* When we read the former, indeed, we tend instinctively to be taken aback by his insistence that the arts be publicly superintended in the interest of promoting good moral formation and stories and poetry censored in order to expunge passages that misrepresent the gods by portraying them as "the cause of evil" or as beings subject to change. And in the case of the latter, having endured the apocalyptic rigors of twentieth-century political life, it is understandable that we should be chilled by the element of thought control that Plato envisaged, with his provision for a "nocturnal council" of magistrates charged with the task of punishing, by death if need be, any infringement of the law against impiety.[28]

But, then, that deeply felt sensitivity to the liberty of the individual conscience, which over the course of centuries has come to be almost instinctive for us, would have been very foreign, indeed, to Plato. We are prone to distinguishing what is morally right from what is socially expedient and to admitting the possibility of a divergence between what is beneficial to society and what may be good for the individual citizen. With Plato, however, as with Aristotle after him, the very possibility of such a divergence is but rarely envisaged and "the rules which make society possible are identified with the rules which make men good."[29]

Should this strike us as odd or extraordinary, that very fact should alert us to the wisdom, as we embark on the long trip down into the Western centuries, of keeping our interpretative compasses firmly set on the magnetic north constituted by the following fundamental assumptions: that despite the presence in the classical Greek world of some personalities of truly heroic stature, the individual depended almost entirely for his status—perhaps even for his very identity—upon the group to which he belonged; that even the great classical philosophers attained only intermittently to anything more than a tenuous grasp of the notion of individual personality;[30] that the approach to social and political life explicit in Plato and Aristotle and implicit in the life of the Greek polis presupposed a general view of the world and of the nature and destiny of man differing radically from that most characteristic of the later western European tradition; that that classical view, accordingly, is less readily comprehensible in the light of what came *after* than of what went *before,* less in the light, that is, of subsequent Western patterns of thought than in terms of the archaic "mythopoeic" pattern in which its roots were so firmly lodged.

Pursuing that very approach, Mircea Eliade once perceptively remarked of Plato that he "could be regarded as the outstanding philosopher of 'primitive mentality,' that is, as the thinker who succeeded in giving philosophic currency and validity to the modes of life and behavior of archaic humanity."[31] Anyone who has read Plato's great dialogue, the *Timaeus,* in conjunction with the earlier Babylonian *Enûma elish* or the Egyptian *Memphite Theology* (all three of them creation myths embracing a theogony, cosmogony, and anthropogony) would, I suspect, be inclined to agree with that appraisal. Despite the seeming freshness of their vision, the world was already old when Plato and Aristotle came to write. It is from their pre-philosophic forebears, then, from the archaic "mythopoeic" pattern of thinking that we would do well to take our start.

I. Prolegomenon
The Cosmic Kingship in Mediterranean Antiquity

1. Historical Orientation
Hellenic, Hellenistic, Hebraic, and Roman Antiquity

IF BY THE EARLY second millennium BCE a mode of life that we are accustomed to calling "civilized" had been established for centuries in the Indus Valley and Minoan Crete as well as among the Hittites of Asia Minor and the Canaanites of Syria and Palestine, it could already lay claim to a much more ancient, indeed millennial, history in Mesopotamia and Egypt and in scattered urban settlements such as Jericho, where we have evidence for the existence of a walled city dating back as early as the seventh millennium BCE. None of these precocious areas of civilized life, however, escaped the great waves of barbarian invasion that broke upon this whole vast region between about 1700 and 1400 BCE. By the time those waves finally receded, Aryan invaders had destroyed the civilization of the Indus Valley and the Achaeans that of Minoan Crete. But despite episodes of barbarian intrusion and periods of barbarian rule, the traditional cultures of Mesopotamia and Egypt contrived, somehow, to survive and with them the historic role those two regions had long played in the diffusion throughout the eastern Mediterranean of civilized forms of life.

Certainly in the wake of those centuries of turmoil, the erstwhile invaders were either assimilated or had themselves chosen to enter upon a version of the cultural heritage of the ancient Middle East. Egypt and Mesopotamia (the latter now under Assyrian rule) began to recover their former strength, and concurrently a powerful Indo-European Hittite empire rose to prominence in Asia Minor. At the same time, the Achaeans, the first Greek invaders of the Aegean, came themselves to develop a civilized mode of life on the Greek mainland. Their political and cultural sphere pivoted on a group of strongly fortified towns, the most prominent of which was Mycenae. Like Crete, it was the center of a web of maritime commercial enterprise reaching out to embrace the whole eastern Mediterranean and serving to forward the complex process whereby a cosmopolitan *Mediterranean* civilization was eventually to crystallize. But that process was not destined to be completed before the Mycenaeans' dependence on bronze had put them at a significant disadvantage when confronted by yet another great wave of barbarian invasions (1200–1100 BCE) stemming from the neighboring desert peoples to the south and the steppe and mountain dwellers to the east and north. Bronze was expensive to produce and favored accordingly the concentration of military expertise and power in the hands of the aristocratic few. The invaders, however, had mastered the art of producing iron weaponry, which, being much cheaper, enabled them to arm and field as soldiers a much larger proportion of their populations. And that appears to have been enough to give them the military edge when they encountered in battle the noble charioteers of the settled kingdoms and empires.

The eventual outcome was the total destruction of the Hittite empire and of the Mycenaean civilization, as well as the severe weakening of the Egyptian and Assyrian empires. And looking forward now to the political developments that were to transpire among the Greeks of the classical and Hellenistic periods, as well as among the Hebrews of the monarchical age, and which, together, were to do so much to shape the political thinking of western Europe, it is upon the Greeks and Hebrews that we will concentrate.

The invasion of Greece, the Aegean islands, and parts of Asia Minor by the Dorian and Iolian Greek peoples not only brought about the final collapse of Mycenaean society, driving some of the population to seek refuge in Asia Minor, but also ushered in what is, historiographically speaking at least, something of a "Dark Age" that was to extend down to the ninth century BCE. During that period, however, in the refugee communities scattered along the coast of Asia Minor (regions later to be called Doria and Aeolia), the foundations were laid for the mode of life that was later to flourish in the poleis or city-states of classical Greece. In Greece itself the development of the polis proceeded at a slower pace, but by the eighth century BCE, and prior to the outward movement that was to seed Greek colonies throughout the Aegean and along the Mediterranean and Black

Sea coasts, new forms of government had evolved and the power of the kings of old was coming to be replaced by regimes of aristocratic stamp.

The fifth and fourth centuries BCE were to constitute the heyday of the polis, with Athens and Sparta being the most prominent among them and the ones about which we today are best informed. So much so, indeed, that we are tempted to overlook the fact that the institution of kingship had not been banished entirely from the Greek world. It was Philip, king of Macedonia, after all, who in 338 brought to a definitive closure the comparatively brief classic era of the polis when he succeeded in extending Macedonian power throughout the heartland of Greece and put an end to Athenian independence. With the subsequent expansionary expeditions of his son, Alexander the Great (d. 323 BCE), Macedonian power was extended to embrace the erstwhile Persian empire, Mesopotamia, and Egypt, bringing into existence a vast cosmopolitan empire centered on the eastern Mediterranean but extending far beyond. As a result, the *direct* governmental legacy of Greece to those who were later drawn into its cultural orbit was to be monarchical rather than republican in nature. Even the Roman republic, as it rose to hegemony in the Mediterranean world during the second and first centuries BCE and became subject to increasing Hellenization, was to enter into the monarchical legacy of Alexander's empire and its successor kingdoms and became itself an empire. Though successfully clothed at first in some of the constitutional forms of the revered republican past, that empire was destined, after the devastating years of military anarchy in the third century CE, to be transformed by the emperors Diocletian (284–305) and Constantine (306–37) into an outright military despotism. Having embraced the ideological legacy of Hellenistic kingship and adopted the imposing regalia (crown, scepter) and exotic ceremonial of the Persian royal court, the later Roman emperors, then, ruled their far-flung imperial territories as sacred figures distant and mysterious, styled no longer as "first citizen" (*princeps*) but simply, and more accurately, as "lord" (*dominus*).

With Constantine's establishment at Byzantium of what was to develop into a dazzling new imperial capital in the East, and when Diocletian's practice of dividing up the responsibilities of rulership among two or more imperial colleagues ceased finally to be an intermittent one, the stage was set for the political developments that were to characterize the medieval centuries. After the emperor Theodosius died in 395, his two sons divided the empire into two parts, eastern and western, which were largely independent of one another and whose histories were destined increasingly to diverge. If imperial unity survived for a while, it did so increasingly as little more than a beckoning fiction.

The Roman empire of the East was to endure down to 1453, almost a millennium after the disintegration of its western counterpart. In that year, the last Byzantine emperor, Constantine XI, met his death as a warrior fighting in a forlorn attempt to stave off the conquest of Constantinople by the Ottoman Turks. In much greater degree than its western counterpart, the Eastern empire was eloquent witness to the enduring vitality of the cultural and intellectual legacy bequeathed by Greek antiquity to the Roman world. But in common with its erstwhile western counterpart and the Germanic successor kingdoms that replaced it, the Eastern empire was also witness to the transformative power of the legacy that Hebrew antiquity handed down to Christian East and West alike.

The wave of barbarian invasions that had destroyed both the Hittite empire to the east and the Mycenaean civilization to the north had had a less devastating impact on the great empires and culture bearers of the south. But it had left Egypt and the Assyrian rulers of Mesopotamia in a momentarily weakened condition. As a result, conditions had been ripe in Canaan or southern Syria for the emergence of an array of petty independent states or kingdoms, among them that of the Hebrews, a semi-nomadic pastoral people who in the twelfth century BCE had begun to infiltrate into Canaan from the bordering desert region and to settle among the agrarian people long since established there. By the eleventh century, the strength of their presence had become such as to lead them into a bitter struggle for control of Canaan with the seafaring Philistines, marauding invaders from Mycaenae who had established themselves in city-states along the Mediterranean coast in the vicinity of what is today referred to as the Gaza Strip. And though various internal developments may also have played their part, it was by way of response to the demand for heightened organization and cooperation evoked by that great struggle with the Philistines that the Hebrews were led to abandon their nomadic traditions of tribal independence and, under two successive warrior leaders—Saul and David—and in imitation of the practices of the surrounding peoples, to accept a form of kingship.

During the long reign of Solomon (c. 961–c. 922), David's son and immediate successor, an attempt appears to have been made to develop the Hebrew kingdom, now pivoting on the fixed cultic center of Jerusalem, into something more closely akin to a sacred despotism of the traditionally Mesopotamian type. But that attempt ultimately failed, and to the united or confederated kingdom succeeded upon Solomon's death two smaller entities—the kingdom of Israel (or Ephraim) to the north, with its capital and cultic center at Samaria, and that of Judah to the south, centered still on Jerusalem. The subsequent revival of Assyrian power meant that the days of both kingdoms would be numbered. In 722 BCE the Assyrians conquered Israel. In 586/7 BCE their Chaldean or neo-Babylonian successors destroyed Judah, deporting many among its more substantial citizenry to Babylon. There they lived in exile until the advent of a newly consolidated Persian imperial power in 538 BCE released them from their bondage and gave them the option of returning to Judah. They survived the exile as a distinct (and distinctive) people and one that was later to prove capable of surviving also the dispersion that followed the Roman destruction of the Temple at Jerusalem in 70 CE and, with it, the ancient tradition of priestly led Temple worship. And, a matter of great historic moment, their survival as a distinctive people ensured the handing down to Christian no less than Jewish posterity of the remarkable (if disparate) collection of narratives, laws, poems, prophecies, and meditations that together constitute the Jewish Bible/Christian Old Testament.

In the context of the ancient Mediterranean world at large, all of this amounted in fact to very small beer indeed. That in the context of a history of political thought there is need to devote any space at all to the Israelite kingdoms speaks less to their intrinsic political importance or the significance of their essentially provincial secular histories than to the powerfully formative influence that the biblical rendering of their religious beliefs, hopes, and yearnings (as it was mediated especially through their Christian successors) was destined to exert over European and Western modes of life and thought. In a profound sense that is true in relation to the history of no other people in the ancient Near East, our own history in the West is continuous with the history of the Hebrews—or, rather, with their own retroactive and providentialist understanding of their remarkable odyssey through time. So much so, indeed, traditional historiographic practice notwithstanding, that the history of Western political thought is not fully comprehensible unless we make a conscious effort to come to terms with that singular fact. Such an effort, then, it will be our purpose to make in the chapters immediately following.

2. Ancient Affections
The Archaic Pattern of Royal Sacrality and the Hellenistic Legacy

IF KINGSHIP AND ITS embedment in the sacred has had an almost universal and certainly millennial history extending from deep antiquity to the very recent past, it was in the ancient Near East that it made its first appearance in the historical record. And while the features characteristic of sacral monarchy in the ancient Near East have many striking parallels among the forms of kingship that arose later on and wholly independently in other widely separated parts of the world,[1] it is from its beginnings in Egypt and Mesopotamia that we must take our departure here. For it was from those beginnings that it was destined to exert a profound influence over the forms of rulership that emerged in the Mediterranean world as well as in its bordering territories. It was also destined to leave an enduring imprint on the political life of the Byzantine East and of Russia, of the neighboring Muslim world, and of the Latin West. We begin, then, with kingship in Egypt and Mesopotamia and with the cosmic religiosity in which it participated and of which it was an historic manifestation.

The Sacral Kingship: Egypt, Mesopotamia, and the Near Eastern and Mediterranean Diaspora

If, for shorthand purposes, one may be permitted to use terms like "primitive," "premodern," and "archaic" to refer to a type of mentality that persisted in some parts of the world into the nineteenth and twentieth centuries, then it may be asserted that at the heart of primitive or archaic "politics" lay one or another form of what I will again for shorthand purposes call "cosmic religion."[2] So much so, indeed, that for the greater part of human history it is an egregious anachronism even to make use of the words "politics" and "religion," the very definitions of which presuppose our modern Western distinction between the religious and the political and inevitably evoke misleading intimations of the modern church-state dialectic. This becomes entirely transparent when one approaches archaic notions of kingship, which was conceived in China, Africa, and Mesoamerica, no less than in the ancient Near East and elsewhere, as an institution "anchored in the cosmos."[3] "If we refer to kingship as a political institution," Henri Frankfort has said, "We assume a point of view which would have been incomprehensible to the ancients. We imply that the human polity can be considered in itself. The ancients, however, experienced human life as part of a widely spreading network of connections which reached beyond the local and national communities into the hidden depths of nature and the powers that rule nature. The purely secular—insofar as it could be granted to exist at all—was the purely trivial. Whatever was significant was imbedded in the life of the cosmos, and it was precisely the king's function to maintain the harmony of that integration."[4] Frankfort speaks here with explicit reference to the ancient Near East, but his formulation is particularly valuable because it refers not only to the state of affairs in Egypt and Mesopotamia alike and during the full range of their millennial histories but also (its rich variety notwithstanding) to the fundamentally sacral nature of kingship worldwide and to the depth of its rootage in the cosmic religiosity. Despite the successive geologic deposits of Taoist, Confucian, and Buddhist patterns of thought, it is the Chinese empire, indeed, that proved to be the most stable and enduring manifestation of that phenomenon. Manifestation, that is, of what has been called the "ontocratic state" or state as "the embodiment of the cosmic totality," with the emperor "identified with the cosmic center, which was also the place of the ancestors."[5] For two millennia and more, and in this independently of analogous developments elsewhere in Eurasia and Mesoamerica, it remained the emperor's duty as Son of Heaven and possessor of the mysterious "mandate of Heaven" to bridge the gulf between heaven and earth and, by scrupulously performing a cyclic round of rituals and sacrifices geared to significant calendric moments, to secure the maintenance of order, cosmic no less than mundane, natural no less than societal. The structure of the altars of earth and heaven to the north and south of the imperial palace at Beijing, at which until 1912 the emperor offered sacrifice on the occasion of the summer and winter solstices, respectively, was "meant to indicate the cosmic totality at the center of which the emperor dwells as the all commanding axis [mundi] on which both the order of the universe and that of all society and the state depend."[6]

To those of us nurtured, intellectually speaking, in the disenchanted cradle of Westernizing modernity and habituated, accordingly, to thinking of causality in mechanical, impersonal terms, such practices, and the modalities of thought that lay behind them, must necessarily seem profoundly alien. Peoples, however, who participated in the archaic or premodern mentality seem characteristically to have attempted to penetrate the all-encompassing mystery of being—not along a strictly causal axis of explanation but rather in essentially symbolic, analogical, or associative terms. They intuited themselves, in effect, as actors in what has well been called an ongoing "drama of being"[7] and participants in a richly variegated community that reached out from their fellow human beings to encompass the world of nature and its countless nonhuman denizens as well as the not wholly distinguishable but more enduring realm of the divine. And they appear instinctively to have been moved, in ways that we are not, by the explanatory power of symbols and analogy. The mainspring of their acts, thoughts, and feelings was the conviction that the divine was immanent in nature and nature intimately connected with society.[8] And it was a point of view that was later to receive a more nuanced and philosophical expression at the hands of Plato in his enormously influential dialogue *Timaeus*.

In that work Plato makes it clear that he viewed the cosmos as itself divine, "a living creature with soul and reason," with the order of that divine macrocosm providing the intelligible pattern in which the analogous order of the individual human soul participated.[9] In the *Republic,* Cornford points out, Plato "had dwelt on the structural analogy between the state and the individual human soul. Now [in the *Timaeus*] Plato intends to base his conception of human life, both for the individual soul and for society, on the inexpugnable foundation of the order of the universe. The parallel of macrocosm and microcosm runs through the whole discourse."[10]

The archaic mentality that lay behind such philosophic views appears in its origins to have been much more thoroughly monistic in sensibility than was Plato's.[11] Indeed, the degree of consubstantiality of the entities that composed the extended community of being was such that it tended to marginalize any distinction or separateness of substance among them. As a result, the sharp distinctions we are accustomed to make between nature and supernature; between nature, society, and man; between animate and inanimate—these were almost entirely lacking. Archaic man was encompassed by darkness, mystery, and a natural world that he appears to have apprehended almost instinctively in terms of his own psyche. "In the significant moments of his life," it was been said, "he was confronted not by an inanimate and impersonal nature—not by an 'It' but by a Thou.'"[12] Nature, then, was alive; it was, as the classical world was later to put it, "full of Jupiter" or "full of gods"; it expressed, both in its benign cyclical rhythms and in its intimidating and catastrophic upheavals, the movements and indwelling of the divine. That being the case, it should come as no surprise that man himself should be conceived less as an individual standing ultimately alone than as an integrated part of society, deriving therefrom whatever value he possessed. Hardly surprising, either, is the fact that political society should in turn be conceived as embedded in nature, as entangled intimately with the processes of the natural world. Hardly surprising, again, that its primary function should be conceived as something that exceeded the powers of any individual—namely, the preservation of the cosmic order by a complex system of ritual and taboo, the prevention of natural catastrophes, the seasonal regeneration of the world via the ritual elaboration of New Year's festivals and the "harmonious integration" of humankind with nature. And, that is to say, nature being itself a "manifestation of the divine," the *primary* function of society (the family, the tribe, the kingdom), the first object of its anxious, daily solicitude, was what *we*, again, would call "the religious."

What was involved, however, was a specific form of religiosity typical of which was the symbolization of our familiar "profane" space and time via the analogy of the all-embracing spatial and temporal order of the cosmos itself, to which it was characteristically related as microcosm to macrocosm. To that cosmic order, to the repetitive movements of the heavenly bodies and the cyclic rhythms of vegetative nature, the forms, laws, and procedures of terrestrial political society were, then, intuited as analogous.[13] So far, indeed, as mundane objects in the external world and human actions alike were concerned, they were understood as deriving whatever value they possessed from their participation in the celestial archetypes and forms of "reality" that transcended them. This was quintessentially the case with such terrestrial structures as temples, royal palaces, cities even, which were regarded as having been fashioned on the model of cosmic or celestial prototypes. So constituted, they were often assimilated, ideologically speaking, to the cosmic mountain that was understood to have emerged from the primordial waters at the creative moment when a god or gods had rescued cosmos from chaos. They were understood, moreover, to be situated at the very *axis mundi*, the hub, center, or navel (*omphalos*) of the world, the numinous intersection of heaven and earth and the point of contact with the gods. In Mesoamerican (Maya) terms, it was the portal of the Otherworld;[14] in Mesopotamian terms, the "gate of the gods." That, after all, is what the name Babylon (Bāb-ilāni) itself means,[15] and the ziggurats of Mesopotamia no less than the pyramids of Egypt, Mesoamerica, and parts of Africa symbolize the primal cosmic mountain and represent the numinous *axis mundi*.

In this respect, the acts of human beings bear some resemblance to the terrestrial structures they erect. "Just as profane space is abolished by the symbolism of the Center, which projects any temple, palace, or building into the same point of mythical space," Mircea Eliade has said, "so [too] any meaningful act performed by archaic man, any real act, i.e., any repetition of any archetypal gesture, suspends duration, abolishes profane time, and participates in mythical time."[16] The New Year festivals of the ancient Near East exemplify this phenomenon particularly well. Such festivals characteristically involved a dramatic ritual in which the king, as earthly representative or son of the creating god, was understood not merely to *memorialize* the primordial creative act, the establishment of cosmos and the defeat of the anomic forces of chaos, but also in some profound sense to *reactualize* that great cosmogonic moment.[17] For it was the king who, as himself a divinity or quasi-divinity (e.g., Japan, Mesoamerica, Egypt) or as son or earthly representative of the divinity (e.g., Mesopotamia, China, and many an African kingdom), was burdened with the responsibility for ensuring by a ceaseless round of ritual and sacrifice the good order, not merely of human society but of the cosmos at large in which human society was so deeply embedded. That that burden sometimes weighed heavily on them is attested to by the report that even in the first half of the twentieth century the Oné (or priest-king) of Ife in Nigeria was "known to object to the abolition of certain sacrifices on the ground that they were necessary not merely for Ife but for the world and that their interruption might have a disastrous impact on the universal course of nature."[18]

Such, their great variety notwithstanding, was the pattern of religiosity that lay behind so many of the kingships that rose and fell in the ancient Near East, including that of the Indo-European Hittites in the second millennium BCE and that of the Persians which rose to prominence in the mid-first millennium BCE.[19] But its priority in time, its extraordinary millennial endurance, and the influence it came to exercise over the understanding of rulership throughout the eastern Mediterranean—all of these call for a particular focus on the history of kingship as it emerged in Egypt and Mesopotamia.[20]

Two easily identifiable dangers, it should be acknowledged, lie in wait for any nonspecialist who takes the liberty of intruding upon this enticingly rich but dauntingly complex stretch of history. First, that of attributing to institutions and ideologies possessed of nothing less than millennial careers some sort of "timeless" quality and of retrojecting later, highly developed forms into their related but more inchoate predecessors. The insensible transformation of institutions and ideologies from within, the repeated waves of invasion from without; in Egypt the seemingly stately progression of successive dynasties punctuated, however, by intermediate periods of chaos and confusion; in Mesopotamia, the bewildering succession of Sumerian, Akkadian, Kassite, Hurrian, Assyrian, Chaldean (or neo-Babylonian) rulers—clearly a great deal of change must inevitably have occurred under the carapace of institutional and ideological forms that from millennial distance can all too easily seem static and timeless. And the second danger is that of being led by the obvious commonalities of pattern between the kingships of Egypt and Mesopotamia to overlook the real differences that distinguished one from the other.

In relation to the first of these interpretative pitfalls, let me simply acknowledge that such shifts and developments obviously did take place and that what little I am able to say here will apply most accurately, so far as Egypt is concerned, to the pharaohs of the Old Kingdom (2575–2134 BCE) and, so far as Mesopotamia is concerned, to the period of the Assyrian and Chaldean or neo-Babylonian empires (c. 1300–539 BCE). At the same time, it is also important to recognize that one of the most striking features of these two ancient civilizations is in fact the remarkable degree of continuity, stability, and uniformity they both contrived to manifest across the *longue durée* of their millennial histories. During that whole span of time they both cherished and handed down patterns of thought that dated back millennia: in Mesopotamia an ideological framework of essentially archaic Sumerian provenance, in Egypt a cluster of fundamental belief structures whose origins can be traced back to the rulers of the fourth millennium BCE, a period marked by the union and consolidation of the "two lands" of Upper and Lower Egypt.

In relation to the second of these interpretative dangers, let me indicate that I incline less to Engnell's evocation, with reference to sacral kingship in Egypt and Mesopotamia (and, indeed, throughout the ancient Near East), of an "organic" or "uniform" culture, than to Frankfort's insistence (real commonalities notwithstanding) on the existence of important differences, especially between the two instances of sacral kingship with which we are concerned here.[21] Fundamental differences between the two kingships certainly did exist. Among Egyptologists there is unanimity about the attribution of divine status to the pharaoh after his death when, as we can see in the so-called Pyramid Texts dating back to the Old Kingdom, the gods greet him with the words:

> Thou art (king) with thy father Atum
> Thou art high with thy father Atum;
> Thou appearest with thy father Atum,
> Distress disappears,

And when it is declared:

> He lives, king of Upper and Lower Egypt
>   beloved of Ré, living forever.[22]

Unanimity crumbles, however, when it comes to the question of the extent to which divinity was ascribed to the living pharaoh or that of the precise nature of the divinity being thus ascribed.[23] But whatever the case with the earlier dynasties, by the time of the New Kingdom (1520–1165 BCE), the cult of the living pharaoh and the emphasis on his divinity had become unmistakable. From the reign of Amen-em-het III (c. 1840–1790 BCE, at the end of the Middle Kingdom) comes a poem urging the worship of "King Ni-maat-Re living forever," for

> He is Ré [the sun god] by whose beams one sees.
> He is the one who illumines the Two Lands more than the
>   sun-disc,

He is the one who makes the land greener than does a high Nile,
For he has filled the Two Lands with strength and life.[24]

And from an inscription on the tomb of Rekhmire, vizier of Thutmose III (c. 1490–1336 BCE, early in the New Kingdom) has come down to us a classic definition of the Egyptian kingship and one that may be said to reflect enduring Egyptian attitudes toward their rulers. "What is the King of Upper and Lower Egypt?" it is asked. And the answer: "He is a god by whose dealings one lives, the father and mother of all men, alone by himself without an equal."[25] The king was seen, in effect, as a god incarnate whose coronation, as Frankfort put it, was not merely "an apotheosis" but rather "an epiphany."[26]

In some profound sense, then, the Egyptian kingship was apprehended not simply as sacred but also as participating in the divine. It was embedded eternally in the sacred order dating back to the very creation of the universe. The ascent of a pharaoh to the throne involved a reactualization of that cosmogonic moment. Just as his dead father was identified with the god Osiris, the reigning king was seen as the living incorporation of the sky god Horus and (at least by the latter years of the Old Kingdom) viewed also as the "Son of Ré," that is, the royal successor to the sun god. In the words of a hymn (or letter) to the pharaoh Mernephtah

Thou sun of mankind, that banishes the darkness from Egypt.
Thou art like thy father Ré, who arises in the firmament.
Thy beams enter (even) into a cavern, and there is no place devoid
 of thy beauty.[27]

The king's exalted status was such that it precluded any direct approach to his person or even any direct reference to him. To circumvent the latter, recourse had to be had to all sorts of circumlocutions, prominent among them the one from which our word "pharaoh" derives—namely, *per–áa* or "the Great House." This was used to refer to the king in a manner somewhat similar to our own use of locutions like "the Elysée," "Buckingham Palace," or "the White House."

The contrast with Mesopotamia is clear enough. There the institution of kingship had been forged during the third millennium BCE in the crucible of internecine conflict among a congeries of city-states centered on temples or sanctuaries. There the king, or *lugal*, was viewed as no more than a man. He was, nevertheless, a very "great man" (the literal meaning of the Sumerian word *lugal*), "the creation of the fingers of the god," a priestly figure, no incarnation of the gods, admittedly, but representative of them, responsible as intermediary to them, and wielding an authority that they were understood to have delegated to him. As it is said in the preamble to the Code of Hammurabi (1728–1686 BCE), the gods "Anum and Enlil named me to promote the welfare of the people, me, Hammurabi, the devout, god-fearing prince, to cause justice to prevail in the land, to destroy the wicked and the evil that the strong might not oppress the weak, to rise like a sun over the black-headed (people), and to light up the land."[28]

As was, of course, the case with Egypt, the Mesopotamian realm disposed of a complex and sophisticated set of institutions—legal, judicial, administrative, bureaucratic, military, and priestly. All of these institutions reflected an extensive delegation of functions and authority to subordinate officials, with the institution of the palace growing in importance across time in Mesopotamia, just as did the offices of *tjaty* (or vizier) and *nomarch* (or provincial governor) in Egypt. In both countries all these officials were subordinated ultimately to the king whose powers in Mesopotamia, however extensive, were not quite so all-embracing as those of the Egyptian pharaoh. In both countries, kings were often depicted as great warriors, heroic and triumphant leaders in battle, and we know some of them, certainly, actually embraced that role. But if we are to understand the nature of kingship here as so often elsewhere, it is important to realize that the most frequent (and in the view of the day) significant battles in which the kings were called to take part were symbolic rather than military in nature, ritual battles of cosmogonic import. For whatever the differences between the two monarchies, both were characteristically taken to symbolize the order of human society by analogy with the order of the cosmos. Both, that is to say, were underpinned by the enduring adhesion of their peoples to styles or variants of the cosmic religiosity.

In both realms, accordingly, the most important responsibilities of the king extended far beyond what we today would classify as "the political." Both, in effect, were viewed as the "shepherds" or "good shepherds" of their peoples—one of the oldest of royal titles that was adopted later by the Persian kings and applied also to the Greek kings, Homeric and Hellenistic alike. We read that in Egypt the pharaoh Amenhotep III (c. 1398–1344 BCE) strove to make the country flourish as in primeval times by the designs of *maat* (a word usually rendered as "truth" or "right order"). But when we render it in that way, we have to realize that what *maat* denoted was not simply truth in the realm of understanding or justice in the societal realm but also (and, sometimes, rather) the order or "inherent structure of the cosmos, of which justice is an integral part." *Maat* was personified as "a goddess," the daughter "of the sun-god Re whose regular circuit is the most striking manifestation of ... [that] established cosmic order."[29] The rotation of the seasons, the annual rise of the Nile, the reinvigoration of the soil and the abundance of the crops which that ensured—all were understood to depend on the pharaoh's faithful discharge of his ritual responsibilities. Playing a central role, either in person or by priestly substitute, at all the major agrarian rituals, he was "the god who brought fertility to Egypt," in one such ritual encircling a field repeatedly in order to do precisely that. Similarly, he controlled the waters on which fertility depended. "The Nile is at his service," it was said, "and he opens its caverns to give life to Egypt." At the pharaoh's specific command, then, committed to writing and cast upon its waters, the Nile began each year to rise.[30]

Given the (comparatively) less exalted status that they enjoyed and the less predictable and frequently hostile natural environment in which they lived, their Mesopotamian counterparts experienced a greater anxiety in their efforts to discharge the similar responsibilities that they were called upon to shoulder. For these kings, the link between their royal person and the fertility of the land was still a direct one; it stemmed not from their divinity but from the success with which they discharged the task of looking after the gods on behalf of their people. This they did by wending their way through a formidable cycle of cult festivals, rites, and offerings, one of the oldest of them being a fertility rite. Linked with the accession of a new king, and in this paralleling similar rites in many other parts of the world, it involved a *hieros gamos*, a sacred coupling of king and priestess who took the roles, respectively, of the shepherd-god Dumuzi Tammuz and the fertility goddess Inanna-Ishtar. What was involved was a marriage, in effect, "of the creative powers of spring," and through this "willed act of man is achieved a divine union wherein is the all-pervading, life-giving re-creative potency upon which depends, as our texts tell us, 'the life of all lands' and also the steady flow of days, the renewal of the new moon throughout the year."[31]

In addition to building enormous pyramids as funerary sites, the Egyptians characteristically situated the holy of holies of their temples in a high place that was raised above the entrance. For similar reasons, the Sumerians and their successors often built their temples on imposing ziggurats or artificial mountains. In so doing, both peoples, like the pyramid and temple builders of Mesoamerica, were echoing the symbolism of the cosmic or primeval mountain, which at the moment of creation was believed to have emerged from the waters of chaos to become the center of the world.[32] And it was the precise purpose of some of the most striking of the rites in which Egyptian and Mesopotamia kings alike were called upon to play a central role to "reactualize" that cosmogonic moment.

Thus, in Egypt, the creation was ascribed to various gods but quintessentially to the sun god Ré. And the latter, before the creation of the primeval or cosmic mountain that was to function as the earth's very center, could be quoted as having said: "Only after I came into being did all that was created come into being.... I found no place where I could stand." "The analogy with Re," Frankfort notes, "is stressed especially at the coronation [of the pharaoh], which can be regarded as the creation of a new epoch,... a situation, therefore, which partakes of the quality of the creation of the universe."[33] In Mesopotamia, similarly, the king, performing for his people a rite of atonement, played a central role in the protracted New Year's Festival celebrated at Babylon. On that occasion and in that city—the "gate," after all, "of the gods"—the king's sacred marriage with Inanna-Ishtar was celebrated. On that occasion, too, was solemnly recited and in its entirety the great Babylonian creation myth, the *Enûma elish,* an almost complete (though much revised) Akkadian text of which has come down to us from the mid-second millennium BCE.[34] The festival evoked, therefore, the analogy between the creation and the renewal or "re-creation," which each New Year involved, and solemnly "reactualized" the cosmogonic struggle between cosmic order and primordial chaos, this last rendered as the victory of the valiant king-god Marduk over "raging Tiamat," the terrifying sea monster who represented the primordial watery chaos.[35]

It is striking testimony to the enduring power that such primordial creation myths should continue to exercise over the minds and imaginations of other (and later) peoples in the eastern Mediterranean region that scholars can plausibly claim the priestly account woven into the postexilic redaction of Genesis to be modeled on the opening lines of the *Enûma elish.*[36] To that parallelism we will return in the next chapter. More to the point now, as we move forward to address the question of how much the classical Greeks inherited from their Cretan and Mycenaean predecessors and the latter, in turn, from the archaic Near Eastern pattern of sacral monarchy upon which we have been dwelling, is another parallelism—that evident in the philosophized version of the creation myth that one encounters in Plato's *Timaeus*. For in that dialogue the divine *demiurgos* or world-maker is depicted in classically archaic cosmogonic fashion as imposing order in the form now of the eternally unchanging Forms, Ideas, or Archetypes on the chaos prevailing "before the ordered whole... came to be" in what he calls "the Receptacle—as it were, the nurse of all becoming."[37]

When commenting that "the Platonic doctrine of Ideas was the final version of the archetype concept and the most fully articulated," and commenting also on "the Platonic structure" of the archaic ontology, Eliade was led to affirm that "Plato could be regarded as the outstanding philosopher of the 'primitive mentality,' that is, as the thinker who succeeded in giving philosophical currency and validity to the modes of life and behavior of archaic humanity."[38] The claim is by no means an implausible one, and in the next section we have to enquire why that should be so.[39]

Hellenic Survival and Hellenistic Revival

In accordance with common practice, I use the term "Hellenic" to denote that which pertains to the Greeks of the fifth- and fourth-century classical era (as well as their immediate predecessors), and "Hellenistic" to refer to Greek history, thinking, culture, and art in the late antique period stretching from the time of Alexander the Great to the beginning of the Christian or Common era. It was during the Hellenistic period, with Alexander's completion of the process whereby Macedonian power was successfully extended over the whole of the land, that kingship returned on an enduring basis to the Greek world at large. Not that it had disappeared entirely during the preceding Hellenic era. Here our obsessive preoccupation with Athens, in some ways a highly unrepresentative polis or city-state, has sometimes contrived to mislead us.[40] What have been called "ethnos-states" embraced, in fact, "a large part of the Peloponnese, and the bulk of the central and northern Greek mainland,"[41] and in one or two of these, Macedonia and the Molossian Epirate realm in northwest Greece, monarchy survived into the classical era. It did so also in such colonies of Magna

Graecia as Cyrene on the North African coast and Lycia/Caria in Asia Minor. Nor had the more familiar Greece of the poleis or city-states altogether lost touch with its own monarchical past, or with the sacral kingship of Minoan Crete or Mycenae on the mainland, which itself appears to have had much in common with that broadcast right across the ancient Near East.[42] Nor had that Greece lost all memory of the less powerful type of kingship exemplified in the great Homeric epics, which, though they are usually dated to around 750–650 BCE, are thought (variously) to evoke memories either of the Mycenaean Age (c. 1400–1150 BCE); or, alternatively, of the later "Dark Age" of Greek migration (c. 1050–900 BCE), which witnessed the destruction of the Mycenaean civilization; or, yet again, of conditions prevailing in both of those ages.

It is obvious that the *Iliad* and the *Odyssey* cannot simply be treated as historical documents. But they do convey precious intimations of the political culture of the archaic past that lay behind later developments in the poleis of the classical era. However limited the powers of the Homeric rulers, they are portrayed as hereditary kings, figures who are "godlike" or "god-supported" (thus *Iliad* 2:445), descendants of Zeus, himself depicted as supreme king of the gods. It appears that these Homeric kings not only led their peoples in battle but served also as their chief priests, performing sacrifices on their behalf. From the eighth century BCE onward the kings were nudged to one side in most of the poleis, and aristocratic, oligarchic, or, in some cases, democratic forms of government came to characterize the part of the Hellenic political landscape to which most attention has historically been paid.[43] But so integral a part of political life were the sacral functions discharged by the old kings that the nonmonarchical successor regimes "continued to regard the divine cult as one of the main bases on which the state should be built."[44]

This was certainly evident in Sparta, where remnants of an archaic dual kingship survived into the classical era, echoing in some ways the pattern of dual kingship to be found right across the globe, from Tonga and Africa to India and pre-Christian Germany. In that pattern one finds two royal partners affiliated with different divinities and charged with different functions and cultic responsibilities. The legacy of the old sacral kingship was also evident among the other poleis of Greece, where Chios, Miletus, Olbia, Siphnos, Ios, and Naxos all retained *basileis* or kingly figures, bereft, admittedly, of what we would call "political" functions but burdened with the discharge on behalf of their fellow citizens of sacral responsibilities.[45] The same legacy was evident, also, at Athens itself, where in the *Menexenus* Plato himself tells us (if the dialogue is, indeed, his) that "kings we have always had, first hereditary and then elected."[46] By that curious statement he meant, as he tells us in the *Statesman*, that "in many of the Greek cities . . . one finds that the duties of making the chief sacrifice on the state's behalf is laid upon the chief officers of state," and that "you have a striking example of it here in Athens, for I am led to understand that the most solemn sacrifices of this nation are the responsibility of the archon whom the lot designates as King-Archon."[47] In that respect, and he was responsible also for presiding over trials involving homicide, the Athenian king-archon (*archon basileus*) has been said to be "the heir of the Mycenaean priest-king."[48]

In some of the city-states, moreover, the degree of continuity with that Mycenaean religio-political tradition is underlined not only by the fact that such religious ceremonies were still being performed by an explicitly *kingly* figure, but also by the specific types of ceremony involved and by the particular sites where they were staged. Thus in many of the poleis, the palaces of the former kings became (or were replaced on the same sites by) temples dedicated to the city's god. Certainly at Athens itself, and as Aristotle tells us in his *Constitution of Athens*, the king or *archon basileus* of whom Plato had spoken was charged among his other duties with the supervision of the Eleusian mysteries. This he did with the assistance of four "curators," two of them chosen, respectively, from the Eleusian Eumolpidas and Eleusian Kerukes—old priestly families which may possibly have been of royal descent. At the Dionysian festival of the Anthesteria, moreover, the king-archon's wife was still required to contract a sacred marriage with the god Dionysus in the Boukolion, a building on the Acropolis that had once been the royal residence.[49] It was possibly on this occasion, or so E. O. James comments, "that her marriage to the king was celebrated, and its object seems to have been to renew and ensure the processes of fertility over which Dionysus had control, as in the other sacred marriages of the king and queen in the seasonal ritual." And his conclusion? Nothing other than the claim that "the widespread and very deeply-rooted fundamental theme of the sacral kingship persisted in Greece in myth and ritual long after the monarchy had ceased to function as a political institution [at least] in the city-states."[50]

Given the traditional intensity of the scholarly preoccupation with the classical period in general and with the glory days of Athens in particular, the Hellenistic era was for long pushed somewhat condescendingly to one side. Despite that fact, however, historians still felt obliged to try to explain the ease with which in the Hellenistic era a return was made (albeit in more philosophized guise) to something roughly akin to the archaic pattern of sacral kingship. If, however, we do not overlook the survival of monarchical forms in so many of the poleis, and if the claim advanced by E. O. James is at all correct, it seems that the explanatory effort might have been devoted more fruitfully to the task of illuminating why it was that the age-old monarchical tradition had come to be punctuated at all by what Cerfaux and Tondriau have called "the republican parenthesis" of the era of city-states. After all, given the antiquity and ubiquity of the royal institution, that punctuation can hardly be taken for granted as something natural or inevitable. In the event, it was destined to come rapidly to an end with the triumph of Alexander the Great over the Persian empire and its incorporation, along with the Greek territories and others, into a vast Hellenistic empire embracing the great landmass bordering on the eastern Mediterranean. With the creation of that great empire, there is a return, as it were, of the quasi-repressed, and belief in the sacrality of emperors and kings came once more to exert a profound influence over the whole of the late classical world.

Rooted already in the successor kingdoms—Ptolemaic, Seleucid, Parthian—to Alexander's empire, that belief in regal sacrality was later to go on, farther to the west, to establish itself in the emerging empire of Rome. We will see that it was able to do so because it came not as an alien heterodoxy but as a return to a form of "politics" the ideological underpinnings of which had never been fully dismantled—not even during Rome's own "republican parenthesis." That was no less true of Greece in the fourth century BCE than it was to be, later on, of Rome. That much, I believe, is certain. But when it comes to the challenging task of parsing the meaning attaching to the sacral or divine status of rulers and the precise nature of the ruler cult, Hellenistic and Roman specialists confront a formidable tangle of problems. Those problems range from what the "divinization" of rulers really meant, or the complex interaction of ideology and expediency so often connected with it, to the differences of practice (and sensibilities) evident in the Greek, Egyptian, and Persian successor kingdoms or, later on, in Italy and at Rome itself. If we should properly acknowledge the intricacies of such interpretative problems, we cannot dwell on them here in any extended fashion.[51] What we should not omit to say, however, is that the difficulty we ourselves characteristically experience as moderns in comprehending what it might conceivably mean to "divinize" a living human being or even to apotheosize and render cult to a deceased monarch springs from the highly exclusive nature of our own conception of the divine. "The boundary [or separation] between gods and men was narrower in Graeco-Roman belief than in ours and more fluid." In late Hellenistic antiquity it became increasingly common to detect intimations of the divine in outstanding men of wholly extraordinary achievement. "The dividing line between hero and god," accordingly, "was in practice neither sharp nor rigid." Nor, so far as the matter of cult was concerned, was that between homage and worship.[52] What we should add, too, is that no sweeping generalizations should be grounded on the celebrated refusal of his Greek and Macedonian soldiers to perform at Alexander's coronation in Bactria (327 BCE) the traditional Persian *proskynesis,* or act of obeisance in the presence of the god-king (or godlike king). That refusal is perhaps less significant than the fact that Alexander's Persian courtiers felt it appropriate to demand it of them. The refusal by the soldiers themselves can be explained as readily by the fact that they were being confronted by an innovation of specifically alien and Persian provenance as by any unambiguous antipathy on their part to the ruler cult as such.

Similarly, the fact that Alexander asked the Greek poleis of the Corinthian League to proclaim his divinity and that they ultimately acceded to that request is more significant than the fact that Athens, at least, initially resisted it.[53] The cult of deceased rulers was by no means unfamiliar to the Greeks and the apotheosis of a living ruler not altogether unknown. Both drew some ideological sustenance from traditional modes of Greek hero and ancestor worship.[54] With the dawn of the Hellenistic age, moreover, such practices were given an additional boost by the charismatic character commonly ascribed to the Macedonian royal dynasty, which in Alexander's own day continued to trace its lineal descent back to Heracles, son of Zeus.[55] Perhaps more surprisingly, even during the classical age of the polis itself, such sacral notions and traditions had resurfaced in the extensive discussion of the strengths of monarchical government that rumbled on at Athens, nourished by the contributions of such notable writers as Xenephon, Theophrastus, and Isocrates.[56]

While, then, archaic associations of the king's ritual performances with the fertility of the land and the abundance of crops had begun to fade,[57] other echoes of the old cosmic religiosity with its alignment of human microcosm with terrestrial macrocosm were still to be heard. With the emergence, certainly, of the characteristic notion of the kingdom as an analogue of the universe, the Greeks themselves fashioned out of Platonic and Pythagorean as well as Near Eastern materials their own, more consciously philosophical, version of sacral kingship. In that version the king was himself represented as an incarnate *epiphaneia* or manifestation of the divine ordering *logos* or reason conceived to be immanent in the universe and analogous to the reasoning power in man. Fragments of Hellenistic political writings preserved by Joannes Stobaeus in the sixth century CE and probably dating to the second century BCE have been helpfully analyzed by E. R. Goodenough. In the remnants of writings by such theorists as Diotogenes and Ps.-Ecphantus the Pythagorean, they convey a vision of the king as "bearing the same relation to the state as God to the world," with the state or kingdom being "in the same ratio to the world as the king is to God" (thus Diotogenes).[58] That vision was reflected also later on in the writings of Plutarch, a man well acquainted with Hellenistic political literature in general (including some pertinent writings now lost to us). It represented the king as "a dynamic and personal revelation of deity," a "living law" (*nomos empsychos/lex animata*), "himself the state, its constitution and its link with the world order."[59] And the same vision found expression also in the claims of the Hellenistic kings—Ptolemaic, Seleucid, and Parthian alike—not only to be the "shepherd" of their peoples but also their "savior" (*soter*), and to be deserving of such further titles as "benefactor," "mediator," *theos epiphanes*—"god manifest" or, perhaps, "god incarnate."[60] This sacral vision of kingship was certainly an elevated one, and for long centuries into the future it was destined to awaken potent echoes in the Western as well as the Eastern political consciousness. But if that was to be the case, it was, above all, because it had proved capable of exerting a profound and progressively deepening influence upon the legal and political thinking of Rome.

Roman Imperial Sacrality

The influence of this sacral vision of kingship, along with the general process of Hellenization of which it was but one aspect, was to reach its peak toward the end of the third century CE. By that time, however, it had already been at work for several centuries—from the late second century BCE, certainly, and in some respects even earlier than that. But if the debt to Hellenistic and, indeed, Near Eastern beliefs and practices was in the end to be a large one, the sacral status of the Roman emperors and the imperial cult attendant upon that status were far from being explicable solely in those terms. Even if we wished to view them as "foreign or exotic" in their derivation (and it is by no means clear that we would be warranted in so doing), we would still have to explain, as Cochrane insisted more than a half century ago, why they "should have been accepted in the new environment."[61] And in any case, as has become increasingly clear since he wrote, it would be improper to view them as nothing more (or nothing other) than a foreign transplantation onto Roman soil.[62] As was the case with Greece itself, if such notions and practices came to thrive at Rome, it was at least in part because they marked something of a return to an ancient orthodoxy, the ideological underpinnings of which had never been completely dismantled.

Reviled though the title of *rex* or king doubtless came to be, there is a sense in which the sacral kingship had never entirely taken leave of Rome. Even during the "republican parenthesis," and as had earlier been the case with many of the Greek poleis, the Roman commonwealth itself remained in a profound sense what we would take to be a "religious" entity. Rather than being totally obliterated, the institution of kingship was instead broken down into its constituent parts and its disparate functions distributed among the "republican" magistrates who succeeded. Thus the old royal *imperium* or supreme power passed into the hands of two annually elected consuls, the first of whom may have been of royal lineage, and who together enjoyed during their term of office unlimited power in war but limited powers of governance at Rome.

At the same time, the most important of the old royal priestly functions appear to have passed in time to the "supreme pontiff" (*pontifex maximus*), a republican office of great importance. Of such importance, indeed, that Octavian himself was to assume it after 13 BCE and make it one of the chief building blocks of the skillfully occluded but essentially monarchical position that, in the guise of "restoring the republic," he constructed from old republican materials.[63] That notwithstanding, it was still felt necessary (as it had been at Athens and other Greek poleis) to retain the office and title of king in the form of the *rex sacrorum,* a priestly figure of lesser importance than the *pontifex maximus* who, while being precluded from the holding of any magistracy, was charged with the performance of certain ritual functions.

From 63 BCE onward, Julius Caesar had held the office of *pontifex maximus* as one of the many titles and honors that conferred on him sacred and, eventually, divine status. All of this proved to be too much for the conspirators who hastened to dispose of him in 44 BCE before he could add to the actual possession of monarchical power the formal title of "king." In the event, however, his assassination, seen by many as a martyrdom, assured his swift deification and the formal establishment of a cult of "the divine Julius" (*divus Julius*).[64] At the same time, Mark Antony's enthusiastic embrace of the divine status so often accorded to monarchs in the East had some precedents in the earlier willingness of Roman proconsular officials in the eastern provinces to go along with the attribution to them of a similarly sacral status along with the cultic practices that accompanied it. Cicero tells us that as proconsul of Cilicia in Asia Minor he himself was hard pressed to prevent such honors being paid to him.[65] But, in this, his reluctance proved to be the exception rather than the rule; certainly, as time went on, reservations such as his became increasingly unfashionable. In the wake, however, of Caesar's impetuous drive for monarchical status, Mark Antony's behavior was not well received at Rome itself, and in the propaganda he directed against him, Octavian worked hard to exploit that fact.

As a result, the approach to power that the latter was led to follow was somewhat more oblique and a good deal more respectful of Roman tradition. In the eastern provinces, it is true, he was viewed as a royal figure, frequently taken to be a "savior" worthy of divine or quasi-divine honors. In Egypt he was "son of Ré," successor to the pharaohs, worthy accordingly of having the great temple that Cleopatra had begun to build for Antony completed as one dedicated, instead, to him.[66] At Rome, on the other hand, and in Italy in general, though he was eventually able to command the realities of monarchical power, he did so in somewhat indirect and deliberately occluded fashion, working in tandem with the Senate, refusing to be addressed as "our Lord" (*dominus noster*), and contenting himself with the titles of *princeps* (first citizen), *pater patriae* (father of the fatherland), and *augustus,* all of them redolent of Roman tradition and all of them conferred upon him by the Senate.

Worthy of note, however, is the degree to which the position in Roman political life to which he attained after Mark Antony's defeat and death was rooted in religious soil. He was, after all, the "son of the god, Caesar" (*divi filius*), an appellation to which he attached great importance. And the titles of *augustus* and *pater patriae,* along with the office of *pontifex maximus,* which he assumed in 13/12 BCE, all of them conferred on him an unquestionably sacral status and elevated him above other men as a person at least *potentially* divine. Any process of official divinization was left to await his death. When that occurred, after an official *consecratio* voted by the Senate, Divus Augustus was formally enrolled in a state cult with the divinity that the poets had so long been promising him, and to that cult was attached a priesthood devoted to his worship.[67]

The practice whereby the Roman Senate acted to deify an emperor after his death (or, for that matter, to deny that status to him) is not to be dismissed anachronistically as "mere ritual" or as a "transparently political" gesture possessed of no truly religious significance.[68] Nor should the elaborate public ceremonies involving the *consecratio* or apotheosis of a deceased emperor, for which the process of divinizing Augustus set the pattern, be similarly dismissed in modern "commonsensical" terms as some sort of a charade, something without relevance to what historians have characteristically viewed as the "realities" of power—war, politics, administration, and diplomacy. Contemporaries, it turns out, appear to have viewed the *consecratio* (as well as its withholding from some of the deceased emperors) "with complete seriousness." Simon Price has argued, indeed, that it constituted nothing less than "the central focus of imperial ideology at Rome for three hundred years."[69]

The same may be said a fortiori for the practice of "emperor-worship," the imperial cult of "Rome and Augustus" to which, in the Roman empire at large, a similar seriousness attached. While what is sometimes referred to (albeit unduly dismissively) as the "conventional" approach to Roman history has tended to "relegate the cult to the sidelines in favour of diplomacy and administration," there is really no reason "to privilege politics over the imperial cult." They were, in fact, intimately interconnected.[70] The dismissive condescension of the Christian commentators of the day to the contrary, the traditional pagan religiosity of the Roman and Mediterranean world retained its vigor right down into the third century CE and beyond. Sometimes coupled with the worship of *dea Roma* (the goddess who personified Rome), the imperial cult derived some of its own vitality from its attachment to that age-old pagan religiosity and its "incorporation into the traditional religious system."[71]

The eventual spread of that imperial cult throughout the provinces of the empire, western as well as eastern, and especially at the very local level, owed as much, it seems, to popular sentiment as it did to official promotion or outright governmental imposition.[72] There is no reason to suppose that it did not involve, and especially so in the eastern provinces, a genuine piety—though, of course, a piety of the antique civic mode.[73] If it was, indeed, a *political* act, it was political not in the modern and (historically speaking) impoverished sense of that term but in the older, broader, more inclusive sense that bore the clear and continuing imprint of the archaic religio-political vision. Polis, republic, Hellenistic kingdom, Roman empire—all of them still remained something more than "states" in the modern sense. Despite our own inclination to disenchanted dismissal of the older civic piety, political thinking and practice in the Roman no less than the Greek classical world continued to acknowledge no real distinction between the political and the religious. The loyalty men owed to their commonwealth was equally a loyalty to their civic gods and quasi-divinized rulers, and that loyalty was in general conceived to be an ultimate loyalty from which there could be no appeal to any higher norm.

At Rome, certainly, as time went on, and as memories of republican sobriety faded and godlike emperor succeeded godlike emperor, the religious character of that loyalty appears to have intensified. By the third century CE the term "divine" (*theios*) was being applied with greater frequency to the emperor; by the end of that century "the relationship of the emperor to the divine ... [had become] ... much closer and immediate" in the panegyrics of the day than it had been in those of the early second century, and the people could be portrayed as invoking in the person of the emperor Maximian "not the god familiar from hearsay, but a Jupiter close at hand, visible and present."[74] By the early fourth century, the emperor

Diocletian (284–306), having put an end to the military anarchy and transformed the empire into a "Dominate," an absolute monarchy of quasi-oriental stamp, and having taken the imperial cult to its apogee, making his own the court ceremonial, elaborate costumes, and other appurtenances of the sacral kings of Mediterranean antiquity, came to rule the empire less as the *filius divi* than as a veritable *divus* himself.[75]

Such was the legacy inherited by Constantine (306–37), who was to become the first of the Christian emperors. But in moving to embrace a version of the Christian worldview, and to do so in his public no less than in his private life, he was also, and in ways that he can hardly have divined, entering into the legacy of a profoundly different way of thinking and feeling. As a result, and for centuries to come, it was to be the fate of those late Roman and early medieval intellectuals who concerned themselves with the ideological underpinnings of politics to have to undertake the ungrateful task of reconciling those divergent legacies. And, as we shall see, the challenge confronting them was, in many ways, that of rendering compatible the contradictory and harmonious the dissonant.

In the long twilight struggle to surmount that challenge, however, their efforts were to be attended by a surprising measure of success. In fact, they were to meet with so great a measure of success as to conceal from themselves (and sometimes from those of us who attempt as historians to comprehend their project) the essential fragility of the foundations on which they were building and the profound geologic fault that lay beneath them. The irruption into the late antique world of the biblical religions was destined eventually to generate seismic activity along that disabling fault and to destabilize the foundations of the edifice of sacral monarchy that Constantine had inherited. But it was to have that effect only centuries later, long after Judaism and Christianity alike had first proved themselves to be in some degree responsive to the allure of the archaic cosmic religiosity and to have been drawn, accordingly and irresistibly, into the strong magnetic field it continued to exert.

3. Abrahamic Departures
The Hebraic and Christian Contribution

IT WAS JESUS, OR SO grumbled Jean-Jacques Rousseau at the end of *Du contrat social,* who "came to establish on earth a spiritual kingdom" and, as a result, "by separating the theological from the political system, made the State no longer one, and caused the internal divisions which have never ceased to agitate Christian peoples."[1] Historians of political thought, however, have not always been as willing as was Rousseau to ascribe to Christian ideas so important a role in matters political or to perceive in them so obvious a source of novelty. To adduce just one prominent example from the middle decades of the twentieth century, George H. Sabine's *History of Political Theory,* a frequently reprinted textbook, which enjoyed a most successful career in the Anglophone world, chose to devote no chapter or discrete section to biblical ideas concerning political life. That omission was clearly deliberate. "In the beginning," Sabine says, "the rise of Christianity did not carry with it a new political philosophy.... So far as political ideas are concerned, those of the [church] Fathers were for the most part those of Cicero and Seneca."[2]

In this respect it was only in the self-conscious nature of his stance that Sabine was unrepresentative of the genre. The norm for general histories of political thought was no more than a page or two devoted to New Testament ideas on matters political, and that, usually, by way of lead-in to a discussion of Augustine of Hippo.[3] Histories devoted specifically to medieval political thinking offered even less. Instead, they tended to pick up the story in the post-Constantinian era, and while they certainly had to deal with the argumentative deployment of biblical texts in the writings of medieval thinkers, they themselves appear simply to have assumed on the part of the reader some general familiarity with such texts. No space was usually devoted, therefore, to an attempt to tease apart the different strands of thinking about political life that one finds complexly interwoven in the pages of the New Testament and which make it so hard to come satisfactorily to terms with its political teaching overall.[4] One should acknowledge, of course, that to that overall generalization there have always been a few important exceptions. They range from the older classic works by Paul Janet and R. W. and A. J. Carlyle down to the recent Cambridge histories. In the latter case, indeed, both the *Cambridge History of Greek and Roman Political Thought* and the *Cambridge History of Medieval Political Thought* contain substantial and helpful chapters devoted to New Testament and early Christian political thinking.[5]

A truly striking feature, however, of almost all such histories is a quiet omission that it is very easy to take for granted and simply to overlook. And that is the failure to devote any attention at all to the political notions prevalent among the ancient Hebrews, and especially the way in which the institution of kingship was understood during the period when monarchies were established in Israel and Judah.[6] Once detected, that omission cannot but emerge as something of an oddity. The history (or theology of history) embedded in the Jewish Bible/Christian Old Testament, after all, helped shape in marked degree the form and sustaining ideology of kingship in the medieval West. So much so that during the early medieval centuries the Franks, who had begun to view themselves and to be viewed by others as the new Israel, or "new sacred people of promise," tended instinctively to see in their own kings the successors of David and Solomon.[7] That being so, and despite its marginal, provincial, and, indeed, evanescent presence in the secular history of the ancient Near East, it is from the Hebrew kingship as we can discern it in the pages of the Jewish Bible/Christian Old Testament that we must take our departure.

Hebraic Departures

Making a start with the concept of kingship as expressed in the Jewish Bible is not an easy task, especially so if one's intention is to attain to some sort of specifically *historical* understanding of the Hebrew kingship. And that is, indeed, my intention. To attain that goal, one has to grope one's way through a low-lying fog of later theological commentary, which can screen from us all too easily the differing historical contexts in which the various "books" of the Bible were produced.[8] Mindful of the great controversies that in the past have swept across the field, one has to pick a nervously cautious way through the poignant litter and lonely detritus left by the scholarly battles of yesteryear. Even then, one has still to grapple with a set of extremely intricate problems concerning the precise dating of the narratives one encounters in those "historical" books of the Bible that speak to the introduction of kingship into an Israel that had previously contrived to do without it. Again, one has to recognize in the final narratives with which we are presented the "Priestly" (post-exilic) conflation of disparate traditions stemming from the northern and southern kingdoms of Israel/Ephraim and Judah, as well as the uneasy presence in the Books of Samuel, stitched together in a seemingly unified account, of both positive and negative takes on the very institution of kingship itself.[9] Finally, all of that accomplished, one has still to assess the degree to which such historical narratives were themselves shaped at the time of their composition or later redaction by considerations that were essentially theological rather than historical in nature.

All of that said, it should be conceded, with a measure of relief, that the problems involved have been rendered somewhat less intractable by a set of contributions made in the mid-twentieth century. Those contributions were the works of groups of British and Scandinavian scholars whose names are associated with what have come to be known as the "myth and ritual" and "Uppsala" schools of interpretation.[10] Both schools made the nature and function of the Hebrew kingship a central focus of their concern, and while their interpretative approach did not fully carry the day, in large measure it did succeed in framing the basic questions around which subsequent scholarly debate has tended to revolve. Both schools were intent on making the case (Engnell, perhaps, most sweepingly)[11] that the ideology we have seen to lie behind the Egyptian and Mesopotamian kingship extended also to other regions in the ancient Near East, finding expression in what amounted to a shared cultic pattern. Included among those regions was the land of Canaan, among whose inhabitants the Hebrews came to settle and with whose religious and political forms they came, accordingly, into intimate contact. Hence the further claim that the ideology that was to undergird the Hebrew kingship itself partook of that general Near Eastern pattern.

Notwithstanding the complex problems posed by the fragmentary nature of the available evidence and exacerbated by the uncertain dating of some of the pertinent texts, the case that the scholars of the myth and ritual and Uppsala schools succeeded in making was a substantial one and one not lightly to be dismissed. Some of them argued, for example, that the myth of primordial man, widespread throughout the ancient Near Eastern world, was the source of the notion of the "Son of Man," which Jesus seems to have appropriated from the apocalyptic literature of the late Old Testament era and which (rather than the word "Messiah" or "Anointed One"—Greek *Christos,* Latin *Christus*) he used as his own title.[12] Again, many of the attributes that the prophet Isaiah (eighth century BCE) and the later (post-exilic) author usually referred to as Second or Deutero-Isaiah (i.e., Isaiah, 40–55, with 56–66 sometimes attributed to "Third Isaiah") ascribed to the future Messiah and the epithets they heaped upon him (righteousness, love of justice, Mighty God, Servant of God, Everlasting Father, and so on) have now come to be acknowledged as being of Sumerian, Babylonian, or Egyptian provenance.[13] Similarly, persuasive parallels have been drawn between, on the one hand, Deutero-Isaiah's suffering Servant of God, a kingly messianic figure destined in the fullness of time not only to "raise up the tribes of Jacob and to restore the survivors of Israel" but also to atone by his death for the sins of others, and, on the other hand, the role that the Babylonian king played on the day of atonement that formed part of the annual New Year's festival. That festival was of crucial cultic significance, and on that occasion, acting as the representative of his people and as the "Servant of God" (a title explicitly accorded to him), the Babylonian king sought ritually to expiate the wrongdoings of his people.[14]

If these illustrations are all messianic in nature, I do not choose them at random. The relation between the messianic motif and the Hebraic as well as the later Christian political vision is more direct than might at first seem to be the case. If the epithets that the prophets applied to the Messiah or the symbols and imagery associated with him betray possible parallels with Egyptian and Babylonian court style, they do so because some of them, while looking to the future or being at least susceptible of an eschatological meaning, were actually applied to or associated originally with the real-life pre-exilic kings of Israel/Ephraim or Judah. In the eighth century BCE, at the time of the prophet who was the author of Isaiah 1–40, and who is often labeled as "First Isaiah," the word "Messiah"/"Anointed One" appears to have referred simply to the reigning king. In this connection, what Eric Voegelin once characterized as "perhaps the most important [event]... in the Old Testament study of the twentieth century" is directly pertinent.[15] What he had in mind was the discovery that some of the psalms (the language and imagery of which echo through Deutero-Isaiah) together form a distinct group of so-called royal or imperial psalms, which rather than being "original expressions of personal or collective piety written in post-exilic or even post-Maccabean times" and themselves inspired by Deutero-Isaiah, derive instead "from hymns, liturgies, prayers, and oracles to be used in the cult of the pre-exilic monarchy."[16] Thus, and for example, in Psalm 110:1 the poet says to the king:

> The Lord says to my lord:
> "Sit at my right hand
> till I make your enemies your footstool."

Here the parallels with the Egyptian court style have been emphasized, for the pharaohs were often represented pictorially as sitting in the place of honor to the right of the god's throne or with their enemies beneath their feet. Again, if the Egyptians portrayed the pharaoh Thutmose being instructed by the god Seth to bend a bow, in Psalm 18:34 the king can say of Yahweh:

> He trains my hand for war,
> so that my arm can bend a bow of bronze.

Yet again, in what was to be over time an enormously influential reference to Melchizedek, the mythical priest-king of Jerusalem, a priestly character is ascribed to the contemporary Israelite king in Psalm 110(109):4 (cf. Genesis 14:18; Hebrews 9:17):

> The Lord has sworn
>   and will not change his mind,
>   "You are a priest forever
>   after the order of Melchizedek."

A great deal of emphasis, accordingly, has been placed on the priestly duties fulfilled by the Hebrew kings of the pre-exilic period and on the parallels between those duties and the comparable responsibilities attaching to the kingship in Babylon. Thus scholars influenced by the myth and ritual and Uppsala schools took the evidence yielded by the royal psalms, along with additional evidence gleaned from the "historical" books of the Bible, as disclosing the lineaments of a pre-exilic Hebrew monarchy well-nigh undistinguishable in style and status from the other sacral monarchies of the ancient Near East.

As a result, the fragmentary nature of the surviving evidence notwithstanding, Mowinckel and others detected in the autumnal festival at Jerusalem (later known as the Feast of Tabernacles) a New Year's festival comparable to that of the Babylonians. At that festival, or so they argued, there took place a solemn repetition by the king of the work of creation in which Yahweh triumphed over the primeval forces of chaos. Having been virtually proclaimed as universal king, and having "renewed" both his covenant with his people and his covenant "with the House of David as represented by the reigning king," Yahweh demonstrated to his followers "that he was prepared to restore their fortunes in the year that lay ahead and, in particular, to bestow upon his people the gift of rain and the blessing of fertility."[17] In the ritual of that festival, they further claimed, the Hebrew king played a priestly, cultic role comparable to that played by his Babylonian counterpart, an absolutely central role as superhuman representative of his people, sacred mediator between them and Yahweh, "the channel through which the divine blessings flow[ed] to the people."[18]

This being so, new significance could be attached to the fact that in an earlier, abortive attempt to establish a Hebrew kingship (c. 1100 BCE), Abimelech, son of Gideon, permitted himself to be anointed king after the Canaanite fashion under a (presumably) sacred oak tree (Judges 9:6). Similarly, the fact that the great Temple which Solomon erected in Jerusalem with the help of Phoenician architects, and which was oriented to the east and the rising sun, reproduced the cosmological symbolism common to the temples and royal palaces of the ancient Near East and, indeed, elsewhere. In accordance with that symbolism, the structure of the Temple itself reflected in microcosm the overarching structure of the macrocosm.[19] Again, a heightened significance would appear to attach also to those biblical texts (e.g., 2 Samuel 21:1–14; 24:10–25) in which natural catastrophes like plague or drought are depicted as consequences of the king's wrongdoing. At the farthest extreme, a case could even be made for assuming that divine status was accorded to the pre-exilic Hebrew kings and for taking simply at face value the extraordinary statement addressed to the *king* in one of the royal psalms (Psalm 45:6)—namely, "Thy throne, O God, endures forever and ever."[20]

These are truly striking claims and not to be ignored. But it has long become clear that there is among Bible scholars nothing even approximating consensus about them. Most normally concede the fundamental importance of the discovery that the royal psalms were of pre-exilic provenance and embedded in a royal cult. Along with that, most recognize also the significance and extent of the bonds linking the Hebrew monarchy with the institution of sacral kingship as it existed right across the ancient Near East. But the attempt to draw firm parallels between the autumnal festival at Jerusalem and the Babylonian New Year's festival has come close to foundering on the skimpy nature of the evidence available on the Israelite side of the equation. There is, moreover, considerable dispute about the nature and reach of the priestly status ascribed to the pre-exilic Hebrew kings, and few if any commentators would now be tempted to read Psalm 45:6 as ascribing anything like divine status to those kings. As long ago as 1932, C. R. North pointed out that in Hebrew the verse in question may mean no more than "Thy throne is [everlasting] like that of God," and he went on to criticize Mowinckel's entire approach on the grounds that "he interprets Old Testament religion as a whole by working inwards from the wide circle of a primitive and general Semitic *Umwelt* (milieu), instead of outwards from the centre of the prophetic consciousness."[21] Mowinckel himself was later moved to concede somewhat to such criticisms. In so doing, he abandoned his earlier claim that the Hebrew king was regarded as a very incarnation of Yahweh and posted a highly important warning as much to himself as to his fellow commentators. On this particular matter, as on others, he said, the "phenomenological 'parallels'" discernible between notions of kingship in Israel and in the ancient Near East as a whole (and clearly there were many) are "liable to be elusive." "If," he went on, "an expression, an image, or a particular idea etc. is found in two different places, in two civilizations and religions, it does not follow that they *mean* the same, even if there is a direct historical loan or influence from one of the sides. Each detail obtains its significance from the structure of the whole in which it has been incorporated, and of which it is a part. The essential question is what significance has been imparted to a borrowed idea in its new context, what the religion of Israel has made of it."[22]

Given his earlier interpretative commitments, Mowinckel was better qualified than were most to issue such a caveat. And it is only, certainly, if we keep it in mind, only if we remember to pose his "essential question," that we will be at all likely to discern the fundamental novelty of the Hebraic (and ultimately, therefore, the Christian) political vision. Despite the numerous and increasingly obvious cultural similarities between the Hebrew political experience and that of the other peoples of the ancient Near East, real differences between them did nevertheless exist. And, in the context of world history and of the development in the Latin Middle Ages and early modern centuries of a distinctively Western mode of political thinking, it is to the differences rather than the similarities that real significance attaches. Seek the roots of those differences, moreover, and one will find them embedded in that particular consciousness of the nature of God and of his relationship with the universe and with humankind, which crystallizes slowly, emerging, it may be, in fits and starts but also with growing insistence and clarity, during the long and turbulent odyssey of the Israelites as a self-consciously chosen but frequently faithless people. That consciousness finds a particularly powerful expression in some of the Psalms, in Deutero-Isaiah, and in so many of the prophetic voices transmitted to posterity via the pages of the Jewish Bible/Christian Old Testament.

So far as the complex blending of similarity and difference is concerned, one may find a pertinent parallel in the way in which the postexilic Priestly redactors of the several biblical traditions that had come down to them shaped what is usually referred to as the "Priestly" account of the Creation (i.e., Genesis 1:1–2:4a). The parallel, nonbiblical material that appears to have inspired them in their work was drawn, it seems, from the verses of nothing other than the Babylonian creation myth, the *Enûma elish*. And that, as we have seen,[23] renders creation in the form of a great cosmogonic struggle between cosmic order (represented by the king-god, Marduk) and the primordial watery chaos (represented by the sea monster, Tiamat). But unlike the *Enûma elish* the Genesis text is nowhere merely "allusive, 'symbolic,' or figuratively poetic." Instead of featuring a bewildering succession of gods, good and evil, the Genesis account "is dominated by the monotheistic concept in the absolute sense of the term."[24] In effect, for the issue involved was far more complex than the tension between monotheism and polytheism, it asserts (or assumes) not simply the oneness of God but also his transcendence and overriding omnipotence. And these, of course, are themes that run through the Bible, finding (again) particularly powerful and eloquent expression in Deutero-Isaiah. In Kierkegaard's words, what is asserted is "an infinite qualitative difference" between God and world. That world, by simple fiat or an untrammeled exercise of his will, God had drawn out of nothingness and into being—or so the words of Genesis, to the bemusement of Greek philosophers, came eventually to be interpreted. As a result, whatever the use made of Babylonian (or, for that matter, of Canaanite and other Near Eastern) materials, in the Priestly account of creation they are subordinated to the exigencies of an understanding of the divine that differed radically from that presupposed by the *Enûma elish* and by the other creation myths of the ancient Near East. Hence, the concomitant reshaping of the very notion of creation into something at once more familiar to us and more novel in its implications than the widespread archaic notion of the imposition of cosmos (or order) upon some sort of preexisting chaos.[25]

In relation specifically to the ideas and practices attaching to Hebrew kingship, the Priestly creation account in Genesis may serve to offer a measure of insight into the ways attitudes and ideas absorbed from the surrounding cultures could gradually be transmuted, under the transformative impact of the Yahwist religion, into something very different. But it should do more than simply draw attention to an illuminating parallelism. Its connection with the Hebrew understanding of kingship was, in fact, more substantive than that. The biblical idea of creation, that is to say, and the notion of God as one, transcendent, and omnipotent, which it both presupposed and entailed, inevitably imposed severe limits on the degree of sacrality that could properly be attached to any truly Israelite king. By destroying the archaic sense that there existed a consubstantiality between God, nature, and humankind, it dedivinized or desacralized the two last, engineering in effect what Schiller in a happy phrase called the "disenchantment of the world." As a result, it had a desacralizing or disenchanting effect also on human society and on the political institutions necessary for the maintenance of that society. In negating the fundamental primitive or archaic notion of a divine continuum linking humankind with nature and (what we call) the state with the cosmos, it undercut as well what we have called the "cosmic religiosity." And that form of religiosity, as we have seen,[26] was itself the very foundation for the archaic pattern of divine or sacred kingship and for the understanding of the state as "the embodiment of the cosmic totality."

Pursuing the same line of reasoning, it may also be said that the biblical idea of creation and the understanding of the divine in which it was embedded served to shift the arena in which the relation between the divine and the human is played out from that dominated by the cyclic rhythms of nature, in which "there is nothing new under the sun," to that constituted by the open-ended succession of unique moments or events in time that we call "history." In that arena there was envisaged the millennial unfolding across the unpredictable vastnesses of time of a salvific dialogue between the uncreated and transcendent God, on the one hand, and, on the other, the human creatures gathered in community who owed their very existence to his inexplicable generosity. Whereas in the arena of nature kings had played an essential mediatory role in the relationship of their peoples with the divine, in the dialogue central to salvation history they possessed no stable or inevitable role. The central players, instead, were God himself and his chosen and covenanted people. For the kingship was seen (or came to be seen) by some as something of an "alien intrusion" into the life of Israel. The covenant that the Lord was believed to have made through their forefather Abraham with his chosen people (Genesis 15) and renewed at Sinai through Moses when he delivered that people from the land of Egypt (Exodus 24:3–8; cf. 6) appears to have bulked far larger in the Hebraic consciousness than the "royal" covenant he was said to have made with King David (2 Samuel 7:8–16; 23:5).[27] And that covenant with the House of David, it has been said, had itself "a wider significance than the monarchy and was independent of the earthly throne since behind it lay the covenant of Yahweh with the nation as a whole."[28]

When all of the above is duly noted, the most remarkable thing about the Hebrew monarchy is not so much the measure in which it retained a religious aura as the degree to which, if only in comparison with other Near Eastern monarchies, it was a *secular* institution.[29] But if, seen in retrospect, there is indeed a marked contrast between the developed religiopolitical vision of the Hebrews and those of the surrounding peoples, it was to take long centuries before the Israelites themselves came to intuit the nature of the discontinuity involved. There seems no good reason, for example, to deny that the pre-exilic Hebrew kings performed *some* functions of a priestly nature—royal cultic functions that, after the Exile and the ending of the monarchy, the high priest (in this it may be not unlike the Athenian *archon basileus*) was destined to continue to perform in combination with his own traditional priestly duties.[30] Even if we were content to indulge in anachronism, we would encounter great difficulty trying to distinguish in any of the Israelite regimes, whether pre- or post-exilic, discrete "religious" and "political" spheres cognate to the modern categories of church and state. We have to be careful, then, not to exaggerate either the extent to which or the speed with which the ancient Hebrews somehow broke away from the archaic sacral pattern of things. Nonetheless, it is extremely unlikely that even the pre-exilic kings laid claim to anything approximating to "divine" status. Nowhere in the Bible, Mowinckel himself was led to concede, do we meet "with a 'metaphysical' unity of Yahweh and the king or a really mythological idea of the king's relationship with Yahweh."[31] Had such a notion been advanced, that fact would surely have been reflected in the form of yet another charge of blasphemy embedded in the protracted polemic that the prophets directed against their kings. And the very existence and strength of that prophetic polemic themselves reflect, after all, the peculiarly uneasy status of the Hebrew kingship and the fragility of its relation with the divine.

Even before the formal introduction of kingship in the person of Saul, Abimelech's flirtation with Canaanite monarchical forms had called forth in the fable of Jotham (Judges 9:1–21) what Martin Buber described (with pardonable exaggeration) as "the strongest anti-monarchical poem of world literature."[32] And the presence, side by side, of two very different attitudes toward the kingship in those parts of the books of Samuel concerned with its later and formal introduction into Israel discloses, perhaps better than anything else, the fundamental uneasiness attending upon the position of the Hebrew kings and goes some way toward illuminating its nature.

Thus, and on the one hand, Yahweh is depicted as having recognized the need for kingship, as having accepted the popular desire for it, and in what amounted to a beneficent divine gift, as having anointed Saul to be "ruler over his people Israel" (1 Samuel 10:1; 12:1–5). The source that lies behind that account is generally believed to have been more or less contemporaneous with the events it describes. On the other hand, Yahweh is portrayed as having regarded the demand of the Israelites that they should have a king to govern them and fight their battles so that they might be "like other nations" as nothing less than a betrayal, a quasi-blasphemous demand derogating from his own eternal kingship. By that demand, the Lord tells Samuel, "they have not rejected you, but they have rejected me from being king over them" (1 Samuel 8:7). This second, more forceful and rejectionist position may well stem from another source contemporaneous with the first and reflecting the presence among the Hebrews, right from the start, of disagreement about the compatibility of kingship with the Yahwist religion.[33] But it has been more common to attribute it to a later period, when actual experience with the faithlessness or tyranny of the Hebrew kings had promoted the fostering of disappointment and doubt.

Whatever the case, the marked ambivalence in attitude toward the kingship evident in Samuel is evident in many other biblical texts, from the fable of Jotham in Judges, via the two books of Kings, to the prophetic diatribes of Elijah, Amos, Hosea, and Isaiah. And it is almost always reflective of the repeated willingness of the Hebrew kings to accommodate (and even to associate with their own Yahweh worship) the fertility rituals and related practices like sacred prostitution embedded in the cultus of the Canaanite agrarian god Baal. Thus, for example, we have what Buber calls "the syncretistic faithlessness of Solomon" (d. c. 922 BCE), who, "as hospitable as a Roman emperor, allotted holy high places" to the gods and goddesses of the Sidonians and Ammonites (1 Kings 11:4–8).[34] Or three centuries later even, the willingness of Manassah (c. 642) to reopen the Baalist shrines and to undertake once more the attempt to amalgamate the Baalist cultus with the worship of Yahweh (2 Kings 21:1–9).

The religious syncretism, then, consequent upon the continuing Israelite penetration into Canaanite society, the related tendency of the Hebrew kingship to become indeed like that "of other nations"—the focus of a royal cult, the mediatorial pivot of a "political" community envisaged as "the embodiment of the cosmic totality"—these things, much emphasized by the adherents to the myth and ritual and Uppsala schools, seem increasingly to have had the effect of stimulating among the Israelites a vein of criticism, first of royal behavior, when their kings went "whoring" after alien fertility gods, and, then, eventually of kingship itself. As a result, that institution came to be portrayed as a failure, a great aberration, a foreign importation incompatible with the Hebrew religious vision, a veritable betrayal of the covenant between God and his chosen people, something ultimately irreconcilable with the true kingship of Yahweh himself. Again and again, prophetic voices were raised defending that true kingship against those deluded human upstarts, monarchs who, worshipping at the "high places" of the old gods, sought to "raise... [their] throne on high," to "ascend to heaven above the stars of God," to make themselves like the Most High (Isaiah 14:12–14). "They made kings," said the Lord to Hosea, "but not through me, they set up princes, but without my knowledge" (Hosea 8:4). If it was in his anger that he had permitted them those kings, so was it in his wrath that he had taken them away (Hosea 13:11).

The hostility to kings and kingship thus expressed, enshrined in the writings or redactions of exilic and post-exilic times, was to survive the destruction of the kingship in Judah no less than in Israel/Ephraim. And it came to inform the thinking of the Hebrews to such a degree that not even the revival of the monarchy in 103 BCE could overcome it or rally the support of the entire nation behind the (non-Davidic) Hasmonean kings—and that despite the fact that those kings had by their military prowess succeeded in reviving the old kingdom of Judah and, at least for a while, in vindicating its renewed independence. Their earlier willingness to flirt with the cosmic religiosity and cosmic kingship notwithstanding, the Hebrews contrived finally to resist its blandishments. That much is reasonably clear. The Hebrew conception of God and the understanding of creation that flowed from it were determinative in undermining the structure of the archaic sacral pattern. But they were still not powerful enough by themselves fully to destroy it. If, for example, the intimate bond linking man with nature and nature with the divine was now severed, we should not be tempted to assume that the immediate outcome, as a result, was a firm appropriation of something approximating the modern conception of individual personality. The absence of any stable belief in individual survival after death is, perhaps, indicative of the prevailing lack of clarity on the matter. So, too, is the marked degree to which the relation of humankind with God continued to be conceived in collective fashion, framed in terms of the "national" covenant and of Israel's history of common fidelities and apostasies as God's chosen people. Moreover, if for that chosen people the archaic pattern of divine or sacral kingship was to be excluded, it should not be forgotten that it was excluded in the name of kingly divinity. Yahweh alone being recognized eventually as truly king, the Israelite governmental ideal was destined to remain what the Hellenistic Jewish writer Flavius Josephus was later on to call "theocracy."

The importance of the point is not to be gainsaid. And for more than one reason. In the first place, some measure of insight into the convoluted history of the idea of Yahweh's kingship is vital for a proper understanding of the political attitudes one finds expressed later on in the pages of the New Testament, especially those clustering around the pivotal notion of the "Kingdom of God" or "Kingdom of Heaven." And it is vital, further, for a grasp of the recurrent theopolitical dreams (or nightmares) that for long centuries were destined to haunt the apocalyptic imaginings of Europeans. As suggested earlier, the relation of the messianic motif to the Christian as well as the Hebraic political vision is more direct than might seem at first to be the case. Intimately connected with the growing sense that the reign of the earthly Israelite kings derogated from the supreme kingship of Yahweh was the anticipation of the latter's final victory over his enemies, the eager expectation that in the providential unfolding of history the great "day of Yahweh" would eventually dawn. With that dawning, it was believed, his supreme kingship would finally be vindicated and the Kingdom of God gloriously realized here on earth.[35] Moreover, and in the second place, closely affiliated with that belief in the coming of the Kingdom was an extensive body of teachings concerning the Messiah (the "Anointed One"), the future mediator between God and his people, the leader whose coming would inaugurate that glorious event. As the word itself suggests, the Messiah was envisaged as a royal figure, an ideal anointed king sprung from the House or lineage of King David, a royal warrior who would recall the Israelites from their faithlessness and decadence, restore their loyalty to the covenant once made with Yahweh, and lead them into glorious victory over their earthly enemies. "Behold," proclaimed the prophet Jeremiah in the dreadful years leading up to the Babylonian conquest of Judah and the fall of Jerusalem, "the days are coming, says the Lord, when I will raise up for David a righteous Branch, and he shall reign as king and deal wisely, and execute justice and righteousness in the land. In his day Judah will be saved, and Israel will dwell securely" (Jeremiah 23: 5–6).

Whatever else such messianic longings did, they had the effect of passing on to future generations a familiarity with the images, epithets, and attributes long associated with the actual sacral monarchs of the ancient Near East, not excluding the Hebrew kings themselves. Given the visitation on the monarchy in 587 BCE of the doom that Jeremiah had foretold, along with the ensuing experience of the Babylonian exile and the bitter disappointments of subsequent Israelite history, it is not surprising that the version of the messianic hope that remained dominant right down to the lifetime of Christ should have been robustly and unambiguously this-worldly in nature. That is to say, it pivoted on the hope against hope that from the House of David would spring the ideal king who, by restoring the national kingdom and delivering the chosen and covenanted people from alien domination, would vindicate the supreme kingship of Yahweh and inaugurate the reign of righteousness so eloquently evoked by Jeremiah. The picture of the messianic king conveyed by the poems known as the "Psalms of Solomon" and dating to the period after the extension of Roman control over Jerusalem (63 BCE) would suggest that the years of renewed independence under the Hasmonean kings (168–63 BCE) had actually strengthened and rendered more concrete the traditionally this-worldly nature of the messianic hope.[36]

By Christ's own lifetime, then, extremists among the Israelites had begun to draw from the ancient belief that Yahweh alone was king of his people the more novel, and certainly more radical, conclusion that "the chosen people should tolerate no other ruler but Yahweh and that his rule should be effectuated via the ministry of his sole authentic representatives, the priests in the lineage of Levi, brother of Moses."[37] On the basis of that conclusion, those extremists, later referred to as Zealots, adopted a posture of opposition to Roman rule so unyielding as to embrace both hostility to the payment of tribute to the empire and, even, advocacy of the violent overthrow of what they regarded as a blasphemous and alien tyranny. This Zealot party was growing in importance in Christ's lifetime, and some scholars, noting that he never explicitly condemned it, have been led to portray him and his followers, if not as Zealots *tout court,* at least as quasi-revolutionary fellow travelers.[38] The fact is, however, that the Zealots were far from being the sole, or even the most prominent, bearers of the messianic legacy. From the core notion of Yahweh's supreme kingship a whole range of differing conclusions had been drawn across time.

Side by side, then, with the attitude typical of the Zealots must be placed at least two others, and it is only by a salutary economy that one can limit the number to two. Thus, in opposition to the revolutionary activism of the political extremists was the messianic quietism that was shared by Pharisees and Sadducees alike, though doubtless in differing ways.[39] And in opposition to Zealot, Pharisee, and Sadducee alike—all of whom shared the traditionally this-worldly understanding of the messianic kingdom—was a subsidiary complex of messianic ideas, glimpses of which can be caught in Deutero-Isaiah, in Daniel 7:13–14, in the Jewish Apocalypse known as the Book of Enoch (first century BCE), and in the writings of the Qumran sect (c. 200 BCE–70 CE).[40] These disparate works were by no means the bearers of any single, unified, or fully coherent system of ideas. Insofar as they ignore the traditionally this-worldly version of the messianic expectation and emphasize instead the heavenly, semi-divine character of the Messiah and the spiritual and universal nature of his kingdom, they do share at least a common tendency. And it is in relation to all three of these positions—Zealot, Pharisee-Sadducee, and quietist—that one must strive for an understanding of the ideas about kingship and the political life that one finds embedded in the disparate body of writings collected together in the Christian New Testament.

The New Testament

Although more than one point of entry is available to anyone setting out to come to terms with such ideas, I choose to begin with those that the four Gospels ascribed to Jesus himself. In so doing, I must necessarily sidestep any attempt to determine the degree to which the statements attributed to him were actually his or stem, instead, from the experiences of the early Christian communities and the impact of those experiences on the authors of the Gospels.[41] The remarks that follow, then, aspire to do no more than describe and elucidate the "political" notions that Christians as early as the Apostolic age (30–110 CE) believed it correct to attribute to Jesus and, having done that, to set them in the context of the pertinent "political" texts broadcast across the New Testament taken as a whole.

Given the fact that what we encounter in the Gospels is a complex amalgam of accounts of Jesus's life and teachings and later interpretations of the same, it constitutes, at least if taken "as a uniform, consistent, and literal record of Jesus's teaching, ... a collection of puzzles." Thus F. C. Grant, who goes on to insist that "the only possible way toward a solution of the inconsistencies is a frank recognition of the *variety* of interpretations reflected by the gospels and their underlying sources."[42] For our purposes, it is significant that he posts this warning while attempting to elucidate the meaning of the expression "the Kingdom of God." It is an expression that occurs more than a hundred times in the synoptic Gospels (Matthew, Mark, and Luke) and over a hundred and forty times in the New Testament as a whole. It conveys a notion that lies at the very heart of Jesus's overall teaching, and it constitutes the key to the stance he adopts to kingship in particular and matters political in general. But here the "variety of interpretation" of which Grant speaks is very much grounded in the complexity of the Gospel texts themselves and over the years has stimulated much disagreement about what exactly they mean.[43]

That disagreement has pivoted largely on two issues: first, whether the kingdom in question is a present or future one, and second, whatever the case, the nature to be ascribed to it. In relation to the first of these questions, it has to be acknowledged that in many Gospel passages (e.g., Matthew 13:24–52) the general emphasis is eschatological. That is to say that the Kingdom is identified with the state of righteousness destined by God's will to arrive at the end of time—Christ's earthly ministry being regarded as the compelling witness to the certainty of the Kingdom's arrival. But there are also passages—quintessentially Luke 17:20: "the kingdom of God is in the midst of you"—that appear to acknowledge at least some sort of tentative equation between the Kingdom of God and the congregation of the faithful or visible church (e.g., Matthew 13:41–43; 16:18–19). If the former, eschatological, emphasis is the safer guide to an understanding of the teaching dominant in the Gospels, it has to be conceded that the eschatology involved is what has sometimes been dubbed as an "inaugurated or realized eschatology." That is to say that the eschatological dimension has in some measure to be qualified by the sense expressed in so many Gospel passages that "the time is fulfilled, and the Kingdom of God is at hand (Mark 1:14–15), that "the decisive turning point" had already begun in Jesus the Christ,[44] that the Kingdom was in some degree a present as well as a future reality—albeit not one destined for full realization until the moment of final consummation (thus Matthew 5:3 and 10, 11:11–12, 12:28, 13:21ff., 18:4, 23:13–14; Mark 1:14–15; Luke 12:20–21).

But if the Kingdom is indeed a present as well as a future reality, then a heightened urgency attaches to the need to come to terms with the second issue that has been the focus of disagreement among commentators—namely, the nature of that kingdom. And here, in fact, though this-worldly, political, and even revolutionary interpretations have exerted an enduring magnetic attraction to scholars, the evidence afforded by the Gospels presents fewer obstacles to understanding. That evidence reveals a Jesus who, while accepting the role (if not the title) of Messiah, was moved to reinterpret its meaning, setting his face firmly against the traditionally "nationalistic" and this-worldly understanding of the messianic kingdom that was dominant in his day and appropriating instead the more spiritual version that we have seen ascribed to Deutero-Isaiah, David, the Book of Enoch, and the Qumran documents—and at the same time clarifying, deepening, and extending its meaning. Thus we should not miss the fact that the Gospels represent Jesus as having lost no opportunity to emphasize the spiritual and universal (i.e., *supra*national) character of the Kingdom whose advent he was proclaiming. It was a kingdom, it seems, that was to transcend all racial and national distinctions and to embrace the righteous from among all peoples, Jew, Samaritan, and Gentile alike. It was a kingdom, too, that was seen as universalizing itself "only through the entrance of one individual after another into it," for Jesus seems to have "recognized the strategic centre of his campaign to be in the soul of the individual man."[45] So that for the earlier dominant stress on the corporate relationship between Yahweh and the chosen people of Israel is now substituted the notion of the direct contact of the individual soul with God, who is conceived not only as all-powerful King but also as loving Father whose will it is that none of his little ones should perish.[46]

Again, even if it is only in the (later) Gospel according to St. John (18:36; cf. 6:15) that Christ's celebrated reply to Pilate—"My kingdom is not of this world"—occurs, the attitude that it expresses is reflected again and again in the other three Gospels. Thus the Kingdom belongs above all to "the poor in spirit," those who "have been persecuted for righteousness' sake" (Matthew 5:3 and 10), those who are "the servant[s] of all" and have become as little children (Mark 9:35–37; Luke 9:47–48). In that kingdom leadership will be a form of *diakonia*, that is to say, it will properly belong to those who *serve*. In it, certainly, there will be no lordship of the type claimed by the quasi-divinized Hellenistic kings of the day who titled themselves "benefactors" (Luke 22:24–30). This last passage is but one of several in the New Testament that can be read as an oblique deprecation of the Hellenistic portrayal of the king as a "living law," political society's "link with the world order," and as such titled appropriately not only as "benefactor," but also as "shepherd," "mediator," and even "savior."[47]

The conception of the Kingdom of God, then, that lies at the heart of the teaching of the Gospels on matters political is one that differs radically from that associated with the messianic views dominant in Jesus's own lifetime. To that fact attests the evident bewilderment both of his own followers, at least one of whom appears to have been a Zealot (Luke 6:15), and of his Jewish opponents, who certainly were not but who at the end sought to convince Pontius Pilate that Jesus had at least to be something of a Zealot fellow-traveler. But Jesus's negativity in matters political, his frequent disparagement of the kings and governments of this world and of their coercive methods, had little in common with Zealot attitudes. The less so, indeed, in that it was directed against *all* the governmental structures with which he had come into contact, Jewish no less than Roman. Nor should we miss the fact that that negativity was balanced, somewhat, by at least some measure of approval extended to governmental authority. Admittedly limited in scope, that approval finds practical expression in Jesus's own obedience to the laws of the land[48] and formal expression in his celebrated statement on the tribute money ("Render to Caesar the things that are Caesar's, and to God the things that are God's"). If that statement evaded the trap being set for him by the Pharisees and Sadducees, it must certainly have scandalized the Zealots. For if the things that were God's had to be rendered unto God, the tribute money, nevertheless, was identified as Caesar's, and Jesus indicated that it had to be rendered unto Caesar.[49] That position was wholly in keeping with his insistence that the Kingdom whose advent he was preaching was "not of this world." And both positions imply (in modern terms) an altogether novel separation of "religious" from "political" loyalties that stands out, in the broader context of the history of political thought and as Rousseau was later to intimate, as a departure fraught with revolutionary implications.

With the political teaching conveyed by the Gospels, then, the desacralizing process so powerfully evident in the thinking of the Hebrew prophets gained further momentum. The Kingship of God—for the Hebrews an unrealized ideal, no doubt, but for most of them an ideal destined for ultimate vindication in a this-worldly messianic kingdom of Israel—was now declared to pertain to a kingdom "not of this world," to a universal and spiritual kingdom that had nothing directly to do with politics or the collective vindication of a chosen people. It was a kingdom, instead, that was destined to augment and increase as God came to reign in the hearts and souls of individual believers drawn from all peoples. As a result, the denial of anything more than a conditional allegiance to the dictate of any earthly governmental authority ceased to be what it had been for the classical Greek philosophers—a prerogative pertaining not to the mass of humankind but only to those few, extraordinary spirits possessed of philosophic insight.[50] At the same time it ceased also to be what it had so often been to the Hebrews—a merely temporary restriction springing from the subjection of the Israelite people to alien rulers and destined for removal in the fullness of time. Instead it became, this denial, a prerogative to which all could aspire and a duty which all should shoulder.[51] It implied, in effect, a dramatic, permanent, and universal limitation on the allegiance that human beings can owe to any earthly society.[52] As Fustel de Coulanges put it, arguing in a classic statement that it was by the teaching of the New Testament that the polis was reduced finally to the status of a merely secular entity and the individual conscience liberated from its age-old thrall to political authority:

> Christianity completes the overthrow of local worship; it extinguishes the prytanea [sacred fire], and completely destroys the city-protecting divinities. It does more: it refuses to assume the empire which these worships had exercised over civil society. It professes that between the state and itself there is nothing in common. It separates what antiquity had confounded. We may remark, moreover, that during three centuries the new religion lived entirely beyond the action of the state; it knew how to dispense with state protection, and even to struggle against it. These three centuries established an abyss between the domain of government and the domain of religion; and, as the recollection of the period could not be effaced, it followed that this distinction became a plain and incontestable truth, which the efforts of even a part of the clergy could not efface.[53]

We shall see, of course, that these implications of the Gospel teaching were to be grasped only after the lapse of long centuries during which Christian peoples assimilated insensibly to more ancient and established ways of accommodating to the demands of governmental authority. Fustel, in effect, overestimated the immediacy of the change that Christianity introduced. He did so because he overlooked, or grievously underestimated, the nature of the difficulties that Christians of the first few centuries were to encounter in their efforts to come to terms with the full implications of the new teaching. The more so once they had ceased to be an intermittently persecuted minority and had come to occupy the favored position of a religion that (having first been tolerated) came now to be accorded the privilege (and the burden) of official establishment. Those difficulties sprang in part from the sheer novelty of the new teaching, which can be seen, at least in hindsight, to have run counter to the political commonsense of millennia. But they sprang also from the challenge involved in attempting to identify, not simply in the Gospels but in the New Testament taken as a whole, any universal or fully integrated teaching on matters political.

Its admitted complexities notwithstanding, so far as the Gospel teaching is concerned, two things stand out in bold relief. First, the fact that archaic notions of sacral kingship have been nudged to one side and, insofar as they implied the actual divinization of earthly monarchs, bluntly rejected. Second, that if memories of such notions actually survive at all in the Gospel setting (and they do), it is by virtue of being drawn into the magnetic field exerted by the central teaching of Jesus on the Kingdom of God and by being transmuted, therefore, into something radically different. But if one moves now to open up the scope of the inquiry and attempts to set the Gospel teaching in the context of the "political" texts broadcast right across the New Testament taken as a whole, one will find, marshaled around those comparatively firm central commitments, a markedly varied array of positions.

Of course, as Cadoux correctly insists, it is "antecedently probable that whatever the early Christians believed on the subject of the State, they regarded as a legitimate interpretation or extension of... [Jesus's] own teaching.[54] But it is equally probable that the particular interpretations or extensions they espoused would reflect their individual personalities and the particular and changing circumstances—religious, national, political, intellectual—in which they found themselves at the time they were actually writing. So far as kingship itself goes, nowhere, it is true, does one encounter any real drawing back from the deprecatory stance that some of the Pauline Epistles (in this like Luke) took toward the claims for sacrality attaching to the Hellenistic regal philosophy. Instead, under threat of persecution or in face of its reality, that attitude can be seen to have hardened, developing now in an apocalyptic direction, indulging the possibility that the last days might well be at hand, and postulating an open and inevitable opposition between the Kingdom of God and the established and fundamentally Satanic powers of this world. Intimations of that development are evident in the fourth Gospel and St. John's First Epistle. But it moved clearly into the foreground in the "Apocalypse of John" (dating probably to the reign of the persecuting emperor Domitian, 81–96 CE), which speaking in the name of the Kingship of God denounced as Satanic the blasphemously divinized emperors of Rome.[55] That position stakes out one extreme. Elsewhere, however, in what is probably the oldest part of the New Testament, we encounter a stance toward political authority that, while still negative in comparison with archaic and classical views, is a good deal *less* negative.

Thus, given his own possession of Roman citizenship and his well-attested willingness to exploit his rights as a citizen and to rely on Roman protection and the legal norms of Roman justice (Acts 16:35–40, 22:23–29, 23:10–35, 25:10–12, etc.), it was perfectly consistent for the apostle Paul to regard the Gentiles as having access, by virtue of their very humanity, to the norms of natural justice.[56] Again, writing his Epistle to the Romans, as he did, during the early part of the emperor Nero's reign (54–68 CE), when stable government prevailed and persecution of the Christian community at Rome had not yet begun, it is understandable that Paul should affirm the legitimacy of the role played by governmental authority. The more so, indeed, if the sort of public suspicion that might spark persecution was to be defused.[57] The earliest Gospel account of Christ's celebrated "Render to Caesar" injunction (that of Mark) probably postdates by about a decade the Epistle to the Romans,[58] and there is no evidence to suggest that Paul had some version of that injunction in mind when he framed the historic statement to be found in Romans 13:1–7. And even if he had, he had clearly understood that injunction in a distinctly positive fashion.[59] In the passage from Romans (13:1–7), which, down through the centuries, was destined to play so formative a role in the shaping of Christian thinking about political authority, Paul insisted that obedience to governmental authority is not to be viewed as driven simply by fear but is required also for the sake of conscience. In the (later) Gospel according to St. John (19:11), Jesus is reported as having said to Pontius Pilate: "You would have no power over me unless it were given you from above." And here Paul, moved by a similar conviction that political authority is itself of divine institution, goes on to insist that rulers, even when punishing the evildoer, are acting as servants of God. "Therefore," he says, "one must be subject, not only to avoid God's wrath, but also for the sake of conscience. Pay all of them their dues, taxes to whom taxes are due, revenue to whom revenue is due, respect to whom respect is due, honor to whom honor is due" (13:5–7).

Such emphatic exhortations, echoed (or paralleled) in 1 Timothy 2:2, Titus 3:1–2, and 1 Peter 2:13–17 ("Fear God. Honor the emperor."), may well have reflected a need, shared later on by the magisterial Protestant Reformers, to preempt the drawing of unwarranted and *politicized* or anomic conclusions from the notion of Christian liberty.[60] Whether or not they did, once Christians had in the fourth century been accorded toleration, those texts were to lay the basis, when taken as the point of entry into Christian thinking about politics, for a much more positive view of imperial authority than that suggested by Christ's teaching on the Kingdom of God. Certainly they were to do so when taken in conjunction with another important element in the New Testament to which we have not thus far alluded.

The element in question was the frequency with which, in both the Gospel attributed to him and the Acts of the Apostles, Luke correlates the Gospel story with the history of the Roman empire at large, emphasizing in particular the coincidence of the birth of Christ with the reign of the first emperor, Caesar Augustus (Luke 2:1ff., 3:1ff.; Acts 11:28, 18:2). The latter correlation Christians came early to view as nothing less than providential. Long before Constantine's conversion in the early fourth century, it served to ease the way for those Christians who dared to look forward with hope to a more positive relationship between church and empire. And after his conversion, taken now in conjunction with Paul's central teaching and with elements absorbed from the old Hellenistic philosophy of kingship, it helped open the way for others to accomplish something even more striking. It was something that the biblical understanding of the divine, the New Testament notion of the Kingdom of God, and its revolutionary separation of the religious from the political might seem to have rendered utterly impossible. It was nothing less, in effect, than an improbable species of Christian accommodation with the archaic pattern of sacred kingship. Hobbes's "old, empty bottles of Gentilism," it turned out, were indeed destined to be filled up with the new wine of Christianity, but that move was to be accomplished, astonishingly, without immediately shattering them.

/ II. The Long Twilight of
the Sacral Kingship
in Greek and Latin
Christendom
(c. 300–c. 1050)

4. Historical Orientation
The Heirs of Rome

THE ROMAN EMPIRE was a Mediterranean rather than a European power. While it survived as a unity, Europe did not yet exist as anything more than a geographical expression denoting the northwest prolongation of the Eurasian continent. Britain, the Rhineland, and even much of France were no more than peripheral appendages of the Romanized Mediterranean world. Ireland, Scotland, Scandinavia, the Low Countries, much of what is now Germany, and the greater part of eastern Europe all lay outside the empire's boundaries. As a result, the emergence of Europe as a cultural entity presupposed the failure of attempts to preserve or reconstitute the unity of the empire as a whole or of the Roman empire of the West. And that failure was determined during the late antique and early medieval period by three successive waves of devastating invasions of peoples from the outside—in complex combinations, peoples of Germanic, Hunnic, Avar, Muslim, Magyar, and Viking origin.

The first of these waves was generated in Outer Mongolia during the course of the fourth century by a confederation of warlike nomads who by sponsoring the displacement of neighboring peoples triggered the westward movement of other nomadic tribes, among them the people who came to be known in Europe as the Huns. Before it broke up in the fifth century the Hunnic confederacy had succeeded in either subjugating or terrorizing the Germanic peoples occupying the territory stretching from the Rhine and Danube frontiers of the Roman empire eastward as far as southern Russia. The outcome was the movement into the empire either by peaceful infiltration or outright invasion of a whole series of Germanic peoples. Though their initial objective was to seek safety behind the imperial frontiers from the dreaded Huns, they eventually obliterated those very borders and destroyed the political structure that we know as the Roman empire of the West. By the end of the fifth century, then, while the empire of the East continued to flourish, the provinces of its western counterpart had passed under the control of the several groups of migrating Germanic peoples—Ostrogoths, Visigoths, Vandals, Burgundians, Suevi, Alemanni, Anglo-Saxons, Franks—who had succeeded in breaching its frontiers.

In so doing, however, they cannot be said to have substituted for the old unity of the Roman Mediterranean world any new unity that could be designated as specifically "European." The Scandinavian lands to the north and the Celtic lands to the west continued to go their separate ways. Slavic people gradually silted into the regions of eastern Europe vacated by the Germans, and a complex amalgam of Germanic successor states replaced the several dioceses into which the Roman empire of the West had been divided. Principal among those successor states were the Ostrogothic kingdom composed of Italy and parts of what are now Switzerland and Austria, the Visigothic kingdom of Spain and Portugal, and the Frankish kingdom, which included much of France, the Rhineland, and part of the Netherlands. No truly common culture as yet united these disparate peoples. Though Ireland was evangelized as early as the fifth century, it was only during the four centuries from the sixth onward that the Anglo-Saxons, continental Saxons, Franks, Frisians, Thuringians, Scandinavians, and Slavs came to embrace Christianity. It is true that the conversion early in the sixth century of Clovis, the Frankish king, meant that all of the great Germanic successor states of Rome had become formally Christian. But that did not necessarily serve to unite them or to win for them the loyalty of their Roman subjects. Only the Franks had accepted the Catholic form of Christianity espoused by those subjects; the others had been evangelized by missionaries adhering to the rival Arian version, which hewed to a Trinitarian doctrine dismissed as heterodox by their orthodox Roman subjects and which served to widen the gulf dividing them from those subjects.

Even apart from such religious differences, moreover, the invading peoples were divided one from another on other grounds. Whatever their shared Germanic heritage, they differed in the degree to which, upon entering the empire, they had already embraced the rudiments of Roman culture or were already motivated by admiration for the splendors of the Roman achievement. Rather than being moved by any sort of aspiration that can properly be called "European," it is understandable that the more Romanized among these peoples should have been instinctively moved by a desire to preserve Roman civilization. Although Odovacar, the German general commanding the barbarian troops in Italy, deposed in 476 the last of the Roman emperors of the West, it was in some sense as representative of the Eastern emperor, and endowed with the imperial title of "patrician," that he ruled the Roman inhabitants of Italy. The same is true of his successor, Theodoric the Ostrogoth (493–526) who, bearer of the imperial titles of consul, senator, and patrician, set out to maintain the Roman system of administration in Italy and to preserve the fabric of Roman civilization.

Theodoric, it is true, may well have toyed with the idea of reestablishing the empire of the West under the rule of a Germanic king, but any hope that he or his successors might have succeeded in so doing was shattered by a change of imperial policy in Constantinople leading to a more direct assertion of (Eastern) imperial authority in the West. In 533 the Eastern emperor Justinian I (517–65) moved to reassert direct Roman rule over the Germanic peoples settled in North Africa, Spain, France, and Italy. The immediate outcome was the reestablishment of Roman rule over North Africa, the islands of the western Mediterranean, some territory in southeast Spain, and for a short time, the whole of Italy. The long-term results, however, were very different in kind. Britain, France, and most of Visigothic Spain still lay beyond the confines of the reconfigured empire, and the second of the three waves of barbarian invasions did much to render abortive even the limited degree of success that the emperor's prolonged and exhausting campaigns in the West actually did achieve. That second wave of invasions occurred shortly after Justinian's death, bringing the Avars (a people of Turkish origin) into the Balkan provinces, turning the attention of his successors from the rigors of the western reconquest to the tribulations of the heartland of the Eastern empire and the very safety of Constantinople itself. At the same time, it brought the Germanic Lombards into Italy, shattering for good the political unity of that peninsula and limiting effective Byzantine control to the south and to a fragile strip of land extending westward to Rome from Ravenna, where the imperial exarch was now headquartered. As a result, the ancient Roman capital was degraded to the status of a frontier town situated at the very end of the long and tenuous Byzantine lines of communication, very much exposed to the danger of renewed Lombard attacks but difficult to reinforce and left increasingly to its own devices.

That this should have been the case is explicable largely in terms of the price Justinian paid in the East for his unrestrained commitment of men and resources to the pursuit of his Western policy. It left him unable to do much more than sustain a holding action in the danger spots and pressure points elsewhere in the empire. As a result, it was left to his successors to cope with the Avar threat to Constantinople and with the Persian menace in the east. And even Heraclius (610–41), one of the greatest of Byzantine emperors, while he succeeded in destroying once and for all Persian imperialist ambitions, was able to assert no more than intermittent control over the Balkan province.

The luster of his great victory over the Persians, moreover, was soon to be dimmed by the dramatic emergence of a new military threat from the south. It was posed by the followers of the charismatic prophet Muhammad (c. 570–632) who, bursting out of their desert fastnesses in Arabia, seized rich territories in Iraq, Syria, Palestine, and Egypt. Within a single century invading armies under Arab leadership had spread from Egypt across North Africa and into the Hispanic peninsula, eliminating Byzantine control of the former and destroying the Visigothic kingdom in the latter. At the same time the Muslims succeeded in conquering the old heartland of the Persian empire and were beginning to push on farther into Asia. By the second decade of the eighth century, then, Spain having passed into the orbit of the Islamic world, Muslim armies in the West were exerting pressure on the southern part of what we call France, in the East were moving into the Indian subcontinent, and in Asia Minor were mounting a great assault on the city of Constantinople. This last endeavor failed, and by the tenth century the East Roman empire was to reach new heights of political strength and cultural achievement. Nonetheless, a great new power had clearly emerged, a Muslim empire, which in the territories it had absorbed had entered into an inheritance at once both Greco-Roman and Persian and which, in the centuries following, gave birth to the great civilization known as Islamic.

During the early Middle Ages, then, there were no less than three claimants to the Roman inheritance. Although neither the East Roman nor Islamic empire was immune to the sort of vicissitudes suffered by the Germanic successor kingdoms in the West, both succeeded for centuries in preserving and developing the type of higher civilization that had flourished in the ancient Mediterranean world and had spread to its periphery. So much so, indeed, that in the early Middle Ages it is Byzantium and the Islamic empire that deserve to be regarded as the more convincing bearers of the Roman legacy. Certainly the second great wave of invasions ensured that any future reconstitution of the Roman empire in the West would necessarily have to take a different and more novel form than that attempted by Justinian.

The Arianism of the Visigoths had alienated from them the loyalties of their Romanized subject population, and any gains made when they converted to the orthodox form of Catholicism were soon obliterated by the Muslim conquest. It was left, then, for the Franks, a less Romanized people, to grasp the future leadership of the West. Having done so, they eventually constructed a quasi-universal empire that not only embraced the greater part of Christian Europe but also expanded the boundaries of Christendom eastward into central Europe and into territory that had never been subject to Rome. Under the formidable leadership of Charlemagne (771–814), Frankish rule came to extend over the whole of Germanic Europe, except for Scandinavia and England, as well as over the greater part of what had been the Roman empire of the West; it also included some sort of suzerainty over the western reaches of the Slavic world in central Europe. Though a certain amount of confusion surrounds both the event itself and the precise intentions of the participants, there was a certain appropriateness, therefore, in the decision of the pope to crown Charlemagne emperor of the Romans in 800 and in the subsequent (if reluctant) decision of the Byzantine emperor to acquiesce in that title, thus acknowledging the reconstitution at least in legal terms of a Roman empire in the West.

When they had invaded the empire, the Franks had been among the least Romanized of the Germanic peoples and among those most hostile to Roman power. Unlike others, they had embraced the Catholic form of Christianity. But the alliance with the papacy that lay behind the revival of the empire had been cemented only in the mid-eighth century. It became effective only after 751 when the pope acceded to the request of Pippin III, head of the Carolingian family and de facto shogun-like ruler of the Franks, that Childerich III, the Merovingian who, though powerless, retained the title of king, be deposed and that he himself be given the Frankish crown. By that time, a confluence of traditions—Irish, Anglo-Saxon, and Latin— had sponsored the precocious flowering of a vigorous, religiously inspired culture which, centered in northeastern England, had overflowed into continental Europe in a dramatic surge of religious and educational proselytization and had laid the foundation for the renaissance of Latin letters associated quintessentially with Charlemagne's palace school and with the work, especially, of the Anglo-Saxon scholar Alcuin.

One of the marked features of this development was the close relationship that existed between the Roman popes and the Anglo-Irish missionary and educational endeavor on the Continent. As bishops of the city that had been not only the old imperial capital but also, it was firmly believed, the episcopal see of St. Peter himself and site of the martyrdom of both Peter and Paul, the popes had long since laid claim, as successors of Peter, to a primacy of honor and even of jurisdictional authority in the universal church. The gap, however, between theoretical aspiration and practical reality remained immense. These same centuries, after all, witnessed the transformation of Christianity into an imperial civic religion, with the Roman emperors themselves vindicating a stronger claim to be the functioning supreme leaders of the Christian world, even in spiritual matters. This remained true even during the pontificate of so active and distinguished a pope as Gregory the Great (590–604). His pontificate marked no definitive break in the pattern of subservience that had usually characterized the relationship of pope to Roman/Byzantine emperor, and as late as 663, that emperor could visit Rome and still be accorded all the honors pertaining to its lawful ruler.

But if to the inhabitants of the provinces still subject to Byzantine rule Gregory and his papal successors for a century and more remained leading dignitaries in what was still an imperial church, to the Celtic and Germanic peoples of the West they represented something different and far more grandiose. They enjoyed a prestige that was grounded largely in the fact that to the new peoples of the West the bishops of Rome represented in unique combination both the lost glamour of imperial Rome and the mysteries of Petrine apostolicity. In the mid-eighth century, then, when the rise of Islam had dealt shattering blows to the empire of the East, when the Byzantine emperors themselves had fomented a schismatic quarrel within the universal church by prohibiting as idolatrous the devotional use of icons and pictures, and when the Lombards had renewed their drive against the surviving Byzantine territories in Italy, the popes finally turned their backs on the East and sought the protection of the Carolingian rulers of the Franks. In so doing they may have hoped to crown their existing moral leadership of the church in the Western countries with the papal headship of a new and universal Christian society. By first recognizing the legitimacy of the Carolingian title to the Frankish throne and then conferring the title of emperor upon the greatest of the Carolingian kings, the popes revealed their willingness to embark on the exercise of some sort of supreme political authority, which if it belonged to anybody, belonged rightfully to their erstwhile masters, the emperors of Byzantium.

But the outcome of their alliance with the Frankish monarchy was perhaps not quite what the popes had hoped for. Although the forged document that became known as the Donation of Constantine furnished the popes with a persuasive (if spurious) title to the central Italian territory known in later centuries as the Papal States (and to a great deal more), it was in fact Frankish armies that in this same period forced the transfer of those nominally Byzantine territories from Lombard into papal hands. With the ascent to power of Charlemagne, who in 774 seized the Lombard crown for himself and who exercised power in matters civil and ecclesiastical with a truly Byzantine impartiality, it soon became clear that the papacy, by linking its fortunes with the Carolingians and committing itself to the exercise of temporal power in Italy, had not necessarily won the freedom of action its position within the Eastern Roman empire had previously denied it. The period of Carolingian hegemony was, however, short-lived. For a few, fleeting years in the late ninth century popes like Nicholas I (858–67) and John VII (871–81) were able not only to insist upon the primacy of honor due to the papacy but also to reassert with considerable force, and in the teeth of Byzantine opposition, its further claim to a primacy that was jurisdictional in nature. They were able to do so, however, only because the revived universal empire of the Carolingians, the power closest to home, was already beginning to disintegrate. And with the cessation in the 870s of effective imperial government in Italy, the bishopric of Rome, like many another lesser bishopric elsewhere in Europe, far from attaining liberty of action, was destined to be delivered into the rapacious hands of the local nobility.

The major cause of the precipitous decline in Carolingian fortunes, apart from dynastic dissension, was the arrival of the third and last great wave of invading peoples from territories lying beyond the European heartland. Viking sea raiders streamed out of Scandinavia from the early ninth century on into the tenth, attacking every European country from Spain in the southwest to what is now Russia in the northeast but concentrating their most devastating attacks on France and the British Isles. At the end of the ninth century and for sixty years more, a nomadic people called the Magyars came out of Asia and raided southern Germany, northern Italy, and as far afield as eastern France. At the same time, Muslim sea raiders from Africa, having gained the upper hand over Byzantine naval power in the Mediterranean, conducted piratical raids along most of the northern coastline and caused great turmoil in Italy and southern France.

The outcome of this devastating renewal of endemic warfare and ensuing loss of security was the withering of the literary and cultural flowering associated with the Carolingian renaissance, the collapse of the reconstituted empire of the West and, indeed, of all large-scale political structures, the concomitant fragmentation of political authority and allegiances, and a marked retraction of the borders of Latin Christendom. By the early tenth century, Corsica, Sardinia, Sicily, and even parts of the Italian mainland had shared the fate of Spain and been annexed to the Islamic world. By about the same date, a large part of the British Isles, Normandy, and the heartland of old Russia had been conquered and drawn into the orbit of a Scandinavian world that was eventually to stretch westward to Greenland and the North American coast and to become the focus of a brilliant and independent Nordic culture. In the territories that remained, however, ravaged and divided though they were, the years of Carolingian hegemony and partnership with church and papacy proved not to have been entirely fruitless. During those years Latin, Christian, and Germanic elements had begun to merge into a new cultural unity that may without question be called "European." The bonds that held it together were admittedly fragile ones. By the late ninth century all hope of matching fledgling cultural unity with any sort of real political unity had been lost. Under attack its boundaries were constricting and its fate hung in the balance. But it survived. By the late tenth century it had ceased to be on the defensive and was poised for the great economic, military, political, and cultural "take-off" that was to characterize the vigorous and creative centuries that we know as the High Middle Ages.

Long before the Carolingian dynasty came to an end, first in Germany (911) and then in France (987), the various Carolingian kings had been reduced to a condition of great political weakness, their powers usurped by quasi-tribal leaders in the east and by the one-time public officials known as counts and dukes in the west. But long before 911, two forces can be seen at least in retrospect to have begun to encourage the restoration of public order in Europe, to promote the quickening of revived prosperity and political strength, and to lay the foundations for later European recovery and renewed expansionism. The first of these was the continuing process of evangelization, which by the early eleventh century had brought Norway, Sweden, Denmark, and Hungary into the orbit of Latin Christendom and had helped curb the unruliness of Viking and Magyar alike. The second was the gradual and piecemeal emergence of a better-adapted and more effective mode of military, social, and political organization to which, lumping together a great variety of constantly evolving institutional forms, we have become accustomed to attaching the name of "feudalism."

The emergence of feudal institutions has often been regarded as something of a retrograde step. They involved, after all, the parceling out of public authority into private hands and the fragmentation of what had been quasi-centralized royal governments into a congeries of localized units. But that itself meant also that political power had now devolved upon those local magnates or "big men" best able to deploy military force and marshal soldiers in sufficient numbers in the localities that were most directly endangered but that the distant royal armies had proved powerless to defend. It was to turn out, moreover, that in the right hands and under the right circumstances feudal institutions could be manipulated and developed in such a way as to promote rather than hinder the emergence of strong central government. That fact was to become evident already in the eleventh and twelfth centuries with the appearance of the powerful states that the Norman dukes were able to create first in Normandy and then, after the conquest of 1066, in England, and that adventurous Norman nobleman, having wrested southern Italy and Sicily from Muslim hands, went on to establish in those lands.

That duly acknowledged, it has to be conceded that the initial impact of feudal institutions as they spread across Europe was to fragment political authority and to undermine the possibility of sustaining effective central monarchies. This process was first and most notably evident in the

Rhineland and northern France, the very heartland of the Carolingian empire. As a result, the most powerful of the regional monarchies that replaced that empire emerged further to the east, in Germany. There both kings and subjects proved to be more robust in defending themselves and their territories, and feudal institutions, accordingly, developed at a slower pace. By 1050, the terminus ad quem of this volume, German kings, first of the Saxon and then of the Salian dynasties, had inflicted crushing defeats on Viking and Magyar alike, had begun at the expense of the Slavs the prolonged process of pushing Germany's frontiers eastward into the lands beyond the Elbe, had acquired Burgundy, asserted a degree of intermittent political control over northern Italy, and assumed the title of emperor of the Romans.

There were marked fluctuations in the ways in which successive German emperors conceived of their imperial titles as well as in the degree to which they regarded themselves as successors to the ancient Roman emperors. Their revived empire could make a less credible claim to universality than could Charlemagne's, but in the late tenth and eleventh centuries it had become the most powerful state in Europe. There was, moreover, a great deal at once both Roman and Carolingian in the way in which these German emperors characteristically conceived of their relationship with the Christian church. Equating that church with Christian society at large and aligning both—at least by fiction—with the Christian empire, neither they nor (usually) their ecclesiastical advisers saw anything odd about the intimate intermingling of the religious and political that characterized their successive regimes just as it had that of Charlemagne or Justinian before them. Nor, given the fact that they had been anointed with the holy oil during the coronation rite, did they see anything odd in believing themselves to be possessed of quasi-priestly powers, in allowing themselves to be called "vicars of Christ," or in regarding themselves as responsible more than anyone else for the guidance and order of the church within their domains.

While much the same could be said of the Anglo-Saxon kings of England and the kings of France, the position of the emperor differed from theirs in two important respects. First, in the claim to universal leadership implicit in their imperial title and the fact that, within its boundaries, the empire included the seat of the bishops of Rome, those other sometime claimants to the legacy of Roman universality. Second, in the strength of the power these emperors wielded, as also in the degree to which that power depended on the enthusiastic willingness of higher ecclesiastics to serve as imperial administrators and, concomitantly, on the ability of the emperors themselves, through the tight control of ecclesiastical appointments, to ensure the loyalty of those administrators as well as continuing imperial access to the military and financial resources that the bishoprics and monasteries possessed. These were important differences, and they were to prove critical for the direction taken by political developments in Europe on into the future.

Also critical for the particular shape taken by that future was the fact that the years of turmoil, insecurity, and confusion inaugurated by the third wave of invasion from the outside had seen the disintegration of ecclesiastical no less than political organizational structures. They had seen the extension of aristocratic control over every level of ecclesiastical office and personnel: the local parishes and their priests, the monasteries and their abbots, the bishoprics and archbishoprics and their incumbents, not excluding the bishopric of Rome itself. The very notion of office, indeed, came to be assimilated to that of proprietary right, and there was, accordingly, an unprecedented growth of clerical disorder and administrative confusion. Manifested most obviously in the twin abuses of simony (the buying and selling of church offices and functions) and clerical concubinage, the latter carrying with it the attendant danger that hereditary succession to church offices might establish itself as a norm.

Family and political interests came to rule supreme, pushing to one side the church's spiritual goals and stifling its original sense of prophetic mission. In this respect, however, the tide began to turn in the late tenth and early eleventh centuries, when two streams of reforming endeavor began to gain momentum. The first of these was clerical in provenance and embraced twin movements centering especially on Lorraine and Burgundy (where the famous monastery of Cluny was its focus), and it had as its objective the elimination of simony, the establishment of clerical celibacy, and the general restoration of order in the church. The second, which enjoyed royal leadership, shared equally conservative goals, and the great reforming effort began to gain real traction after the year 1049 when the emperor Henry III (1037–56), who had earlier deposed three rival claimants to the papal office and installed successive candidates of his own, intervened once again and appointed Pope Leo IX (1049–54). Himself a representative of the Lorraine movement, Leo set out to provide the reforming forces with unified guidance and control, abandoning the preoccupation with local Italian politics characteristic of his immediate predecessors and appearing in person at a whole series of synods in France and Germany to investigate, to judge, and to legislate. In all of this Leo enjoyed the enthusiastic support of Henry III, and he did not contest the degree of control which that ruler, even more than the kings of France and England, continued to exercise over the churches within his realm. After Henry's death in 1056, however, and the destabilizing imperial minority that ensued, Leo's papal successors finally broke with the conservatism of his reforming stance. The challenge that Gregory VII (1073–85) handed down both to the old ideology of regal sacrality and to the age-old custom of imperial control of the church was nothing less than revolutionary in its implications. And it was destined to usher in a new and markedly different era in the history of European political thought.

5. Patristic Affirmation
The Greek Fathers and the Eusebian Tradition in Christian Rome, Byzantium, and Russia

THE HEBRAIC CONCEPT of God and the notion of creation that flowed from it, however determinative they may have been in undermining the archaic pattern of royal sacrality, did not suffice by themselves to destroy it. That much is already clear. At this point, however, we would do well to pause for a moment and take at least fleeting notice of the fact that on this matter the evidence to be gleaned from the Jewish Bible/Christian Old Testament does not stand alone. It is buttressed, in addition, by what we can learn from the religio-political attitudes prevailing in the vast region extending from the Pyrenees in the west to northwest India in the east that in the course of the seventh and eighth centuries CE had become the sphere of Islam, the third of the great "Abrahamic" religions. The monotheism of Islam's dominant Sunni or "orthodox" tradition is notably firm; so, too, is its insistence on the transcendence, omnipotence, and creative force of God. Even in its Shiite tradition, antipathy to archaic notions of sacral kingship has never been lacking.

Of that we were forcefully reminded less than forty years ago. When, at Persepolis in 1971, the shah of Iran (*Shāh ān Shāh;* "King of Kings") was unwise enough to indulge a moment of imperial triumphalism and to laud the virtues of 2,500 years of Persian kingship, his future nemesis, the Ayatollah Ruholla Mussaui Khomeini (d. 1989), responded from bitter exile by denouncing as un-Islamic the very title of "King of Kings."[1] In so doing, he was reflecting the worried ambivalence toward kingship in general that was early embedded in the Islamic tradition. Beyond that, he was also echoing the early Muslim juristic view that that particular title represented a blasphemous human usurpation of a prerogative that properly belonged to God alone. "The very title King of Kings," he asserted, "is the most hated of all titles in the sight of God." But when, warming to his theme and sharpening his attack, he then went on to claim that "to the whole notion of monarchy . . . Islam is fundamentally opposed," he was brushing to one side as a deviation or declension from some original and more purely Islamic norm long centuries of monarchical rule in the Muslim world.[2] By so doing he was, in effect, and in this like so many of the *'ulamā* (scholars and teachers) before him, ignoring the rich complexities of Islamic history in order to bring it into conformity with the urgencies of his own exacting (but contemporary) religio-political ideal.[3]

The fact is that by Khomeini's day, modern writers had long since slipped into the habit of taking at face value the "formal theological disputes and debates over the nature of political authority" that *medieval* Muslims had projected onto an earlier, largely empty, and concomitantly receptive screen. The Quran itself had had precious little to say about government or politics as such. And not a great deal more was to be elicited from the *hadīth*, or body of reports, traditions, or narratives conveying to posterity the actions and sayings attributed to Muhammad and his companions, which the emerging cadre of *'ulamā* had assembled (largely) in the mid-eighth century and of which they eventually succeeded in making themselves the authoritative interpreters. As a result, during the centuries immediately subsequent to Muhammad's death in 632, the Muslim thinkers and leaders on whose shoulders descended the burden of framing a mode of polity congruent with Islamic aspirations were understandably led to draw also (perhaps rather) on the vast repertoire of inherited bureaucratic practices in the newly conquered territories, as well as on ideological, ceremonial, and iconographic motifs elaborated over long millennia in the kingdoms of the ancient Near East, and especially those of Persian origin.[4] For Islamic political life that ancient Near Eastern inheritance was of enormous importance. And that holds true whether one is thinking of the mode of kingship attaching in the early centuries (c. 661–850) to the Umayyad or Abbāsid caliphs or that attaching in the modern period to the Safavid shahs of Persia or the sultan/caliphs of the Ottoman empire. On this particular point, the historian Aziz al-Asmeh is notably adamant: "Elements derived from the slight Arab tradition of kingship, heavily impregnated by Byzantine and Iranian paradigms, were combined with the enduring heritage of Semitic religion, priesthood and kingship. Muslim forms did not arise *ex nihilo,* nor quite simply from the writ of a Book; to propose otherwise is absurd in the light of historical reason."[5]

Ironically enough, however, it was an inheritance with unimpeachably Quranic roots that was to ease the way for the partial penetration into Muslim thinking about political life of Near Eastern notions of royal sacrality. That inheritance was destined to impress a distinctive stamp on Muslim political thinking and to set it apart from the principles fundamental to the political thinking (if not always the political practice) of the later Christian world. What I have in mind is the *umma* or community that Muhammad established at Medina, which has "remained the one unifying factor amidst the diversity of the peoples of the Islamic empire."[6] In Western terms, the *umma* would be classified as a "religious" community as well as a "political" organism. And the union of the religious and political that characterized it is "symbolized in the institution of the caliphate as the essence as well as the natural form of the *umma*." So that "Islam knows no distinction between a spiritual and temporal realm, between religious and secular activities. Both realms form a unity under the all-embracing authority of the *Shari'a* [the law].[7] . . . Politics is part of religion, so to speak; . . . [it] is the scene of religion as life on this earth so long as the law of the state is the *Shari'a*. The state is the *khilāfa* [caliphate] or *Imāma* [imamate or realm of the *imām,* chief or leader in prayer], and if we must operate with our western terms, it may be defined as a spiritual and temporal unity."[8] That being so, not even the purity of its monotheism or its adamant insistence on the transcendence and omnipotence of God altogether sufficed to immunize Islam against infection by notions deriving from the archaic pattern of sacral kingship with which in the conquered territories of the Near East, most notably in Iran, it came into such intimate and enduring contact. The essential "biblicism" of its basic theological commitments and the traditionalist and juristic temper of the majority Sunni community ("the people of the Community and Tradition," as it was sometimes called) tended to preclude anything more than intermittent episodes of oblique flirtation with elements of the cosmic religiosity underpinning that archaic pattern of sacral kingship. But such episodes did indeed occur. It early came to be assumed, for example, that the accession to the throne of a new caliph would bring with it rainfall and a general revival of the natural world, and that "when rulers act wrongly, the heavens dry up"—this last a saying attributed to Muhammad himself.[9] Later on, the belief spread that "the person of the caliph was a support of the order of the universe. If he were killed the entire universe would lapse into disorder, the sun would hide its face, rain would cease, and plants would grow no more."[10]

If in Sunni Islam such notions were little more than "popular conceptions" apt to be dismissed by the "Muslim theologians who . . . [dealt] with the theory of the caliphate,"[11] they were destined to enjoy somewhat freer play in the Shiite branch of Islam, with its proclivity for esoteric interpretation and its fervent stress on the central role of the imam, the "pillar of the universe," the "gate" through which God is approached, the leader upon whom the mass of the faithful depended for their knowledge and understanding of revelation.[12] It is certainly the case that at times when and in places where Shiite rulers grasped the reins of imperial power, essentially archaic notions of royal sacrality did indeed enjoy something more than rhetorical free play. Thus it was under the Fatimid caliphate centered on Egypt (907–1171), for example, that the degree of veneration of the ruler began to press against the limits set by the fundamentals of Quranic belief. And with the portrayal of the caliph al-Hakim bin Amr Allah (d. 1021) as an incarnation of the divine, those limits were destined finally to be transgressed, leading to the establishment among those known as the Druzes of what was a new syncretistic religion rather than anything properly identifiable as an Islamic sect.[13]

But even if religio-political conclusions falling far short of that Fatimid extreme cannot be regarded as representative of mainstream Islam, the pertinent point for us to grasp is this: if adherents to a religion in the Abrahamic tradition that dismissed the Christian doctrine of the Trinity as a blasphemous denial of the divine unicity were nevertheless not totally unresponsive to notions inherited from the archaic pattern of sacral kingship, then it would be surprising, indeed, if Christian thinkers proved to be any less responsive. Of course, they did not prove to be less responsive, and it was to be the achievement of one notable strand of thinking that runs through the body of early Christian writing that we are accustomed to calling "patristic" to have accomplished the difficult task of filling up again Hobbes's "old empty bottles of Gentilism" with the "new wine of Christianity" and to have succeeded in so doing without immediately breaking them.[14]

The Alexandrian Axis: Philo Judaeus to Origen

In 303, worried by the gradual siltation of Christian believers into the ranks of those holding high civil or military office, and viewing the characteristic Christian reluctance to participate in the public cult of Rome and Augustus as a potential threat to the unity and peace of the empire, the emperor Diocletian took what was to be for the growing Christian community a very threatening step. Having first sought to deflect whatever danger their presence might pose by dismissing Christians from the imperial service, he then moved more forcefully by launching what was to be the most widespread and thoroughgoing persecution the Christian church had yet experienced. The failure of that great persecution, Constantine's extension of toleration to Christianity in 312, and his subsequent policy of conferring an increasing measure of outright favor to its followers brought with them challenges of a type altogether different from those they had earlier confronted. Among those challenges, the most testing may well have been that which the new state of affairs came to pose for faithful adhesion to the core commitments of normative or biblical Christianity.

Over the centuries, and as we have seen, Hellenistic notions of kingship had progressively reshaped the Roman understanding of the imperial office, and the process of transformation had quickened in the wake of the barbarian onslaughts, visitations of plague, and descent into military anarchy that had turned the empire upside down during the disastrous half century running from 235–85. During the years of recovery that ensued, the very constitution of the empire came to be transformed into something akin to a military despotism, though one clothed in the elaborate court ceremonial and other appurtenances characteristic of the sacral kingship of Mediterranean and especially Persian antiquity. The favor Constantine came increasingly to extend to Christianity did little or nothing, of itself, to modify that transformative process. He did not divest himself of the old pagan priestly office of *pontifex maximus* or abandon the ceremonial trappings that served at once to underline his regal remoteness and to impart something of a religious aura to his person and official doings.[15]

To such imperial pretensions one might have expected Christians to react with a measure of prudent reserve at least comparable to that evinced by the mature Augustine a century later.[16] Their predecessors, after all, had had to endure for three centuries as a marginalized and intermittently persecuted sect. And the memory of the most bitter of those persecutions was still painfully fresh. In the early fourth century, however, Christians were far from betraying any such reserve. It is tempting to ascribe that surprising fact simply to an understandable sense of euphoria in the wake of so dramatic an improvement in their public fortunes. But in the context of the history of political thought it has to be attributed also to the impact of a factor less dramatic in nature and less apt to be recognized; namely, the development over the previous century and more of a theological (or theopolitical) tradition, the presence of which in their thinking meant that they were not altogether bereft of ideological resources when called upon to decide how they should properly relate to an imperial authority that had now come to clothe itself in Christian garb.

Surprisingly enough, that theopolitcal tradition was not itself lacking in biblical roots. It is true that the range of political ideas to be found in the New Testament did not, even in its most positive reaches, equip early fourth-century Christians very well when they were confronted with a situation in which they clearly had to find a way to come to terms with contemporary theories of imperial rulership, with their characteristic stress on the exalted and sacred status of the emperor. New Testament teaching clearly ruled out the possibility of ascribing *divine* status to any human ruler, however exalted. And the negativity it showed toward such and affiliated notions went further than that. Thus, though the point is contested, some scholars have detected in Luke 22:24–30 a further deprecation of the traditional Hellenistic claim that the monarch, being a living law, the very foundation of justice, the kingdom's link with the *logos* (or quasi-personified divine ordering reason) and, therefore, with the cosmic order, should appropriately enjoy such titles as "shepherd," "savior," "mediator," "benefactor" and so on.[17] Present also in the Lukan texts, however, was something else that, while not itself explicitly political, was susceptible of political interpretation. And that was the repeated correlation of the Gospel story with the history of the empire and the emphasis placed on the coincidence of the birth of Christ, prince of peace, with the reign of Caesar Augustus and the dawn of the Augustan peace.[18] For those Christians of the pre-Constantinian era who had dared, somehow, to look forward to a more cooperative relationship between Roman emperor and Christian church, that set of correlations, with its providentialist overtones, proved to be enormously influential. The more so in that the New Testament itself had appropriated and applied to Christ, not only the royal title of *Kyrios* (Lord) but also those other Hellenistic royal titles: "shepherd," "savior," and "mediator." Whether or not those latter titles had been appropriated by way of polemic *against* the prevailing ruler cult remains unclear. But even if they had, the very commonality of the language involved may itself (ironically enough) have paved the way toward a measure of accommodation with that cult.[19]

In the writings of the second-century Apologists, the fragmentary nature of the evidence notwithstanding, Francis Dvornik has detected "instances of Hellenistic infiltration into Christian thought."[20] And in the third century, notions drawn from Hellenistic political philosophy came to be mainstreamed into Christian thinking. That that mainstreaming was the work of the great Alexandrian church fathers is no accident. For a great and persuasive example had already been set for them by their distinguished compatriot, Philo Judaeus (c. 30 BCE–c. 40 CE).

Writing almost contemporaneously with the lifetime of Christ, Philo had been called on to undertake the urgent task of reconciling the biblical monotheism of the great Alexandrian Jewish community with the Hellenistic vision of rulership espoused by their Roman masters. He did so, it has been said, by "absorbing all the elements of the Hellenistic doctrine on kings, except for their actual deification."[21] Thus picturing the universe in Stoic terms as a great polis but one over which God rules as king, and going on to correlate monarchy with monotheism, he argued (as had Diotogenes)[22] that the king bore to his kingdom the same relation as did God to the universe. Rulership itself he saw as being in the image of God, and as if to underline that parallelism, he applied to God as the supreme king the traditional royal titles of "benefactor" and "savior." Going beyond mere parallelism, he went on to assert that even when tyrannically exercised, such rulership is a "special gift" from God. Hence the king's high priestly functions and his role as a living law; hence, too, his obligation to live in community with God and to conform himself to the *logos* of God (which, in one text, Philo identifies with the divine law). Thus Moses, in whom all royal virtues were exemplified, Philo presented as king and priest, capable of governing the people "because he himself is governed by the Logos." And going further, he presented Melchizedek as nothing less than king, priest, and *logos* alike "for he has the Really Existent as his portion."[23] Drawing back from the brink, however, he is careful to insist that no king, not even the emperor himself, however exalted his status, was to be accorded divine honors. If "he has no equal on earth" and "by the dignity of his office... is similar to God who is above all," nonetheless, "by his body the king is like any other man" and "as a mortal... must not be extolled."[24]

Central to Philo's thinking about rulership is the way in which he evokes and displays the notion of the *logos*. The term itself possessed the twin denotations of "reason" and "word," and Philo, who never formally defined it, used it at various times with different shades of meaning. The Stoics had equated it with the divine ordering reason immanent in the universe, and sometimes he veered toward that view. More characteristically, however, he took care to distinguish *logos* from God, speaking of the former, rather, as a created being, an "image of God," or a quasi-personification (God's "first-born son," "shepherd") of the divine reason, the presence of which in God's creation and governance of the world is the guarantor of its order and intelligibility.[25] And, in subsequent years, this was to resonate with those Christian thinkers who, in so many ways, trod in his footsteps.

Encouraged, in their turn, by the fourth Gospel's identification of the *logos* with Jesus Christ himself (John 1:1–18), those Christian thinkers were later to appropriate the *logos* doctrine and bend it to their own purposes. Prominent among those purposes was the pressing need to make the New Testament's varying statements about the nature of Christ and his relationship with the Father coherent and intelligible to themselves no less than to the world at large. From the time of the second-century Apologists onward, then, the Greek fathers of the church were led to exploit the *logos* doctrine in their ongoing attempt to shape and clarify their Trinitarian and Christological beliefs. They did so in a body of argumentation that is exceedingly complex and formidably dense, any real engagement with which would inevitably lead us to veer well away from the intellectual shipping lanes usually plied by works in the history of political thought. But one aspect of those recondite debates that was to prove pertinent to the development of fourth-century Christian theopolitical thinking may properly engage our attention here. Namely, that to the extent to which the Hellenizing motif was dominant in these patristic debates, to that extent the emphasis in the understanding and presentation of Jesus was not placed on the vivid historical figure one meets with in the New Testament accounts—the incarnate Christ, Man of Sorrows, crucified redeemer, heir to the messianic prophecies of the Jewish Bible/Christian Old Testament, proclaimer of the messianic kingdom, eschatological king. Instead, the emphasis was characteristically placed on Christ viewed as a cosmic figure, eternally preexistent *logos* or Son of God, mediator between that transcendent God and the created universe, the means by which alone the ineffable One could come into contact with the concrete Many, the simple with the complex, the necessary with the contingent, the unconditioned with the conditioned. Christ was presented, in effect, in such a way as to make plausible the historic conflation of the distant and abstract deity of the late antique philosophers with the God of Abraham, Isaac, and Jacob; the personal God of power and might who had deigned to create and govern the world and to reveal himself to humankind as a providential ruler; the God from whose omniscient purview not even the fall of a sparrow escaped (Matthew 10:29) and against whose miraculous intervention not even the might of a Nebuchadnezzar was proof (Daniel 3). A quite stunning conflation in effect, that involved the precarious insertion of essentially atemporal philosophical notions of archaic provenance into the ineluctably historical modality of thinking that stemmed from the Bible.

The Philonic legacy and the early Christian intellectual tendency described above came powerfully to the fore in the writings of the Alexandrian church fathers Clement (c. 150–c. 215) and Origen (185–c. 254). Their propensity for viewing Christ as primarily a cosmic figure, the eternally preexistent *logos,* encouraged them to clothe him with royal attributes derived less from the Bible or the tradition of eschatological Jewish messianism than from the contemporary and characteristically Hellenistic picture of the ideal king. And in this both theologians revealed the impress on their thinking of the writings of their great Jewish predecessor at Alexandria: "Through the identification of the Son with the Logos of Hellenistic philosophy," Per Beskow has said, "it becomes possible . . . to apply the ideas of a Philonic political metaphysics to Christ."[26] In comparison with Philo, it is true, Clement of Alexandria was not particularly interested in politics. But, in accord with his efforts to harmonize Christian claims with the Greek philosophical tradition and moved by the example of Philo, he proved, nevertheless, to be the thinker who "introduced Hellenistic notions of kingship into Christian speculation on the state and its rulers."[27] And that proved to be the easier in that, like Tatian and Justin Martyr before him (as well as Origen and Eusebius after him), Clement believed that it was from Moses and the Old Testament that the Greek philosophers had derived some of their most characteristic teachings. Thus, lauding God as the supreme king, he spoke in Hellenistic fashion of a "purely rational and divine kind" of kingship, one modeled on the divine archetype. Similarly, evoking the model of Moses, ruler and legislator, to whom he applies the standard Hellenistic royal terminology and whom he describes as having always been "guided by the best *logos,*" Clement went so far as to toy with the idea of the good ruler as being, akin to him, an "animate law" (*nomos empsychos*) and "the good shepherd" of his people.[28]

Well schooled though he was in the Greek philosophical and literary learning of the day, Origen, Clement's Alexandrian disciple, was to be somewhat more restrained in his embrace of Hellenistic political notions.[29] To God he frequently applied the word *basileus* (or "king"), evoking thereby the Hellenistic practice of seeing a parallelism between divine and human regality. But the only kingship with which he was willing to associate the notion of "animate law" was that of Christ the *logos* himself, and he was similarly restrained in his application of the Hellenistic royal titles to earthly rulers. Two aspects of his thinking, nonetheless, were to prove to be of great importance to the successor who, under the changed conditions of the early fourth century, succeeded more than anyone else in framing the first coherent Christian political theology.[30]

The first of these is the degree to which, in his reply to the attack which the Platonist Celsus had earlier launched against Christianity, Origen foregrounded the "Lukan" tradition, attributing a providential role to the Roman empire and the dawn of the Augustan peace in the dissemination of the Christian message.[31] "Bear in mind," he said, "that Jesus was born in the reign of Augustus, who, I would say, united into one *basileia* the many nations of the earth. The existence of many kingdoms would have been a hindrance to the spread of the teachings of Jesus throughout the world."[32] The second pertinent aspect is not in itself "political." It is the degree to which, while insisting that the divine Son or *logos* is truly divine, he contrives also, by calling him a *creature,* to convey the sense that he is less than or subordinate to the Father. Operating as they were with more developed Trinitarian formulae, later commentators of the post-Nicene era were prone, as a result, to view Origen as an Arian before the fact or to label him, even, as "the father of Arianism."[33] More to the point, at least for our purposes, is the way in which this "weak" or "subordinationist" Christology served, when picked up by his fourth-century sympathizers, to lessen somewhat any sense of a conceptual gap dividing Christ, the eternal *logos* and savior, from those more traditional saviors, shepherds, benefactors, and manifestations of the *logos* who went by the title of emperors of Rome.

Notable among those sympathizers was Eusebius, bishop of Caesarea (260/70–339). However prominent as a churchman and scholar (and he was the author of the *Ecclesiastical History*, to which we are primarily indebted for whatever we know about the Christian church of the first three centuries), Eusebius is far from being a household name in our histories of political thought. But it is in that very context that his thinking warrants close attention. His writings have well been described as "the point of confluence of all Oriental, Hellenistic, and Ante-Nicene Christian conceptions of kingship"[34] and the "first clearly stated ... political philosophy of the Christian Empire."[35]

The Eusebian Political Theology

By temperament and talent historian and scholar rather than philosopher or theologian (of any originality, at least), Eusebius trod very much in the footsteps of the great luminaries of the Alexandrian school from Philo to Origen.[36] Expelled by his bishop from Alexandria, Origen settled for the rest of his life in the Palestinian coastal city of Caesarea, which his pupil Pamphilus and, in turn, the latter's students had succeeded in transforming into a leading center of Christian learning. Among those students Eusebius, adopted son of Pamphilus and after 313 bishop of Caesarea, stood out as the most distinguished. In common with Pamphilus he viewed himself, quite self-consciously, as one of the bearers of Origen's intellectual legacy. And Origen's influence, certainly, is clearly evident in his writings. Of those writings, the two most pertinent to any attempt to come to terms with his political ideology are his *Life of Constantine* and his *In Praise of Constantine*, this latter being an oration delivered in the emperor's presence in 335 on the occasion of the thirtieth anniversary of his reign.[37]

Over the years, scholars have disagreed mightily about some very basic issues pertaining both to these works themselves and to the historical context in which Eusebius wrote them. The points at issue range from the very size of the empire's Christian population (and the extent to which, therefore, an emperor needed their goodwill in order to be able to rule effectively), to the nature and sincerity of Constantine's conversion, to the degree to which Eusebius's evident admiration for the emperor involved anything more substantial than the sycophancy of an established (or compromised) house or court theologian. In the absence of statistical evidence, opinions continue understandably to vary about the size of the Christian population.[38] But on the questions concerning Constantine's conversion and the nature of Eusebius's relationship with him, the scholarly labors of recent years have effected a considerable measure of clarification. Against the more critical views of yesteryear, they have converged on a more positive appraisal of the sincerity of Constantine's conversion and have come to emphasize its gradual nature.[39] At the same time, they have served to underline the fact that Eusebius, far from being "a court propagandist" or even one of the emperor's intimates, can actually have met him on no more than four occasions. If he was certainly an admirer of the emperor, he had to have been no more than "a distant admirer," and he deserves to be viewed not as some sort of court sycophant but rather as "a basically honest writer."[40]

That duly acknowledged, and despite his personal experience of the last great persecution, which had claimed as a martyr none other than Pamphilus himself, Eusebius can be seen to have remained faithful in the works to which we must attend to his earlier, remarkably optimistic viewpoint. That is to say, his appraisal of the role to be played by and the status to be claimed for the Roman imperial authority remained a fundamentally positive one. For him, in effect, "it was the persecution not the triumph of Christianity that was the aberration from the predictable course of history."[41] In this, he still reflected the attitude of his Alexandrian Christian predecessors. And like Themistius, his pagan contemporary, who also saw kingship as modeled on the divine celestial prototype (in his case, that of Zeus), he was very much in line with the course followed, three centuries earlier, by their great predecessor Philo.[42] His own point of departure, however, was a more historical one than Philo's: nothing other, in effect, than the Lukan tradition, which had earlier found expression in a whole series of Christian thinkers culminating in Origen himself. But Eusebius's position was somewhat more complex and rounded out than was Origen's. To the Lukan tradition he wedded the Philonic belief (shared also by Themistius) in the existence of a correlation between monotheism and monarchy, human kingship and the archetypal kingship of the supreme and sovereign God.[43]

It was a matter of simple fact, Eusebius noted, that the men of old suffered from the chaos and anarchy that followed ineluctably from the division of humankind into a multiplicity of warring tribes, principalities, and powers. And "you would not miss the mark," he added, if you were to "ascribe the reason for these evils to [the impact of the] polytheistic error."[44] Such, however, were the miseries attendant upon that state, and so gravely was "the whole race of mankind" oppressed by that "ancient malady," that "the benevolent Logos of God," moved by a divine compassion, "instilled" in them, "by... instructions of all kinds, certain preambles and elements of divine worship," imparting "the knowledge of the One God" and heralding alike "to Greeks and barbarians and all men" throughout the world "the one kingdom of God." He did so first by the ministry of pious men, later by that of the Hebrew prophets, and finally by condescending "to commune and converse with mortals through the instrument of a mortal body." Thus "now that the causes of the manifold governments had been abolished," the Roman empire "subdued... [those] visible governments in order to merge the entire race into harmony and concord." And it is not to be denied that "the synchronising of this with the beginning of the teaching of our Saviour is of God's arrangement."[45] "At the same time, then, and by the working of divine providence one empire also flowered everywhere, the Roman, and the eternally implacable and irreconcilable enmity of nations was completely resolved. And as the knowledge of One God was imparted to all men and one manner of piety, the salutary teaching of Christ, in the same way and at one and the same time a single sovereign arose for the entire Roman Empire and a deep peace took hold of the totality."[46] This "profound peace," this "deepest peace," the *pax Augusti*, which had lasted "from our Saviour's birth until now," Eusebius considered to be "the proof irrefutable that the prophet refers to the time of our Saviour's coming among men."[47]

Attaching as he did so great a significance to the advent of a unified Roman empire under the leadership of Caesar Augustus, it is not surprising that Eusebius should attach an even greater significance to Constantine's inauguration three centuries later of a *Christian* empire. Recognizing in that empire an even closer approximation to the archetype of divine monarchy, he viewed it as not merely a continuation of the Augustan initiative but, further than that, as an extension (or completion?) of the work of Christ himself. Constantine's imperial position was to be regarded as sacred in nature, and Eusebius leaves us in no doubt that the emperor himself was personally close to God. To him, we are told, God has often vouchsafed revelatory insights, along with "frequent enlightening visions of... [Christ's] divinity." So much so, indeed, that it would be "presumptuous to attempt to instruct the emperor in matters pertaining to the sacred mysteries."[48]

Far from representing him as an ordinary lay believer, then, Eusebius portrays Constantine as a quasi-priestly figure, "like a universal bishop appointed by God," one deeply involved in ecclesiastical government—convoking, supporting, presiding over, and participating in the councils of the church, not least among than the historic Council of Nicaea which assembled at his bidding in 325.[49] On more than one occasion he explicitly compares the emperor with Moses, the figure in whom Philo and Clement of Alexandria had seen all the royal virtues exemplified, and his great victory at the Milvian Bridge over his imperial rival Maxentius is rendered as an explicit parallel to the destruction during the Exodus of pharaoh and his host in the Red Sea.[50] From time to time, moreover, and perhaps more arrestingly, Eusebius would appear to be hinting that with the advent of Constantine and the unification once more of the entire empire, the world might be witnessing at long last the dawning of the messianic era that, as the Scriptures had foretold, was destined to succeed to the reign of Antichrist. The great palace banquet that Constantine staged on the occasion of the twentieth anniversary of his reign and at which he feasted the bishops whom (he hoped) he had reconciled at Nicaea, Eusebius describes in the *Vita Constantini* as "beyond all description," an event suggestive of the messianic banquet itself. "It might have been supposed," he adds, "that it was an imaginary representation of the kingdom of Christ, and [that] what was happening was 'dream not fact.'"[51] And in a passage in the *Oration* attributing to Constantine a victory, which in a comparable passage in the *Theophany* he ascribed to the *logos*-Christ, he presents the emperor very much in the guise of a quasi-messianic figure, the "invincible warrior and Attendant" of God the "Supreme Sovereign" and "the image of the One Ruler of All" who has finally vanquished the manifold forces of evil.[52]

In terms even of the most positive strand of New Testament thinking about politics, comparisons of this sort are really quite startling. What renders them understandable is a recognition of the degree to which Eusebius was indebted to Philo's theopolitics and of his own evident sympathy with the type of *logos*-theology espoused (under Philonic influence) by the Alexandrian church fathers. His familiarity with Philo's Judaized version of Hellenistic sacral kingship is not open to question, and it has been asserted, indeed, that his "imperial ideal and Philo's conception of the monarchy coincide entirely."[53] Nor, though it is surely incorrect to label him as an Arian *tout court*, is the "weak" or "subordinationist" nature of his Christology in doubt.[54] In the *Oration*, as in other of his writings. Philonic indebtedness and Christological subordinationism are alike very much on display. In that work, God the Father is portrayed very much as the supreme royal figure, "the one who is truly supreme...Above the Universe, the Highest of All, the Greatest, the Supreme Being," the "Supreme Sovereign, indeed, of all eternity."[55] "Ungenerated, above and beyond the universe, beyond description, beyond understanding, unapproachable, living in unapproachable light," he is the God of the late antique philosophers, and as such, if he is also to be the biblical God, creator of all things visible and invisible, he needs to project an intermediate power between himself and those merely created and "perishable" beings that are so far removed from his ineffable perfection. That intermediary is, of course, Eusebius's second royal figure, "the hidden and invisible Logos," the "Only Begotten of God" whom the creator "ordained Captain and Pilot of this universe" and who "now directs and turns it by an incorporeal and divine power, expertly handling the reins in the way he deems right."[56]

Attendant upon such formulations, at least in post-Nicaean terms, is, admittedly, a certain uneasiness. But Eusebius is far from denying the divinity of the *logos*. Nor does he fail to affirm that without changing "from His natural deity," the "divine" or "inspired Logos of God," "the Common Saviour of All... condescended to commune and converse with mortals through the instrument of a mortal body, with the intention of saving mankind through the resemblance."[57] Thus, by means of that "mortal" or "physical instrument" he revealed himself as "the benefactor and salvation for all," descended to earth, was crucified, died, and rose from the dead. In the *Oration* he persistently favors such terms as "divine logos," "logos of God," "All-Ruling logos of God and Universal Creator" and speaks but briefly of the historical Jesus. Moreover, when he feels moved to offer reasons for the Incarnation, Crucifixion, and Resurrection, it is significant that he leans most heavily (and, it seems, instinctively) on the explanation that they were necessary, above all, if the *logos* was to be able by means of a mortal body to proclaim to all the doctrine of the one God and to overcome *ignorance* by conversing with men. Thus, by taking upon himself the weakness of mortal flesh, by suffering, dying, and rising again, he was able "to reveal Himself [as] stronger than death" and to impart to men not simply "by words and speeches" but also by "the very act [of resurrection] itself" the saving doctrine of the "immortality and life with God that is our common hope." The emphasis, then, is on knowledge and enlightenment. Only in a third, and subsidiary, explanation does he allude to the notion of Christ's having suffered and died as a sacrificial victim to atone for the "earthbound and guileful error" of our human ways. In effect, and as Maraval correctly notes, in these explanations Eusebius tends to construe the role of the incarnate Christ-*logos* less in terms of redemptive acts than in terms of the revelation of eternal verities.[58]

In the *Oration,* addressed as it was to a pagan as well as a Christian audience, Eusebius manages to avoid evoking explicitly the name of Christ. Faithful in this to the Alexandrian tradition, his Christlike figure is above all the eternally preexistent *logos,* creator, governor, "Framer and Organizer of the universe," sole revealer of the "Heavenly Father," or "Supreme Sovereign" but distinct from and subordinate to him. Thus, although the Christ-*logos* is the "world-creating" and "All-Ruling Captain and Pilot of this universe," Eusebius contrives nonetheless to associate very closely with him, and not least of all in the role of drawing men to the knowledge of the one, true God, that other ruler and regal pilot, the earthly emperor of Rome.[59] For the *logos* "has modelled the kingdom on earth into a likeness of the one in heaven, toward which He urges all mankind to strive, holding forth to them this fair hope." And in this hope, "God's friend," the divinely favored Constantine, who "has patterned regal virtues in his soul after the model of . . . [the divine] kingdom" is destined henceforth to participate. He stands, therefore, as Eusebius's third royal figure, one positioned in a uniquely intimate relationship with the "all-pervasive Logos of God, from whom and through whom bearing the image of the higher [divine] kingdom, [he, this] sovereign dear to God [and] in imitation of the Higher Power, directs the helm and sets straight all things on earth."[60] And, like Eusebius's further application to Constantine of the ancient sun symbolism, such sentiments are, of course, redolent of the Hellenistic vision of sacral kingship.

Nowhere is the depth of Eusebius's commitment to that vision more notable than in the *Oration*'s second chapter. There, without ascribing divinity to the emperor or identifying him as an incarnation of the *logos* and, as such, a "living law" (*nomos empsychos*), he contrives nonetheless to correlate his activities and powers very closely with those of the (Christ)-*logos* and to draw a striking series of parallels between their respective functioning, salvational as well as governmental. Thus, for example,

> The Logos, being the Pre-Existent and Universal Saviour, has transmitted to His followers rational and redeeming seeds, and thereby makes them rational and at the same time capable of knowing his Father's kingdom. And this friend [the emperor], like some interpreter of the Logos of God, summons the whole human race to knowledge of the Higher Power, calling in a great voice that all can hear and proclaiming for everyone on earth the laws of genuine piety. [Similarly], the Universal Saviour throws wide the heavenly gates of His Father's Kingdom to those that depart hence for there; the other [i.e., the emperor], in imitation of the Higher Power, has cleansed all the filth of godless error from the kingdom on earth, and invites bands of holy and pious men into the royal chambers, taking care to preserve intact each and everyone of all those entrusted to his care.[61]

And if following in this the Scriptures, Eusebius accords to the *logos* such Hellenistic royal titles as savior, benefactor, and good shepherd, he does not refrain from attributing similar qualities, functions, and titles to Constantine himself. In his *Life of Constantine* he reports that the emperor's soldiers had done likewise,[62] and in the *Oration* he represents the emperor, a "good shepherd," as "seeking to emulate in royal deeds the benevolence [*philanthropia*] of the Higher Power." He portrays him, indeed, as a sort of imperial savior, a priestly and Christlike figure who, "entirely dedicated" to that divine power, "has himself rendered a great offering, the first fruit of the world with which he is entrusted."[63]

What is involved, then, is a thoroughgoing resacralization of the imperial office in quasi-Christian terms. It is doubtless an exaggeration to claim that Eusebius's political theology "puts the immanent emperor in the place of the transcendent Christ." But by understanding in mimetic fashion "the terrestrial empire as an image of the heavenly kingdom," it certainly contrived to situate "the Christian Roman Empire in the economy of salvation."[64] As George Williams rightly insisted, "Christians of the Ante-Nicene period had for the most part recognized the Roman state, even when it persecuted them, as an order of *creation,* but emphatically not as an order of *redemption*.... But now in the fourth century with the emperor a Christian, the state would seem to have significance as an ally of the Church or indeed as itself a secondary instrument of salvation."[65] Eusebius clearly interprets Constantine's victory "in terms of the history of salvation," and he portrays the emperor as being obedient not to the earthly, incarnate Jesus Christ, whose authority lives on in the church, but to the eternal *logos.*[66] It would be pointless, accordingly, to expect to find in his political theology any clear distinction between church and Christian empire. To the contrary, and as the subjects of the empire embraced Christianity, Eusebius saw those two social structures moving toward unity, with the Christian society thus produced standing in direct and close relation with the Kingdom of God.[67]

In a classic essay written under the shadow of the Third Reich with its totalitarian promotion of a "positive Christianity" and stimulated also, it may be, by Carl Schmitt's earlier evocation of the notion of a "political theology," Erik Peterson argued that every purportedly "Christian" political theology, the Eusebian version included, was destined to be negated by the triumph in the fourth century of orthodox Trinitarianism.[68] Though historically grounded, Peterson's central point was theological rather than historical in nature. But that notwithstanding, sympathizers with his general point of view have not proved to be lacking among subsequent historical commentators.[69] Evoking Peterson's work and arguing in somewhat schematic fashion, G. H. Williams postulated an intimate connection between the respective Christologies of the Arian and Nicene-Catholic churchmen, on the one hand, and, on the other, their characteristic attitudes toward the empire. Thus with "the Catholic insistence upon the consubstantiality of the Son" he linked "the championship of the independence of the Church of which he is the Head" and the insistence that "the emperor is within the Church." And with "the Arian preference for Christological subordinationism" he linked "the Arian disposition to subordinate the Church to the State" and to view the emperor as "bishop of bishops." The former position, with its "sense of disparateness between the Christ-founded Church and the God-ordained Empire" was destined to become "a permanent feature of Western Christianity," while the latter had some sort of affinity, at least, with "Caesaropapism," or what Jacob Burckhardt had earlier labeled as "Byzantinism."[70]

While no doubt helpful in the demanding attempt to find a coherent path through the tangled complexity of fourth-century thinking about the way in which Christians might properly come to relate to a sacralized imperial authority, the neatness of this sort of schematic approach generates its own rigidities and confusions. It is true that to the degree in which the Eusebian political theology was dependent on a subordinationist Christology, to that degree one might expect it be vulnerable to the Nicene insistence that Jesus Christ was the Son of God, consubstantial with (or the same essence as) the divine Father. And in some measure, at least, that may well have been the case.[71] But more telling than any specifically theological motif was the fact that the chastening political circumstances of the mid-fourth century began themselves to make apparent how vain had been the Eusebian imaginings that the looming silhouette of the millennial kingdom of the prophets was to be discerned in the newly Christianized empire of Rome.[72] It was under the impact of the embrace of the Arian heresy by the emperor Constantius II that such supporters of the Nicene orthodoxy as St. Athanasius (d. 373) in the East and St. Hilary (d. c. 367) in the West began openly to criticize imperial interference in ecclesiastical affairs. And when, at the end of the century, the emperor Theodosius's religious policy "placed the Arians in the conflict situation previously occupied by the [Nicene] orthodox," they, too, Christological proclivities notwithstanding, were similarly disposed to criticize imperial interference. As Beskow has rightly concluded, "political considerations were often of greater significance than the basic theological attitude in these matters."[73]

It would be incorrect to suppose, however, that the disposition to adopt a less uncritical attitude toward the claims and policies of the emperors in matters religious necessarily entailed any wholesale abandonment of the Eusebian political vision. *Christomimesis* may well have succeeded to Eusebius's own more ambiguous and more purely Hellenistic *Logomimesis,* but his general vision, with its beguiling evocation of the parallelism between divine and human regality, was destined for an extraordinarily long life. Even in the Latin West, and as we shall see in the following chapter, the strength of its appeal is evident in the writings of a series of Christian thinkers: the anonymous fourth-century writer usually known as "Ambrosiaster" or "Pseudo-Augustine" (in many ways the Western counterpart of Eusebius), or the great St. Ambrose, bishop of Milan (d. 397), or, most of all perhaps, the Spanish author Orosius (fl. early fifth century). And in the Byzantine East where, in the fourth and fifth centuries, the Eusebian vision was clearly reflected in the writings of St. Gregory Nazianzus (d. c. 389), Gregory of Nyssa (d. c. 394), and St. John Chrysostom (d. 407), it was destined to enjoy nothing less than a millennial career.[74]

Byzantium, Russia, and the Eusebian Legacy

In relation to Byzantine political thinking, scholars have been apt to emphasize continuity rather than discontinuity and have insisted, with no little unanimity, on the marked stability evident across the centuries in the overall conception of the imperial authority and its central place in the Byzantine world view. Fair enough, it may be, so long as one is appropriately mindful of the degree to which the unfortunate deployment of terms like "Byzantinism" and "Caesaropapism" has tended to promote a somewhat foreshortened vision of Byzantine political thinking, encouraging us to see that body of thought through the distorting lens of distinctively Western categories and to project onto its shifting and millennial complexities a mystic sense of timeless stasis.[75] But those complexities are real and "stasis" is hardly descriptive of the realities on the ground. And while it has to be recognized that the type of change involved was conservative in nature and gradual in its emergence, it has also to be admitted that such complexities did indeed serve in their own way to promote it. It should take little more than a nodding acquaintance with the tangled skein of East Roman history to disabuse one of any notion that Byzantine attitudes on matters political were monolithic and resolutely unchanging, or that the emperor possessed a measure of control over the apparatus of ecclesiastical life such that the assertion by clerical dignitaries of the ultimate spiritual independence of the church was totally inconceivable.[76]

During the centuries, especially, that preceded the definitive ending of the iconoclastic controversy in 843, some attributes traditionally ascribed to the emperors and some actions periodically taken by them did become the focus of occasionally sharp contestation between them and the clerical and monastic leadership of the day. So far as moments of tension between emperors and the clerical and monastic leadership are concerned, two matters in particular gave rise to periodic controversy. First, attempts by successive emperors to circumvent the normal recourse at moments of doctrinal disagreement to the decisive agency of an ecumenical council acting as the legitimate arbiter in such matters, and to impose on the faithful, instead, their own preferred solutions. Across the centuries and right down to the extinction of the empire in the fifteenth century, such attempts proved to be endemic. The most egregious of them was the protracted effort from 730 to 780 by the emperors Leo III, Constantine V, and Leo IV to suppress as idolatrous the customary cult of venerating images, to prohibit their presence in the churches, and to bring about their destruction.[77] As was almost invariably the case with imperial intrusions into the realm of doctrine, that attempt conformed to the pattern of short-term success followed remorselessly by long-term failure. Indeed, this particular exercise in "imperial heresy" (as it was sometimes called) marked something of a turning point in the way in which the relation of the imperial authority to the inner reality of the church was viewed. Moved usually by considerations of political expediency, subsequent emperors certainly did not refrain from comparable attempts to engineer doctrinal change. But the fact remains that in the eyes of the faithful no ultimate legitimacy appears to have attended upon such efforts.[78]

The second matter responsible for generating tension in the ongoing relationship between emperor and clergy was the traditional claim that the former was in some sense himself a priest. The Arian inclination to portray the emperor as "bishop of bishops" proved evanescent. But according to Eusebius, Constantine had called himself "bishop for those outside the Church,"[79] and a kind of hieratic character did indeed cling to the imperial personage.[80] The adoption by St. Ambrose in the West and St. John Chrysostom in the East, in the fourth century, of a more critical stance toward the claims of the emperor in matters religious may have reflected a felt need to discriminate between the ill-defined type of priesthood ascribed to the emperor and the more exclusive priesthood in matters sacramental possessed by the ordained clergy.[81] But even on that score, and more than a half century later, Pope Leo I (440–61), who stands out for having advanced quite striking claims on behalf of the papal primacy, could still ascribe a priestly character to the emperor.[82] Even in the West, it is not until the end of the fifth century that we encounter in the celebrated statements of one of his papal successors, Gelasius I (492–96), an unambiguous denial of that imperial sacerdotal status. That much about the contested views of Gelasius is certainly clear. But little else is, and given the conflicting interpretations that Western commentators were to give to his views over the course of the next millennium, it is necessary now to pause for a moment and to try to come to terms with what exactly it was that he had to say.[83]

Evoking as an example the mysterious figure of Melchizedek, referred to in the book of Genesis (14:18), Gelasius acknowledged that "before the coming of Christ... certain men, though still engaged in carnal activities, were symbolically both king and priest." "But when He [Christ] came who was true king and true priest, the emperor no longer assumed the title of priest, nor did the priest claim the royal dignity." Christ, in effect, "distinguished between the offices of both powers according to their own proper activities and separate dignities," so that a "healthful humility" would prevail, neither would be "exalted by the subservience of the other, and each profession would be appropriately fitted for its appropriate functions." And that argument Gelasius sought to bolster with the historically inaccurate suggestion that it was only the pagan emperors who had used the title of *pontifex maximus*.[84]

It should be remembered that Gelasius was writing under unusual circumstances, in the wake of the Gothic incursion into Italy, at a moment when the Byzantine emperor was possessed of no more than theoretical authority at Rome itself, and when the papacy had already embarked on the process of elaborating in legal terms its nascent claim to a primacy of jurisdiction in the universal church.[85] It has to be realized, too, that Gelasius was also writing under conditions of crisis precipitated by the emperor Zeno's unilateral attempt to impose an imperial doctrinal solution to the recrudescent Christological disputes of the day.

Under such circumstances, by dismissing the commonplace notion of the emperor's priesthood and by affirming a dualism of powers that was certainly more in keeping with the New Testament vision of things, Gelasius's aim was to try to eliminate the theoretical underpinnings for imperial intervention in religious matters. That much is clear. What remains unclear, however, and certainly much disputed, is whether or not he intended to go further than that and, if so, how much further. During the medieval centuries, many a controversialist in the West believed that it was his intention to do nothing less than claim for the priesthood in general and the papacy in particular a superiority even in matters temporal. And on the basis of the most subtle analyses, some modern scholars have not hesitated to affirm that that is certainly the conclusion to be drawn from the further (oft-quoted) statement made in a letter of 494 to the emperor Anastasius (and in response to that emperor's complaint that Gelasius had not notified him about his election as bishop of Rome):

> Two there are, august emperor, by which this world is chiefly ruled, the sacred authority of the priesthood and the royal power [*auctoritas sacrata pontificum et regalis potestas*]. Of these the responsibility of the priests is more weighty in so far as they will answer for the kings of men themselves at the divine judgment. You know, most clement son, that, although you take precedence over all mankind in dignity, nevertheless you piously bow the neck to those who have charge of divine affairs and seek from them the means of your salvation, and hence you realize that, in the order of religion, in matters concerning the reception and right administration of the heavenly sacraments, you ought to submit yourself rather than rule.[86]

Much of the controversy over this particular text has turned upon the precise meanings to be given to the terms *auctoritas* and *potestas*. Disagreement persists as to whether the words were simply being used here as synonyms or, rather, as terms bearing the technical meanings attaching to them in the Roman law. Even if the latter is taken to be the case, much still depends on whether by the *potestas* ascribed to the emperor is meant effective, sovereign power or merely a species of power delegated by the (papal) possessor of *auctoritas* to execute orders from above. If the former is the case, the ascendancy in the relationship between the imperial and papal offices tilts toward the emperor; if the latter, it tilts toward the pope.[87] But technical arguments of this sort have not proved to be very fruitful,[88] and attention paid to the statements of Gelasius taken as a whole and to the context in which they were framed shows more promise of opening up a route to the resolution of the issue.

Take that tack and it speedily becomes clear that there is little ground for the conclusion (to which many a medieval nonetheless subscribed) that Gelasius had himself intended to accord an inherently superior authority to the priesthood and a merely delegated power to the emperor even in matters temporal. Little ground, that is, unless one is committed to the prior assumption that when he ascribed a weightier responsibility to priests in that they will have to answer for kings at the divine judgment, he had in mind not the ruler simply as another member of the faithful but the emperor in his public, imperial capacity. The letter as a whole, which is quite deferential in tone, certainly does not lend itself to such an interpretation. The less so, indeed, when read in its historical context and in tandem with Gelasius's other principal statement on the two powers discussed earlier. For the context, it should not be forgotten, was one of crisis in which it was the pope who was on the defensive and the emperor who had broken with tradition by attempting, on his own authority alone, to impose on the church a particular doctrinal position. Seen in this way, then, and with the exception of his denial to the emperor of any sacerdotal office, Gelasius's views do not appear to have constituted any marked break with Eusebius's half-Christianized version of the Hellenistic philosophy of kingship.[89]

Moreover, even had his views constituted such a break, and however much medieval political theorists in the West were later to make of them, it remains the case that Gelasius's immediate successors at Rome appear to have been unmoved by them, inclining instead to ease back into more traditional attitudes.[90] Still less did his views generate any reverberations in the East. There the attribution to the emperor of some sort of priestly role was to persist for centuries, surviving even the turmoil of the Iconoclastic era and defying efforts to disentangle it in clear and definitive fashion from the specific range of powers possessed by the ordained priesthood. To the emperor Justinian (d. 565), a priestly character was routinely ascribed, as it had been to his predecessors Constantine and Theodosius. If the Christian emperors had eventually relinquished the old pagan title of *pontifex maximus,* that did not prevent Anastasius I in 516 from calling himself *pontifex inditus*—"eminent priest." As late as the ninth century, indeed, the iconoclast emperor Leo III is reputed to have flung in the face of Pope Gregory II the blunt affirmation: "I am emperor and priest."[91]

Although clarity was never fully to be attained on the question of what such claims might precisely entail, two developments that took place in the wake of the iconoclastic turmoil did something to dispel the confusion and are worthy of note. The first concerns the intense use made of Old Testament analogies by the partisans alike of emperor and patriarch of

Constantinople. On the imperial side, the maximalist habit of trying to place the emperor in a king-priest lineage going back to the mysterious figure of Melchizedek was to fade away by the tenth century.[92] And if it was still common to place him (as leader of the chosen people) in the lineage of Moses and, after him, King David, the supporters of the patriarchs did not fail to remind people that Moses had relinquished his priestly role, conferring it instead on his brother Aaron and thence on the members of the tribe of Levi. Thus represented as being in the lineage of the Levite priesthood, the patriarch and the ordained priesthood which he represented were equipped with their own Old Testament credentials. In the rhetorical eulogies of the patriarchs, the "comparison between the two pairs, emperor and patriarch, Moses and his brother Aaron ... [came to be] the norm,"[93] thereby fostering the notion of the patriarch's partnership with the emperor.

The second pertinent development was an ongoing (if fluctuating) attempt to analyze and tease apart the several strands in the complex relationship between the emperor and the ongoing religious life of the empire. The customary practice whereby he enjoyed the privilege of playing a specific role in the sacred liturgy normally denied to laymen was not called into question. Nobody claimed for him, however, the sort of role that the ordained priesthood played in the administration of the sacraments,[94] and the clerical and (especially) monastic leadership never accepted as legitimate his periodic aspiration to a personal role in the determination of matters doctrinal. But clerical grumbling notwithstanding, the emperors did not relinquish what amounted to a dominant role in the organization and governance of the church. His it was to appoint and depose patriarchs, to change the boundaries of dioceses, to legislate on matters ecclesiastical, to convoke general councils, to validate their enactments, and so on. The overall nature of his religious and ecclesiastical role was perhaps best caught in the application to him of the title *epistemonarches*. Used originally in the context of monastic life of the official charged with enforcing the disciplinary rules governing the outward behavior of monks, its use was expanded in the twelfth century to cover the role of the temporal power vis-à-vis ecclesiastical discipline at large. Finally, in the thirteenth century, Demetrios Chromatianos, in an attempt to define the emperor's precise ecclesiastical status, entitled him "the general *epistemonarches* of the churches." By so doing, he clearly intended to imply (as had other canonists) that the emperor was "the wise defender of the faith and regulator of order in the church." More precisely, or so he added, the emperor "defends the decrees of the councils and regulates the hierarchy of the church. With the single exception of the sacramental office, all the other privileges of a bishop are clearly represented by the emperor, and he performs them legally and canonically."[95]

By calling on the battery of canonistic distinctions that church lawyers in the Latin West were hammering out at about the same time in their own efforts to elucidate the nature of ecclesiastical power, one can try to render in the following way what Chromatianos had in mind. What was being *denied* to the emperor (or, rather, what he was *not* claiming) was the "power of order" (*potestas ordinis*), the power of conferring sacraments, which bishops and priests possessed by virtue of having themselves received the sacrament of holy orders. Also being denied, at least implicitly, was the affiliated "power of jurisdiction in the internal forum" of the individual conscience (*potestas jurisdictionis in foro interiori*), a power exercised quintessentially in the sacrament of penance, one directed to the private good and exercised only over those who voluntarily submitted themselves to its sway. What, on the other hand, was being *accorded* to the emperor in his dealings with the church was the "power of jurisdiction in the external forum" or public sphere (*potestas jurisdictionis in foro exteriori*), a coercive power pertaining to a public authority, exercised even over the unwilling and directed to the common good of the faithful—in effect, a truly governmental power over the externalities of the church.[96] To this translation of Byzantine practice into contemporary Latin terminology one qualification, however, must be appended. Canonists in the medieval West (unlike their modern successors) viewed the power of jurisdiction in the external or public forum as one that included the magisterial power or authority over the definition of true doctrine. But as we have seen, any Byzantine emperor who regarded his own power of ecclesiastical jurisdiction as embracing the right to intrude unilaterally into the doctrinal sphere tended, sooner or later, to run into an unyielding wall of clerical and especially monastic opposition. For by so doing, he would be viewed as having shattered the *symphonia* or harmony with the patriarch of Constantinople, the "amiable dyarchy" that represented in such matters the enduring Byzantine ideal.[97]

Such complexities, shifts, and tensions duly signaled, and despite a certain strengthening across time of the spirit of clerical independence, we may return now to the underlying degree of continuity and stability that was so striking a characteristic of Byzantine political thinking. So striking, indeed, that there is little reason to fault the firmness of Norman H. Baynes's judgment to the effect that what one finds in the *Oration* of Eusebius, clearly stated and for the first time, is "the political philosophy of the Christian Empire, that philosophy of the state which was consistently [to be] maintained throughout the millennium of Byzantine absolutism." And its basic tenet was "the conception of the imperial government as a terrestrial copy of the rule of God in Heaven."[98] Hence the persistent Byzantine consciousness of the proximity in which the Christian empire stood to the Kingdom of God. Hence, too, the uninterrupted and intimate intermingling of the political and ecclesiastical orders in the political life as well as in the legal and political thinking of the Byzantine world. It is significant that in the Greek "political" vocabulary the word "Christendom" had no cognate; the church, taken to be coterminous with the empire, was itself the all-embracing entity.

Right at the start, and accordingly, the legislative activity of the emperor Justinian had extended into almost every corner of ecclesiastical life. Never abandoned, and despite moments of tension, was the ideal of a fundamental *symphonia* between the imperial authority and the clerical priesthood. To that ideal Justinian had given influential expression even if he had not always honored it in the actual exercise of his power. It was his conviction, or so he affirmed in one of his decrees, that "the priesthood and the *imperium* do not differ very much, nor are sacred things so very different from those of public and common interest." And it was equally his conviction that "our chief concern... [should be a focus on] the true dogmas about God and the saintliness of priests." Speaking thus, he went on to affirm that he regarded the imperial authority no less than the priesthood as a gift of God to man, and that he believed it to be a fundamental part of his imperial mission to lead his people to God, to concern himself with their spiritual welfare, and acting of course in harmony with the priesthood, to take whatever steps were necessary to preserve the true faith.[99] And though Justinian nowhere elaborated it in systematic fashion, behind such commitments lay the old Hellenistic philosophy of kingship. So powerfully did it influence his thinking indeed that, abandoning even the muted qualifications of a Eusebius, he went so far as to embrace the ancient notion that God had sent the emperor to humankind to serve as an "animate law" (*nomos empsychos*).

That being so, it is understandable that remnants of the old vocabulary of imperial divinity, lingering on at Byzantium, were to generate echoes in the legal code itself, or that something akin to a Christianized version of the old ruler cult should remain embedded in the elaborate ceremonial of the imperial court and in such practices as the veneration of the imperial image in the churches of the empire. Though it later became common to represent the emperor and patriarch standing side by side in the guise of Moses and Aaron,[100] in the earlier Byzantine centuries the preference was to portray the emperor as a "new David" or a "new Solomon" and to compare him not only with Moses but also (Gelasius to the contrary) with the archetypal priest-king Melchizedek. Certainly in the great mosaics of San Vitale, Ravenna, Melchizedek is depicted in the robes of the *basileus,* and elsewhere David appears in the same guise. Nor did Byzantine iconography fail to reflect at least the somewhat chastened, post-Nicene theopolitical tradition, the imperial majesty thus being brought into close relation with the royal attributes of Christ.[101]

This last point brings us back, in effect, to beginnings. For it was largely via their Christological thinking that Christian theologians like Clement of Alexandria, Origen, and Eusebius had contrived to domesticate Philo's version of the Hellenistic philosophy of kingship within the alien confines of Christian belief. In that effort they had succeeded, and they had done so in spite of the disruptive impact of the Judaic conception of God and of Christ's reinterpretation of the messianic hope. By so doing, moreover, they made possible what Christian political attitudes of the Apostolic era might well have seemed to render impossible—namely, the construction of a Christianized version of the archaic sacral pattern. That version was to preclude the emergence in the Byzantine East of any firm distinction between what we in the West have become accustomed to calling "church" and "state." Indeed, it even came close at times to affirming that the realization of the Kingdom of God on earth was somehow linked with the expansion of the Christian empire. Across the centuries, certainly, it consistently presupposed that that empire somehow stood in close relationship with that heavenly kingdom.

As evidence in support of this last claim one may adduce two celebrated letters, one written by a Roman emperor, the other by a patriarch of Constantinople, and separated from one another, astonishingly, by a more than millennial interval. The first, with which Eusebius acquaints us, was written in 324/5 by Constantine himself, and in his own hand, to Shapar, king of Persia. Constantine wrote in support of the well-being of Persian Christians, by so doing revealing that "he fancied himself the Caesar of every Christian in the world, claiming a power that would rest only on an identification of a universal Church and a universal empire," as well as on the presupposition that "since there was only one God in Heaven, only one emperor should represent him on earth."[102] The second letter, written over a thousand years later and at a time when a shrunken empire possessed no more than tattered remnants of its former power and glory, witnesses powerfully to the remarkable tenacity with which such ideas persisted at Byzantium. Written around 1395 by Antonius IV, patriarch of Constantinople, to Vasili I, grand duke of Moscow, and in response to the latter's assertion that he recognized the authority of the patriarch but not that of the emperor, it fervently insisted that:

> The holy emperor has a great place in the Church: he is not as other rulers and governors of other regions are; and this is because the emperors, from the beginning established and confirmed true religion (*eusebeia*) in all the inhabited world (*oikumenē*).... My son, [because of that] you are wrong in saying "we have a church but not an emperor." It is not possible for Christians to have a church (*ekklēsia*) and not to have an empire (*basileia*). Church and empire have a great unity (*henōsis*) and community; nor is it possible for them to be separated from one another.... Our great and holy sovereign (*autokratōr*) by the grace of God, is most orthodox and faithful; he is the champion, defender, and vindicator of the Church: and it is not possible that there should be a primate who does not make mention of his name.[103]

The ideological gulf separating such views from those characteristic of the contemporary counterparts of the patriarchs in the Latin West is unmistakable. Less clear, however, is the degree to which such views, Patriarch Antonius to the contrary, came to be at home in the Russian East. Contemplating in 1945 the markedly aggressive and unqualified understanding of the reach of royal power evinced by Ivan IV (the "Terrible," 1533–84) and Peter the Great (1682–1725), one that went well beyond the claims made for the absolute monarchies of western Europe, the late Arnold Toynbee was moved to assert, "The Soviet Union today, like the Grand

Duchy of Moscow in the fourteenth century, reproduces [nothing other than] the salient features of the medieval East Roman Empire." "In the Byzantine *totalitarian* state," he added, "the church may be Christian or Marxist so long as it submits to being the secular government's tool."[104] Toynbee's formulation is, of course, a characteristically extreme one, and in response, having properly questioned the validity of his characterization of the Byzantine tradition, his critics have sometimes gone further than that. Noting that it was Peter the Great who abolished the Moscow patriarchate and reduced the church, legally speaking and in matters organizational and administrative, to nothing more than a department of state, they have insisted to the contrary—that "the seeds of [modern] Russian totalitarianism... far from being inspired by Byzantine models" instead reflected Western Lutheran practices and "were sown" no earlier than the eighteenth century "by Peter the Great" himself.[105]

But even if one were to bracket that particular issue and to focus on the sacral dimension so persistently attaching to the office and person of the Russian tsar (Caesar) in the earlier period, the validity of the (sixteenth-century) claim for an essential ideological continuity with the Byzantine past is surprisingly difficult, it turns out, to assess, and it would be all too easy to wander disconsolate in the no-man's-land that lies between affirmation and denial. Two things, certainly, stand in the way of any unhesitating affirmation of such a continuity. First, the impact on Russian patterns of thinking about matters political that was only to be expected from the experience of two centuries and more of Mongol or Tatar overlordship or rule (c. 1240–1480), a period during which Moscow was drawn into the ideological orbit of a powerful, central Asian culture. Second, the degree to which the later Russian stress on Byzantine roots reflected a certain amount of retrojection on the part of the Russian Orthodox clergy, an archaizing exercise, if you wish, in cultural wish-fulfillment.[106]

So far as a putative Mongol inheritance is concerned, it is important to be aware of the fact that to the office and person of the Mongol *khan* (or king), no less and even more than to the Byzantine *basileus,* a certain sacral aura attached. Divine or sacred ancestry, certainly, was ascribed to the great Genghis Khan himself who, in the Chinese fashion, bore the title of *T'ien-tze* or "Son of Heaven." He was viewed, and viewed himself, as possessed of "the mandate of heaven" and as divinely charged with the noble mission of bringing peace to humankind by absorbing the disparate nations into an overarching unity. The very title of tsar, regularly applied to Russian rulers from the time of the coronation of Ivan IV in 1547 onward, had earlier been applied not only to Byzantine emperors but also to the Mongol khans descended from Genghis Khan. Hence the sense that their rule, too, was divinely ordained. Hence, too, as Michael Cherniavsky argues, the gradual process whereby in Russia "the image of the Khan overlapped that of the [Byzantine] basileus" and became "vaguely fused" with it. Hence, again, the related process whereby the "golden cap" or cap or crown of Monomachus (*shapka Monomakha*)—of central Asian rather than Byzantine provenance and originally "an expression of the sovereign position of the Tatar khan"—became the primary piece of royal regalia in the Russian state. "For Russians of the sixteenth century," then, "the title of 'tsar' was firmly connected with the image of the khan, more so than with that of the basileus." And that image was perhaps preserved in the idea of the Russian ruler as the conqueror of Russia and its people, an *autokrator* "responsible to no one."[107]

Such Mongol influences duly acknowledged, it must still be insisted, so far at least as the specifically sacred characteristics of the Russian tsars are concerned, that the Byzantine legacy, whether real or supposed, appears to have been the dominant one. During the reign of Ivan III (1462–1505), in the wake of the Turkish conquest of Constantinople, the concomitant demise of the Byzantine empire, and the contemporaneous decline of the Mongol overlordship in Russia, the Russian orthodox clergy set out to obliterate the memory of the khan-tsar, to foreground instead the notion of the tsar-basileus as rightful successor to the erstwhile Byzantine emperors, and to position him as obvious claimant to the supreme leadership of the Orthodox Christian world.

In the early sixteenth century, accordingly, the notion began to gain currency that, just as Constantinople had been the new or second Rome, so now was Moscow "the third Rome" and the rightful bearer of the Roman/Byzantine legacy.[108] Around the same time, moreover, three other links with Byzantium came to be stressed. Having married Sophia Palaeologa, niece of Constantine XI (d. 1453), last of the Byzantine emperors, Ivan III could well claim to stand proudly in the Roman/Byzantine succession. So, too, could his royal successors. Those successors came also to claim that when, centuries earlier, Vladimir I, prince of Kiev, had embraced Orthodox Christianity (c. 988), the Byzantine emperor, giving him the hand of his sister Anna in marriage, had given him also an imperial crown. And they claimed, too, that his son, Vladimir II (son also of a Byzantine princess) had received some further pieces of imperial regalia. These two latter testimonies to the antiquity and intimacy of the Byzantine connection appear, in fact, to have been no more than legends. But that did not prevent their incorporation into the Russian coronation ceremony, and they were to serve across the years to reinforce the widespread Russian belief in the existence of a basic continuity between the second Rome and the third.

But if that was to be the case, at least insofar as it spoke to the sacred nature of the tsar's office, it may well have been so because that element of continuity, however nurtured by clerical propaganda, was not wholly the stuff of legend. Instead, it did possess some real historical foundations and ones that had been laid down already in the early days of the Christian principality of Kiev. Though parts of the document may well have been of later date, the church statute attributed to Vladimir I and issued allegedly in 996 "established an extensive precedent for the acceptance of Greek canon law." It was to provide a model, in later times, for similar Russian statutes. And it was to be bolstered by the later appearance in Russia of collections of canon law translated from the original Greek into Slavonic.[109] The circulation of such collections had a broader significance than the term "canon law" might readily suggest. Such collections served to mediate to Russians an acquaintance not only with Byzantine imperial laws concerning ecclesiastical affairs but, beyond that, with some key elements of the old, Eusebian vision of kingship. An enduring familiarity, that is, with the conviction that the emperor was nothing less than "the image of God," the "final link between the power of man and the power of God."[110] And, along with that, the belief in the interdependent nature of the relationship between emperor and priesthood, the ancient ideal that there should properly exist an ultimate *symphonia* or harmony between what, in the modern era, we have become accustomed to calling church and state.[111]

6. Patristic Reservation
The Latin Fathers from Tertullian to Augustine

DESPITE ALL VICISSITUDES, the Eusebian vision of the Christian Roman empire as a vehicle or manifestation of the Kingdom of God contrived in the Greek and Russian East to cast a long shadow down through the centuries. In the Latin West, which until the seventh century, it should not be forgotten, meant North Africa as well as western Europe, the ideological situation was a good deal less clear-cut. In this connection, it would be easy enough and not altogether inaccurate to play off Augustine and the "Augustinian tradition" against Eusebius and the Eusebian. And that has often, in fact, been done. But not, it must be insisted, without generating something of a misrepresentation of the way in which religio-political ideas actually unfolded in the world of late antique and early medieval Christianity. It is true that the astringent vision of the mature Augustine stands out in bold contrast with that of Eusebius. But in order to be able to appreciate its originality, we have first to grasp the fact that it came into focus in a cultural context in which Eusebian or quasi-Eusebian ideas formed the ideological commonsense of the day. And in order to appreciate its historic singularity, we have to recognize that it actually failed in the early medieval centuries to insert itself successfully into the minds of those who framed the religio-political thinking characteristic of the era. If it succeeded at all in making its way, it was only by virtue of being transmuted into a pattern of thinking that differed radically from that which the mature Augustine seems himself to have intended. And that mutation reflected the degree to which early medieval authors had accommodated his actual views to a pattern of thinking shaped, even in the Latin West, by the salience of ideas that had something in common with those characteristic of the Eusebian tradition in the East. Before attempting to come to terms, then, with the thinking of the mature Augustine we would do well to acquaint ourselves with the outlines, at least, of the ideological "commonsense" prevalent among the Christians of his day. In his earlier years he had more or less shared that commonsense, and it was in dialogue with it that he was moved finally to make his singular departure.

"Eusebian" Harmonics in the Latin West: Tertullian, Ambrose, Prudentius, Orosius

In its totality the Eusebian political theology was not destined to enjoy a career in the Latin West, but some of the features of early Christian thinking that had helped shape it (notably what we have called the "Lukan" tradition)[1] did indeed maintain a continuing presence in the thinking of Christian writers in late Latin antiquity. Of those writers we can focus on no more than an illustrative handful.[2] And we begin with Gibbons's "zealous African," Quintus Septimus Tertullian of Carthage (c. 160-c. 230), "the first theologian of the West" or the first, at least, to elaborate in writing an extended theology.[3]

Writing a full century before Eusebius, confronting an imperial authority that might well choose to make further martyrs of Christians, and tempted, it has been suggested, to view "the notion of a Christian Caesar ... [as] a contradiction in terms,"[4] Tertullian in his *Apologeticus* nonetheless proclaimed, "We [Christians] respect the judgment of God in the Emperors, who has set them over the nations." He emphasized, accordingly, "the religious awe, the piety of Christians, where the Emperor is concerned" and argued that "we must needs respect him as the chosen of our Lord" and commend him to God to whom alone he is subordinate.[5] Hence, evoking the authority of Paul (1 Timothy 2:2), he is at pains to insist that "we are ever making intercession for all the Emperors. We pray for them long life, a secure rule, a safe home, brave armies, a faithful senate, an honest people, a quiet world and everything for which a man and a Caesar can pray."[6] For "we know," he adds, "that the great force which threatens the whole world, the end of the age itself with its menace of suffering, is delayed by the respite which the Roman empire means for us."

And, elsewhere, edging further along the trajectory that was later to lead to the widespread identification of Christian interests with the destiny of the empire, he hinted at the Lukan emphasis on the quasi-providential significance of the dawn of the Augustan peace.[7]

A century later, St. Ambrose of Milan (c. 334–97), Roman aristocrat as he continued to be and responsive also to the Hellenistic political vision, was to emerge as "a supremely representative voice, a reverberant spokesman for the instincts of the Western Church in a formative moment."[8] Ambrose was moved to edge the process of accommodation still further, pointing now in the direction of a religio-political commonsense in terms of which "Christian" was to be aligned with "Roman" and "Roman" with "Christian."[9] His writing is somewhat diffuse, and one finds in it no systematic statement of his views concerning the empire and the imperial office. But one can, nonetheless, intuit the drift of his thinking from scattered observations (*dicta*) and from the actions he himself took as bishop. Thus, on the one hand, in the context of the attempt in 385–86 of the court at Milan to appropriate for Arian use some of the city's churches, and in that of his insistence in 390 that the emperor Theodosius I do penance for having ordered a massacre carried out in Thessalonica, Ambrose stubbornly advanced in classic and influential fashion the essentially pastoral principle that at least as an individual Christian the emperor was "within the Church not above it."[10] A few years earlier, moreover, in response to the petition of Symmachus and other pagan senators that the Altar of Victory be restored to the Senate house and along with it the previously expropriated stipends, endowments, and revenues originally intended for the public maintenance of the old pagan cults, he had gone somewhat further than that. He had done so by appealing to the emperor Valentinian II to refuse in his official capacity any such official support to pagan cultic practice.[11] Thus "beyond wanting to set up moral standards for the personal conduct of Christian emperors," Markus has noted, "Ambrose [seems to have] envisaged the Roman empire as a society which was, or should be, a radically Christian society, and the Church as called upon to mould its public life and institutions."[12] He clearly resonated to the inclination, widespread in the fourth century among Christian thinkers, Western as well as Eastern, that led them to view the empire as fulfilling the prophecies of old and its history as unfolding within the broader framework of salvation history itself.[13] In that connection he, too, evoked the Lukan theme of the coincidence between the birth of Christ and the Augustan peace, whereby "all men, living under one earthly sovereign, learnt to confess the sovereignty (*imperium*) of one God almighty."[14]

That whole sense of the providential destiny of the Christian Roman empire was to be given a strengthened charge at the start of the next century (and after the emperor Theodosius had proscribed pagan worship throughout the empire) when the Christian poet Prudentius entered the lists. He did so in retroactive response to the case Symmachus had made twenty years earlier in connection with the Altar of Victory affair. He spoke very much as spokesman for the "progressivist" tradition of theopolitical thinking that went back via Eusebius to Origen and beyond.[15] Whereas "in Ambrose's answer to Symmachus's arguments," it has well been said, "we hear the confidence of aggressive enterprise," "in Prudentius's treatment of the same themes the confidence is born of a sense of achieved success," and his words disclose "a boundless confidence in the future."[16] Evoking in terms that were by now traditional the providential rule played in salvation history by the dawn of the Augustan peace, he assured his readers that: "For the time of Christ's coming... was the way prepared which the general goodwill of peace among us had just built under the rule of Rome. For what room could there have been for God in a savage world and in human hearts at variance, each according to its different interest maintaining its own claims, as once things were."[17] As a result of "the great successes and triumphs of the Roman power," which has not "grown feeble with age," the world is now in harmony, and "his earth receives Thee, now, O Christ, which peace and Rome hold in a bond of union."[18] For she (Rome) "has devoted herself to Thee and placed herself under thy governance." She has withdrawn "from her long-standing errors and... [shaken] the murky clouds from her aged face, her nobles ready now to essay the everlasting ways, to follow Christ at the call of their great hearted leader, and cast their hopes into eternity."[19] Only lacking here is the further (quasi-Eusebian?) move evident in the assertion of the anonymous contemporary whom we know as Ambrosiaster to the effect that the imperial entourage stands in relation to the emperor very much as the angels stand to God. The emperor is God's vicar and is to be reverenced (*adoratur*) on earth as such. For (more enigmatically now) "the king has the image of God, just as the bishop has that of Christ."[20]

Among the Latins, however, it was to be the Spaniard Paulus Orosius (fl. early fifth century) who, having fled from Spain after the Vandal invasion and writing at a time of mounting calamity, gave what is perhaps the most forceful expression, nonetheless, to the tradition of providentialist optimism. He did so in his *Seven Books of Histories against the Pagans* (*Historiarum adversum paganos. Libri VII*), which he completed in 417 and which, as the first general Christian history, was destined to exert a powerful influence in the medieval West.[21] Almost a millennium later, it is true, Petrarch was to describe Orosius as "that collector of the evils of the world."[22] And there is something to the charge. His aim was to give a comprehensive account of the odyssey of humankind from the Creation to the present. His story, accordingly, is a story of human tribulation and divine judgment. But necessarily so, in Orosius's view. For "we are taught," he says, "that sin and its punishment began with the very first man.... [E]ven our opponents, who begin with the middle period and make no mention of the age preceding, have described nothing but wars and calamities. What else are these wars but evils which befall one side or the other? Those evils which existed then, as to a certain extent they exist now, were doubtless either palpable sins or the hidden punishments for sin."[23]

That said, it is his purpose to convey to the reader the fact that, being embedded in salvation history, the story of humankind is to be understood as something more or other than an unremitting sequence of calamities. Willing enough to concede that human suffering is a constant in history, he sets his face firmly, nonetheless, against the classical intuition of ongoing declension and decay. The remorseless alternation since the Creation of "periods of good and bad times" are but part of a salvific divine discipline.[24] Against the pagan critics of the day, Orosius argues that contemporary calamities, including even the fall of Rome to the Goths in 410, represent no historically unique concatenation of disasters but a measure of turmoil that in the past has not only been paralleled but even surpassed. He himself had discovered, even, "that the days of the past were not only as oppressive as those of the present but they were the more terribly wretched the further they were removed from the consolation of true religion."[25] For the darkness of the law is now illumined by the flickering light of divine providence. Destructive though they may have been for the Romans, the barbarian invasions were the divinely appointed means whereby so many of those untutored peoples encountered the saving teachings of Christ.[26]

Having said that, and inviting the reader (as it were) to step back from overanxious preoccupation with the localized miseries of the moment and to take in with him the broader sweep of universal history, Orosius continues, in the footsteps of Eusebius, to infuse the darkness of calamities and confusions past with a progressivist glow of Christian optimism. Taking as his framework the succession across the ages of four dominant monarchies (a notion earlier Christian writers had based on Daniel 2 and 7), kingdoms, or empires, which he depicted as "preeminent" in successive stages at the four cardinal points of earth, to wit the Babylonian kingdom in the east, the Carthaginian in the south, the Macedonian in the north, the Roman in the west,[27] and believing it to be the divine will that all the competing kingdoms of the earth should eventually be subjected to the rule of one supreme kingdom,[28] he focuses intently on the emergence of the Roman empire to universal predominance. About that, of course, there was nothing accidental. "This quiet, serenity, and peace throughout the entire world," came "not from the greatness of Caesar, but by the power of the Son of God, Who appeared in the time of Caesar."[29] Many an earlier Christian writer, and Eusebius quintessentially so, had depicted the ascendancy of Rome in similarly providentialist terms and stressed, in Lukan fashion, the coincidence between the birth of Christ and Caesar Augustus's vindication of a monarchy that was truly universal. But it was left to Orosius to elaborate those ideas in the most systematic fashion, setting out to do nothing less than demonstrate "in every respect that the empire of Augustus had been prepared for the advent of Christ."[30] And he achieved his purpose to such a degree that Erik Peterson was moved to attribute to him (disapprovingly) nothing other than the elaboration of a "whole Augustus-theology." For Orosius, in effect, "Roman Empire and Christianity became a unity." "Augustus was Christianized and Christ Romanized."[31]

"Practicing historians of the Middle Ages," it has been said, taking it to be "an authoritative expression" of St. Augustine's views, are "more apt to read *The Seven Books of Histories* than *The City of God.*"[32] The enormous popularity of the former is reflected in the fact that it was handed down in almost two hundred manuscript copies.[33] As a result, its providentialist ideas and the theology of history they reflected echoed down through the medieval centuries and beyond. In his great *Chronicle,* Otto, bishop of Freising (c. 1115–1158), who certainly made use of Orosius's work, did not fail to emphasize the providential coincidence of the birth of Christ and the Augustan peace and to assert that "the reign of Augustus was in many ways a prophecy of the birth of Christ."[34] Five centuries after that, though a specific Orosian connection is not demonstrable, Jacques Bénigne Bossuet (1627–1704), bishop of Meaux and tutor to the dauphin, representing in his *Discours sur l'histoire universelle* the course of history as unfolding in accord with the dispensation of divine providence, and seeing the French kingdom as having entered into the inheritance of the Roman empire, also evoked in similar and classic fashion the coincidence between the birth of the Savior and the dawn of the *pax Romana*.[35]

Augustine of Hippo (354–430)

In his *Policraticus* John of Salisbury (c. 1115–80) described Orosius as "a disciple of the great Augustine,"[36] and many modern authors, indeed, have subscribed to the same judgment.[37] Orosius, after all, had studied with Augustine from 414 to 415, and he himself tells us that it was Augustine who had asked him to undertake the writing of the *Seven Books of Histories against the Pagans*.[38] When he finished the work in 417, it was to Augustine that he dedicated it, and its very survival and circulation may have been taken in the Middle Ages as confirmation of the fact that Augustine had approved of its contents.[39]

In his earlier years, in fact, he might well have been tempted to do so. The conversion experience that he describes so movingly in the *Confessions* was a conversion to Christianity, certainly, but, under the formative influence of St. Ambrose, to a form of Christian belief itself impregnated with Neoplatonic modes of thinking.[40] At that point in his life (386), and for some years thereafter, he was not moved to question the validity of the accommodation being made between the biblical message and the Greek philosophical inheritance. Still less was he moved to question the viability of the theopolitcal "commonsense" of the Theodosian era, which viewed the rise of the Roman empire as a divinely engineered *praeparatio evangelica* and saw in the transition to a Christian empire a truly decisive moment, the realization of the messianic prophecies of old and the dawning of the reign of God on earth. At Milan in 386, it has been suggested, Augustine was converted to something akin to "the serene, optimistic, cultivated" Christianity of the Pelagians to come and against whom he was later to turn—the Christianity, in effect, of a Roman gentleman still resonating to the classical frequencies of the ancient culture.[41] At that moment in his life he leaned as far as he was ever to lean in the direction of the old, classical view of political life as a school for character, a vehicle of moral formation, an instrumentality in man's striving for the good life in all its fullness. A revelatory straw in the wind indicative of that leaning is his inclination in the 390s to see in the current triumph of imperial Christianity the fulfillment of such prophecies as that of Psalm 72(71):11 ("May all kings fall down before him, all nations serve him"), prophecies that Eusebius before him had been bold enough to apply to Constantine himself.[42] Similarly, the fact that in his *De gratia Christi et de peccato originali* the younger Augustine had been moved to write as if the empire's embrace of Christianity and its deployment of imperial power to marginalize pagans and schismatics alike could work to produce a just and even a "*Christian* empire."[43]

This last phrase, however, appears but this once in Augustine's writings, and that fact is significant. It reflects, I believe, the great sea change that began to take place in his thinking during the last decade of the fourth century. No allusion to that change is made in his *Retractationes*, the effort he made in his last years at cataloging and commenting on the vast body of his writing. But it had a profound and reshaping effect on his attitude toward the status of the Roman empire, its place in history, and its alleged contribution, once so widely celebrated, to the dynamics of salvation history. Completed no later than 405, that shift in attitude predated the chain of disasters that overtook the western provinces of the empire from 406 to 410, culminating in the Gothic sack of Rome and shattering the serene assumption of the Theodosian age that some sort of Christian millennium was dawning with "the whole world ... [having] become a choir praising Christ."[44] It was a transformative shift, generated not by the impact of such external upheavals but by the inner turmoil of the spirit, by his reabsorption, after experiencing the humane Christian *Romanitas* of Ambrose's Milan, back into the passionate and febrile religiosity of his native Africa, which seems to have fed what has aptly been called "his appetite for transcendence."[45] The key factor in the whole process appears to have been the degree to which, in the years after his ordination in 391, he came to immerse himself in the Bible and especially so in the depths of what seems to have been in the mid-390s a transformative encounter with the Pauline Epistles. In the complex dynamics of that encounter, Markus has argued, lies the real source of "Augustine's increasingly stark vision of human history in terms of a simple dichotomy of those predestined to be saved and the reprobate." And that dichotomy was destined soon to eclipse the idea, widespread among the Christians of the day, "of a progress through the successive ages of God's unfolding plan 'educating mankind.'"[46]

The fundamental shift involved, then, was in effect a shift in Augustine's understanding of the way in which the millennial course of history had unfolded and would continue to unfold, from the very Creation itself, that moment of inexplicable divine generosity with which it had all begun, on to the moment of dread divine intrusion with which it was all destined to end. Almost alone among Christian writers and apologists he no longer saw either the conversion of Constantine or the earlier dawn of the Augustan peace (which he mentions only in passing)[47] as pivotal moments in the providential unfolding of salvation history. The sacred history of redemption he viewed now as confined to the biblical narrative itself. Roman history, in contrast, was radically desacralized. What he called the sixth or last great age of man—the *saeculum* or present age extending from the birth of Christ to his second coming and the end of time—he now saw as at once both homogeneous and "secular." Homogeneous because it betrayed no intimations of the providential punctuations so dear to Eusebius and many another Christian writer of the day, "no signposts," as it were, "to sacred meaning, no landmarks in the history of salvation."[48] Secular because he saw it as falling neither into the sacred nor the profane but into a distinctive, more neutral category. The *saeculum*, the intermediate age in which human beings until the end of time are destined to pursue their temporal affairs, is, in effect, the realm of the "secular." During this age imperial society, its goals and institutions are neither, Eusebian fashion, to be sacralized nor, as in the Revelation of John, repudiated as demonic or profane. Though it does not permit of a common religious platform, the *saeculum* does provide a space wherein a bleak measure of social consensus, some shared values, and the rudiments of a common culture can be preserved. Such, then, was the state of mind of the mature Augustine when in 413 he embarked on the writing of *The City of God*. The history of the church being no longer for him a part of sacred history, still less so was the *Christian* Roman empire (if, indeed, there could even be such a thing). Accordingly, the prophetic biblical texts that he had once been willing to interpret as referring to the hegemony of Rome and the inauguration of the *pax Romana*,[49] he now interpreted in eschatological fashion and without any reference to Rome. And scholars like Peterson, Cranz, Mommsen, and Markus, writing over the course of the past half century and more, have succeeded in persuading us now "to see at least part of the central concern of Augustine's argument in that work as lying in his *rejection* of the [optimistic] Eusebian Rome theology."[50]

But rejectionist in this sense though he may have been, Augustine still stands out as the principal architect of Christian theology in the West, Protestant as well as Catholic. He stands out also as the greatest of the church fathers to address himself to what we classify as matters political, the thinker with whose voluminous writings subsequent theologians and writers on ecclesiastico-political problems felt they had to come to terms. Not that Augustine, despite his appropriation of Neoplatonic modes of thought, set out to elaborate any systematic philosophical position in general or to frame in particular any coherent theory of what we would call "the state." His temperament and his training as a rhetorician did little to encourage such an undertaking. Even had that not been the case, as a conscientious bishop charged with the pastoral care of his flock during a turbulent period when the Roman West was succumbing to barbarian attacks from without and his own North African region was being torn apart by religious dissension from within, Augustine would have been hard-pressed indeed to embark upon any truly systematic expression of his ideas.[51] Instead, his multitudinous writings are nearly always occasional pieces written in haste and in response to one or another external challenge. They possess their own internal force and cohesion but are often punctuated by the lengthy digressions so dear to the rhetoricians of the day. And that is quintessentially true of the writings of his maturity in which, more than in any others, he addressed himself to matters political and from which, more than any others, we have to quarry what we are prone to labeling as his "political ideas." The works in question are *The City of God* and the several tracts he directed against his dissident fellow Africans, the passionate Donatist advocates of a "church of the pure."

Although it was a full thirteen years (413–26) in the writing and shared with the public piecemeal, *The City of God* was occasioned by a specific event—the Visigothic capture of the city of Rome in 410. Rome—the Rome that Virgil had promised was to be eternal—had remained inviolate for some eight hundred years, and for many its fall seemed to herald the collapse of civilization itself. The psychological impact of that event, then, was traumatic, and the pressing need that inhabitants of the empire felt to locate it in some structure of explanation is readily comprehensible. Such an explanation many Romans of the day were moved to discern in a change of attitude ascribed to the old civic gods. To their goodwill, assured by the regular performance of the civic cult, men had once been accustomed to attribute the endurance and worldly triumphs of Rome. To their anger, accordingly, brought on by the neglect of that cult under the Christian emperors, some leading pagans sought now to attribute Rome's decline. It was such an argument that Augustine set out to refute in the first ten books of *The City of God.* In those books it was his purpose, above all, to establish the utter powerlessness of the pagan gods to contribute to man's felicity either in this world or the next. Thus "the first five books," he tells us, "have been written against those who imagine that the gods are to be worshipped for the sake of the good things of this life." And the latter five, in turn, written "against those who think that the cult of the gods should be kept up with a view to the future life after death."[52]

In the remaining twelve books of the work, however, grounding himself explicitly in sacred Scriptures, "writings of outstanding authority in which we put our trust,"[53] Augustine sets out to construct and elaborate an alternate and less fragile explanatory structure. He does so by unfolding a specifically Christian vision of the course of world history, moving from God's creation of the angels, the world and man, via the catastrophe of the Fall and the redemptive moment of the Incarnation, on to the Last Judgment and the end of time. The focal point of that great vision is the story of "the rise, the development and the destined ends" of what, invoking scriptural warranty, he calls "the two cities, the earthly and the heavenly ("earthly city" and "city of God"—*civitas terrena, civitas dei*), which we find "interwoven as it were, in this present transitory world, and mingled one with another."[54]

While it is perfectly appropriate, then, to describe this whole "huge work" (*ingens opus*—his own description) as "the last and greatest of the Apologies for Christianity produced by the early Church,"[55] Augustine's very choice of terminology suggests that it is an apology not without relevance to the history of what we are accustomed to calling "political" thought. But with that terminology itself, unfortunately, problems of interpretation immediately arise. As Augustine suggests at the beginning of the eleventh book and elsewhere, the notion of the two cities is a biblical one reflective of the enduring division between those moved by the love of God and neighbor and those who are in thrall to the lust (*libido*) for merely temporal goods. It is manifest, therefore, in the contrast between Abel and Cain and symbolized by the opposition between Jerusalem and Babylon. There are passages that clearly suggest that he saw this opposition as being realized in his own day in the overt contrast between Roman empire and Christian church. Thus he can tell us that the Assyrians in the East and the Romans in the West are the "two empires [that] have won a renown far exceeding that of all" the "great number of empires" into which "the community which we call by the general name of 'the city of this world' has been divided."[56] Similarly, he can say that he himself is engaged in "defending the City of God, that is to say, God's Church" (*civitatem Dei, hoc est ejus ecclesiam*); can insist that "we, his City," are God's "best [and] ... most glorious sacrifice," the "mystic symbol" of which "we celebrate in our oblations, familiar to the faithful"; and can assure us that "it is completely irrelevant to the Heavenly City" what dress its faithful members wear or what manner of life they adopt "provided that these do not conflict with the divine instructions."[57]

That being so, and some sort of identification clearly being made in these particular texts between Roman empire and *civitas terrena*, on the one hand, and Christian church and *civitas dei*, on the other, one is encouraged to expect that it may be possible to extract directly from *The City of God* an explicit teaching on the relation between the temporal and spiritual authorities. Given the fact, moreover, that Augustine assures us that "the Church even now is the kingdom of Christ and the kingdom of heaven,"[58] one is also nudged in the direction of concluding that that teaching will represent something of a departure from the essentially dualistic stance we have seen to be adopted in the pertinent texts of the New Testament itself.[59]

These passages in *The City of God* are fairly explicit. They cannot simply be ignored. Nor do they lend themselves readily to any effort to explain them away. The less so, indeed, in that they can be seen to have helped to shape the way in which *The City of God* has been understood (or, rather, misunderstood) over the course of the long centuries since it was written. That is true not only of the medieval centuries, when it was not common practice to read the work in toto, but also in subsequent centuries, including the twentieth, when influential historians of political thought in the Anglophone world have not always been averse to aligning themselves with an essentially medieval take on Augustine's intent.[60] But it must be insisted that only a casual or selective reading would support the conclusion that the institutional identifications that these texts imply represents Augustine's overall or controlling thinking. Indeed, a closer look at the last one cited above underlines the caution with which such texts must be read. For the kingdom that is to be identified with the church as it is "in this world" is clearly Christ's kingdom only in a qualified sense. The "Church as it now is" is a kingdom in which the tares have still to be separated from the wheat. It is a "kingdom at war, in which conflict still rages with the enemy," one that must be distinguished from "that kingdom of perfect peace... where the king will reign without opposition," namely, the eschatological kingdom at the end of time from which, at the Last Judgment, the sinful have been eliminated, the tares separated from the wheat and, having been gathered together, consigned to the fire.[61]

The particular chapter involved is not, in general, an easy one to construe, and it should be acknowledged that Augustine is struggling to cope here with a set of difficult apocalyptic texts drawn from the Revelation of John. Insofar as he is willing fully to identify the church with the kingdom of heaven, it would not seem to be (invoking now the terminology of later centuries) the *visible* church of this world that he has in mind but, rather, the church understood as the body of the elect, the community of saints who partake fully in the reign of Christ. Again, it is this latter, necessarily *invisible,* church that he has in mind when he identifies the *civitas dei* with the church. For to the ambiguity in his usage of the term "kingdom of Christ" corresponds also (and perhaps necessarily) an ambiguity in his use of the term "church."[62]

The importance of recognizing this becomes clearer if one focuses also on the central position occupied in Augustine's thinking by Adam's revolt against the will of his Creator, by his concomitant fall from grace, and by the devastating impact of that fall upon the subsequent condition of the human race, moral no less than physical.[63] Augustine's thinking on the matter underwent across time a certain development. And it was in the course of his struggle against what he took to be the views of Pelagius (c. 354–c. 418) and his followers that he hammered out what I take to be his mature, controlling teaching.[64] Pelagius was a Romano-British theologian who had become a fashionable teacher at Rome during the early years of the fifth century and who, around the year 410 and along with his pupil

Coelestius, had spent some time in North Africa. By temperament a moralist, he had apparently been shocked by the low standard of moral conduct that he had observed among Christians at Rome. He had similarly been dismayed by what he seems to have regarded as a demoralizingly pessimistic view of what could realistically be expected of human nature. The belief that man did not have it within his natural powers to avoid sin struck him as derogating from the very power and goodness of the God who had created humankind. Hence Pelagius's rejection of Tertullian's teaching that as descendants of Adam the souls of all human beings had somehow inherited the damaging effects of that progenitor's original sin. Hence, too, his disdain for the idea that as a result of the Fall the human will had any intrinsic bias toward sinfulness, and his concomitant tendency to downplay the role of divine grace in the process of salvation. It is not by God's favor but by their own merit that people progress in holiness. Indeed, it is possible for man in the freedom of his will and by his own natural powers to avoid sin and, by a strenuous and persistent effort of the will, to attain perfection. As Coelestius is said to have put it, "If I ought, I can."

To Augustine the African bishop, the mature Augustine whose own position on the matter appears to have hardened in the mid-390s in the course of his transformative encounter with the Pauline Epistles, such views were simply anathema. Because of the moral and spiritual struggles of his earlier life—struggles whose anguish and intensity he conveys so movingly in the *Confessions*—he himself was in no way prone to doubt the reality of original sin or the searing impact of Adam's fall on the souls of his descendants. As a result of that unhappy event, or so he had come to believe, human nature itself was scarred so deeply and corrupted so fearfully that it had become enslaved to sin, to ignorance, and to death. The ability to refrain from sin and to attain the good—the natural prerogative that Adam had enjoyed in the state of innocence—was now lost and recoverable only by the merciful infusion of God's grace. While this does not mean that man has also forfeited his own free will, what it does mean is that the inevitable use to which he puts that free will is to do wrong.

Hence the almost instinctive hostility with which Augustine reacted to the teaching of Pelagius and his (sometimes more assertive) followers. It was the challenge which that teaching posed that spurred him on, in the second decade of the fifth century, to state his own doctrine in its harshest, most repulsive, and most uncompromising form. Left wholly to himself, he argued, man can do absolutely nothing to achieve his own salvation. Without divine help he can no more turn to God than he can turn away if God, by an irresistible grace, chooses to turn to him and, as a veritable Hound of Heaven, to pursue his deliverance. Left wholly to himself, man can be said, shifting the metaphor, to be shipwrecked on the sin of Adam, drifting disconsolate and helplessly into sin, at the mercy of the turbulent seas of his own fallen and depraved nature, incapable of even hoisting a sail or charting a course for land. From such a desperate plight he can be delivered only if God, of his infinite and incomprehensible mercy, reaches out, raises him up, and draws him to himself. Hence, of course, Augustine's further commitment to the grim doctrine of double predestination. It is up to God to determine which men and women (a minority) will be the recipients of that gratuitous mercy and which will not. This, Augustine believed, he has done from all eternity, basing his dread decision not upon his foreknowledge of the lives, good or bad, that people may contrive to lead, but on a secret and inscrutable justice that transcends the categories of any merely mortal equity. While since the coming of Christ, God has committed himself to using the church as the necessary vehicle for gathering together the elect, it has still to be remembered that the (visible) church comprehends not only the elect but also those who belong still to the ranks of the reprobate. And no Christian, however devoted, can really be sure that he himself is numbered among the body of the elect destined for eternal salvation.[65]

The implication of all of this for the meaning to be ascribed to the duality *civitas dei/civitas terrena* is clear and immediate. When Augustine speaks of the city of God, what in fact he has in mind is the body of the elect, a transpacial and transtemporal community that embraces the good angels and the saints of yore as well as those people among the living and yet unborn who are predestined to join the ranks of the blessed.[66] Similarly, when he speaks of the earthly city, he has in mind a parallel but opposed community that embraces Satan and the fallen angels as well as the unredeemed sinners, the reprobate majority of humankind—dead, living, and yet to be born.[67] Both "cities," then, are communities that transcend any merely temporal organism to such a degree that even when we limit ourselves to talking only about things as they are here and now on earth, it is not permissible to identify these communities with any existing social structures.

It should not escape our attention, however, that in terms at least of their relation to the commonwealths and civil communities of this world there is a certain asymmetry between the members of the city of God and those of the earthly city. Whereas within those civil communities the former can do no more than sojourn as aliens or "pilgrims," the latter, in effect, are very much at home. That is to say, they actually share the merely temporal aspirations of such communities, are not constrained to see them as merely a means to some higher end, and are content with their merely temporal satisfactions. For Augustine, it seems, the earthly city stands in a closer relationship to the empires and commonwealths of this world than does the city of God to any worldly community, the visible church not excluded. Because of that, and as we have seen, he is sometimes led to envision those empires and commonwealths as in some sense *divisions* of the earthly city. That duly acknowledged, we should also note the fact that his use of the term "earthly city" is often shadowed by an ambiguity that permits (or encourages?) him, without signaling the fact, to deploy it with two different meanings. While he certainly uses it in its strict, eschatological sense as denoting the transpacial and transtemporal community of the damned, he also uses it more loosely to refer to the empires and commonwealths of this world, themselves constituting, as it were, what may be called "the visible earthly city." And whereas the former belongs unambiguously to the realm of the demonic or profane, the latter belongs, rather, to the realm of the secular.

Between the two, then, there can be no ultimate identification. Some of the citizens of the *visible* earthly city constituted by those empires and commonwealths, rulers, it may well be, as well as subjects may in fact be members also of the city of God, as it were her hidden citizens to be.[68] Correlatively, the only church which can truly be identified with the city of God is the invisible church of the elect, not the church of here and now, visibly present in this world. By virtue of the fact that in that visible church the city of God "produces citizens here below," it may be said to be "on pilgrimage [in this world] until the time of its kingdom comes." But until that time, this pilgrim city of Christ the King, in so far, at least, as it is the new Israel, is not much more than a foreshadowing of the (true) city of God.[69] We should not forget that in the ranks of the visible church here below there lurk, unrecognized it may be by their fellow Christians (perhaps also unbeknown to themselves), numbers of the reprobate, members of that earthly city the profane boundaries of which cut across and exceed the familiar divisions between what we today call "state" and "church."[70] Thus, adamantly opposed though the two cities may be, the line of demarcation between them is not a visible one; their memberships are not destined to be separated until the end of time, and they remain commingled in this world to such an extent that Augustine is at pains even to admit the possibility that "certain men belonging to the city Babylon [the earthly city] do order matters belonging to Jerusalem [i.e., sinful men occupy positions of authority in the Church], and again certain men belonging to Jerusalem do order matters belonging to Babylon [i.e., good men, members of the city of God, occupy positions of power and authority in earthly states]."[71]

That said, it should not be necessary to belabor the fact that there can be no *direct* deduction from Augustine's discussion of the relationship between the two cities to any theory of the relationship between the spiritual and temporal authorities of this world. There may, however, be an indirect one, though it will emerge only if we change tack and approach *The City of God* from a different direction, posing, as we do so, a different question. Thus, accepting the fact that Augustine's whole conception of the two cities is shaped by his overriding preoccupation with the effects of original sin and his insistence that only the grace of God, gratuitously given, can counteract those effects, and accepting also the corollary that the elect and reprobate remain inextricably commingled in all the societies of this world, we can still ask of him what position, what dignity, is *under such circumstances* to be accorded to the civil community, to the empires and commonwealths of this world. And in the reply that Augustine yields to this question, he succeeds in being responsive not only to the several strands, positive as well as negative, woven into the Christian pattern of thinking as it emerges from the New Testament but also to some strands of Hellenistic political thinking and even, in more muted fashion and going back still further, to the Platonic vision of the ideal republic capable of assuring to its citizens true peace, concord, harmony, and fulfillment.

In so doing, however, he is responsive also to the complexity of the Gospel teaching about the Kingdom of God. He recognizes, that is to say, that according to that teaching the Kingdom of God is at once a spiritual kingdom coming into existence as Christ comes to reign in the hearts of the faithful and, at the same time, a transcendent society, a kingdom not of this world, one not destined for complete realization until the ending of time. And by that recognition Augustine firmly endorses the New Testament's forthright rejection of the archaic sacral pattern and its revolutionary reduction of what we call "the state" to the position of a merely secular entity. The Platonic political vision, the nobility of which is not to be gainsaid, he sees, accordingly, as an ideal destined for realization in no earthly political community but only in that kingdom whose king is Christ, that is to say, in the city of God itself.[72] With the other church fathers, it is true, he does find a place for the Hellenic belief that social life is natural to man, and again like the other fathers, and indeed St. Paul, he also embraces the notion of a natural law accessible by virtue of their very humanity to the reason of all men and dictating to them the norms of moral conduct.[73] But because of the Fall and the concomitant corruption of human nature, not only has there been a palpable dimming in man's perception of those norms but, beyond that, and even when he recognizes them, a catastrophic diminution in his ability to follow them. Only among the ranks of the redeemed, by God's inexplicable mercy and the gratuitous bestowal of supernatural grace, can now be attained the peace and harmony that, in the state of innocence, man had enjoyed as his natural condition. As for the rest of humankind, their very survival depends on the protection of new institutions and new laws of an essentially political nature appropriate to their fallen condition. Those laws and institutions are designed in part to mitigate, at least, the horrors attendant upon the incessant struggle of humankind for mutual domination and to make possible, via the coerced suppression of conflict, the achievement of a minimal external peace and the reverberation through society of at least a dim harmonic of justice. And even the redeemed, condemned as they are to journeying in this life as pilgrims among the unregenerate majority of humankind, cannot be secure in the peace and harmony that is properly theirs without the supervention of those same legal and political instrumentalities, from the institution of private property to the very existence of what we today call "the state."[74]

For Augustine, then, subjection to political authority enters the picture not as something natural to man but, like slavery or for that matter death itself, as an outcome of Adam's primordial fall from grace.[75] Far from being a means of redemption, or a school for character, or even an agency capable of securing for humankind a good quality of life, the commonwealth or empire is a remedy, indeed a punishment, for sin, and it has in all humility to be accepted as such. For it is appointed by God for those very ends. Nor does the rule of tyrants constitute any sort of exception to that generalization. Even to cruel despots like the emperor Nero "the power of domination is not given except by the providence of God, when he decides that man's condition deserves such masters."[76] But if a punishment for our sinful condition, the commonwealths and political institutions of this world are also in some measure a remedy for it. For they strive to effect a "harmonious agreement of citizens concerning the giving and obeying of orders," even if it is one limited, in effect, "to the establishment of a kind of compromise between human wills about the things relevant to this mortal life."[77] And in this, that fragile measure of agreement is of service not only to the reprobate, the members of the earthly city who constitute the mass of humankind, but also to those members of the city of God who dwell as aliens in their midst. Hence it is in the interest of the latter to make use of the earthly peace "for so long as the two cities are intermingled we [the members of the heavenly city] also make use of the peace of Babylon." And "that is why the Apostle [Paul] instructs the Church to pray for kings of that [earthly] city and those in high positions, adding these words: 'that we may lead a life of quiet devotion and love' (1 Timothy 2:2)."[78]

The spirit, nevertheless, in which the pilgrim members of the heavenly city render obedience to their earthly rulers differs from that of the reprobate mass of their worldly neighbors. For the latter, the earthly peace which it is the function of the powers that be to assure is not regarded as a means to any more ultimate end; for the former, it is. As Augustine insists,

> The heavenly city—or rather that part of it which is a pilgrimage in this condition of mortality, and which lives on the basis of faith—must needs make use of this [earthly] peace also, until this mortal state, for which this kind of peace is essential, passes away. And therefore, it leads what we may call a life of captivity in this earthly city as in a foreign land, although it has already received the promise of redemption, and the gift of the Spirit as a kind of pledge of it; and yet it does not hesitate to obey the laws of the earthly city by which those things which are designed for the support of this mortal life are regulated; and the purpose of this obedience is that, since this mortal condition is shared by both cities, a harmony may be preserved between them in things that are relevant to this condition.[79]

It is possible to preserve this harmony, however, only "provided that no hindrance is presented thereby to the religion which teaches that the one supreme and true God is to be worshipped." The things that are God's have to be rendered to God, and in response to any governmental attempt to impose on Christians "laws of religion [held in] common with the earthly city," the pilgrim city of God "in defence of her [own] religious laws" is "bound to dissent from those who... [think] differently and to prove a burdensome nuisance to them." Thus, he adds, until her own numbers grow, "she has to endure their anger and hatred, and the assaults of persecution."[80] Such dissent should never go so far as to take the form of active resistance to the powers that be. For as they are ordained of God, that would be contrary to the divine ordinance. Instead, it is the bounden duty of the pilgrim members of the heavenly city to confine themselves to nothing more than passive disobedience and to follow, if need be, in the footsteps of the martyrs who, having confessed and proclaimed their faith, "endured all their suffering for their religion with fidelity and fortitude, and... died with a devout serenity."[81]

The central thrust, then, of Augustine's mature theopolitical thinking, as we encounter it in *The City of God,* is to make unambiguously clear the fact that the "state" or civil authority, however vital its function, is nothing more than a secular instrumentality adapted to the evanescent conditions of the *saeculum* or present age, an essentially limited and necessarily coercive force that lacks both the authority and the ability to reach beyond the imposition of a merely earthly peace and a merely external order to mould the interior dispositions of men. For "even peace is a doubtful good, since we do not know the hearts of those with whom we wish to maintain peace, and even if we could know them today, we should not know what they might be like tomorrow."[82] Certainly there is no longer any reverberation here of his earlier tendency to resonate to the progressivist Christian optimism of a Eusebius or his ideological fellow travelers in the Latin West. But despite that, and despite the concomitant miseries Augustine is at pains to associate with life in civil society,[83] he is also careful to insist that we must still acknowledge political authority to be of divine institution. And in all of this, unlike Eusebius, Ambrose, Prudentius, or Orosius, he manages to do full justice to the whole spectrum of New Testament political attitudes—with the exception of those apocalyptic utterances that identify Roman power directly with the profane or demonic, with the power, that is, of Satan.

Of course, and as those very utterances so forcefully remind us, the political thinking we can glean from the pages of the New Testament was in considerable measure geared to a situation in which political authority was in the hands of pagan rulers indifferent—or even positively hostile—to Christians and Christian belief. It may well be felt, then, that those views can be no more than indirectly relevant to the changed political conditions of Augustine's own day, when pagan emperors had been succeeded by Christian, and when Christianity had finally been established as the official religion of the Roman empire. That being so, it behooves us to change tack yet once more and to put yet another new and different question to Augustine. To ask, in effect, and his rejection of Eusebian progressivist optimism notwithstanding, if he would not after all accord to the specifically *Christian* empire a higher status, and to Christian rulers a greater dignity than we have seen him accord to their pagan forebears. Or, put differently, to ask him if the somber political vision we have been describing at such length is one pertinent only, after all, to the conditions of life in a pagan or non-Christian society.

This question is undoubtedly a crucial one to answer. It is so not only because of the response that medieval thinkers characteristically understood him as giving to it, but also because of continuing scholarly disagreement about the nature of the answer that we today should properly ascribe to him. The nature of that answer hinges upon the interpretation given, above all, to three texts or groups of texts. First, and most important, those classic texts in the second and nineteenth books of *The City of God* bearing on the relation between justice and the commonwealth (*respublica*). Second, the celebrated portrait of the ideal Christian emperor to be found in the fifth book of the same work. Third, those tracts written against the Donatists in which he explores the nature and extent of the Christian ruler's responsibility for the preservation of the true religion in the lands subject to his sway. These three sets of texts we will take up in turn.

Here the interpretative stakes involved are very high indeed. If, after all, the works of Augustine's maturity yield a *positive* answer to the matter in question—if, that is, he there accords to Christian regimes a higher dignity than he would to pagan—then he will clearly be qualifying the desacralizing thrust of the teaching inherited from the New Testament, evincing once more something akin to the sympathy of his earlier years with a progressivist Christian optimism of Eusebian or Orosian stamp,[84] and opening up a route that could lead to a "respiritualization" of politics. And that is certainly what he would be doing if, as his medieval interpreters usually assumed and as some modern scholars have continued to insist, he went along with most of the other church fathers[85] and endorsed Cicero's definition of a commonwealth (*respublica*), in accordance with which justice was to be of its very essence, while at the same time insisting that only specifically Christian civil communities could be truly just. For in that case no pagan civil community, lacking justice, could strictly speaking be regarded as a true commonwealth.[86]

But despite claims made to the contrary by later "clericalist" interpreters (sometimes defended on the grounds that otherwise one would have to assume that "medieval theologians were less able to understand Augustine than modern critics),[87] I propose to argue that this Augustine simply does not do. Justice being "that virtue which assigns to everyone his due,"[88] it is clear that there can be "real justice" or "true justice" (*justitia vera*) only in the community where the one, true God is given his due, and where he "rules an obedient City according to his grace, forbidding sacrifice to any being save himself alone; and where in consequence the soul rules the body in all men who belong to this City and obey God, and the reason faithfully rules the vices in a lawful system of subordination; so that just as the individual righteous man lives on the basis of faith which is active in love, so the association, or people, of righteous men lives on the same basis of faith, active in love, the love with which a man loves God as God ought to be loved, and loves his neighbour as himself."[89] This being so, Rome, of course, necessarily lacked "real justice" or "true justice," so that, if one sticks with Cicero's definition, it was never a true commonwealth at all.[90] The same is true of the empires that preceded Rome "when they exercised imperial rule, whether on a small or a large scale, in their commonwealths." And it remains true of "any other nation whatsoever" that, because God does not rule in it, is "devoid of true justice."[91] But, then, to say that is not to say a great deal. After all, if it is really *true* justice that we are seeking, we will not find it in any earthly commonwealth, for "true justice (*vera justitia*) is found only in that commonwealth whose founder and ruler is Christ; if we agree to call it a commonwealth, seeing that we cannot deny that it is the 'weal of the community.' However if this title [*respublica*], so commonly-used elsewhere with a different sense, may be too remote from our usual way of speaking, we may say that at least there is true justice in that City of which the holy Scripture says, 'Glorious things are said about you, City of God.'"[92]

It was necessary, therefore, to reject Cicero's definition and to adopt a different and "more probable" (*probabilior*) definition which refrains from regarding justice as being of the very essence of the polity. And in accordance with this more probable definition (which Augustine refers to as his own [*definitio nostra*]), all of the polities that he had described as being devoid of true justice were still to be regarded as commonwealths for they were all "an association of some kind or other between a multitude of rational beings united by a common agreement on the objects of its love."[93]

Throughout his discussion of the relation between justice and the state, then, Augustine makes no major departure from the attitude toward political life hammered out in his maturity and ascribed to him earlier in this chapter. Believing as he did that the Fall, however catastrophic, had not utterly extinguished man's capacity to apprehend the natural law or totally obliterated his ability to frame his actions in accordance with its norms, Augustine was not prepared to deny that the states of this world, even pagan states, could retain at least some pale semblance of justice. For did not their citizens possess some "bond of concord," some "common agreement on the objects of its love"? States, he was perfectly willing to admit, will be better or worse in character according to the objects that their citizens pursue. "The better the objects of this agreement, the better the people; the worse the objects of this love, the worse the people."[94] But having insisted that true justice, by its very definition, is not to be found in any society other than the city of God itself, and having denied that the city of God could be equated with any earthly community (not even the visible Church Militant), it would be odd, indeed, if he were then to turn around and suggest that even a state governed by a Christian ruler and composed of professing Christians could possess true justice. Not all who say "Lord! Lord!" are destined to enter the kingdom of heaven, and the Christian state, in this like the visible church, will always harbor among its membership numbers of the reprobate, people whose true citizenship is that of the *civitas terrena*.

Of course, it is very much to the point that nowhere in this whole complex discussion does Augustine suggest that the distinction between pagan and Christian polities is at all pertinent to the matter at hand. If this has often been missed, it is largely because of the fact that elsewhere in his multitudinous writings—including, as we have seen, some of his earlier ones—he did not hesitate to make quite a lot of that distinction. But not, in any marked degree, in *The City of God*. And that is directly pertinent to the portrait of the ideal, "happy" Christian emperor who belongs "to the kingdom of God" that he paints in the fifth book of *The City of God*, a portrait destined to be much flourished in the Middle Ages and one that fitted into the Hellenistic and medieval genre of political writing usually known as the "Mirror of Princes" genre.[95] In the passage in question, Augustine is not describing how Christian rulers do in fact behave but urging that such emperors "rule with justice" and "put their power at the service of God's majesty"—fearing him, loving him, and worshipping him, seeking to extend his worship far and wide, and "more than their earthly kingdom," loving "that realm where they do not fear to share the kingship." But when he says that, he is professedly seeking to describe (and promote) those attitudes and policies in which an individual emperor's personal duties as a Christian will be fulfilled and in which, as a result, his own true happiness will reside. What he is doing, in effect, is reminding such an emperor "of his duties as a Christian who is seeking to win eternal salvation." And what he is certainly *not* doing is "discussing what a state must do if it is to be a state." Nor is he explicitly reneging here on the view of his maturity that "the basic fundamental task that the state is expected to perform" remains "the maintenance of earthly justice and temporal, external peace and order—the peace of Babylon."[96]

All of that said, it has to be conceded that the type of exhortation embedded in Augustine's portrait of the ideal Christian emperor could conceivably introduce a measure of distortion into an otherwise clear and somber vision of the state as a lowly institution concerned with gritty externalities and, being unable to see into the hearts of its subjects or citizens, lacking the ability and authority to touch their consciences. And it could do so especially if read (as it seems so often to have been read) in light of the position to which Augustine eventually found his way during the latter years of his long and bitter struggle (391–417) with the Donatist advocates of a "church of the pure." That struggle took place both in his own diocese and in the North African province at large, where, or so recent scholarship has suggested, the views of the Donatists rather than those of their Catholic opponents came close "to being the normal form of Christianity."[97] By the end of that bitter struggle he had been led to make a quite radical shift away from his earlier rejection of the idea that the Christian church, in its efforts to cope with schismatics and heretics, could move beyond persuasion and call upon the coercive power wielded by the temporal authorities.[98]

That shift he made only gradually, and not without uneasiness and hesitation. Threatening though the Donatists undoubtedly were in the 390s to what, at Hippo certainly, was a Catholic minority, Augustine still resisted the notion that the coercive power of the imperial authority might properly be invoked to nudge them out of the error of their ways and shepherd them back into the one, true fold. And if early in the next decade he began to waver on the issue, his grounds for so doing reflected the felt need for state protection to shield the Catholic minority from the violence of some Donatist factions rather from any commitments to the principle that the temporal authority had any duty to enforce orthodox belief. Only in the latter part of that decade (406 onward), having observed the effectiveness of coercion, even in matters religious, did he concede to a change of heart and begin to vindicate the imposition of legal penalties on those who were simply heretics and had committed no criminal acts. "Coercion," he was now willing to say, was "in and of itself neither right nor wrong." The fundamental principle involved when it came to the invocation of force was not the matter of coercion itself but "'the nature of that to which he is coerced, whether it be good or bad.'"[99] As a result, he was led eventually "to elaborate a general defense of the *principle* that Christian rulers are duty-bound to use their power and authority to punish those men whose views on doctrine and organization are declared to be heterodox by the leaders of the Church."[100]

This crucial shift in position Augustine defended on more grounds than one. But the ground most relevant to our concern is surely his invocation of the dramatic change in condition since the Apostolic age when the Roman emperors were still pagan and his own era when they had embraced the Christian faith and now strove to "serve the Lord with fear, with trembling" (Psalm 2:11). This change he saw prefigured in the Old Testament, invoking Daniel's depiction of the contrast between King Nebuchadnezzar's earlier persecution of the "pious and just men" who would not worship his image, and his later behavior when, "being converted to the worship of the true God, he made a decree throughout his empire, that whosoever should speak against the God of Shadrach, Meshach, and Abednego should suffer the penalty which their crime deserved."[101] Nebuchadnezzar's decree, Augustine adds, was read before Christian emperors as an example for them to follow, "that they should show themselves religious by belief in God ... [and should] consider what decrees they ought to make in their kingdom, that the same God ... should not be treated with scorn among the faithful in their realm."[102] For it is the case that in such matters, "kings, just as it is divinely prescribed to them, serve God as kings, if in their kingdoms they prescribe the good to be done and proscribe the bad, *not only in those matters that pertain to human society, but also indeed in those that touch upon divine religion.*"[103]

Arguments of this sort certainly indicate that during the Sturm und Drang of successive bitter struggles with Donatists and Pelagians, Augustine was prepared to accord at last a somewhat higher status to Christian rulers than to pagan. Such a position may conceivably have been in concord with his earliest views when he still seems to have shared the progressivist optimism of the day concerning the providential redemptive mission of the Christian Roman empire. But surfacing as it did in the context of the chastened sobriety of his latter years, it was unquestionably in tension with his refusal in the works of his maturity to assign to the temporal powers much more than a limited authority over the external actions of subjects and citizens in things that pertained to their earthly well-being. If that "unresolved tension" or inconsistency seems largely to have escaped his own attention, it may well be—or so Markus has helpfully suggested—because nowhere in Augustine's discussions of religious coercion or his exchanges on the matter with imperial officials "did he ever consider Christian rulers and civil servants as parts of a governmental machinery, of the 'state.'" Instead, he was prone to thinking of them as "members of the Church," so that it is by means of them that the church (not the empire) "coerces" or "uses power." What was involved, in effect, was "a theory of coercion by the Church, not by the state."[104]

The implications, nonetheless, remain theocratic, with the imperial administration being viewed, in some measure at least, as a piece of legal machinery serving higher ends stipulated by the church. Such theocratic implications were certainly at odds with the teaching on matters political that was faithful to the desacralizing thrust of the New Testament and which we have represented as the product of Augustine's maturity and as his controlling teaching on matters political.[105]

Augustine's Conflicted Legacy and the "Political Augustinianism" of the Middle Ages

One does not necessarily have to agree with Figgis that "the De Civitate Dei needs for its interpretation the writings against the Donatists"[106] in order to admit that what the *De civitate dei* had to say has all too often been understood in the light of those writings—and never more strikingly than during the Middle Ages. But in order to understand why that should have been the case, it is not enough simply to take note of the fact that Augustine's struggle against the Donatist schismatics led him to justify recourse to governmental coercive force in order to nudge them back into line with Catholic orthodoxy. Instead, one has to probe more deeply into the basic doctrinal issues at stake, to ask what exactly it was that he sensed to be unorthodox about the Donatist position, to describe what it was that he himself took to be the orthodox norm in the ecclesiological issues at stake, and to identify the definitive stance that the church was finally led to take vis-à-vis such competing claims.

Of the four marks of the church designated in the Nicene Creed—one, holy, catholic, apostolic—the mark of holiness had appeared earlier and more often in the various creeds than had the other three. It had also been the characteristic that had given rise to some of the earliest ecclesiological controversies. All agreed that the church—the body of Christ, the body wherein, via the sacraments, the saving grace of God was mediated to sinful human beings—*had* to be holy. But how was that holiness to be defined and what did it imply for the sacraments of baptism and penance? On this issue the contribution of Augustine was to prove to be determinative. And what prompted him to make that contribution was the need to come to terms with the standpoint adopted by the Donatists in his native African province where, already by his lifetime, it had come to split the Christian community into bitterly opposed Catholic and schismatic churches.

Its point of departure had been the great persecution launched by Diocletian in the early fourth century under the pressure of which some of the clergy had become *traditores*. That is to say, they had handed over their copies of the sacred scriptures and had thereby apostatized. In the wake of that persecution, a group of African zealots had challenged the authority of the bishop of Carthage (on the grounds that he had been ordained by a *traditor* who had repudiated his faith and lapsed thereby into mortal sin), had questioned in general the validity of the sacraments administered by clergy of immoral or unworthy behavior, had adopted the position that the church had forfeited its claim to be holy if it tolerated within its ranks members guilty of the cardinal sin of apostasy or clergy morally unworthy of their high office, and had insisted, in effect, on making "the unity and catholicity of the church contingent on its prior holiness."[107] For these men, who came to be known as "Donatists," that holiness was to be judged solely in terms of the moral rigor with which the individual members conducted their lives. The church was for them to be a church of the pure, the membership of which was to be restricted to the ranks of the righteous—it was, in effect, in Ernst Troeltsch's sociological terms, to be a "sect."[108] That being so, the Donatists, as they achieved something close to a preponderance in the African church, came to reject the self-styled "Catholic" Christianity of the universal majority as "the synagogue of Satan." And they also became willing eventually to claim that their own church, limited though it might be to the African province and schismatic at that, alone possessed valid sacraments, the primary instrumentalities through which grace was mediated, and alone could properly claim to be the one, true Catholic church.

But if the Donatists had made the unity of the church contingent upon its holiness, Augustine, by way of reaction, went a long way toward making its holiness contingent upon its unity. For him, it was schism more than the individual unworthiness of its ministers that struck at the very life of the church. Cut off, indeed, from "the unity of the body of Christ" and, as a result, from the grace that by divine ordination the church and its sacraments mediate to man, nobody could attain true holiness. For the holiness of the church did not reside in the subjective righteousness of its individual members but rather in its own institutional sanctity as the locus of the regenerative working of divine grace. "The church is one, and its holiness is produced by the sacraments," Optatus, another anti-Donatist had said. "It is not to be considered on the basis of the pride of individuals."[109] The emphasis, therefore, was on the objective and the sacramental, and the authenticity and holiness of the sacramental channels of divine grace were not seen to depend on the moral worthiness of either minister or recipient. In his subsequent (post-411) confrontation with Pelagianism, it is true, Augustine would be led to state his belief in predestination in a particularly uncompromising form, thus identifying the true church not with any institution or visible fellowship of men but with the invisible body of the elect foreknown to God alone—the members, if you wish, of the city of God. In his earlier writings against the Donatists, on the other hand, he had come to identify the visible, institutional church, with its saints and sinners, hierarchy and sacraments, as the one true Catholic church and the sole ark of salvation. If the membership of that church is more inclusive, strictly speaking, than that of the "essential" or "invisible" church, it is not God's will that we, like the Donatists, should presume to do what he himself will not undertake to do before the Last Judgment—namely, to separate the wheat from the chaff, the saints from the sinners.

In an even more direct and thoroughgoing fashion than his doctrine of grace, Augustine's teaching on the church was to succeed in defining the terms of medieval orthodoxy and establishing the boundaries within which ecclesiological discussion, if it aspired to be orthodox, had necessarily to be conducted. But it should be realized that Augustine himself had developed his doctrines of the church and of grace independently of one another and at different points in his life. By 411–12, when he wrote the first of his treatises against the Pelagians, he had long since developed his anti-Donatist doctrine of the church. Early in 411, indeed, that doctrine had been adopted at the Council of Carthage as the official teaching of the church. He made little or no reference to it in his subsequent anti-Pelagian writings, and yet when the two doctrines are brought into mutual contact, the tension between them is palpable. Pushed to its logical conclusion, his affirmation of predestination and the irresistibility of divine grace could conceivably have the effect of depriving the sacramental ministrations of the visible hierarchical church of their central importance in the economy of salvation. It could do so, that is, at least in the sense that for a believer predestined to eternal damnation, not even the most assiduous exploitation of the sacramental channels of grace would do anything at all to promote his salvation. Augustine did not, of course, push that position to its logical conclusion and the tensions we ourselves detect between his anti-Donatist and anti-Pelagian teachings may have been altogether foreign to him. But the fact remains that whereas in the context of his writings on grace and salvation he was moved to define the church as the invisible body of the elect foreknown to God alone, in the context of his writings against the Donatists it was the visible, institutional church that he emphasized as the necessary vehicle of salvation.

During the centuries after his death the medieval church did not attempt to reconcile these two conflicting positions. But whereas Augustine's anti-Donatist teaching on the church was fated to become the prevailing and enduring orthodoxy, his views on grace and predestination were admitted only with modifications. And what was to prove significant for the characteristically medieval interpretation of what it was that he had had to say on matters political was the fact that those modifications served (though they were not necessarily consciously intended so to serve) to bring those views on grace and predestination into line with his teaching on the church. What emerged, then, was a modified version of Augustine's own teaching, a form of "Augustinian traditionalism" that, while affirming man's inability to engineer (Pelagian fashion) his own salvation, attributed to human beings instead the power and burdened them with the responsibility of *cooperating* with the workings of divine grace. Affirming also the necessity of grace, this modified version went a long way to confining its dispensation to those channels of grace called sacraments, which had in most cases to be administered by the ordained priesthood. And their efficacy was understood to be guaranteed *ex opere operato,* "by the sheer performance," that is, "of the act itself."[110] It was this modified version of Augustine, packaged and popularized in the Latin West by the influential writings of Pope Gregory the Great (590–604) and underpinning the power and prestige of the priestly hierarchy, that was to form the bedrock of medieval orthodoxy.[111]

As a result and insofar as political thinking was concerned, the Augustine whom one characteristically encounters in the Middle Ages is the Augustine of *The City of God* only insofar as that work was read or reinterpreted in light of what he had to say in his tracts against the Donatists. Medieval churchmen, after all, did not fully share his somber doctrine of grace; they rejected his sternly predestinarian division between the reprobate and the elect; they saw instead in every member of the visible Church Militant a person already touched by grace and potentially capable of citizenship in the *civitas dei*. More familiar with the anti-Donatist writings, in which Augustine had ascribed to the Christian emperor a distinctive role in the vindication of orthodoxy, than with the sober, limited, and essentially secular conception of rulership conveyed in his *City of God,* those churchmen were also apt, it may be, to assimilate the historical vision embedded in the latter to the optimistic Christian progressivism that Orosius had made (influentially) his own. They were led, accordingly, even while invoking Augustine's authority, to depart from his mature and controlling political vision. That is to say, they broke down the firm distinction between the city of God and the Christian societies of this world that we have seen him draw so firmly in all but a handful of texts in *The City of God* itself. Instead, and what he actually had had to say about justice and the commonwealth to the contrary, they understood him to have asserted that it is the glorious destiny of Christian society—church, empire, Christian commonwealth, call it what you will—to labor to inaugurate the Kingdom of God and the reign of true justice in this world.

As a result, and for example, it is on Augustine's glancing (and prescriptive) portrayal of the ideal Christian emperor (*DCD* 5:24), that "happy" ruler who sees his power as essentially *ministerial* and uses it for the extension of God's worship, that the Carolingian scholar Alcuin was to build the vision of Christian rulership with which he associates the reign of Charlemagne. And it was on that same portrayal that Pope Gregory IV (822–44) believed that the emperor Louis the Pious might most properly focus his attention. In a similar vein, Pope Nicholas I (858–67) and other ninth-century churchmen who deployed Augustine's authority contrived unwittingly not to render the precise thinking of Augustine himself, but rather to place his texts at the service of what, in a classic interpretation, H.-X. Arquillière called "political Augustinianism."[112] By that term he meant an essentially theocratic pattern of thought, within the modalities of which there is a marked tendency to respiritualize politics, to absorb the natural order into the supernatural, the profane laws of civil society into the sacred laws mediated by the ecclesiastical order (whether under imperial, royal, or episcopal/papal leadership) and, as a result, to interpret kingship as a divinely ordained and essentially *ministerial* office incorporated within, and at the service of, the Christian church. In effect, and by one of those superb ironies in which the history of ideas abounds, the name and prestige of Augustine became one of the instrumentalities whereby archaic notions of sacral kingship—to all intents and purposes excluded by the New Testament vision of politics (as well as by Augustine's own mature political thinking)—were nevertheless able to survive in Latin Christendom and, though in somewhat modified guise, to renew their vitality, just as, in the form of the Eusebian vision, they had been able to survive in the Byzantine East. Charlemagne himself, certainly—and Einhard, his biographer, tells us he was particularly fond of Augustine's *City of God*—felt, like Constantine before him, that he had an especial responsibility for the welfare even of those Christians who lived beyond the boundaries of his Christian empire. And some scholars, indeed, have been bold enough to assert that "he considered it his mission to build the City of God on earth."[113]

Whether or not that was indeed the case, and the supportive evidence is admittedly scant, we have seen that in the thinking of the Augustine of *The City of God* there were some hesitations that rendered that work susceptible of being used to support "political Augustinianism." But only, it must still be insisted, if its readers were predisposed so to interpret it. And it is in vain that one would search the pages of the New Testament or of *The City of God* itself for the roots of that predisposition. They must be sought, instead, elsewhere: in his own anti-Donatist writings, certainly, but also and beyond that in the ideological groundsoil of early medieval western Europe into which his ideas were destined soon to be transplanted.[114]

7. The Early Medieval West (i)
Sacral Kingship in the Germanic Successor Kingdoms

IF IT IS INDEED IN the ideological groundsoil of the Germanic successor kingdoms of the West that we must seek the roots of the stubborn medieval predisposition to transpose the bleakly secular political melodies of Augustine's *City of God* into an essentially theocratic key, we must recognize the fact that those roots tapped into three very different layers deposited sequentially across time. The first of these was the set of religio-political attitudes characteristic of the peoples of western Europe, Celtic as well as Germanic, during the centuries before their embrace of Arian or Catholic versions of the Christian faith. The second was the sweeping transformation in status undergone by the Christian church during the late Roman era, a transformation advanced still further by the complex nature of the Christianizing process and by the religio-political conditions that came to prevail in the Germanic successor kingdoms from the fifth to the eighth centuries. The third was constituted by the attempts that rulers, clerical thinkers, and others made during these and subsequent centuries to come to terms with that changed status and those prevailing conditions via an earnest exploitation of the fragmentary patristic materials handed down to them and of the Old Testament texts that seemed to speak so directly and so startlingly to the conditions of their own day. Of these "layers," it is the first (and deepest) that has most persistently been plagued by controversy and dissent. With it, accordingly, it is appropriate to begin.

Celtic and Germanic Kingship in Western and Northern Europe Prior to the Advent of Christianity

I have suggested that the way in which medievals characteristically understood Augustine depended in no small measure on what was on their minds when they sat down to read him. Something similar, I believe, may be said of modern scholars as they have edged up, some more nervously than others, to a moment of decision concerning the precise nature of the religio-political attitudes characteristic of the Celtic and Germanic peoples in the pre-Christian era, and the degree to which those attitudes enjoyed a continuing half-life in western Europe during the early medieval centuries and as the process of evangelization quickened. In the case of some historians, certainly, a stubborn sense of European or even Germanic exceptionalism seems to have served as a conceptual screen precluding recognition of the fact that the element of sacrality attaching to kings worldwide might conceivably have attached also to Germanic kings.

It was during the period stretching from the fourth to the eleventh centuries that Christianity spread far and wide to become the dominant religion in western and northern Europe. It took hold first in the lands that were (or had been) provinces of the Roman empire, spread thence into Ireland, Scotland, and (later) northwestern and northern Europe at large, with the culminating evangelization of Norway and Sweden gathering momentum in the tenth century and reaching its term in the course of the eleventh. Scholars attempting to assess the nature of Celtic and Germanic kingship in the pagan era before those centuries of evangelization and the degree to which it partook of sacrality have found themselves, given the nature, provenance, and paucity of the surviving evidence, confronting interpretative challenges of an unusually testing kind. Generalization has proved frequently to be difficult; agreement among philologists, anthropologists, historians, and students of comparative religion stubbornly elusive. A comparatively high degree of confidence attaches to what may be said about the insular Celtic periphery and (though in somewhat lesser degree) the Scandinavian north, for it was in Ireland and Iceland that oral tradition came to be committed to writing. Unavoidable though it is, generalization about the Germanic continental center remains, however, at least for historians if not for anthropologists or students of comparative religion, something of a high-risk venture.

Not in dispute is the essentially sacral character of the kings of pre-Christian Ireland. The Celts in general did not commit their lore to writing, and in this the pagan Irish were no exception. The pertinent evidence has, instead, to be teased out from the interstices of the ancient Irish law tracts and from the epic tales and traditions that later Christian redactors and writers were careful to record for posterity. While in that process a good deal of Christian "overpainting" occurred, in the writings they produced ancient pagan commitments were not altogether erased, and the outlines of the picture that resurfaces once the overlay is carefully removed is comparatively clear and consistent. According to D. A. Binchy, what "the Irish law tracts" disclose is "a rural society consisting of a congeries of petty kingdoms, each governed by a *rí* (king)," a ruler selected from among "the royal kindred," those possessed of the inherited royal blood.[1] If the specifically priestly and judicial functions of kingship were later to pass into the hands of a caste of learned specialists, that does not appear to have been the case earlier on. In the primary territorial unit or *tuath*, it was the king who functioned not only as leader in war but also as lawgiver and judge; and not only as its representative in dealings with the other petty kingdoms of the day but also as its representative before the gods. He served, in effect, as its sacral mediator with the divine forces upon which the well-being of his people depended, and the centrality of that religious function among the king's varied responsibilities is attested to by the importance that was attached to the solemn rites of royal inauguration.

We know such rites to have taken place at multiple sites broadcast across Ireland and traditionally viewed as sacred. Each of them, in a manner familiar to us from practices in other cultures,[2] was identified as the center of the world, marked by the *bile* or great tree, which stood in microcosm for the very *axis mundi* or hub of the universe itself. Tara was the most celebrated of these sites. Situated in *Midhe* (i.e., "middle"), the central province of Ireland at the confluence of the other four provinces, it functioned as the center of "a cosmographic schema which has parallels in India and other traditions." Indeed, "the traditional accounts of the disposition of the court of Tara," reveal it to have been "conceived as a [microcosmic] replica of this cosmographic schema."[3] At that center or numinous point of contact with the divine was periodically held the great *Feis Temhra* ("feast of Tara") at which was celebrated the inauguration of a new king and his ritual or symbolic mating with the (earth) goddess Medb. The inauguration was referred to as *banais righi,* "the wedding feast of kingship," and comparable rites of inauguration and related fertility rites took place in the other Irish kingdoms. They served to affirm the sacred character of the king; to encourage, doubtless by taboos of one sort or another, the well-attested restrictions on his freedom of movement; and to strengthen the degree to which he was held responsible for the fertility of the land, the favorable nature of the weather, and the abundance of crops.[4] And while it is not to be supposed that Irish patterns of thought and behavior were simply identical with those of the Brythonic Celts of neighboring Britain or the Celts of continental Europe, the fragmentary evidence we do possess for the lives of these related peoples in the pre-Christian era is strong enough to suggest that their kings, too, were sacral figures and to warrant Binchy's conclusion that "we are entitled to speak of a 'Common Celtic' type of kingship."[5]

On balance, it is safe, I believe, to say something similar about the prevalence of sacral kingship in the pre-Christian Germanic world, both in the Scandinavian north and the continental center. It is true that after a sweeping attack on what was threatening in his day to crystallize into a viable learned consensus, the East German scholar Walter Baetke concluded bitingly that "the religious nimbus" with which contemporary scholars were seeking to envelope the Germanic kingship was nothing more than "false gold."[6] But while he is persuasive enough in his insistence that the old Nordic kings were not seen to be "divine" in the sense that they were not themselves the object of a religious cult, his target in this case is something of a straw man. Far less persuasive is his concomitant attempt to deny them any sacral status at all. The less so, as he himself had had to concede the fact that by virtue of their position they certainly played a mediatorial role in the religious cult of their peoples.[7] If the Scandinavian kings played so prominent a role in that religious cult it was, after all, because they were embedded in a traditional society possessed of its own version of the cosmic religiosity characteristic of the archaic world. In their case, the cosmic tree Yggdrasill was seen to mark the center of the divine world, upholding the universe while at the same time reaching down with its roots both to the world of man and to the world of the dead. In such a setting, kings were certainly called upon to perform *blót* or sacrifice, and they were called upon to do so not simply "in order to provide for a good and fertile year . . . but [beyond that] to provide for a year to come," serving thereby as the very "creator of a new year."[8] Regarded as being of divine descent, they were sometimes revered as gods after their death and, in accord with the pattern familiar to us from so many other parts of the world, were held responsible for the rotation of the seasons, the fertility of the land, and the general well-being of their subjects. Such notions were so deeply ingrained, indeed, and their half-life so very long, that as late as 1527 King Gustavus Wasa could complain bitterly at a meeting of the Reichstag of Västerås that "the Swedish peasants of Dalarna blamed him if bad weather prevailed as if he were a god and not a man."[9]

Although the exaggeration is doubtless real, there is then something to be said for the claim to the effect "that kingship in Old Scandinavia is entirely sacral is nowadays considered as a mere matter of fact."[10] And that fact is directly pertinent to the stance one chooses to adopt vis-à-vis the Germanic kingship in western, central, and southern Europe during the late imperial era and the subsequent age of barbarian invasions.[11] For that issue consensus has proved elusive. In the extensive German literature on the subject one encounters something of a standoff, for instance, between a Baetke or Graus, on the one hand, and a Höfler or Hauck on the other.[12] The period crucially involved being one of great turbulence, the picture that emerges is understandably more varied, complex, and confused than that of the Scandinavian north. The evidence from which it has to be constructed is much scantier, and the interpretative challenge is exacerbated by the fact that the fragmentary written record is powerfully shaped by the essentially Roman or Christian perceptions and preoccupations of the writers involved. Given the fact, however, that the Germanic peoples shared a common Indo-European inheritance with the Celts and were also, over an extended stretch of time, close enough (and even intermingled) neighbors with them for some of their traditions to develop in tandem, it would surely be natural enough to start with the assumption that a form (or forms) of sacral kingship prevailed during the pre-Christian era among them, too. The more so, indeed, if one is willing to take into account the later evidence from the Scandinavian north as well as the testimony of the cultural anthropologists and students of comparative religion to the quasi-ubiquity and extraordinary staying power of that archaic institution. And it is the case that some historians of late antique and early medieval Europe have proved willing to embrace such a conclusion.[13]

Some, admittedly, but by no means all. Others, and especially those with a professional focus on legal and political history, continue to balk at such a step, taking their stand on the paucity of the direct (historical) evidence from the continental center available to support it, and, while so doing, brushing aside the validity of any appeal to cross-cultural analogies and even to the comparatively abundant (but admittedly later) Scandinavian evidence.[14] But given the ubiquity and longevity of forms of sacral monarchy, and weighing the importance of argumentative tactic, perhaps one is justified in insisting that the burden of proof should properly lie not on the shoulders of those who acknowledge the likelihood of its presence among the Germanic peoples of the pre-Christian era south of the Baltic, but rather of those who adamantly persist in denying it. The more so in that by so doing they are, in effect, insisting on a species of Germanic "exceptionalism" behind which would appear to lurk shadowy remnants of the old Teutonic myth. The belief, that is—as Bishop Stubbs had put it in 1880, evoking the authority of Caesar's *De bello gallico* and Tacitus's *Germania*—that the English had somehow inherited freedom with their German blood, and that in "the common germs of Germanic institutions," notably the selection and limitation of rulers by the assemblies of the *Volk*, were to be found the origins of the practices of representation and consent destined for so glorious a future in the providential flowering of English constitutionalism.[15]

But if one is indeed moved to evoke historical parallels with the Germanic *Thing* or folk assembly, rather than looking forward to the modern European future one would do better to delve deeper into the earlier Indo-European past. Make that move and one will encounter among the Hittites in the thirteenth century BCE, and in what has been called "the first Indo-European contribution" to the development of ideas of kingship, a form of monarchy at once both sacral and in some degree limited. The Hittite king was unquestionably a fundamentally sacred and priestly figure "regarded during his lifetime as the incarnation of his deified ancestor" and himself worshipped after death as a god. And yet, in the Old Kingdom at least, there existed a *pankuš* or assembly of nobles or notables that *may* have had a voice in the making of kings and certainly had power to limit his actions, possessing "jurisdiction over the king if the latter committed a crime."[16]

There is no ground a priori, then, for simply assuming with Baetke that because Scandinavian and Germanic kings were so often chosen or "elected" by the *Thing* or folk assembly, or because limitations of various sorts were placed upon the exercise of their power, that they should not also be regarded as truly sacral figures. The *Thing* was itself, after all, a sacred, cultic assembly through which flowed to the monarch the sacred power of the whole community. It is not to be viewed anachronistically as some sort of "secular" or even "democratic" body.[17] Nor should we be tempted to assume that the act of "election," even apart from the limitation of choice to members of certain families viewed as throne-worthy by blood-right (*Geblütsrecht*) in virtue of their claim to divine descent, was itself devoid of a sacral dimension. To Schlesinger, indeed (and speaking specifically of the choice of Swedish kings), "election" was an essentially "magical act."[18] And as for limitations on the power of pagan Germanic kings in western and southern Europe, the most definite evidence that has come down to us suggests that such limitations, like those suffered also by Irish and Scandinavian kings, sprang not from some sort of primordial "constitutionalism" but precisely from their sacral status. The king of the Burgundians, as the fourth-century Roman historian Ammianus Marcellinus tells us, "according to an ancient custom, lays down his power and is deposed, if under him the fortune of war has wavered or the earth has denied sufficient crops; just as the Egyptians commonly blame their rulers for such occurrences."[19]

Notwithstanding, then, the persistence on the matter, and especially so among legal and political historians, of what amounts almost to an instinctive skepticism, there really seems to be no compelling reason for denying to the Germanic kings of the pre-Christian era in the territories south of the Baltic a sacral status in some sense analogous to that which we know their Celtic counterparts to have possessed, and also, if centuries later, their royal counterparts in Scandinavia. In archaic Germanic society the workings of sacral forces appear to have been recognized as omnipresent. And "when the Germanic peoples entered the sphere of Christendom," it is not to be supposed, Otto Höfler has insisted, that they arrived "as a religionless multitude, but [rather as a people] shaped by an order of life in which the operation of religious forces and experiences can still be recognized."[20] So far as kingship is concerned, the operation of such forces can be discerned in the care with which a whole series of Germanic peoples—from the Ostrogoths to the Anglo-Saxons—handed down genealogies tracing the ancestry of their royal families back to mythical divine progenitors, most notably the god Woden.[21] It can also be discerned in the notion of sacred qualities inherent in the blood by virtue of which the choice of kings was in fact limited by *Geblütsrecht* to selection from among the throne-worthy members of the divinely descended royal kindred—those, in effect, who were possessed of the royal mana, or what German historians have sometimes called *Geblütsheiligkeit.* How very seriously this was taken can be strikingly illustrated by calling to mind the story related by the Byzantine historian Procopius about the two successive embassies that the Heruli, then living in Roman territory, sent back in the sixth century to their original homeland in the Germanic north in order to find among the members of the ancient royal family the type of king they felt they needed. The perceived legitimacy of the king so chosen proved to be so potent that the entire army of the rival Heruli king (who had in the meantime been appointed with the approval of the emperor Justinian) proceeded to desert him and to rally to the cause of the contender who was secure, after all, in his possession of the requisite *Geblütsheiligkeit.*[22]

It is commonplace to dwell on the differential measure in which the various barbarian peoples who settled within the perimeters of what had been the western Roman empire accommodated over the course of time to the patterns of life, institutions, legal norms, and political ideology prevailing among the surrounding Roman or Romanized populace with which they came into such intimate contact. But looking to the patterns of religio-political thinking that eventually rose to such prominence in the Germanic successor kingdoms—most notably in the Frankish realm—it is important to acknowledge also the degree to which the Roman populace proved, in turn and over the course of time, to be itself receptive to the archaic beliefs and traditions that their Germanic neighbors, Christian though they might now be, found it so hard to relinquish. Speaking interestingly of what he calls the process of "re-archaization" taking place in the late antique and early medieval centuries and of "the simplification of Roman political theory and philosophy," itself reflective of "the simplification and change of... Roman institutions," Herwig Wolfram has noted that, as time went on, "irrational and mystical concepts of blood, innate power, and virtue became more and more important with the ruling Roman class itself, and not just with the Germanic kings and noblemen who were considered to be incarnations of, or at least derived from, Woden and other pagan gods."[23] He is right to do so, and that fact should not be forgotten as we attempt to make sense of the complex process of accommodation with archaic sacral patterns that went into the formation of notions of kingship in the early medieval West.

Ecclesia Dei: From Voluntary Society to Public Authority

During the late Roman and early medieval centuries, the Christian church in the empire's western provinces and in the newly evangelized territories lying beyond the borders of Romania was destined to undergo a sweeping change of status.[24] When we use the word "church" today we think instinctively in terms of a corporately organized voluntary society, one akin in civic status and in relation to the law of the land to such other voluntary societies as colleges and universities, fraternal or professional organizations, trades unions, and the like. And during the first three centuries of its existence, though intermittently persecuted and of questionable legal status, the church—or, rather, the loosely affiliated communities of Christians—had enjoyed a status at least roughly analogous to that. As early as the third century, and even before they had become the beneficiaries of official toleration, bishops had begun to act as legislators, administrators, and arbitrators in the churches under their supervision. But they had done so as leaders of private, voluntary societies, organizations that were directly concerned with only one segment of human activity, and their decisions as leaders possessed binding force solely in the degree to which they had proved able to touch the consciences of the faithful. No more than the leadership of any modern private organization could they lay claim to any public, coercive power.

With the conversion of Constantine, however, the concomitant extension of toleration to Christians and, at the end of the fourth century, the proscription of paganism and the "establishment" of the new faith, Christianity had come to be transformed from the proscribed religion of a suspect minority into the official religion of the empire, taking the place, therefore, of the civic cult of pagan antiquity. As a result, ecclesiastical authority, supported increasingly by the public force of the imperial administration, was well on the way now to becoming political and coercive in nature. Led at the Roman center by aristocratic bishops serving very much as successors to the old senatorial class, and in the western provinces and in territories that had never been subject to Rome often by clerics of royal or noble descent (who were in close touch with their lay kinsfolk), the apparatus of ecclesiastical administration also began to reach out into areas that we today would recognize as pertaining to the state. That is to say, it began to assume the burden of public functions in the realm, especially, of what we today would call health, education, and welfare. This was very much the case, under the unstable conditions of the day, at Rome itself during the pontificate of Gregory I (590–604), as well as in the nominally Byzantine provinces of central Italy. Such developments intensified during the two centuries ensuing, and as overt paganism was suppressed or died out, membership of what we would call "the church" and membership of what we would call "the state" gradually moved close to being coterminous. The church ceased, in effect, to be a voluntary, private organization comparable to other social organizations and became instead a compulsory, all-inclusive and coercive society comparable to what we would call the state and, in its totality, well-nigh indistinguishable from it.

That state of affairs was evident alike in the western provinces of Romania and in the newly Christianized territories that had never been subject to Roman rule. It was evident, that is, in what Peter Brown, emphasizing the "profound regionalization" of the Christian churches of the sixth and seventh centuries, has referred to felicitously as "a patchwork of adjunct, but separate, 'micro-Christendoms.'"[25] Thus by the late seventh century, in one such micro-Christendom—that of Ireland and western Scotland—great fortified monasteries presided over by abbots often of royal descent "recreated, in Christian form, the great high places that had [earlier] acted as intertribal meeting points." There Christianization had meant the bold appropriation of the pre-Christian culture by a new religious caste, the monks and clergy who had succeeded to the role once played by the druids. And under such conditions, Brown has said, "the pre-Christian past continued in the present with a self-confidence that was inconceivable in Continental Europe."[26]

Nonetheless, on the Continent, too, the progressive coalescence into a single society of what we would distinguish as state and church was by that time well advanced. It was notably evident in the "micro-Christendom" that, after its conversion from Arianism in 589, the Visigothic kingdom came to constitute in Spain. There the kings came to rule in close collaboration with the Catholic bishops and their noble confrères, presiding over (and ratifying the decrees of) the seventeen great provincial councils assembled over the years at Toledo. In that kingdom, the celebrated encyclopedist Isidore of Seville (c. 560–636) equated church and society, portraying the king as "servant of God" (*minister dei*) divinely appointed to rule that unitary society with an authority that extended, accordingly, to matters religious in general and to clerical discipline in particular. Of early medieval authors, Isidore may well have been the most widely read (he was certainly one of the most frequently cited), and his apprehension of the facts on the ground and recognition of the new state of affairs was doubtless widely influential.[27]

With the destruction in the early eighth century of the Visigothic kingdom at the hands of Muslim invaders, and the subsequent rise of the Frankish people to leadership in the West, the process whereby the church had come to be identified with the entire social and political community reached its maturity. Under the magisterial rule of Charlemagne and the Frankish revival in 800 of the empire in the West, the several micro-Christendoms of western Europe were finally fused into a single Latin Christendom, a single, public society—church, empire, Christian commonwealth, call it what you will—a universal commonwealth that was neither voluntary nor private. To that commonwealth all Europeans, even after the collapse of the Carolingian empire, still felt that they somehow belonged. So far as the ecclesiastical body went, its leadership was by then deeply involved in affairs of state, its laws supported by the coercive power of the civil ruler, and its membership well-nigh indistinguishable from that of civil society itself. And the beckoning vision of a universal commonwealth, coterminous with Christendom, sustained in theory by periodically revitalized memories of ancient Rome and guaranteed in practice by the prestige of the Roman legal inheritance and by the universal and international character of the ecclesiastical structure itself, was to linger on to haunt the purlieus of the European political imagination long after the rise to prominence of an array of de facto national monarchies—until, with the advent of the Protestant Reformation, the unity of that ecclesiastical structure was itself finally to be destroyed.

This gradual but ultimately sweeping change that the Christian church underwent during the nearly half millennium separating the emergence of imperial Christianity from the later era of Carolingian hegemony went hand in glove with a complex set of accommodations with age-old notions concerning the sacrality of kings. It could hardly have been otherwise given the complex, varied, and shifting nature of the process of Christianization itself and of the ways in which contemporaries understood it.[28] That process was punctuated by periodic moments of drastic discontinuity, such as Charlemagne's desecration in 772 of "the great [Saxon] intertribal sanctuary of the Irminsul, the giant tree that upheld the world," or St. Boniface's felling in the 730s of the Oak of Thunor at Geismar, using its sacred timbers to construct a Christian sanctuary where once it had stood.[29] But the norm appears rather to have been a more ambivalent process involving a (sometimes conscious) willingness to effect accommodations of one sort or another with the beliefs and practices of the pagan past. We catch a glimpse of this in the celebrated instructions which Pope Gregory the Great sent to the Benedictine missionaries in England ordering that the temples of the idols there were not to be destroyed but "purified from devil worship, and dedicated to the service of the true God. In this way, we hope that the people, seeing that its temples are not destroyed, may abandon idolatry and resort to these places as before, and may come to know and adore the true God.... For it is certainly impossible to eradicate all errors from obstinate minds at one stroke, and whoever wishes to climb to a mountain top climbs gradually step by step, and not at one leap. It was in this way that God revealed himself to the Israelite people in Egypt, permitting the sacrifices formerly offered to the Devil to be offered thenceforward to Himself instead."[30]

It comes as no surprise, then, that in the unfolding process of evangelization Isis suckling the baby Horus could mutate in Coptic Egypt into the Virgin Mary suckling the infant Jesus, or in the Germanic world, that the name of a pagan goddess *Eostre,* nudging aside the Latin *Pascha,* could come to be attached to the most sacred of Christian feasts. As a further concession to the demands of local circumstance (and as the very date chosen for Christmas attests),[31] it seems to have become common practice to substitute Christian feasts for seasonal pagan celebrations and, similarly, to substitute (as at Geismar) churches for pagan shrines and the cult of some Christian saint for that of a local spirit or deity. But while that was viewed, it seems, as a shrewd and not inappropriate tactic, it was destined to have enduring consequences. When St. Boniface cut down the sacred oak at Geismar, he himself was attempting, it turns out, to cope with such consequences, for he had found himself dealing in a supposedly Christianized region with religious syncretism of the crudest kind.[32] Similarly, as we read in Augustine's *Confessions,* the African Christians of his day, like so many other Christians elsewhere in Europe, regarded it as a devout practice "to take meal cakes and bread and wine to the shrines of the saints on their memorial days." His own mother, Monica, abandoned that practice only when they went to Milan, where St. Ambrose, a quintessentially Roman figure, recognizing it for what it was—a survival in barely Christianized guise of the ancient cult of the dead—had forbidden it.[33] If that prohibition was in any way distinguished, it was so mainly by its precocity.

In the centuries that followed, churchmen were called upon again and again to issue comparable prohibitions. Northumbrian penitentials, the great Visigothic councils at Toledo, Carolingian capitularies later on—all of them witness alike to the worries generated among the leadership, lay and clerical alike, by the survival of pagan cultic practice and its continued appeal to the general populace. Outright sacrifice to the old gods, the stubborn persistence of votive offerings made to idols, the continuing practice of cremation, these and other *paganiae* or remnants of paganism were all of them the occasion of repeated prohibitions.[34] But more telling than such specific survivals, and deeper still, was the degree to which in the rural fastnesses of Europe "an untranscended [pagan] past perpetually shadows the advancing footsteps of the Christian present."[35] The later records of ecclesiastical visitations, Lutheran as well as Catholic, and the modern sociologically oriented investigations that have made use of them, have raised serious doubts, indeed, about the degree to which some of the more remote rural areas of western Europe can really be said to have been Christianized at all.[36] As one might expect of a society that was overwhelmingly agrarian, the old nature religion, with its instinctive sense of "something far more deeply interfused," of the indwelling in the natural world of the divine, its rites for the promotion of fertility, and its nostrums for the prevention of natural disasters, proved to be exceedingly robust. So much so, indeed, that little understood remnants of such beliefs and practices were to survive in the legends and folklore of European peasant society right down into the nineteenth century.

That being the case, and given the marked degree to which Christian missionary effort was focused initially (and strategically) on kings rather than their subjects, it is understandable that an analogous measure of continuity and religious syncretism should be present in the way in which early medieval Christians understood the nature and role of their kings. It was clerics, after all, who preserved in writing the solemn genealogies tracing the royal, god-sprung lineage back to Woden. And Wolfram and others have emphasized the importance of such genealogical credentials in ensuring that a sense of the sacrality of kings survived the transition from the pagan world to the Christian era.[37] It was clerics, too, who in France and England were later to domesticate within the boundaries of official ecclesiastical approval the tenacious belief in the healing power of the royal touch, even if in order to do so they had to risk stretching the framework of Christian belief itself. Advanced already on behalf of the Merovingian king Gunthram (592) and asserted officially on behalf of the French and English kings from the eleventh to the eighteenth centuries, such a notion would have been inconceivable apart from the survival into the Middle Ages of pre-Christian notions about the sacred qualities attaching to kings.[38] And it was a cleric, again, the Venerable Bede who, in his *Ecclesiastical History of the English Nation,* attested to the miraculous properties attaching to the very soil on which King Oswald of Northumbria (633–41) had fallen in battle.[39] Later on, not even Alcuin, the great Anglo-Saxon scholarly luminary at Charlemagne's palace school, was able to refrain, when writing in 793 to the Northumbrian king Aethelred, from associating with that king's own virtue a mild climate, the fertility of the land, and the health of his people.[40]

King Oswald was one of the first of what proved to be during the medieval centuries, and right across Europe from the Anglo-Saxon to the Slavic world, a wholly extraordinary number of royal saints. Some scholars have seized on that fact in order to make a case for continuity between pagan royal sacrality and Christian dynastic sanctity. But even they have had to acknowledge the existence for centuries of a certain rivalry between the claims made for the Christian saint and those advanced on behalf of the sacred ruler, as well as the wariness often evinced by the ecclesiastical authorities toward the popular cult of royal saints. So far as pagan royal sacrality and Christian dynastic sanctity are concerned, the available evidence is not such as to support any compellingly *direct* connection between the two. The most that can be said with any degree of confidence is that the royal cult may, in certain instances at least, have incorporated notions stemming from the old pagan cult of kingship and that the existence of ecclesiastical wariness may itself attest to the fact that contemporary churchmen detected in the new cult of royal saints the penumbral remnants of pagan commitments.[41]

Looming much larger, certainly, than the phenomenon of royal sanctity in the intricate process whereby a viable and durable accommodation was arrived at with inherited notions of royal sacrality was something more fundamental and, oddly, much more direct. Nothing other, in fact, than the authority of the Old Testament itself, which handed down a vivid and compelling account of the triumphs and tribulations of the chosen people and of the prototypical, if ambivalent, accommodation that the Israelites themselves had made with Near Eastern notions of sacral kingship.[42] For a whole array of peoples—Ethiopians and Irish, Britons, Anglo-Saxons and Franks, even in some measure the East Romans themselves—the history they encountered in those Old Testament texts, and the way of life evoked there, seems to have possessed a freshness, familiarity, and immediacy with which the receding memories of imperial Rome could not quite compete. In marked degree, those texts succeeded in colonizing the imaginations of early medieval peoples.

Thus, writing in the early sixth century his *De excidio et conquestu Britanniae* (*On the Ruin of Britain*), the British cleric Gildas portrayed the beleaguered Britons as an erring people of Israel, and himself as their Jeremiah, threatening for their sins divine punishment at the hands of the Saxons.[43] A century later, the celebrated Irish legal collection the *Senchas Már* mediated to Christian contemporaries the hallowed laws of pagan Ireland by seeking to present them very much as an appendix to the Old Testament. Meanwhile, as they reeled under the impact of successive Muslim onslaughts, Byzantines of iconoclast sympathies were coming to fear that through their traditional veneration of icons they, like the ancient Hebrews or chosen people, had drifted along with their biblical forebears into idolatry and had, accordingly, been abandoned by their God. But all of this notwithstanding, as the eighth century wore on it was to be the Franks who, reaching out for leadership in the West, came quintessentially to see themselves as a "blessed people," like the Israelites of old a chosen people of God, and to interpret their destiny and that of their kings in terms of that beguiling vision.

Rex Dei Gratia: The Ministerial Conception of Kingship in the Eighth and Ninth Centuries

Products as they were of aristocratic societies in which the presence of god-sprung kings loomed large, it is understandable that early medieval commentators were prone to seeing the political conditions of their day as cognate to those so vividly conveyed in the narratives of the Old Testament. At the same time, it is understandable, too, that as they brooded over the books of Samuel and other biblical "historical" texts, they were not prone to focusing on the passages that witnessed to Yahweh's displeasure with the Israelites for blasphemously demanding a king "like other nations."[44] What caught their attention, instead, was the overall depiction of divinely sanctioned kings charged with the solemn duty of being good shepherds to their people in the spiritual no less than the temporal domain. Accordingly, and already in the opening years of the seventh century, Isidore of Seville had prototypically depicted the role of the (now safely Catholic) Visigothic king as that of being a minister or servant of God, a ruler entrusted with the duty of exercising over Christians, with piety no less than justice, a divinely appointed office. Around the same time we encounter in Frankia, in the persons of Chlothar II and his son Dagobert, Merovingian kings who were clearly possessed of the conviction that the power they wielded was in some sense God-given. During that same century one also begins to encounter comparisons between those kings and their prototypical biblical predecessors, David and Solomon, and, eventually, between the Frankish people themselves and the divinely chosen people of Israel.[45] Early in the eighth century, Ine, king of Wessex (d. 725) was to describe himself as king "mid Godes gife," a direct parallel to the lapidary formula *rex dei gratia* (king by the favor of God—still inscribed on British coinage), which was destined in the latter part of the eighth century to become with the Carolingian rulers of Frankia the standard formulation of the notion that kings ruled by divine ordination.[46]

Attempts, therefore (à la Fritz Kern's), to postulate some sort of dramatic ideological revolution dating to 751 when Pippin III (the Short), the Carolingian mayor of the palace (or de facto shogun-like ruler), deposed Childerich III, the last of the "do-nothing" Merovingian kings, and himself took the title of king of the Franks do not really measure up to the complexity of the facts on the ground.[47] Already by the early eighth century, developing church practice, in its intermingling of the civil and ecclesiastical and especially in the authority so readily conceded to kings in matters religious, already reflected a considerable degree of accommodation with the archaic, pagan pattern of sacral kingship. It was simply left to the clerical shapers of opinion in the Carolingian realms, along with their counterparts in Anglo-Saxon England and their successors in East Frankia under the Ottonian and Salian king-emperors, to exploit the biblical texts and patristic materials available to them in an attempt to make some sort of theological peace with this state of affairs. In that attempt the clerical liturgists in particular proved to be resourceful, creative, and successful. Their legacy, as a result, was the robust theoretical framework within which the theocratic form of Christian kingship that emerged in the course of the eighth century as the dominant political institution in early medieval Europe was able, for the next three centuries and more, to flourish.

In connection with that legacy, the events of 750/51 that mark the end of Merovingian and the beginning of Carolingian royal rule may best be seen as the culmination of a century and more of complex development. But they did succeed in bringing the nature of those earlier developments into comparatively sharp focus. They may serve, then, as an appropriate point of departure for a brief examination of the nature of the Carolingian kingship that emerged in their wake.[48] It might well seem that what those events involved was nothing more than a forthright and formal acknowledgment of where the realities of power had long since come to reside. But that was not the way in which they appear to have been viewed at the time. And it would be hard to account for that fact without recognizing the stubbornly sacred character which, despite the Christianization of Frankia and their own loss of real "political" power, had continued to cling to the Merovingian kings.

From about 687 to 751 those kings had characteristically stood to one side while the actual power of the kingship came to be wielded by the successive Carolingian mayors of the palace. In this, however, they were, historically speaking, by no means unique. Similar instances of seemingly do-nothing kings are to be found in times and places as widely separated one from another as, for example, the contemporaneous kingdom of Axum (in Ethiopia), or the tenth-century kingdom of the Volga Bulgars, or the nineteenth-century South Pacific island kingdom of Tonga, or, quintessentially, from the late twelfth century onward under the Kamikura and then the Tokugawa shogunate in Japan. In all of those cases the mana of royal legitimacy lay not with the actual wielder of political power but with the "do-nothing" king.[49] The same was true of the later Merovingians. Their insistence on wearing their hair long (they were called the *reges criniti*) may well have been of religio-magical significance (an interpretation supported by Vandal and Norwegian parallels), as also the custom whereby they traveled around (like the German fertility goddess Nerthus) in a wagon or sacred chariot drawn by white oxen.[50] Certainly the fact that after Charles Martel's death in 741 and after a prolonged interregnum, it was felt necessary to install on the throne another "do-nothing" Merovingian, Childerich III, underlines the sacral aura still attaching to the dynasty. Similarly, the precise way in which, a few years later, the Carolingian mayor of the place, Pippin the Short, went about the business of disposing of that hapless king, and the extreme caution with which he approached that delicate task, does suggest that he viewed it as fraught with some sort of danger. His moves, therefore, as he went about the business of appropriating the Frankish kingship for himself and his own dynasty were very deliberate in nature.

It was only after he had consulted the pope and been assured that the person wielding the actual power should be possessed of the royal title[51] that Pippin proceeded to depose the last Merovingian king. He went about it, moreover, by having Childerich and his son shorn of their long hair and incarcerated in a monastery. At the same time, in what (Fredegar to the contrary) was for the Frankish kingship a novelty, he himself was ritually anointed as king, first by St. Boniface, functioning as papal legate, and then, three years later, by Pope Stephen II himself. Given the dating, brevity, and conflicted nature of the surviving sources, it is admittedly difficult to be sure about the precise significance that contemporaries (as opposed to commentators in subsequent centuries) attached to these moves.[52] But the tonsure can plausibly be read as a ritual deprivation of the sacred power inherent, as it were, in the blood of the old Merovingian royal family. Similarly, the unction or anointing with chrism—the ancient Near Eastern rite for the transference of a person from the sphere of profane into that of the sacred—can be identified as "a piece of church magic"[53] intended to serve as a Christian substitute compensating the Carolingians for their lack of *Geblütsheiligkeit*. As Fritz Kern put it long ago, alluding to the sacred aura of the *reges criniti*, with the introduction in 751 of royal unction "an ancient pagan symbol [now] gave way to a modern theocratic one."[54]

It was because it had been preserved and hallowed alike by Old Testament example and Christian liturgical practice that the ancient rite of unction was at hand to serve such a purpose. It had found an important place in Hebraic ceremonial, and Christians had adopted it for their own purposes, folding it into the ceremonial rites associated with baptism, confirmation, the ordination of priests, and (eventually) the consecration of bishops. As we have already seen,[55] with the establishment of the Hebrew kingship, the Israelites had adopted it for the inauguration of their own kings. Those biblical parallels clearly worked their magic on the early medieval imagination. As a result, and however ironically, it was the Bible itself that, as Marc Bloch put it, "provided [in the West] the means of reintroducing into the lawful ceremonies of Christianity the sacred royalty of past ages."[56] Anointing had become part of the ceremonial inauguration of the Visigothic kings of Spain as early as the seventh century and in the opening years of the eighth; it *may* have been added for a while to the essentially pagan inaugural rites of the Irish kings.[57] Certainly after its appearance in Frankia in 751 and England in 786/7, and after a period of fluctuating usage, it went on in the latter part of the ninth century to become the norm in the various Carolingian kingdoms. It spread thence, eventually, throughout the greater part of western Europe, and notwithstanding the persistence of some local differences, the usages prevalent in West and East Frankia and in Anglo-Saxon England came to influence one another in complex and intricate ways, converging in the end on liturgical forms that were genuinely international in character.[58]

In Frankia the fortunes of the Carolingian monarchs depended not only on their high status vis-à-vis matters religious but also and in marked degree on the closeness of their affiliation with the aristocracy.[59] In that connection, then, no little importance attached to the way in which the papacy itself linked the anointing of the Frankish kings with the peculiar destiny as a holy and chosen people of the Frankish nation as a whole. If other early medieval peoples had thought of themselves in similar terms, it was the Franks who came to do so quintessentially. Ever since their conclusive victory early in the eighth century over the Arab invaders of Gaul, Ernst Kantorowicz has noted, they "had begun to think of themselves as the new people chosen by God. The 'new sacred people of promise,' as they were styled by the Holy See." They began, accordingly, to find "the roots of their history ... not in the profane evolution of the Greco-Roman world, but in the sacred tradition of the Old Testament." So that, in effect, they "endeavored ... to wheel into Church history as the continuators of Israel's exploits rather than into Roman history as the heirs of pagan Rome."[60] To the promotion of such a vision the rite of royal anointing was admirably suited. Along with its introduction into the Frankish realms went an increasingly common proclivity for seeing the position and attributes of the

Frankish monarchs as paralleling the sacral position and priestly attributes of the Old Testament kings, as well as those of such figures as Moses and Melchizedek, the mysterious king of Salem and priest of the most High God.[61] This development became more strikingly evident as the Carolingian era wore on, and as contemporaries became prone to portraying the Frankish kingdom as itself "the kingdom of David" and the Frankish king as a new Moses, a new David, a new Solomon, a truly sacred monarch worthy of being acclaimed by the clerics of his kingdom assembled in 794 at the Council of Frankfurt as nothing less than "king and priest."[62]

Given the degree to which the political atmosphere was saturated with the language and imagery of the Old Testament and charged with the idealized memory of Davidic kingship, contemporary history must sometimes have felt like a replay of biblical history. In such an atmosphere it is understandable that the desacralizing thrust of the New Testament (or of Augustine's texts so far as they were read) should have been blunted. Nor is it surprising that there should have grown up around the Carolingian rulers and their successors (or analogues) in more than one part of western Europe what amounted to a reworked version of the archaic ruler cult. Rather than being cosmically oriented, however, that cult was now transposed into an essentially biblical historical key, to be played out along the axis of a salvation history that was at once recognizably Christian and distinctively Western. Thus the *Laudes regiae,* the liturgic acclamations of the Carolingian rulers drawn up in the late eighth century, constitute in many ways a replication of "acclamations [once] tendered to the Roman emperors," and a "medieval equivalent of ancient ruler-worship." Portraying the hierarchy of royal, noble, and clerical rulers on earth as a reflection or counterpart of the heavenly hierarchy, they "display, as it were, the cosmic harmony of Heaven, Church and State, an interweaving and twining of the one world with the other and an alliance between the powers on earth and the powers in heaven."[63]

That being the case, the later distinction between ecclesiastical and temporal governance understandably remained as remote from the thinking of these theocratic kings and their successors in western Europe for the next two or three centuries as it had been from the thinking of those Israelite kings in whom, by virtue of their common unction, they tended to perceive as their direct forebears. In the 877 liturgical *ordo* for the royal consecration, which was destined to enjoy a millennial currency, the "holy church" is simply equated with "the Christian people" entrusted to the royal charge. Almost a century earlier, in the preface to the *Libri Carolini*, an important piece of royal propaganda, Charlemagne had been designated as the governor of "the kingdom of the Holy Church" (*regnum sanctae ecclesiae*).[64] No idle words, these, as the defeated Saxons learned when Charlemagne gave them the choice of baptism or the sword. He clearly viewed religious responsibilities as lying at the very heart of his royal charge. He was crowned "emperor" in 800, and whatever his empire was—Frankish or neo-Roman—it was certainly a community of belief and he the imperial ruler of a Christian people.[65] As the modalities of his administrative oversight no less than his legislative activity and court propaganda reveal, Charlemagne regarded himself as charged with the task of leading his subjects to their eternal salvation. Not even doctrinal matters escaped his scrutiny or failed to reflect his decisive influence. Of the Carolingian Latin capitularies Mayke de Jong has said that they are "documents with a profoundly religious perspective in which kings and their clerical and lay magnates all had a stake." Of one such set of instructions that Charlemagne gave to his *missi dominici* (agents of the central administration) as they made their supervisory rounds visiting those charged with the governance of the various imperial territories, Arquillière, noting their stress on virtuous living and eternal salvation, was moved to exclaim: "This document ... is not an administrative text: it is an apostolic act!"[66]

Under such circumstances, it is readily comprehensible that during the early medieval centuries Augustine's essentially secular understanding of the role and status of civil rulers should be lost sight of, and that the prestige of his name should come to be attached not to the somber and New Testament-oriented Augustinianism of *The City of God* but to the essentially theocratic pattern of thought to which Arquillière gave the name of "political Augustinianism." Testimony to that fact is the ease with which the works of the fourth-century author "Ambrosiaster," whom we have seen to be something of an ideological counterpart in the West of Eusebius in the East, could nevertheless circulate under the name of Augustine.[67]

But although some ideas of Romano-Hellenistic provenance did come to cluster around it, it was above all the cultus of biblical kingship that provided the ideological underpinnings for the early medieval kingship and continued for long centuries thereafter to impart a distinctive tonality to that institution. That particular form of kingship flourished not only in

England and in what, after Charlemagne's coronation as emperor in 800, we can now call the Carolingian empire, but after the latter's disintegration in the late ninth century, it also became the norm in the successor kingdoms of France, Italy, and Germany and found a more indirect parallel in Spain. It flourished not least of all under the Saxon and Salian rulers of Germany who, from the moment of the imperial coronation of Otto I at Rome in 962, were destined to rule that revived transalpine "Empire of the Romans," which in the fullness of time came to be known as the *Sacrum Imperium* or Holy Roman empire.[68] To the biblically inspired cultus that developed around these kings the sacrament of unction (or rite of anointing) was central. The notions that clustered around it found broadly influential expression in the great liturgies elaborated for the coronation of European kings as well as in the iconographic representation of such events.[69] A prayer dating from Charlemagne's reign, and destined early to find its way into widespread use in those liturgies, well catches in brief compass the royal ideal envisioned. Beginning with the words "Look out with clear eyes, omnipotent God, for this most glorious king" and conveying the fundamental idea that royal power was God-given, it petitioned for the bestowal of divine grace on the king, that he might triumph over his enemies both at home and abroad; extend himself with magnanimity to the nobles, leaders, and "faithful men of his kingdom"; secure peace and abundance for the realm (affording generous protection especially to its churches and monasteries); and, not least of all, that he be blessed with royal heirs and, his royal duties discharged, be deemed worthy at the end of an eternal reward.[70]

Flourishing as it did over so wide an area and for so long a time, the ideology that underpinned this type of theocratic kingship understandably betrayed more than one variation. Two, in particular, deserve mention because they were characteristic of the way in which that ideology developed over the course of time as the West Frankish monarchy became more fragile, as its East Frankish counterpart struggled to establish a firm foothold, and as the type of supernatural sanction conveyed by the anointing of kings became, accordingly, more and more important. The first of these variations, evident from the late ninth century onward, is the increasing *clericalization* of the royal office. The second, by no means unknown in the Carolingian era[71] but evident especially in tenth- and eleventh-century Germany, is the increasing tendency to understand kingship not merely in generally theocentric terms but also in specifically *Christocentric* fashion. And both were to be reflected in paradigmatic fashion in the writings of an unidentified cleric now usually known as the Anglo-Norman Anonymous. To those writings, accordingly, we must now turn.

The Anglo-Norman Anonymous: Christomimesis and the "Liturgical" Kingship of the Tenth and Eleventh Centuries

Although evocations of the mysterious Melchizedeck, king and priest, were far outnumbered by parallels drawn between the Frankish kings and their Davidic predecessors,[72] a priestly aura came gradually to be associated with the Carolingian monarchs. Early on in their royal career, Pope Stephen III (768–76) had not hesitated to label them as "a holy race, royal and sacerdotal." And as we have seen, the bishops assembled in 794 at the Council of Frankfurt had likewise acclaimed Charlemagne himself as "king and priest."[73] The turbulent political conditions of the late ninth and early tenth centuries in West and East Frankia alike had imparted a heightened charge to the legitimating force of anointing. Needing it more, kings came to accord it greater value. And with unction now established as an integral part of the royal and imperial coronation ceremonies of western Europe, it was in the tenth and eleventh centuries that the clericalization of the royal office became increasingly marked. Anointed like bishops with the holy chrism in a ceremony of inauguration modeled on and strikingly similar to that for the consecration of a bishop, the king came to be regarded as endowed thenceforward with a priestly or clerical status.

By the mid-eleventh century the view had become widespread that the anointing of a king, like the consecration of a bishop, constituted a sacrament. The nature of the clerical status it was taken to confer was not, admittedly, precisely defined. It would be tempting here, as with Byzantium and by way of elucidation, to call upon the later (twelfth century) canonistic distinction between the powers of order and jurisdiction and to confine the king's priestly role to the jurisdictional.[74] But as we will see, the witness of the Anglo-Norman Anonymous would imply that to do so might be anachronistically restrictive. Lack of precise definition, moreover, was not to preclude the explicit liturgical affirmation of the king's clerical status. Thus in the coronation *ordo* of the tenth-century German kings, it was stipulated that the archbishop of Mainz should adjure the king to "receive the crown of the realm at the hands of the bishops... and through this thy crown know thyself as partaker in our office." And from the tenth century to the twelfth (when it was quietly dropped), the formula "and here the lord pope makes the emperor-elect into a cleric" was included in the liturgy for the imperial coronation. All of this, as Wido of Osnabrück emphasized in 1084–85, because "being anointed with the oil of consecration," he participates in the priestly ministry "and is removed from the realm of the laity."[75] In this connection, there comes irresistibly to mind the fact that the coronation and anointing of Queen Elizabeth II in 1953, in a liturgical rite modeled closely on the Edgar *ordo* of 973, stimulated a flurry of impatient (but not altogether inaccurate) complaints about the *sacerdotalization* of the English monarchy.[76]

With this process of clericalization should properly be affiliated the second of the noteworthy developments calling for our attention. Namely, the tendency for the ideology of western European kingship in the tenth and eleventh centuries to move beyond the merely theocentric and become specifically Christocentric in nature. In the eighth century Cathwulf, an author about whom we know very little but who clearly vibrated to the same ideological frequencies as had Ambrosiaster, could address Charlemagne as the vicegerent of God, whereas he relegated the bishop to "the second place" as "only the vicegerent of Christ."[77] A century later, moreover, Smaragdus of St. Mihiel could similarly describe the king very much as a sacred figure who stood in the place of Christ.[78] By the tenth century that appellation ("vicar of Christ") had become more common. Under the influence, perhaps, of the growing clericalization of the royal office and, certainly, of what Kantorowicz called the "uncompromisingly Christocentric" nature of contemporary monastic piety, the kingship of the Ottonian and Salian rulers of Germany and of the rulers of Anglo-Saxon England had become, in effect, what he called "liturgical." That is to say, it had come to be centered not, as usually in the Carolingian era, on God the Father but on Christ, the God-man whom they imitated and represented.[79] In the eleventh century, Peter Damiani stressed the fact that in the person of the king, Christ is to be recognized as truly reigning. In the same century, the historian Wipo depicted the archbishop of Mainz as having said to the German king Conrad II in 1031: "You are the vicar of Christ. No one but his imitator is a true ruler."[80] And in the previous century, in the celebrated miniature produced in the Abbey of Reichenau and incorporated in the Gospel Book of Aachen, the emperor is depicted as elevated to heaven, enthroned in glory, as not merely the vicar of Christ, "but almost like the King of Glory himself." "It is," Kantorowicz adds, "as though the God-man had ceded his celestial throne to the glory of the terrestrial emperor for the purpose of allowing the invisible *Christus* in heaven to become manifest in the *christus* [imperial anointed one] on earth."[81] In arguing thus he leans heavily on an intriguing set of writings that witness both to the clericalization of the royal office and to the degree to which it had slipped its theocentric moorings and been drawn into the orbit of Christocentric notions. The writings in question reflect no less in thought than in language the influence exerted by the contemporary coronation *ordines* and related liturgical texts. They give classic theoretical expression, accordingly, to the ideology of "liturgical kingship."

These writings, which date to around 1100, are drawn from the *Tractates* of an unknown Norman or Anglo-Norman cleric who, on the assumption that he might have been Gerard, bishop of Hereford and later archbishop of York, it was once customary to refer to as the Anonymous of York. The *Tractates,* more than thirty in number, not widely known in their own day, came down to us in a single codex.[82] The variety of topics that they address—and the tensions and quasi-contradictions evident among the various positions they adopt—have sometimes been taken to reflect multiple authorship. But the current scholarly consensus supports their attribution to a single, Norman author, whose identity remains unknown but who was probably writing at Rouen.[83]

Some of the *Tractates* are focused on contemporary disputes and issues of considerable specificity, and some are no more than sketches or fragments. But in a few of them, and most notably in his lengthy *De consecratione pontificum et regum et de regimine eorum in ecclesia sancta* (*Concerning the Consecration of Pontiffs and Kings and Their Rule in the Holy Church*), the author sets forth "the christocentric theory of kingship in its most concentrated, and most extreme form."[84] While it was once the norm to regard these *Tractates* as looking back to a world of ideas already disintegrating by the time of their composition, scholars are sometimes disposed now to viewing them as expressing not simply the theopolitical ideas of the tenth and early eleventh centuries but even the avant-garde ideas current in their own day.[85] And they certainly constitute a peak expression of the complex and slowly evolving movement of thought which—out of Germanic, Romano-Hellenistic, patristic, and, above all, Old Testament materials—had fashioned another Christianized but, this time, distinctly Western theory of sacral kingship and embedded it firmly in the unfolding saga of salvation history. Their somewhat esoteric nature and periodic lack of clarity notwithstanding, as a striking illustration of a remarkable theopolitical phenomenon and as a fitting conclusion to this discussion of early medieval Latin forms of sacral monarchy, the *Tractates* clearly warrant a measure of closer scrutiny.

There is something of a parallel between the general approach adapted by the Anonymous and what may loosely be labeled "the Ambrosiaster tradition." But he does in fact depart somewhat from that tradition, and his departure is an intriguing one. Whereas Ambrosiaster in the fourth century, Cathwulf toward the end of the eighth, Hugh of Fleury in the early twelfth century, and others, indeed, later on all portrayed the king as the image of God and the bishop as (no more than) the image of Christ,[86] the image of kingship advanced by the Anonymous was quite explicitly Christocentric. If that was so, it was because, like Eusebius before him, he had developed a Christology of a quite specific kind. In Eusebius's case, that Christology had been (helpfully) subordinationist;[87] in the case of the Anonymous it was at once more orthodox (in Nicene/Chalcedonian terms) and more convoluted. At the point of entry into his thinking, as elaborated in the *De consecratione,* stands the mysterious figure of Melchizedeck, king and priest, and king, he says, "of righteousness" (*rex justitiae*). For "to Christ was it said 'You are a priest for eternity ... according to the order of Melchizedeck'" (Psalms 110:11; Hebrews 7:17).[88] But for the Anonymous, if Jesus of Nazareth was indeed the true Mechizedeck, king and priest, he was king "by reason of his eternal divinity, not made, not created, nor inferior to or different from the Father, but equal to and one with him," creator and ruler of all things "through all eternity" (*in eternum et ultra*). He was priest, however, only in time—only, that is, "up to eternity" (*in eternum non ultra*), for he was such "by reason of his assumption of humanity, constituted in accordance with the order of Melchizedeck, created and, therefore, less than the Father."[89]

With this distinction of natures, the Anonymous correlated a further distinction that enabled him to speak of Jesus both as a "Christ by nature" in virtue of his divinity and as a "Christ by grace" in virtue of "the grace of unction and the consecrating benediction."⁹⁰ The "Christ by nature," uncreated eternal king, the Anonymous regards as equal to God the Father. In Jesus's functioning as creator of the universe and regenerator of fallen man, the Anonymous represented him, therefore, very much as indistinguishable from the Father. As such, he is not to be confused with the "Christ by grace" who, in assuming a created humanity and concealing thus his royalty, became a priest; less, therefore, than the Father and indeed subordinate to him.⁹¹

In the context of the history of political thought, and as, indeed, in the earlier case of Eusebius of Caesarea, the temptation is strong to push such Christological considerations to the margin of attention as remnants of hopelessly recondite theological esoterica. Any such temptation, however, is to be resisted. Upon such considerations, in fact, rests the whole structure of the Anonymous's political theology. For it is on the foundation of "the high Christology of the Eternal Christ," George Williams has correctly noted, that the Anonymous proceeds to ground the power of kings: "Thanks to his two Christologies the Anonymous's political theory, while seemingly *Christ*ocentric will tend to be *Theo*centric, because the Person of the Humbled [incarnate] Christ has been reduced in significance and may no longer be said to exercise a predominant influence over the conception and image of the God of the Universe. On his 'low' Christology of the Humbled Nazarene *sacerdos* [priest] who put off or rather conceded his royal nature the Anonymous bases clerical authority."⁹²

The way in which this political theology is worked out is complex enough to defy any attempt at summary encapsulation. What one can do, however, is by way of background to sketch in two fundamental lines of argument that (at risk, it may be, of a little distortion or oversimplification) can be said to control or dominate the Anonymous's entire pattern of thinking. And further than that, looking ahead to the great ideological struggles of the eleventh century between reforming popes and staunch defenders of the traditional religio-political role of kings, to dwell finally on a significant corollary attaching to the second of those two main lines of argument.

Serving as backdrop to both is an observable tendency and an outright conviction. The former, readily evident if one approaches what the Anonymous has to say keeping in mind the later canonistic distinction between ecclesiastical *power of order* and *power of jurisdiction*,⁹³ is a tendency to emphasize in relation to the priestly office the jurisdictional rather than the sacramental power.[94] The latter is his conviction that baptism is the fundamental sacrament, possessed of such overriding efficacy that it can be said, in a sense, to comprehend all the other sacraments, priestly ordination not excluded. For he who is baptized, putting on as he does the very sacerdotal nature of Jesus Christ, is transformed by that sacramental moment into a species of priest or cleric. And as such, he is not to be classified in derogatory fashion as a mere layman (*laicus*)—for the Anonymous, clearly, a term of ignominy that he equates with the *vulgar* (*popularis sive publicanus*).[95] That said, and the "priesthood of all believers" in effect affirmed, he focuses intently and at great length on another sacrament, that of unction or anointing with the holy oil, a sacrament of which kings and priests alike were the recipients.[96] In so doing he draws heavily on the theological notions embedded in the coronation liturgies inherited from the great formative era during which the Anglo-Saxon, Carolingian, and Ottonian-Salian *ordines* had been developed. Indeed, he goes so far as to incorporate in the latter part of the *De consecratione* the Edgar coronation *ordo* of 973.[97]

According to the first main line of argument, then, the Anonymous notes that under the New Testament dispensation, no less than that of the Old which prefigured it, king and priest alike are both "sanctified with holy oil and by chrism and divine blessing consecrated." Both, accordingly, imaging the Christ by nature, are themselves now christs (i.e., anointed ones) by grace; "one with God and his Christ, they are [themselves] Gods and Christs through the spirit of adoption." "[T]hrough them speak also Christ and the Holy Spirit, and in them he [Christ] finds his representatives and office; through them he sacrifices, reigns over and rules his people." So that "each is in the spirit Christ and God and in his office is the figure and image of Christ and God. The priest of [Christ] the Priest; the king of [Christ] the King. The priest, of Christ's lower and human office and nature, the king of his higher and divine office and nature. For Christ, who is God and man, is the true and highest King and Priest."[98] But Christ's divinity being "greater and higher than his humanity," so, too, is his royal power superior to his priestly power. Whence it follows that among men the king and the royal power are "greater and higher" than the priestly, modeled as they are on the superior power of Christ's divine nature. As a result, there is nothing at all unjust about the priestly dignity's being "instituted by the regal or subordinated to it, because in Christ the dignity of the priesthood was instituted by his regal power through which he was equal to the Father."[99]

Human kingship is thus related to the "Christ by nature" (i.e., the eternal, royal Christ), and, as a result, to God the Father, with the human priesthood being related, in contrast, to Jesus of Nazareth (i.e., the humbled, human, priestly, and distinctly subordinate "Christ by grace"). If from that fact is drawn the appropriate conclusion, then the essentially sacred character of kingship and its superiority in matters ecclesiastical are, concomitantly, enhanced. And they are enhanced still further by the second principal line of argument that the Anonymous pursues. According to that, the Christian king, by virtue of the sacrament of unction which makes of him a new person and transforms him into a "Christ by grace," now becomes not only an image of the royal God-Christ but also, in addition and in common with the anointed bishop or priest, an image of the sacerdotal Christ-man. As a result, the priesthood conferred already by baptism having thus been enhanced, he becomes now after the fashion of the biblical Melchizedeck, priest as well as king—as Williams puts it, a veritable "national Melchizedeck."[100] And as such, the Anonymous further asserts, he is possessed not only of the responsibility for guiding the church but also of the power to remit sins and to offer the bread and wine in sacrifice, as, indeed, he does as part of the solemnities of his coronation day.[101]

The Anonymous advances these last claims in the context of drawing on the words of the Edgar coronation *ordo*. That being so, it is conceivable that when he referred to the remission of sins he may have had in mind nothing more than the granting of the usual coronation amnesty. Similarly, in the case of the royal offering, he may have been envisaging nothing more than the English king's entering the sanctuary after the coronation (in this like the Byzantine and German emperors, for that matter) and presenting the elements of bread and wine to the clergy officiating at the Mass. And those elements, unlike ordinary lay recipients, he would himself receive under both kinds at the Communion. The texts, however, though not fully clear on this point, seem to suggest at least that something more was intended. In the case of the royal offering, it may be that the Anonymous was casting the king in the role of representative communicant receiving the Eucharist on behalf of the collective Christian people of God. And by the reference to his remission of sins, it may also be that the solemnly consecrated and "deified" king was being conceived in a fashion redolent of pagan sacral monarchs propitiating for the sins of his people, mediating between them and God, serving in fact—and by virtue of the transformative grace bestowed upon him—as in some sense their "savior."[102]

Bold claims, of course, to make in behalf of any Christian political leader, but of course they serve to underline the fact that the king was being conceived as something far more than a "political" leader in our modern constricted sense of that term. And they serve also to confirm the fact that the society over which the king ruled was conceived as something other and, indeed, more than a merely civil society. It was, instead, a species of united church-kingdom, a coupling of kingdom and priesthood "glued together," as it were, by the action of God.[103] Driving that point home, and in the teeth of Gelasian dualism, the Anonymous does not hesitate to equate "the Christian people" over which, by virtue of his sacred anointing, the king was divinely authorized to rule with "the holy church of God" itself (*mundum hic appellat sanctam ecclesiam, que in hoc mundo peregrinatur*). When centuries earlier Pope Gelasius had spoken of the two powers, sacerdotal and royal, that rule "this world" (*hoc mundum*),[104] what he had really meant, the Anonymous now insists, was in fact nothing other than the "holy church... which is on pilgrimage in this world." Accordingly, the kingdom over which the king is called to exercise the supreme power is to be identified with the church, "which is," we are then told, "the Kingdom of God" or "Kingdom of Christ" in which the royal and sacerdotal powers are no longer divided and in which the king (Melchizedek *redivivus*) reigns "together with Christ."[105]

When Williams comes to summarize this whole position he sees in it a sharp contrast with the original Gelasian claim that "Christ had expressly severed the regal and the priestly powers out of recognition of their abuse when united in any but the divine.... [Instead] the Anonymous asserts the divinity of kings by consecration, the fusion of two natures, divine and human, and hence the king's Christlike competence in both the temporal and spiritual realms. The Anonymous holds that the Celestial Christ so far approves of the rejoining of the royal and sacerdotal functions that the king, by virtue of the apotheosis [resulting from the royal anointing], may be said to co-rule with Him."[106] This being so, there should be little occasion for surprise in the Anonymous's further willingness to portray the coronation feast in Eusebian fashion as a kind of messianic banquet, to depict the king as mediator and shepherd-redeemer, to accord him the messianic prerogatives and to apply to him the messianic sayings set forth in Isaiah (22:22; 42:7). Nor should there be much to surprise in the fact that for him "the earthly kingdom under its *rex et sacerdos,* tends to replace the *ecclesia* as the instrument of salvation." Or, for that matter, in the sense he persistently conveys that the Kingdom of God is, at least in part, being "realized within history through the progressive achievement of the royal *christi.*"[107]

It seems fair to conclude that in all of this there are at least some echoes of Ambrosiaster and more than one harmonic of the Eusebian rendition of the Hellenistic philosophy of kingship, which was destined to endure for centuries at Byzantium. And yet it has to be conceded that the *Tractates* themselves contain little evidence to suggest any *direct* appropriation of such notions. The Anonymous bases himself, instead, on biblical precedent, on ideas drawn from the old collections of canon law (especially the decrees of the Toledan councils of Visigothic Spain),[108] and, most fundamentally, on what he believes the sacrament of royal unction to entail. His version of "royal messianism," it has rightly been said, "is demonstrably dependent on the Edgar *ordo* of 973."[109] The observation is a telling one, the more so if one calls to mind Marc Bloch's admonition about the drawback of depending too much on theorists and theologians if one truly aspires to penetrate the type of mentality that sustained the regal "idolatry" of the era.[110] If behind the arguments of the Anonymous did not stand the supportive framework provided by the firm structure of liturgical practice and symbolic gesture buttressed also by the royal and imperial iconography of the era,[111] it would be tempting to dismiss those arguments as wholly unrepresentative, as the product of abstract clerical speculation with no real grounding in the life of the times. But as becomes increasingly clear, those arguments were more representative of the thinking of the Anonymous's own era and of the two centuries preceding than it was usual in the past to concede. Clerical in origin and inspiration such notions may have been, but it would be unwarranted to conclude from that that even Saxon and Salian noblemen, however difficult and rambunctious they could often be, were necessarily prone to scoffing at them or brushing them to one side. If kings and emperors were anxious to proclaim and "stage" royal or imperial majesty, we should not overlook the desire of nobles, as the ruler's faithful men, to partake in the effulgence of the royal majesty. Proximity to the royal *christus* (*Königsnähe*) was something that they unquestionably valued.[112]

Our somewhat obsessive concern in the last three chapters, though interrupted by the intrusion of the mature Augustine's stern dissent, has been with the series of complex accommodations that the Christian intellectual leadership sought to make with the notions of sacral kingship they had inherited from their Greek, Roman, Celtic, and Germanic precursors. And if, taking a moment now to stand back a little from the rich complexity of the Western ideology of kingship on which we have been dwelling, we move to readmit the Byzantine experience into the orbit at least of our peripheral vision, the temptation to align the Anonymous with Eusebius becomes admittedly quite strong. And that should come as no surprise. However different their overall inspiration and the particular materials out of which they constructed their respective positions, the general thrust of their argumentation is not dissimilar. Recognition of that fact may serve to underline the extraordinary tenacity of the dominion that archaic notions of royal sacrality clearly exercised over the late antique and early medieval imagination. More specifically, it may serve to underline also the degree to which messianic notions and Christological concerns opened up a route whereby such pagan notions, linked originally after all with the cosmic religiosity and inspired by the cyclic rhythms of nature, were able to penetrate and inhabit a Christian consciousness that was fundamentally historical in its orientation. Beyond that, moreover, and insofar as the thrust of their argumentation leads both Eusebius and the Anonymous to assign to kings and emperors a central role in the unfolding of the drama of salvation history, and to see the kingdoms and empires of this world as standing in close relation to the Kingdom of God, it also leads them both (and in this in common with Orosius) to adopt a stance diametrically opposed to the controlling position that the mature Augustine had attained to in close accord with the teaching of the New Testament itself.

We must now acknowledge, however, that the ideas of the Anonymous were destined for a much less successful career in the West than that enjoyed by the Eusebian political theology in the East. And we should properly attribute that fact less to any comparative lack of cogency or firm rootage in contemporary patterns of thought than to the presence in the West during the early medieval centuries of a range of factors differentiating the climate of opinion and conditions of political life there from those prevailing in the Byzantine world. Among those factors two must be singled out for specific attention. And having (implicitly) bracketed them in the chapters preceding, where the principal focus has been on the sacral dimension of kingship, it will be my purpose now in the two chapters ensuing to take them up in turn.

The first of these factors is the centrality of the role played by the nobility in Carolingian, Ottonian, and Salian government and the significance of "fidelity" and "consent" in their relationship with king and emperor. Similarly, the equally central (if subsequent) importance for western European political life and thought of the intricate web of personal and institutional relationships, which gradually extended to encompass the leading magnates and kings alike, and which the squeamishness of current historiography permits us to label as "feudal" only under the cover of a veritable embarrassment of quotation marks.[113]

The second factor in question is the crystallization during the early medieval centuries of a clerical "order" or caste, increasingly distinct in status from ordinary lay folk, and, within that caste, the rise to prominence of a unique locus of divinely conferred authority and power—namely, the papal institution at Rome. By the time the Anonymous sat down to write his *Tractates* both processes were well advanced. He himself, however, had clearly set his face against them. We have already noted that he vigorously resisted the attempt to deny to the ordinary faithful Christian, transformed as he was by the saving waters of baptism, a certain sacerdotal status and to consign him in derogatory fashion to the status of a *laicus*. And to that we should now add that the Anonymous pursued the logic of his position somewhat further in order not only to affirm the subordination of bishops and priests to the royal *christus* but also to deny any legitimacy to the mounting claims of the bishop of Rome to a position of jurisdictional superiority to the other bishops in the universal church. By virtue of their common unction there is an essential parity among all bishops. The lower clergy, regular (i.e., monastic) as well as secular (i.e., diocesan), are hierarchically subordinate to them. But "the hierarchy is properly completed *above* the archiepiscopal rank, not by a primate and the pope, but by the sacerdotal king who is no layman, but *rex et sacerdos* and *presul princeps et summus* ['king and priest' and 'foremost and highest prince']."[114]

Though it was to find some resonance in England later on, the Anonymous's position on this particular issue was destined to be nudged off the screen in the twelfth and thirteenth centuries. With the rebound of Europe in the late tenth and the eleventh centuries from the devastation, chaos, and confusion engendered in both political and ecclesiastical life by the last great wave of "barbarian" invasions (Scandinavian and Magyar) to break upon the West, and with the convergence on Rome in the mid-eleventh century of the twin reforming movements (royal and monastic) intent upon the restoration of church order, both of the factors mentioned above began to come very much to the fore. And they did so with consequences for the evolution of political thinking even more far-reaching than the previous rise to prominence of the characteristic notions of kingship upon which we have dwelt in this chapter.

Those consequences were to be constitutionalist in nature. If in some ways early medieval theocentric theories of kingship can be seen to point forward in the direction of early modern aspirations to divine-right absolutism,[115] the religio-political conditions of these early medieval centuries also bore within themselves seeds that were destined to germinate in the thirteenth, fourteenth, and fifteenth centuries into those institutional arrangements for constitutional restraint upon the abuse of executive power that we will be called on to address in subsequent volumes and which ultimately had so profound an effect upon the political life and thought of Europe. Our concern in the final two chapters of this volume, however, must necessarily be limited to probing the institutional and ideological soil in which those later developments were later to take such firm root.

8
The Early Medieval West (ii)
Fidelity, Consent, and the Emergence of "Feudal" Institutions

---

OUR FOCUS IN THE LAST chapter was very much on the king or emperor himself and on the way in which the nature of his position came to be conceived in the Germanic successor kingdoms of early medieval Europe. In that choice of focus we were very much at one with those writers of the period who began, after the start of the Carolingian era, to concern themselves more or less explicitly with matters political. Prominent among the writings involved were the *De institutione regia* (*On the Institution of the King*) by Jonas of Orléans (c. 780–842/3); the *Via regia* (*Royal Way*) by Smaragdus (fl. early ninth century); the *De regis persona* (*On the Person of the King*) and the *De ordine palatii* (*On the Government of the Palace*), both by Hincmar of Rheims (c. 805/6–87); and the *De rectoribus christianis* (*On Christian Rulers*) by Sedulius Scottus (fl. 840–60). Most of these works were in some degree responsive to the promptings of Gregory the Great's *Regula pastoralis* (*Pastoral Care*), a tract intended especially for the guidance and instruction of bishops but read as being applicable to rulers in general, and concerned above all to inculcate in them the virtue of personal humility. Their characteristic preoccupation, then, was not so much with matters pertaining to the community at large as with the moral deportment of the individual ruler.

As their titles suggest, these works belong to the *speculum principum*, or "mirror of princes," genre of political writing. That genre was devoted to the instruction or moral formation of rulers and, as such, drew characteristically on the royal example set by such paradigmatic Old Testament figures as David and Solomon. Thus Jonas of Orléans, for example, urged the king to read the book of Deuteronomy in order to learn "what a king ought to be and of what he must beware." "The justice of a king exalts his throne, and the government of peoples is secured by truth." "A king's injustice," on the other hand, "not only darkens the countenance of the present reign, but casts a shadow over sons and descendants whose tenure of the realm is threatened. For Solomon's sin the Lord took the kingdom of the house of Israel from the hands of his sons, and for King David's merit he left a lamp for his seed forever in Jerusalem."[1] Or again, as Sedulius Scottus insists, "What are the rulers of the Christian people unless ministers of the Almighty?" It is only proper that "the most upright and glorious princes rejoice more that they are appointed to be ministers and servants of the Most High than lords or kings of men." For that very reason, after all, "blessed David, an illustrious king and prophet, often called himself the servant of the Lord."[2]

And so on. But the intensity of the focus on the person of the king, his sacred legitimation, and his moral deportment should not be taken to suggest that these centuries knew no distinction whatsoever when it came to kingship between the individual royal personage and the impersonal and enduring office that he occupied. That distinction had been reflected clearly enough in the legislation of the seventh-century Visigothic kingdom, responsive as it was to the legal terminology inherited from Rome, though some of that clarity was, admittedly, to be lost later on when, as Janet Nelson has put it, "a whiff of the household clung to the Carolingian notion of 'ministry' (*ministerium*)."[3] Nor, again, should the focus on the royal person be taken to presuppose the total absence from the political thinking of these early medieval centuries of what Ernst Kantorowicz called "the transpersonal, public character of the *respublica*" or commonwealth.[4] In so doing, admittedly, he was speaking of the degree to which John of Salisbury in the twelfth century gave expression to the new ways of thinking about matters political associated with what historians have sometimes described as "the rebirth of the state"[5] that were coming to the fore in his own lifetime. Similar notions suggestive of the fact that the kingdom or empire was being conceived as a public entity subsisting independently of any given ruler may have come to be marginalized in the tenth century after the fragmentation of Carolingian power. But they had been evident enough in its heyday when "the empire of Charlemagne and his immediate successors disposed of the necessary central organs of government and local officials to ensure that minimum of security, administrative adjudication and legislation which we associate with the very concept of a state."[6]

It is possible that memories of Rome evoked after 800 by the revival in the West of the imperial title may have provided added sustenance for such transpersonal political notions. But the idea of "empire" or "emperorship" was not always anchored in memories of Rome or, for that matter, clearly distinguished from "kingship." It was sometimes evoked (as later on) in relation to Anglo-Saxon or French kings, or to the king of Léon in Spain either as a simple honorific or in explicit recognition of the hegemony they enjoyed over other subkingdoms or subject peoples. Thus the Venerable Bede and the Carolingian scholar Alcuin both acknowledged an imperial quality in the overlordship exercised by the Anglo-Saxon kings.[7] It should be noted, too, that neither Charlemagne himself nor his son Louis the Pious vibrated at all enthusiastically to Roman frequencies, and that neither used the title "Emperor of the Romans." When it came to the legitimacy of his own new imperial title, Charlemagne was by no means disposed to view his acclamation by the Roman people or his coronation by the bishop of Rome as in any way constitutive. Right from the start, of course, the popes may well have thought otherwise. But not until the late ninth century did the notion that the papal coronation was constitutive in the making of emperors come definitively to the fore. And not until the reign of the German emperor Otto III in the mid-tenth century, with its programmatic endorsement of a *renovatio imperii Romanorum* ("renewal of the Roman Empire"), did the imperial office become firmly (and, it turned out, permanently) attached to Rome and an indissoluble link forged between Roman emperorship and German kingship. Such renewed memories of Rome did, it seems, have the further effect of nurturing a transpersonal understanding of the realm as grounded in law and subsisting apart from the person of the ruler. And that understanding is reflected in the words that Wipo, his court chaplain, put into the mouth of the emperor Conrad II (1024–39). Speaking of his recently deceased predecessor Henry II (1002–24), Conrad proclaimed to the citizens of Pavia: "Even if the king is dead, the kingdom remains, just as the ship remains whose helmsman has fallen."[8]

A transpersonal dimension should also be recognized in the complexly evolving structures of a range of other "medieval solidarities," communities of one sort or another—villages, counties, towns, and, later, even the "community of the realm"—associations that constituted autonomous or quasi-autonomous entities possessing a life of their own and governed by their own bodies of customary law.[9] The ongoing significance of such "solidarities" and of the role they played during the early medieval centuries in preserving the frail tissue of public order is not, then, to be gainsaid. But neither can we overlook the fact that within and beyond them ties of a different sort were making their presence felt. One has, indeed, to acknowledge also the central importance for the cohesion of society during these troubled centuries of the intricate network of *bilateral* ties of fidelity and obligation among men, ties that were essentially personal in nature. The existence of such ties, their evolution across time, and their quasi or explicitly contractual nature were destined in the long haul to exert a profoundly shaping force on late medieval and early modern constitutional thinking in general and on the crystallization of notions of representation and consent in particular. They warrant, therefore, and at this point, a measure of closer attention.

Fidelity and Consent

In a celebrated but now unduly neglected attempt to pattern out and reduce to order the teeming complexities of medieval political thinking and to identify the great engine driving the changes that had come by the fifteenth century to transform it, the Cambridge historian Walter Ullmann developed and elaborated in the mid-twentieth century a lucid but highly schematic approach to the subject.[10] Originally trained himself as a lawyer rather than an historian, preoccupied with what gave legitimating force to law, and thinking almost exclusively in terms rather of the source than of the end or purpose of lawmaking and political authority,[11] he intuited the drama of medieval political thinking as residing in its domination by two competing "conceptions of government and law," conceptions that, being "diametrically opposed" to one another, were mutually exclusive. These he referred to as the "ascending" and "descending" themes or theses. According to the former of these, which he designated also as the "populist" conception and viewed as nothing other than the "natural" way of thinking about matters political, "governmental authority and law-making competence" are attributed to the people or community and ascend to the top of the political structure "from the broad base in the shape of a pyramid." With this theme, at least in the fullness of its development, Ullmann associated consent, representation, and the notion of the individual as *citizen,* as participant in public government occupying within society a status characterized by autonomy and independence, endowed, therefore, with a battery of "inalienable rights" proof even against the encroachment of the powers that be. According to the latter, "descending," thesis, on the other hand, all power is located ultimately in God, who, by means of an earthly vicegerent himself endowed with a plenitude of power, distributes it downward via a hierarchy of officials "again in the shape of a pyramid." In the context of this theme, "as a result of the overpowering influence of Christianity" in early medieval Europe, faith is substituted for consent, the "extra-human" for the "earth-bound and human," the notion of office delivered from above replaces that of representation, and instead of the autonomous rights-bearing individual, we encounter the faithful Christian, recipient of the favors of an absolutist government, *subject* rather than citizen.

The attempt Ullmann made to carve out this commanding approach was a noble one. At its service he placed a formidable wealth of learning garnered from a lifetime's acquaintance with the pertinent texts, especially those of a legal nature. But less than fifty years later, it seems now generally to be conceded that the pertinent historical data, in all their rich complexity, cannot be made in convincing fashion to respond to the rigidities of the schema he proposed—or at least cannot be made to do so without recourse to an unacceptable measure of textual coercion. One of the rocks on which his attempt foundered (it is the rock most pertinent to our concern now with fidelity and consent) was the way in which he deployed the distinction between the *natural* and *supernatural*. That distinction, which presupposes a commitment to the exclusivity of the biblical understanding of the divine, made its appearance only in the fourth century CE.[12] And yet Ullmann uses it to help characterize the political thinking of Aristotle, even though the latter's understanding of the "natural" was one that can itself be said to have comprehended in some degree that which under the influence of the Christian tradition we ourselves have become accustomed to classifying as "the supernatural." Similarly, and more directly pertinent to the point at hand, even though the Germanic peoples of the pre-Christian era knew no sharp distinction between the natural and supernatural and intuited the world of nature itself as pulsating to the rhythm of the divine,[13] Ullmann did not hesitate to characterize the role of the ancient Germanic folk assembly in the choice and making of kings as an expression of the ascending "natural" theme—and that in contrast to the later Carolingian notion of kingship "by the grace of God," which he depicts as lying at the very heart of the supernaturally grounded, Christian descending thesis. So that, over against the "theocratic" kingship of the Carolingian era and its aftermath (divine appointees ruling by "the gift of God," by virtue of "divine intervention" and "the transmission of divine grace") he sets those earlier Germanic rulers whom he characterizes as the products of merely "natural-biological forces," their kingship resting only on foundations "of a physical and purely human kind"—heredity, that is, and consent.[14]

The fact that he should be betrayed into so doing reflects the shaping impact of a further (if implicit) assumption that the conceptual relation between forms of kingship rooted in the divine and those shaped by heredity, rooted in election, and limited in some way by popular will had necessarily to be one of opposition or contradiction.[15] So that because medieval Scandinavian kings and their ancient Germanic forebears were often "elected," or because there were limitations of one sort or another on their power, it followed that they were not to be regarded as truly sacral kings. But that assumption and that implication we have already seen to be questionable.[16] The pagan Germanic and Scandinavian kingship, in effect, was by no means as unqualifiedly "populist" (in Ullmann's sense of that word) as he would have us believe. And that being so, it is hard not to entertain severe misgivings about the allegedly "theocratic" purity of the medieval Christian monarchy that he contrasts with it as a manifestation of the descending rather than the ascending theme.

Ullmann, of course, was far from being alone in suggesting that the Christian emphasis on the derivation of the king's power from God, symbolized so effectively in the royal anointing and the adoption of the title *rex dei gratia,* involved also the suggestion of a certain independence in the king's relationship with his people. Fritz Kern said as much earlier and in a statement of classic balance.[17] But Kern was also at pains to emphasize the interdependence during the greater part of the Middle Ages of the divine and popular sanctions that the monarchy enjoyed, insisting that the royal dependence on God "was broadly enough conceived to allow the monarch to be dependent also upon the will of the community in so far as monarchy itself was based upon a popular as well as a divine mandate."[18] If this formulation sits ill with the categorical exclusiveness of the ascending-descending schema, it accords better with the complexities of the actual medieval situation. Certainly, to return now to a focus on the Carolingian era, it carries greater conviction than does Ullmann's characteristic dismissal of the title that Louis the Stammerer adopted in 877—"King by the grace of God and through election by the people"—as a futile attempt "to reconcile... two irreconcilables."[19]

The fact is, and as the Carlyles rightly insisted long ago, referring especially to the documentation concerning the succession of Charles the Bald in 869 to the kingship of the East Franks, that "the right of the legitimate heir, the appointment of God, and the election of the nation," all of these were involved in "the conception of a legitimate claim to the [Carolingian] throne."[20] Thus in 817 Lothair, the eldest son of Louis the Pious, was chosen by vote "of the whole people" to be his colleague and successor in the imperial office. Similarly, in 876, when Charles the Bald was elected as ruler of the Italian kingdom.[21] Or again in 877, and as we have seen, when Louis the Stammerer came to the throne and was consecrated by Hincmar, bishop of Rheims. And just as complementarity rather than opposition marked the relation between clerical consecration and noble choice in the legitimation of kings, so too does a similar relation hold in the day-to-day work of royal and imperial government between the theocratic stamp placed upon Carolingian, Ottonian, and Salian kingship and its dependence in practice upon the collaboration, fidelity, and consent of the great magnates of the realm, both clerical and lay.[22]

That need for noble collaboration and a degree of consensus was no Carolingian novelty. It dated back to an immemorial Merovingian past. If it finds less of a reflection in the written record than does the theocratic notion of rulership, that record reveals, nonetheless, one or two straws in the wind signaling the importance of their contribution to the success of royal government, notably when it came to the matter of legislation. In continental Europe, it is true, the tenth and eleventh centuries saw little in the way of new lawmaking. But the Carolingian era had been replete with it, as was Anglo-Saxon England, whose kings, from Ine (689–726) to

Canute (c. 995–1035), were notable lawgivers. Here the documentary record makes it clear that the king, in order to promulgate new laws, had first to seek a measure of popular concurrence at the great assemblies of king, noblemen, and leading clerics that the Carolingian rulers convened with such regularity for the discharge of the public business of the realm.[23] Thus, and for example, in his *De ordine palatii* (*On the Government of the Palace*), Hincmar of Rheims states that laws are indeed made by the king but promulgated with "the general consent of his faithful subjects," and in the Edict of Pitres of Charles the Bald (864), law is actually defined as being made "by the consent of the people and the constitution of the king."[24]

At the assembly which promulgated that edict, the king was at pains to express his gratitude to the noblemen in attendance for their *fidelitas*, and the documentary record in general leaves little room for doubt about the central importance of fidelity in the relationship of the aristocracy with their ruler. Following Merovingian precedent, Charlemagne more than once exacted from all the free men in his realm an oath of fidelity. In 802 he added to that oath the words "[faithful] as a man ought in right [*per drictum*] be faithful to his lord," signaling thereby that faithfulness was "deeply rooted in contemporaries' values."[25] Certainly it lay at the very heart of the mutuality and collaborative nature of the relationship between king and aristocracy in the business of governing. That was so much the case, indeed, that additional, as it were targeted, oaths of fidelity were sometimes exacted of particular groups of key *fideles*.[26] Thus Louis the German extended into East Frankia the West Frankish tradition of holding regular assemblies of the notables of the land, as well as the traditional practice of demanding from all freemen an oath of fidelity. Beyond that, moreover, he demanded of his bodyguard and of an array of royal officials a further oath of "vassalage" whereby they became his "men." Of his greater magnates—bishops, abbots, and the most important of benefice holders—he demanded assent to the creation of "a more intense personal bond," sealed by "the ritual of 'joining hands' and the solemn swearing of an oath of fidelity while placing their hands on a holy object," recognizing him thereby as their lord. If by so doing such magnates committed themselves to serving the king in fidelity and giving him the benefit of their aid and counsel, he in turn pledged never, in the absence of just cause, to mistreat or dishonor them.[27]

Vassalage doubtless imposed specific additional obligations on those who chose to enter into that specific relationship with the king. But the more common relationship pivoting simply on the commitment to fidelity entailed its own more global pattern of obligation, and under the troubled conditions of the ninth century, that pattern tended to become less one-sided, more mutual, and even quasi-contractual in nature. It came to make demands not only on the king's faithful men but also on the king himself. It imposed limitations on him in the exercise of his royal power, thereby opening up the possibility of lawful resistance to him if he were deemed to be abusing that power. All of which, of course, summons up the resilient shade of the institutional pattern that by long tradition we have been accustomed to calling "feudal"—though "feudo-vassalism" or "vassalic-feudal system" have been canvassed without success as more exact alternatives.[28] Much scholarly ink has been spilt over the question of whether or not it is legitimate to apply such terminology to the Carolingian practice of granting tenures of land to vassals in order to enable them to maintain themselves and discharge the services (usually military in nature) that went with their status. Much of that ink appears now to have been spilt in vain, especially so in light of the new wave of agnosticism that has broken of recent years over the very notion of "feudalism" itself, calling harshly into question the viability, historically speaking, of that very term. It is not a question that we need to enter into immediately. What is called for first is some commentary on the nature of the institutions usually designated as "feudal," the pattern of ideas affiliated with them, and their eventual and formative impact on western European constitutional and political thinking. The fullness of that impact was to be felt only centuries later, and in a period lying beyond the boundaries of the present volume. But if the legal codification of "feudal" practices and ideas was not to take place until the late twelfth and early thirteenth centuries, the formation of the institutions themselves and the crystallization of the pattern of ideas that went with them took place during the period running from the eighth to the eleventh centuries. It is appropriate, then, to address them here, even if it means transgressing at times the chronological limits set for this volume.

Feudal Institutions: Their Emergence and Political Significance

Unlike the divine-right monarchs of the sixteenth and seventeenth centuries, the sacred kings of the early medieval period were unable even to aspire to rulership of an absolutist stamp. If that was so, it was less because of any theoretical restrictions on their authority (though such existed) than because of the lack of adequate systems of communication and administration and because, within their realms, they were confronted in their dukes, counts, and lesser nobility by rival possessors of real and extensive governmental powers whose fidelity, as we have seen, they labored assiduously to ensure, and upon whose loyalty, collaboration, and consent they were obliged, willy-nilly, to depend. Such restrictions on the uninhibited exercise of royal power were the deliverance of an age-old Germanic and Christian past. But without the last wave of attacks and invasions from without—Viking, Magyar, Saracen—and the concomitant disintegration of the Carolingian empire, such limitations would scarcely have come to be as formidable as they became in the late ninth and tenth centuries. And without the emergence of the institutional forms we have become accustomed to labeling as "feudal," it is hard to imagine such inherited limitations as having left as deep and permanent an imprint on Western legal thinking and political institutions as they in fact did. What the disintegration of the empire meant is clear enough: in matters economic, a further retreat into local self-sufficiency and a concomitant acceleration in the shrinkage of anything approximating a money economy; in matters political, an increasing inability on the part of the central royal or imperial government to have its authority recognized in practice throughout its realms and to extend the benefit of its protection to all of its subjects; in matters social, the growth of public disorder, the periodic loss in one region or another of any sense of security and the increasing degree to which the mass of small men came to be at the mercy of the more powerful. What the emergence of feudal institutions meant, however, is a good deal less clear, primarily because of the exceedingly problematic status of the term "feudalism" itself.

The particular word is of post-medieval provenance and, in this, like that other problematic word "humanism," achieved general currency only in the nineteenth century. But persistent debate and controversy about the set of phenomena it purported to denote long predated its moment in the sun, with roots reading back into the thirteenth century and a period of flowering among lawyers and humanists alike in the sixteenth. In 1792 the legal commentator Michael Bellius still felt himself obliged to concede that "the historical origin of the fief, to what period and what nation it should be attributed, is somewhat obscure," a concession evoking from

Donald Kelley, who cites him, the wry but telling comment that "over five centuries of discussion by lawyers had not—and over four centuries of discussion by historians have not—radically altered this conclusion."[29]

The legacy of protracted disagreement about the origins and nature of feudalism did not, however, preclude in the nineteenth and twentieth centuries an enthusiastic proliferation of complementary or conflicting usages. Of these, the least helpful though most enduringly popular has been the employment of the adjective "feudal" as a broad-gauged term of derogation, ready at hand for condescending application to any sociopolitical system one happens to judge reactionary. More defensible, perhaps, at least in terms of its own presuppositional framework, is the Marxist/universalist usage denoting the type of society that is built upon "precapitalist" modes of production and exchange. Or again, the appropriation of the term by sociologists and comparative historians to denote, in comparably ecumenic fashion, a supposed phase in the development not only of European society but of a broad array of societies elsewhere: Byzantine, Islamic, Chinese, Japanese, and so on. While this last usage has not been without its appeal to some historians concerned primarily with medieval Europe (Marc Bloch and Robert Boutrouche, for example),[30] others among them, conscious of the definitional strain involved when a single term is stretched to accommodate a shifting variety of institutional arrangements in an array of vastly different cultures, have either avoided the comparative dimension or pushed it, at least, to the margins of their concern.[31] These latter historians have preferred to confine the term "feudalism" to a set of institutional phenomena appearing in their totality in western Europe alone. Even then they have differed about the precise range of phenomena to be encompassed by the term. Some have stretched it to cover the organization of society at large, including therefore its economic dimension.[32] Others have confined it to the legal dimension. Still others, staking out middle ground, while still excluding matters economic, have viewed the term as appropriately extending beyond legal relationships to embrace also the military and political spheres.

This last being the approach to the matter most congruent with the history of political thought, it is the approach I propose to adopt here. "Feudalism," then, I will use to denote a set of political institutions, legal relationships, and military arrangements that emerged between the ninth and thirteenth centuries in western and central Europe, as well as in England and in the Latin principalities established in those parts of the Middle East that fell under western European control. Within this large area there was, of course, a considerable degree of local institutional variation. But if we accept the pertinent definitional profile finally arrived at by the American medievalist J. R. Strayer,[33] the characteristics fundamental to feudalism throughout that broad region can be summed up under three headings. First, "the fragmentation of political power," with the county as "the largest effective political unit" in a good deal of western Europe and itself, even then, riddled with independent jurisdictions belonging to other and lesser lords that eluded the court's control. Second, "public power in private hands," the fragmented political power being itself regarded as a property right, an essentially private possession susceptible of being bought, sold, inherited, mortgaged, divided, and so on. Third, a state of affairs in which, despite the continued and perhaps predominant use of less specialized folk armies of infantry, "a key element in the armed forces [as a whole]—heavy-armed cavalry—is secured through individual and private agreements," through private contracts between the lord and his knights, even if the lord in question happened also to be the king.

If we accept and go on to work with this definitional profile, then, clearly we are using "feudalism" to denote not a set of broader social and economic arrangements but, rather, "a method of government, and a way of securing the [armed] forces necessary to preserve the method of government." Thus defined, too, it refers to a set of political, proprietary, and military arrangements in which only the aristocratic minority—in classic medieval parlance, "those who fought"—directly participated. This is not to suggest that the military aristocracy existed in a vacuum or to deny that that aristocracy, in this like the clergy ("those who prayed"), depended on the economic efforts of others ("those who worked") to sustain its own expensive and (in economic terms) unproductive activities. But the agrarian system of great estates farmed by a dependent peasantry long predated the rise of feudal institutions, at least as we have been defining them here. Similarly, feudal institutions survived under the changed conditions of an expanding money economy.[34] Thus the relation between the seignorial or manorial economy and feudalism was one of congruence rather than necessity. To choose, as we have, to define feudalism as a set of political and military arrangements is not to deny that congruence; it is simply to insist that what was novel and distinctive about the European society of the ninth to twelfth centuries was not its economic system but its particular mode of governance.

That said, not even historians whose sympathies align them with this, comparatively precise, definitional tactic find themselves altogether immune to moments of nervousness about the tightness of its "fit" with the varied local specificities evident in so vast a region. And that is especially so given the evident degree to which those specificities were subject to change across an almost half-millennial stretch of time. Hence the extent to which the argumentative channel has come to be narrowed by a veritable siltation of cautious qualification. Of the qualifications in question I would note three. The first is spacial in nature, with wide institutional variation being seen to exist across Europe at large, and with the characteristics identified with feudalism being seen, accordingly, to be limited in their fullness at least to the lands of the north, the region between the Loire and the Rhine that had constituted the heartland of the Carolingian realm. The second is temporal in nature, conceding the importance of change across the centuries characterized by the dominance of feudal institutions and distinguishing, accordingly, between a "first" and a "second" feudalism, or at least between earlier and later stages in its development,[35] with the latter part of the twelfth century witnessing an acceleration of change. The third, while also reflecting change across time, emphasizes the need to take into account differences "in social standing and in function during the early medieval period." Feudalism is seen to exist, accordingly, "on two levels, the level of the armed retainers who became feudal knights" but who, until the eleventh or twelfth centuries, wielded no political power, and the more aristocratic level of "the royal officials (counts and their deputies, and *vassi dominici*) who became rulers of feudal principalities, counties, and castellanies."[36]

Specificity of definition, ongoing refinement of description, and cumulative complexification of the overall picture being painted have not proved, however, sufficient to blunt the skepticism of those medievalists who, of recent years, have launched a frontal assault on the continued deployment of the very notion of feudalism itself. It is nothing other, they say, than a "tyrannous construct," one that (whatever its overweening pretensions) simply cannot convincingly aspire to the status of an empirically based generalization, and one that, standing between us and the infinitely varied facts on the ground, cannot but distort our perception of the complex realities of medieval life. As a result, or so they argue, we would be far better off if we simply decided to do without it.[37]

The case these critics make is in many ways a powerful and at times, even, a compelling one. But it is fueled, it seems, by a species of radical historiographic nominalism that leads them to call into question not only the notion of feudalism as a purported empirical generalization but, further than that and far less convincingly, the more readily defensible evocation of the feudal concept as a species of Weberian "ideal type" or model, one constructed in theoretical fashion "with a rational consistency which is rarely found in reality."[38] Possessed, it may be, of a greater unity and cohesiveness "than has ever been the case in the flux of [its] actual development,"[39] and standing self-confessedly at a certain distance from the teeming institutional variety of history and the stupefying scramble of events, the ideal-typical approach to feudalism was deployed classically by Max Weber himself and, among historians, by Otto Hintze.[40] Adopted in what follows here, it has the advantage of highlighting or laying bare the inner coherence and logical implications of feudal institutions, at least in the legally rationalized form they had come to attain by the thirteenth century.

Of course, the ultimate historical roots of that whole institutional complex lie much further back in the past, in the centuries predating the rise of the Carolingian empire. During those centuries, with the disruption or decline of the tribal bond among the invading peoples and the decay among their Roman (or Romanized) subjects of loyalty to anything as abstract as the state, there was a growth in the practice by which lesser men, some of them warriors, attached themselves by bonds of personal loyalty to the most powerful men in their local communities. This practice, with precedents in both the Roman and German past, was the source of the first and most basic component of the feudal complex, that of the personal dependence of the warrior or vassal upon his lord. In the Merovingian Gaul of the sixth and seventh centuries, the vassals in question—strong-arm men who fought on their lord's behalf in return for protection, maintenance, and a share of the spoils—were by no means aristocratic figures. In the eighth and ninth centuries, however, vassalage appears to have risen steadily in status, and that process was accelerated as it came to be linked with the holding of a benefice (*beneficium*) or fief (*feodum*) as it came eventually to be called.

Vassalage in its inception had nothing to do with landholding. Vassals had usually been maintained in their lord's household. Such landless "household knights" were to be found throughout the Middle Ages; as late as the tenth century they may have outnumbered by far their fief-holding brethren. The institution of dependent land tenures, however, had grown up independently, though side by side with vassalage. In a time of troubles, the less powerful landholders had often found themselves unable to protect their property and had had to resort to the stratagem of surrendering the full ownership of the land to a powerful aristocrat, receiving it back from him as a protected tenant who, in return for stipulated rents and services, could continue to cultivate it and enjoy its fruits. At the same time, it had become common for the great landowners to lease out part of their lands to dependents who would render them rents and, perhaps also, stipulated services in return for protection and the right to enjoy the fruits of that land. In both cases the property title remained with the lord and the tenancy was for a restricted period of time. Such tenancies, however, seem usually to have been renewable, and a tendency for them to become de facto hereditary quickly set in.

At the outset there was no connection between such dependent tenancies and the institution of vassalage, nor was the service that the dependent tenants owed military service. Had not the nature of Frankish warfare begun gradually to change, it is conceivable that the tripartite linkage of vassalage to fief holding, and fief holding to military service might not have come about. Although most of their soldiers had fought—and were to continue to fight—on foot, the Franks, in common with their adversaries, had always been horsemen and made some use of cavalry in battle. With the passage of time, however, and during the period of Muslim invasions in the eighth century, they appear to have concluded that it was vital to stiffen the traditional bodies of free peasant foot soldiers with stronger contingents of cavalry. The availability of wealth and the pertinent organizational skills being the determining factors, it was probably not until the tenth and eleventh centuries that such strengthened cavalry contingents evolved into the type of "shock force" of knights that the Normans were to deploy so effectively.[41] Whatever the case, although in theory it might seem easy enough to turn vassals from foot soldiers into mounted knights, in practice it proved to be forbiddingly expensive. Mounts, remounts, attendants, complex equipment, and years of training—all of this cost a great deal. In an era of scarce money but abundant land, it is understandable that the solution arrived at from the mid-eighth century onward involved turning the vassal into a dependent tenant and conferring on him as a benefice a manorial estate cultivated by its own peasantry, which could provide him with the revenue necessary to maintain himself as an effective cavalryman in the service of his lord. Full title to the benefice remained in the hands of the lord. But there was an understandable tendency for son to succeed father and for the arrangement gradually to become a hereditary one.

The combination of vassalage with fief holding tended to enhance the social status of those warriors who had thus been elevated to the position of lords of the manor. As the lingering social stigma attaching to the status of vassalage itself came gradually to fade away, it came to be regarded as a form of personal dependency about which there was nothing ignoble. During the ninth century, therefore, as the Carolingian realms came under increasing attack and Carolingian rulers sensed a weakening of their control over the dukes, counts, and margraves who served in the localities as their great imperial officials, they moved to strengthen that control. They did so not only by the repeated insistence on oaths of fidelity in general but also by the further establishment of a more specific and personal bond, that of lord and vassal. As a result, dukes and counts came also to be royal vassals. But whatever gains accrued to the king or emperor from that transformed status were offset by a comparable transformation of the way in which the public offices of those dukes and counts came gradually to be apprehended. What occurred was something of a blurring of the crucial distinction that the Romans had made (and that we ourselves make) between the holding of office and the ownership of property, a mingling that came later to be reflected in the medieval use of a single word, "dominium," to denote both proprietary right and governmental authority.[42]

As a result, kings themselves began to slip into the habit of speaking about granting a benefice or fief to a vassal when what they were actually doing was bestowing a countship (an office akin to that of the modern military governor) on an appointed public official. Office (a focus of public duty) was gradually coming to be thought of as property (a source of private income or benefit) and, like property, susceptible of being bought, sold, mortgaged, inherited. When Charles the Bald, king of West Frankia, was about to set off in 877 on an expedition into Italy, he issued a decree (the Capitulary of Quiercy), which, though it involved no startling novelty and established no permanent legal norm, was at least a straw in the wind signaling the degree to which expectations of heritability were already threatening to become attached to public office.[43] Over the long haul, certainly, office holding was destined to be assimilated to vassalage and the office to the fief. The outcome was the dispersion of royal governmental authority among the dukes, counts, and margraves who now came to rule, in everything except theory, as independent magnates, dominating their districts from fortified strongholds, providing military protection for the local inhabitants, administering justice, collecting taxes, and pocketing the proceeds thereof. In order to do so, however, they themselves had to be able to count on the loyalty and military prowess of their own personal vassals. As more and more of those vassals became fief-holders and important figures in their own smaller and more readily defensible localities, it became concomitantly harder for great public officials to retain their monopoly over the governmental powers they had made their own. The outcome, more advanced in some regions than in others, was a further fragmentation of that power and the dispersal of part of it into the hands of a whole range of lesser members of what was now emerging as a fairly cohesive feudal military aristocracy.

By the twelfth century, then, one can discern shadowy anticipations of the entity rendered so familiar by our textbooks—namely, the feudal hierarchy, the continuous ladder of lord-vassal relationships reaching from the myriad of lowly, fief-holding knights at the base, via their immediate lords and the lords of those lords, all the way up to the king who, as feudal suzerain or supreme lord of lords, resided in lonely eminence at the apex of the pyramid of power so constituted. The realities, of course, were a good deal more complex than such a symmetrical model would seem to suggest. It was not until the twelfth century, with the deployment of the historical fiction that all political power had been delegated in hierarchical fashion from king to superior lord and thence to lower lord, that the type of legal systematization presupposed by the notion of the feudal pyramid became possible. Even then, not all vassals were fief-holders; not all important landowners everywhere were necessarily caught up in the feudal nexus. A single knight could often accumulate several fiefs from different sources, thus becoming the vassal of more than one lord, and so on. And long before the great lords and academic lawyers began to pursue the process of systematizing feudal institutions, administrative, fiscal, and judicial powers that had once been public and that we today would classify as governmental had passed into a multitude of private hands and were being wielded in a myriad of jurisdictions, large and small.

The political consequences of this state of affairs are obvious enough. While the emergence of feudal institutions may itself have sponsored a degree of anarchy, it also represented a creative response to the daunting challenge of how to get the basic political tasks performed during a period of invasion, confusion, and public disorder. That it should have had the long-range constitutional consequences it did is, however, a good deal less obvious. Those consequences presupposed in no small degree the possession by European feudalism of two particular characteristics that comparative historical studies suggest are more singular than we may be tempted to assume. The first is the fundamentally contractual nature of the feudal relationship; the second, the personal involvement of the king himself in the feudal nexus.

In the early days, when most vassals lived as household knights or retainers, the obligations they incurred when they swore fealty and did homage to their lords were onerous and ill defined. They were to serve their lords at all times and in whatever manner was congruent with their own status as free men. The arrangement, nonetheless, was a reciprocal one. The lord was committed, in turn, to protect and maintain his vassals. But as the grant of a fief became the customary way to discharge that obligation of maintenance, and once it became accordingly more common for men of high social status to undertake the bonds of vassalage, there was a corresponding inclination on their part to try to define with greater precision the nature and extent of the services demanded of them, and to do so restrictively.

As systematization progressed in the course of the twelfth century, the feudal contract came generally to be held to involve, on the lord's part, the maintenance and protection of his vassal and, on the vassal's part, the giving of aid and counsel to his lord. By counsel was meant both advising the lord on governmental matters and being present at or participating in the hearing and settling of judicial cases that came before his court. By aid was meant, above all, personal military service, eventually by convention not to exceed forty days, and involving also, in the case of powerful vassals, the contribution of a contingent of knights for a similar period of service in the lord's army. By aid was also meant, however, the financial assistance the vassal was obliged to extend to his lord on those occasions when the latter's financial burden was recognized by local or regional custom to be heavy—as, for example and classically, on the occasion of the marriage of the lord's eldest daughter. Especially when involved in war, a lord might wish to levy further "aids" (or taxes) beyond the customary ones, and powerful lords were indeed able to do so. Such further aids, however, were regarded as "gracious aids"—that is to say, they were aids that had to be asked for. In theory, they were to be granted only at the goodwill of the vassals; they were, in effect, contingent upon the freely given consent of those vassals.

In all of this the feudal contract was backed by legal sanctions. If the vassal failed to live up to his obligations, he was subject, after trial by his peers in the lord's court, to the forfeiture of his fief—as King John of England was famously reminded in 1202 when he was deprived of the great French fiefs he held of his overlord, King Philip II of France.[44] But if, on the other hand, the lord failed in his duties to the vassal, the latter had at law the formal right to break faith with the lord (*diffidatio*), thereby dissolving the feudal tie that bound them together.

That such legal sanctions could hardly be invoked in the absence of a willingness (and capacity) to resort to force of arms should not be allowed to obscure the significance of the fact that they existed at all. And that significance, of course, was enhanced immensely if the faithless lord in question happened also to be king. Without the latter's entanglement in the network of feudal relationships, without his casting in the role of paramount lord, legally bound by bilateral contractual relationships with his principal subjects, feudalism would not have attained to the enduring constitutional importance it eventually did. Because of that role as lord of lords, the king, regarded already by the Germanic peoples as in some sense subordinate to the customary law of the folk and bound to his sworn *fideles* by a hallowed sense of reciprocal obligation, came now to be burdened with the further weight of specific legal obligations and restrictions: the subordination to an increasingly codified feudal law, the rights and liberties guaranteed to his great vassals (including freedom from taxation without consent), and the undermining presence of a right of resistance to his commands should those commands be deemed illegitimate or excessive.

All of this is familiar enough from our standard textbook accounts. So familiar, indeed, that one is tempted to take it more or less for granted. But it would be a mistake to give in to that temptation, and here the comparative, world-historical study of "feudal" institutions can serve us well. And especially so if we call to mind the contrast afforded by Japan, among non-Western societies the one that is usually conceded to have come closest in its "feudal" phase to the western European model or ideal type we have been detailing. Despite all its remarkable similarities to the medieval West, Japan in fact lacked a truly bilateral contract between vassal (*gokenin*) and lord (*tono*). The vassal's submission to the lord appears to have been much more complete than was that of his European counterpart, and the nature of the lord's obligations toward his vassal was at the same time not at all clearly defined. Rather than being comprehensible in the precise legal terms that eventually came to be characteristics of western European feudalism, the whole relationship was essentially familial in nature.[45] It "rested strongly on unwritten custom publicized by ceremonial observance; it relied less on written or oral contract which specified individual duties or privileges."[46] Again, and in the second place, it is important to recognize the significance of the fact that in Japan the feudal hierarchy, which did indeed exist there, culminated not with the emperor but with the shogun, the generalissimo to whose office accrued for long centuries nearly all the political functions and concrete powers of the imperial government. Nevertheless, however powerless in day-to-day practice, an imperial court and a civil nobility survived side by side with the feudal warrior structure. The emperor remained in theory the sovereign of his people, and his legitimating function was eventually to find regular and formalized symbolic expression at the accession ceremonies at which each successive Tokugawa shogun assumed his executive rule.[47] The divine emperor, the lineal descendent after all of the sun goddess, Amaterasu-ōmikami, was too sacred a figure, it seems, either to be dispensed with altogether or to be domesticated within the network of feudal relationships, even though those relationships turn out not to have been contractual in nature. Monarchical and feudal relationships coexisted side by side, as they did in Europe. But in Japan the two failed to interpenetrate, and the sacral isolation of the emperor precluded the possibility of the type of constitutionalist legacy that European feudalism bequeathed to the West.[48]

We should not overlook the possibility that had the comparable duality between Merovingian "do-nothing" king and Carolingian mayor of the palace persisted, a similar sort of situation might have arisen in Frankia. By 751, after all, the king, who was still endowed with a sacral aura, wielded no practical, governmental power, whereas the mayor of the palace, about whose position there was nothing sacred, was the true possessor of political power. In contrast with Japan, however, the sacral status of the king was rooted in a pagan past that was by then half forgotten. That status had survived the triumph of Christianity but had been able to derive no ideological sustenance from the new religion. In the favorable judgment of the papacy, moreover, and by the introduction at his own coronation of the biblically validated sacrament of unction, Pippin the Short, in contrast to the Japanese shogun, had succeeded in finding the type of independent and countervailing religious sanction he clearly needed in order to displace his Merovingian rival and himself assume the office of king. But the kingship he assumed and to which his descendants succeeded was now, at least in comparison with the archaic past (and the oriental present), one somewhat diminished in sacral status. As a result, that status turned out to interpose no insuperable barrier to the kingship's being drawn into the secular network of feudal relationships and regarded as itself limited by the obligations arising from the feudal contract. Indeed, the type of ecclesiastical sanction that the Carolingian and other European monarchs came to enjoy, while it contrived, on the one hand, to confer on them a sacred status of new Christianized type had, on the other hand, implications of a constitutionalist type that comported very well with the limitations on executive power sponsored by feudalism. By the ninth century, Frankish ecclesiastics, while teaching that the authority of the king was of divine origin, did not hesitate to insist that, precisely because of that, it should not be exercised in an irresponsible fashion but only in accord with the norms of justice, divine or natural, of which they themselves were, of course, the rightful interpreters.[49]

Over the years historians have oscillated in their assessment of the constitutional implications of feudal institutions, with the current tendency, I would judge, inclining somewhat in the direction of an austere underestimation.[50] But the swirl of interpretative crosscurrents and the shifting tide of historiographic fashion should not be permitted to cloud our recognition of the simple fact that great feudal magnates proved capable of joining forces more than once during the medieval centuries to wrest from a recalcitrant king some sort of formal acknowledgment of his obligation to govern with their advice and in accordance with the laws of the land. The organized opposition of the English barons to the failed policies of King

John is only the most historic of those instances, the Magna Carta, the peace treaty with those barons to which John appended a reluctant signature in 1215, only the best-known outcome of such baronial efforts.[51]

Focusing for a moment on that particular document, it would be all too easy to read too much into it, and much that is not there has at one time or another been read into it—including, indeed, most of those constitutionally guaranteed liberties that only after centuries of subsequent travail did English people actually secure. As a result it has been customary to post stern warnings to the effect that the Charter was essentially a feudal document, one designed by feudal magnates to define and restrict the rights of the king in his capacity as feudal suzerain, one above all intended, therefore, to protect their own interests as members of a feudal aristocracy that constituted only a small and highly privileged minority of the total English populace. Apart from the celebrated promise of what we would call "due process" made in chapter 39 to every freeman in the land,[52] the Charter, it is insisted, had little to say about the rights of Englishmen at large. Some of its provisions moreover, were no more than temporary in nature; it did not establish a constitution, it made no provision for representative government, and the machinery of enforcement outlined in its last chapter depended on nothing less crude than a legalized resort to arms against a recalcitrant king.

Such caveats are entirely to the point. Despite the dramatic circumstances attending its signing and the more than symbolic importance attaching to it in England from the seventeenth century onward, there was in fact little in the Magna Carta that was entirely novel and much that reflected assumptions about the powers of kings that were no more than feudal commonplaces. But it is precisely because of that that the Charter (and its continental analogues) stands as an eloquent witness to the importance of feudal institutions in the development of Western constitutionalism. To the older Germanic belief that the king was responsible for the welfare of his people and in some sense accountable if he failed in that responsibility, and to the quasi-reciprocal nature of the bond between the king and his *fideles* so often reaffirmed by oath during the Carolingian era, feudalism eventually added the more specifically legal conviction that the king as feudal lord of lords was himself bound by the laws and customs of his kingdom. Admittedly it gave pride of place to the laws and customs that protected the property rights and interests of the great magnates; but, then, those same rights served to block the free exercise of the royal taxing powers in the absence of which no king could aspire to despotic authority. The Great Charter (ch. 12; cf. ch. 14) clearly affirmed, for example, the characteristic feudal insistence that the king could levy no "gracious" or extraordinary aids without the consent of his tenants-in-chief. Even though that stipulation was dropped from subsequent reissues of the Charter, English kings clearly felt they could not afford to ignore it in practice. In the thirteenth and fourteenth centuries it was, above all, their urgent need to acquire that consent that led not only the English kings but rulers all over Europe to turn to representative assemblies, whether on the national or provincial level. And it was those assemblies that ultimately provided the means whereby the theoretical limitations on executive power that most accepted might be vindicated without recourse to the armed violence that most apparently deplored.

The upwelling of baronial resolve in England from 1213 to 1216 could all too easily have dissolved into the dysfunctional pursuit of individual private grievances. That that did not happen, and that baronial grievances coalesced instead around what amounted to a commonly shared reform project, is another matter that should not be taken for granted. It is testimony, among other things, to the clarity of mind, good judgment, and leadership skills of Stephen Langton, papally appointed archbishop of Canterbury, who succeeded in uniting the barons and directing their opposition to the king's policies. His ability to do so reflected, doubtless, his own remarkable personal qualities. But it presupposed also the rise in importance right across the early medieval centuries of a distinct clerical order. And the circumstances that thrust him into the maelstrom of English politics during these particular years—the great clash between King John and Pope Innocent III leading at one point to John's excommunication and the imposition of a papal interdict on England—witness powerfully to the dramatic rise to international preeminence during the twelfth and thirteen centuries of the papal monarchy itself. On these clerically related developments, alluded to only in passing in the chapters preceding and fundamentally important as they will prove to be for the later unfolding of medieval political thinking, it is time now to focus more intently.

9. The Early Medieval West (iii)
The Clerical Order and the Rise of the Papal Monarchy

EVER SINCE THE HUMANISTS of the Renaissance era came up with the notion of a "Middle Age" separating from the perceived glories of classical antiquity their own era of revived interest in humane letters, the shadow of the present has weighed heavily on the centuries destined henceforth to be known as "medieval" and envisioned initially as a veritable night of barbarism and ignorance.[1] This tendency was perhaps never more obvious than when the focus of interest is the nature and evolution of the Latin or Western church's hierarchical structure presided over by its papal monarchical head.[2] Here the habit of transforming the foreign into the familiar is particularly well established. Given the fact that formal treatises devoted to ecclesiology (the branch of theology concerned with the nature and structure of the church) made their appearance only at the start of the fourteenth century, the danger of "retrojecting" into the earlier centuries ideas and developments that were, in fact, of later provenance is accordingly especially acute. In approaching those earlier centuries, then, we should be more than usually alert to the need to keep any preconceptions we may have about the role of the clergy and the position of the papacy on a particularly short leash.

The Crystallization of a Clerical Order

Should we be tempted simply to take as some sort of universal medieval "given" the existence of a distinct clerical order laying proud claim to a higher status than that occupied by mere lay folk, the witness of the Anglo-Norman Anonymous (c. 1100) dating to a later period of great ideological turbulence may serve as an appropriately chastening wake-up call. For the Anonymous, stressing the overriding importance of the sacrament of baptism, rejected even the application to lay folk of the derogatory term *laicus*.[3] In this, however, he was fighting something of a losing battle against the papally led ecclesiastical reformers of his day whose views, within a half century, were destined to receive classic formulations in the enormously influential works of the canon lawyer Gratian (d. c. 1160) and the early Scholastic theologian Hugh of St. Victor (d. 1141). Both assure us that among Christians there are basically *two* types of people, clergy and laity, the former superior in dignity and power to the latter. As Hugh puts it, "inasmuch as the spiritual life is of greater worth than the earthly and the spirit than the body, so does the spiritual power surpass in honor and dignity the earthly or secular power." Similarly, as Gratian insists, the members of the clerical order bear the tonsure as a "crown," a "sign of the kingdom that is expected in Christ," and "ruling themselves and others in virtues, are themselves kings and have thus a kingdom in God."[4]

Such standard formulations were far from being "the hasty product of a day" but were rather the outcome of several centuries of somewhat fluctuating development. By the third century it had become common to apply the words *clerus* and *clericus* to the cadre of people who, within the larger Christian community, had been entrusted with the task of leading and presiding over the community at worship.[5] From the sixth century onward, tonsure rather than ordination to a specific liturgical "order" (priest, deacon, subdeacon, and so on down through the "minor orders") came to be the means of ceremonial incorporation within that distinctive cadre, order (*ordo*), or group discharging a specific function. By the fourth century, moreover, Constantine had extended to the Christian clergy exemptions from taxes, the jurisdiction of imperial courts, and other public burdens. He had also conferred upon them certain privileges, including the right to receive salaries or stipends calibrated to their particular rank.[6] Such concessions and exemptions not only foreshadowed the array of privileges that were to become normative for clerics in the High Middle Ages[7] but served also to symbolize the distinction between minister and congregation as well as those differences of rank among the clerical cadre that pointed in the direction of the later hierarchical structure.

But the early Middle Ages still lacked the sharpness of distinction between the clerical and lay orders that, later on, the Gregorian reformers of the eleventh century were to work so hard to establish; it was their clear purpose to redraw "the boundaries between the secular and the sacred" and to claim "the latter as the exclusive domain of the clergy."[8] For, or so they claimed, the centuries immediately preceding had been scarred by an unacceptable intermingling of things secular and ecclesiastical.[9] The realities on the ground lent some credence to that claim. At the top end of the social scale, and as we have seen, kings had themselves come in marked degree to be clericalized. Deploying the standard image of the church as the bride of God, the Anglo-Saxon scholar Alcuin had slipped easily into referring to it also as the bride of Charlemagne, who, as king and priest, was also its "governor" (*gubernator ecclesiae*).[10] At the same time, and at the other end of the scale, local custom and customary arrangements governed all. Sacerdotal status notwithstanding, rural priests (and sometimes bishops, too) were all too often at the mercy of lay proprietors, subject accordingly to sudden deprivation and dismissal. Early in the ninth century, Agobard of Lyons, in his *De privilegio et jure sacerdotii,* deploring the menial status that was so often the lot of priests in the society of his day, insisted on the need for lay submission to clerical leadership. But later in the same century, in a capitulary of 857, Charles the Bald himself unwittingly conceded the abysmal conditions under which so many poor priests still had to function when he ordered that they were not to be "dishonored" or "flogged" or "thrown out of their church without the agreement of their bishop."[11]

In the early medieval centuries, however, even such tentative attempts to establish a clear and hierarchically ordered divide between clergy and laity were doomed to remain in the realm of aspiration. During those centuries it appears to have been less common to see society as divided simply between clerical and lay order than to see it divided among lay folk, monks, and bishops or, in another tripartite classification, between those who prayed, those who fought, and those who worked.[12] Only when the ecclesiastical reform movement began finally to take firm hold in the middle of the eleventh century did the starker bipartite division of society into clerical and lay orders begin to gain the upper hand. And it really succeeded in doing so only after the reform had reached Rome and popes of reforming stamp had committed themselves to vindicating the dignity of the clerical *ordo* and to liberating it from its previous subservience to the members of the lay *ordo* to which it was in fact superior. That great effort was to go hand in hand with the related attempt to vindicate also, but this time *within* the clerical *ordo* itself, a hierarchical structure analogous to that believed to prevail among the celestial choirs of angels and one that culminated on earth, at least, in the monarchical supremacy of the vicar of St. Peter, the pope or bishop of Rome.

The Rise of the Papal Monarchy (i): Ideological Formations

However important the doctrinal tradition that undergirded the papal monarchy, and however significant the foundations for that tradition laid down already in the earliest centuries of Christian history, we should begin by acknowledging two things. First, the underrecognized fact that the papacy as we know it today, an essentially monarchical power possessed of sovereign authority over the entire Roman Catholic Church worldwide, is very much the product of the second thousand years of Christian history. Indeed, in the degree to which, via effectively centralized governmental agencies, mechanisms, procedures, and instrumentalities of communication, it is actually able on a day-to-day basis to impose its sovereign will on the provincial churches of Roman Catholic Christendom, the papacy is the achievement, more precisely, of the past two hundred years at most, and may be said to have reached the peak of its prestige and the apex of its effective power within the universal church probably no earlier than the pontificate of Pius XII (1939–58).[13] We should not be too ready, then, to discern the firm profile of the modern papacy, itself the product of long centuries of complex maturation, in the shifting uncertainties of a much earlier era.

Second, we should also acknowledge the ease with which, when dealing with the medieval no less than the modern centuries of papal history, one can be betrayed into overemphasizing the centrality of ideological factors. Across all those centuries, the gap between sweeping assertions at Rome of a papal primacy in the universal church and the fustian realities of the effective power popes were actually able to wield, while doubtless fluctuating in extent, has often been enormous. That was to remain true, perhaps surprisingly, well into the modern era. In 1799 an obscure Camaldolese monk, Fra Mauro Cappellari by name, published a work of triumphalist pro-papal advocacy—*The Triumph of the Holy See and the Church over the Attacks of the Innovators*.[14] The work was a great rallying cry of resistance to what Cappellari viewed as the satanic forces unleashed by the French Revolution. In it he pictured "a papal church whose unchangeability enabled it to stand firm against the storm of changing times and turn back the attacks of all innovators." Like the great conservative propagandist Joseph de Maistre a few years later, he aligned "papal infallibility with papal sovereignty" and advanced the twin notions that "the pope is infallible 'independently of the Church' and that the Church is dependent only on the pope, not the pope on the Church."[15]

Doubtless it was an important straw in the wind and one prophetic of the train of events that was to pick up steam in the 1830s and culminate in the triumph of ultramontanism at the First Vatican Council in 1870. In terms, however, of the realities of papal power on the ground, Cappellari was writing at a very dark moment in the history of the papacy and in a decade that saw one pope die while imprisoned by Napoleon and his successor bullied into accepting a compromising concordat with France. It was a decade, also, that saw the papal office itself threatened with the same dire fate as actually overtook the office of Holy Roman Emperor in 1808 when Napoleon moved brusquely to terminate its existence.[16] That the papacy should instead have survived to attain by the mid-twentieth century an all-time peak in its spiritual preeminence and jurisdictional power within the Latin Catholic Church was the outcome less of any purely ideological development (though such development there certainly was) than of a series of historical contingencies that had the effect of clearing the way and making straight the path for the successful assertion in mid to late century of high-papalist claims.

Prominent among those contingencies was the enormously destructive impact of the Revolution upon the French national church, for centuries past the most prosperous, best-endowed, and most powerful church in Latin Catholic Christendom, as also its proudly independent intellectual and spiritual leader. Only a little less important (and part on the international scene of that same erasure of the traditional political and ecclesiastical regime that had enabled royal and imperial churches to maintain so marked a degree of independence from Rome) was the fragmentation of the German church and its reorganization into smaller dioceses in the wake of the 1815 Congress of Vienna. One outcome of that reorganization was the disappearance of the powerful elector archbishops of Cologne, Mainz, and Trier, who had functioned as proudly independent bulwarks against the extension into Germany of direct papal jurisdiction.[17] Similarly, the accommodation that Pius VII (1800–23) arrived at with Napoleon in 1801. Viewed at the time as a humiliating defeat for the papacy, it involved what has been dubbed "the liquidation of the French past,"[18] the coerced papal deposition of the entire French episcopate and its replacement by a new one functioning now within a restructured distribution of bishoprics. But it was to redound ultimately, nonetheless, to the benefit of the papal curia rather than to that of the emperor. For it was eventually recognized for what (ironically) it really was: nothing less than an historic and wholly unprecedented exercise of direct papal authority over the universal church. And as such it was to set the tone for the vigorous expansion of papal jurisdictional power worldwide that was to mark the middle and latter years of the century.[19]

That such factors were to be so prominently at work even as recently as the nineteenth century may serve to alert us to the fact that analogous factors were almost certainly and even more obviously in play during the late antique and early medieval centuries. There, as we shall see, the contrast between the developing papal claims to primatial preeminence and the chastening limits on the power that popes themselves were able to wield in practice was even more marked than it was destined to be under the ancien régime.[20] Though they did not always find a receptive audience in the loose association of regional churches that together constituted the universal church, such claims in one form or another came early to be voiced at Rome itself. Reflecting the belief that it owed its foundation to the great apostles Peter and Paul, such claims were advanced first on behalf of the church at Rome. Later on, after it had become common to stress the importance of the apostolic succession of bishops, they came to be advanced also on behalf of the bishop of Rome himself, viewed now as the successor of Peter. But the primacy of jurisdiction (or power of governing) that from the thirteenth century onward the popes were to succeed in vindicating within the orbit, at least, of Latin Christendom is not to be read back into the ill-defined primacy of honor that had come by the fifth century to be accorded to them among the several patriarchates[21] of Christian antiquity. Still less is it to be confused with the loose coordinating role that the Roman see had come to play as a "unifying center of communion" in a universal church conceived, above all, as a family of local episcopal churches, participants alike in a sacramentally based community of faith uniting believers with their bishops in given local churches and, beyond that, uniting all the local churches of the Christian world one with another. The characteristic institutional expression of those bonds of communion was that complex pattern of collaborative or collegial episcopal governance and synodal activity that stands out as so marked a feature of the earliest Christian centuries. Later on, as the Roman emperors transformed Christianity into a de facto and eventually de jure official state cult, thrusting upon it "the role of a universal administrative order,"[22] the old synodal mode of governance was to find its culmination at the level of the universal church in the succession of ecumenical councils stretching from Nicaea I (325) to Nicaea II (787). And while in the convocation and deliberations of those great councils the role of the emperor was routinely far more prominent and decisive than that of any of the popes of the day, it was during that era of conciliar governance, and especially so in the late fourth and fifth centuries, that the papacy began to press its claims to a position of primacy within the universal church that was not merely honorific but rather jurisdictional in nature.

In earlier centuries, the authentic tradition—that which had been believed "everywhere, always, and by everyone"[23]—had furnished believers with the rule of faith. But with the imperially sponsored introduction into the church of an overarching administrative order a momentous shift toward legalism began to occur. Conceptualizing this shift as involving a growing tension between *tradition,* or "the concept of a *continuum* of authentic knowledge," and *discretion,* or "the idea of spontaneous administrative authority," Karl Morrison has argued that from the fourth century onward "many thinkers" began to transfer the function of tradition in providing the bond uniting "true believers and [setting] them apart from the rest of the world" to "the bearers of tradition" instead. As a result of this shift, he says, "Roman thought became a 'Janus complex' of tradition and discretion."[24]

This becomes particularly evident in the development of primatial claims that got underway in the late fourth century. It did so via the prompting of a series of popes beginning with Damasus (366–84) and culminating with Leo I (the Great, 440–61), whose classic formulations constituted the high-water mark for papal claims in Christian antiquity. Having first borrowed as a mode of authoritative communication with communities beyond Rome the imperial practice of issuing decretals (letters handing down juristic decisions in particular cases), Pope Siricius (384–99) had justified their universally binding force by emphasizing (in Morrison's terms) discretion over tradition and by arguing that St. Peter lived on and ruled through his papal successors at Rome.[25] In that view of Rome as the font of authoritative unitary tradition and of decisive judgment in matters of faith,[26] Siricius's immediate successors appear to have concurred. Pushing on further, indeed, they conferred a degree of legal precision on papal claims to an authority that was, in fact, administrative in nature. With Leo I, "the most complete theologian of primacy in the first millennium" and the pope through whom "the primatial monarchic theme received its final theoretical stamp,"[27] the complex blending of legal, scriptural, and ecclesiological argumentation becomes markedly evident.

By Leo's day the terms "apostolic see" and "see of Peter" had come to be applied to Rome, and Boniface I (418–22) had declared that the papacy "occupied the 'apostolic height' (*apostolicum culmen*) from the verdict of which no appeal lay to any other authority or tribunal."[28] With Leo, the tension already present in the Roman church between tradition and discretion, along with the growing tendency to privilege the latter over the former, became even more evident. He did affirm the ancient view that the authentic tradition pertaining to the substance of the faith as well as to its practice had been handed down from the apostles themselves via "the preaching of the Holy Fathers" in unbroken succession to the present. At the same time, however, he also insisted that development took place in the way in which that tradition was humanly understood. So that "in its administrative and magisterial character" it "received elaboration."[29] Here his emphasis on the pyramidal nature of church government came forcefully into play. And the vision involved was one of a hierarchy of prelates ascending from the multiplicity of ordinary bishops, via the rulers of great provincial churches who were known as metropolitans up to the bishop of Rome himself who, at the apex of the pyramid and as successor of St. Peter, presided over the whole universal church. To the scriptural basis for his formidable vision two classic texts were central. The first, Matthew 16:18–19, where, in response to Peter's confession of faith in Jesus as "the Christ, the Son of the living God," Jesus, having declared him "blessed" went on to say: "You are Peter, and on this rock I will build my church, and the powers of death shall not prevail against it. I will give you the keys of the kingdom of heaven, and whatever you bind on earth shall be bound also in heaven, and whatever you loose on earth shall be loosed in heaven."[30] To this text, which had been evoked at Rome in support of papal claims as early as the third century, Leo adjoined 2 Corinthians 11:28 where the apostle, having described his endless journeyings, imprisonments, shipwrecks, and miseries, added: "And, apart from other things, there is the daily pressure upon me of my anxiety for all the churches." Walter Ullmann emphasized the impact on papal thinking of the degree to which, in his translation of the Bible into what was to become known as the standard Latin "Vulgate" version, St. Jerome (c. 331–419/20) had employed in many a text terminology drawn from the Roman vocabulary of law. The "binding" and "loosing" in Mathew 16:19 is a case in point, for here Jerome rendered the Greek with the legal terms *ligare* and *solvere*.[31] And Leo himself, certainly, did much to shift in the direction of concrete legal rights and responsibilities the older notion of the Roman church as the "unifying center of communion."

He did so, moreover, in a quite specific way. Distinguishing the pope as holder of the papal office from the pope as individual person, Leo drew on Roman legal principles as a way of rendering more precisely what he himself took the Petrine succession of the Roman bishops to imply. As officeholder, the pope was "heir" to St. Peter, which meant that, in accordance with the law of inheritance, he came into direct possession of Peter's rights and responsibilities, among them his crucial power of the keys. If Peter was the vicar or representative of Christ, the pope as bishop of Rome is the "vicar of Peter." In a mysterious sense, Peter lives on in him. As bishop of the Roman church, which is the head (*caput*) to which the other churches of Christendom are attached as members, he is charged with the *solicitudo* or "care" of all those churches, possessed of a primacy that involves a "fullness of power" (*plenitudo potestatis*) and to which Leo viewed it as appropriate to apply the term *principatus*. The significance of that choice of word should not escape us. Since the time of Caesar Augustus in the first century, *principatus* had been the constitutional term used by the emperors to designate their own monarchical power. It was now used also to designate henceforth "the supreme jurisdictional status which the papacy claimed to exercise within the Christian community, within the Church."[32]

In the churches of the East, such papal pretensions, insofar as they were received at all, were taken with a grain of salt. Even in the West, and as we shall see,[33] the complex political realities of the centuries ensuing provide little sustenance for Leo's interpretation of the papal office in so monarchical a fashion. Some of his successor popes, indeed, played down such explicitly monarchical aspirations. Gregory I himself (590–604) is a distinguished case in point. A great and vigorous leader he undoubtedly was, and a man unquestionably committed to the precedence of the Roman church. But humility and collegiality bulked larger in his thinking than it had in Leo's, and he did not view the unity of the universal church as pivoting on the preeminence of Rome in any legal or jurisdictional sense. Indeed, "his emphasis on the Petrine commission in the conventional Roman sense was qualified by the eastern understanding that the rock upon which the Church was built was not St. Peter, but Christ Himself."[34] Nevertheless, the ideological foundations for papal monarchy laid down in earlier centuries were not to be forgotten in the centuries ensuing. The less so in that by the time Pope Nicholas I (858–67) moved vigorously to vindicate the old Leonine monarchical theme and to develop it still further, those foundations had been strengthened by a series of important writings that were destined to exercise a formative influence over the mature papal ideology as it came to be elaborated in the central Middle Ages. None of them, in fact, was papally generated and all of them involved either incorrect attribution or outright forgery. But that notwithstanding, their significance proved to be great.

The first of them, *On the Celestial Hierarchy* and *On the Ecclesiastical Hierarchy*, were purported to have been written by Dionysius the Areopagite, pupil of St. Paul in the first century CE, who enjoyed a certain cachet because of that attribution. In reality, however, they were produced toward the end of the fifth century by an anonymous author of Neoplatonic sympathies whom historians know as Pseudo-Dionysius (or Dionysius, the Pseudo-Areopagite) and whom medievals dubbed as the *doctor hierarchicus*. With good reason, for the whole "Dionysian universe" pivots on the notion of hierarchy, a term that the author himself is credited with having introduced into the ecclesiological vocabulary, and in accordance with which all powers emanated from the one God, with power transmitted downward via a succession of ranks calibrated according to function.[35] This divinely established hierarchical order was seen to pervade the celestial no less than the ecclesiastical world, with the latter (very much in Hellenistic fashion) echoing or mirroring the former. Thus the choirs of angels—cherubim and seraphim, principalities and powers—were seen to find their analogues in patriarchs and metropolitans, priests and deacons, and so on.[36] Being of divine ordination, the hierarchical ordering of higher and lower ranks among the clergy was not to be challenged or broken, and it is easy enough to discern the potential congruence between such a sweeping vision of things and the more juristic orientation of the Leonine papalist ideology.

The second set of writings also dated to the same era, being produced around 500 presumably by followers of Pope Symmachus, who, by virtue of his support for the Arian king Theodoric the Goth, had alienated a powerful faction of the philo-Byzantine Roman clergy and was seen, accordingly, to be threatened by synodal deposition. The writings in question were outright forgeries but purported to reproduce decrees dating back to the early fourth century. Those decrees involved, among other things, a particularly succinct formulation of the notion, bruited already by some of the popes, to the effect that the pope and his decisions were not subject to judgment or reversal by any superior court. Via the lapidary formulation embedded in these Symmachan forgeries—"the first [i.e., Roman, Apostolic] see is [can be?] judged by no one"—the principle of papal judicial inviolability had found its way by the ninth century into the canon law itself, to be embedded later on in Gratian's *Decretum* or *Concord of Discordant Canons* (becoming thereby the focus of an enormous amount of canonistic commentary) and, as a result, living on into the 1917 *Codex Juris Canonici* and the 1983 revised *Code of Canon Law*.[37]

In these latter, twentieth-century legal codifications, both framed under the long shadow cast by the First Vatican Council (1870), the principle is stated in absolute, seemingly watertight, terms. But that had not been the case before the codification of the canon law in 1917. In the Middle Ages, the frequency of disputed elections to the papacy, the possibility that the office had been acquired illegitimately through simoniacal intrigue, and the further possibility (readily admitted) that the papal incumbent, however legitimate, might still have lapsed into heresy, all of these conspired to impose qualifications on the basic principle. And in Gratian's *Decretum*, a particular qualification relating to that last possibility was appended to that principle in historic fashion and in a way that was destined to give rise to enduring constitutional tensions in the church. For in that work, to the classic formulation that "no mortal shall presume to rebuke [the pope's] faults, for he who is above all is to be judged by no one" was added the crucial qualification "unless he is caught deviating from the faith."[38]

The third writing, another forgery but dating, this time, to the mid-eighth century, is the *Donation of Constantine,* so called because it takes the form of a brief charter in which the emperor Constantine supposedly described his conversion to Christianity, his confession of faith, and his later move to endow the Roman church (this last the "donation" proper).[39] Though a powerful attempt has recently been made to assign a Frankish origin to the document, the currently prevailing tendency, understanding it as a private (rather than a macropolitical) instrument, is to view it as a fictitious foundational charter or legend produced by a cleric at the Church of St. John Lateran in order to bolster the standing and reputation of that church, which was at that time being challenged by the growing popularity among pilgrims of St. Peter's in the Vatican. Despite such seemingly limited intentions, the document was destined eventually to enjoy a more high-profile career in the larger arena of European political life. And not surprisingly so, for in it Constantine is portrayed as having recognized the preeminence of the see of Rome over all other churches; and when he himself was moving his seat of power to Constantinople in the East, as having endowed Pope Sylvester I and his papal successors with the rulership of Rome, Italy, and the western provinces of the empire at large; and as having transferred to him also the use of the imperial regalia—scepter, crimson cloak (*cappa rubea*), crown, and *phrygium,* this last being in fact a piece of white, pointed headgear of Byzantine origin.[40] As a result, the *Donation* came eventually to be taken to depict the pope as occupying a position equal in status with that of the emperor, as placed at "the centre of the concept of empire," and as clothed with all "the splendor which surrounded the earthly *imperator.*"[41]

Finally, and of greater importance than any of the others, the fourth piece of writing in question, something of a potpourri of conciliar documents and fictitious as well as authentic papal decrees, is the historic compilation that has gone down in history as the *Pseudo-Isidorean* or *False Decretals* and which, testimony to its currency and importance, survives in almost a hundred medieval manuscripts. Folded later on in the twelfth century into the pages of Gratian's *Decretum,* it constituted about a tenth of that great and much-perused textbook.[42] Ascribed to a certain Isidore Mercator (frequently confused later on with Isidore of Seville), the compilation purported to include all the papal decretals issued down to the pontificate of Pope Gregory II (715–31) and all the principal decisions of the church councils down to the Thirteenth Council of Toledo in 783. Authentic decretals promulgated by popes from Damasus (366–84) to Gregory I (590–604) were preceded by around sixty spurious decretals attributed to the very earliest popes and conveying the impression that the papacy had reigned supreme over the church from its very inception.

Although they were later to lend their authority to the magnification of papal power, the *False Decretals* were not themselves of Roman provenance. They were forged around 847–52, it now seems likely, and in the ecclesiastical province of Rheims. Those responsible appear to have been enemies of Archbishop Hincmar of Rheims, and their "immediate intent... was not the strengthening of Roman authority." Instead, it was their purpose to magnify and "make use of the acknowledged authority of Rome in order to break the much closer and more dangerous authority of the metropolitans."[43] In effect, their target was to undercut the metropolitan power of rulers of ecclesiastical provinces—like Hincmar himself—who were now claiming a distinctive position and one superior to that of the ordinary bishops. It was, therefore, their desire to protect those bishops that led the forgers to invoke and magnify papal power. Hence their insistence that a bishop on trial had the right at any moment of that process to appeal beyond the local court in question to that of the pope, thus adumbrating the legal principle that it is to Rome alone that the prerogative of deposing bishops properly pertains. In the same vein was their stipulation that councils and synods, once the unquestionable expression of episcopal collegiality, were properly to be viewed as deriving their very legitimacy from papal approval and confirmation.

The truly telling impact of all four sets of writings on the subsequent elaboration of the high papal ideology dates really to later centuries that lie beyond the purview of the present volume. It was only in the late eleventh century, at the hands of the Gregorian reformers, that the *False Decretals* came into their own as a valuable piece of papal weaponry. Similarly, there are few references to the *Donation* in the first three centuries of its existence (750–1050), and one of them was its dismissal by the chancellery of the German emperor Otto III as a forgery. The Gregorian reformers did make some use of it in their struggle to assert their sovereign control over the papal states in central Italy and to vindicate their own independence from imperial control. But it was to lend itself to extensive use by the defenders of a broader papal sovereignty in matters temporal only after Pope Innocent IV (1243–54) had reinterpreted it. He did so in order to portray it as describing not so much a *conferral* of sovereign power on the popes as a *restitution* to them of a sovereignty or "royal monarchy in the apostolic see" that Christ himself had originally conferred on his papal vicar.[44]

In the course of the ninth century, nonetheless, all four sets of writings had at least begun their gradual ascent to prominence. The corpus *Dionysiacum*, in which the *Ecclesiastical Hierarchy* was embedded, was first translated into Latin in 832, and the fact that more than a dozen further translations were made attests to its currency and popularity during the medieval centuries. Similarly, it was from the ninth century onward that the Symmachan formulation that the pope could be judged by no one became a fixture in the various compilations of canon law—though accompanied by the crucial qualification alluded to earlier. Again, it was by virtue of its inclusion in the mid-ninth century in the *False Decretals* and its twelfth-century folding thence into the *Decretum* of Gratian[45] that the *Donation* became readily available for exploitation by papal propagandists. And, so far as the *False Decretals* themselves were concerned, questioned though the authenticity of some of these writings were (and by none other than Hincmar of Rheims himself), they had begun to find a place in papal argumentation by the ninth-century pontificates of Leo IV (847–55) and Nicolas I (858–67). Nicholas may have refrained from actually quoting them, but he did not hesitate to refer to them and that very fact may have worked to promote their currency and establish their authority in Frankia.

Short though it was, it has been claimed that in the history of the papacy the pontificate of Nicholas I stands at the same level of importance as those of Gregory the Great before him and Gregory VII (1073–85) after him.[46] Few papal letters survive from the first half of the ninth century, and while those of Gregory IV (827–44) and Leo IV do reveal their commitment to the view that the universal church's unity pivoted on the hierarchical preeminence of Rome, they articulate no fully developed papal ecclesiology. So far as the ninth century goes, it was left to Nicholas I to undertake that task. He did so with great brio and in a manner that set the example for the reformed papacy of the late eleventh century and the imperial papacy of the thirteenth.

Nicholas's tendency was to think of the church as, above all, a discrete sacerdotal community.[47] It was a community ruled by its papal monarch, heir as he was to the "principate of divine power" (*principatus divinae po-*

testatis), which had been given, admittedly, to all the apostles but preeminently so to Peter.[48] While Nicholas certainly venerated "apostolic tradition," in his writings (to use Morrison's terms) "discretion" tends to trump "tradition." Or put differently, he inclined to collapse the latter into the "tradition of the Apostolic See," to view Rome, in effect, as "the font of tradition for the whole Church," and to see the pope as its authoritative interpreter.[49] And by virtue of their alignment with apostolic tradition as he interpreted it, he viewed the prerogatives of the Roman see as extending beyond the magisterial into the legal and jurisdictional realms. That see possessed the power to judge not only bishops but also synods whose very legitimacy depended on its approbation. Being itself subject to judgment by no one, the first see's own judgments were themselves subject neither to reversal nor review. As Nicholas put it in one of his letters, "if anyone disregard the teachings, mandates, prohibitions, sanctions, or decrees beneficially promulgated by the head of the Apostolic See for the catholic faith, for ecclesiastical discipline, for the correction of the faithful, for the improvement of wrongdoers or for the prohibition of imminent or future evils, let him be anathema."[50]

The force of such claims Nicholas was prone to matching with a willingness to deploy papal power in order to vindicate them. He did so in a variety of particular cases, large as well as small. Thus he betrayed no hesitation about entering into conflict with the archbishop of Ravenna, or the great Frankish metropolitan Hincmar of Rheims, or the Carolingian Lothar II, king of Lotharingia (whom he went so far as to excommunicate), or even the Byzantine emperor Michael III himself. No succeeding pope until Gregory VII himself advanced such sweepingly monarchical claims on behalf of the papacy, and none, certainly, until Leo IX (1049–54) was to succeed in integrating papal power so effectively in the life of the universal church.

The Rise of the Papal Monarchy (ii): Contextual Factors

Having moved as early, it seems, as the fourth century to establish a chancery modeled on imperial practice, a papal archive housed at the Lateran, as well as papal registers housed in that archive and logging in mail, both incoming and outgoing,[51] popes were understandably not prone to forgetting much about bold primatial claims advanced by their predecessors. When afforded occasion to push such claims, they were unusually well positioned, accordingly, to buttress the case they were making with precedents (whether plausible or implausible) drawn from the past. During the first millennium of Christian history, however, such occasions did not present themselves with any great frequency. And the uneven, stop-go fashion in which the papal ideology developed itself reflects that fact.

Given the grandeur of the claims advanced on behalf of the papacy's primatial role by such popes as Nicholas I in the ninth century or, before him, by a Leo I or Gelasius I in the fifth, it is something of a chastening experience when one turns to the political context in which popes had perforce to operate from the fourth to the eleventh centuries. When one does that, one is forced to recognize the markedly stringent limitations on the power they were actually able to wield. For the whole period from the fourth to the eighth centuries, with the exception of the years between 476 and 536 when they were subject in Italy to Ostrogothic rule, they had to function within the confining framework of the Roman/Byzantine imperial structure and of a universal church that was embedded within that structure.

The moments, then, when papal assertiveness was a real option were few and far between. When Leo I advanced his bold claims on behalf of the papal primacy, he was able to do so because imperial power was collapsing in the West, and he did so only after he himself had been forced in Italy to assume on behalf of the beleaguered populace a leadership role that was as much temporal as spiritual. Similarly, when Gelasius I was moved to deny any priestly status to the Byzantine emperor,[52] Rome was subject not to Byzantine but to Ostrogothic rule. In the wake, however, of Justinian's campaigns of reconquest in Africa, Spain, and Italy, Rome and Ravenna became subject once more to Byzantine rule. As a result, from 556 on into the eighth century the legal form of papal election was itself determined by imperial decree, with the Byzantine exarch in Ravenna possessing a supervisory role and confirmation by the emperor (or, later, the exarch) being required before an elected candidate could actually be consecrated.[53] Nor was the traditional role of the emperor in matters religious the only factor imposing restraint on the implementation of papal power. After all, until the Muslim conquests of the late seventh and early eighth centuries, western Christendom still embraced within its orbit the great churches of northern Africa and of Visigothic Spain. Both of them were markedly independent in spirit. The great councils assembled by the Visigothic kings at Toledo did not hesitate to promulgate doctrinal decrees without seeking advice, let alone confirmation from Rome. And even in Italy itself papal authority by no means went unchallenged.[54]

The demise of these two great churches, both of them in some ways counterweights to Rome, was followed later in the eighth century by the growth of tension between the papacy and the Byzantine imperial government. An imperial summons in 711, accompanied by a guarantee of safe conduct, brought Pope Constantine to Constantinople. But that proved to be the last of such papal visits to the seat of imperial power. Renewed intrusion into doctrinal matters by successive emperors culminating in the adoption by Leo III (726) of an iconoclastic policy proscribing the use of images in public worship[55] nudged the papacy steadily in the direction of a final break with Byzantium and a novel alignment, instead, with the growing power of the Frankish kings.

In itself, this realignment did not necessarily mean release from the type of pressure that temporal rulers were prone to exerting. The prerogative of confirming papal elections, exercised first by the Byzantine emperor himself and then by his exarch at Ravenna, passed for a while under the new Frankish protectorate to the Frankish kings.[56] If we can believe his biographer Einhard, Charlemagne himself appears to have viewed the bishopric of Rome as nothing more than the leading metropolitan church in his empire.[57] Only in the mid-ninth century, with a weakening in the position of Charlemagne's Carolingian successors, was the papacy able, during the remarkable pontificate of Nicholas I, not only to flourish anew and to extend the papal primatial claims in theory but also, and as we have seen, to vindicate them in practice.[58]

That bold implementation of the papal primacy notwithstanding, two countervailing forces came rapidly into play in the wake of Nicholas's pontificate, forces that were destined over time, though at differing moments, to undermine the position of the papacy and to impose severe constraints on the effective exercise of papal power over the church at large. The first, evident already in the ninth century among some at least of the Frankish bishops, was a species of what has often been dubbed "episcopalism."[59] That is to say, it was an ecclesiological stance that challenged the notion that the authority of Peter still held sway via the rule of his papal successors, insisting instead and in more collegial fashion that all bishops were alike "vicars of God" and successors to the apostles. Those who took this stance argued that the "rock" referred to in Matthew 16:18 was Christ himself, not Peter, and that Matthew 16:19 was to be understood in the light of Matthew 18:18, where the evangelist made it abundantly clear that the power of binding and loosing was conferred not on Peter alone but on all the apostles.[60] Hence the concomitant insistence on the legal priority of the ancient canons handed down by tradition to the authority claimed by such as Nicholas I for decrees grounded merely in the exercise of papal discretionary power. Hence, too, the stubborn measure of hostility evinced toward the renewed papal drive for monarchical centralization on Rome.[61] This type of episcopalist collegiality projected on into the future a version of the ancient ecclesiological vision harking back to an era when every bishop had been viewed as a successor of Peter, "joined" with all his fellow bishops, as Cyprian of Carthage had put it in the fourth century, "by the bond of mutual concord and the chain of unity" and with them responsible in solidarity and via the practice of vital synodal cooperation for the well-being of the entire Christian church.[62] Over the years it was destined to rise and fall in importance, but over the long haul it proved to possess considerable lasting power, enduring in one form or another down to the very eve of the First Vatican Council in 1870[63] and succeeding in the 1960s in generating a qualified harmonic in the Second Vatican Council's teaching on episcopal collegiality.

The second countervailing force—the disastrous Europe-wide political conditions of the late ninth century and at Rome itself the rivalries of local aristocratic factions and their intrusion into papal electoral politics—doomed the papacy, after the forceful pontificates of Nicholas I, Hadrian II, and John VIII (858–82), to a century and more of turmoil, scandal, and obscurity. During the tenth century, no less than fourteen popes and antipopes were imprisoned, driven into exile, or assassinated.[64] That being so, it is understandable that during this dismal period no pope contributed anything to the assertion or further development of papalist theory. And it is understandable, too, that with the revival of the imperial office by the Ottonian kings of Germany the papacy found itself subjected, once more, to the heavy (if intermittent) hand of imperial power.

Thus in 962 the newly crowned emperor Otto I (936–73) descended on Rome and, responding to the treachery of his erstwhile collaborator Pope John XII (955–64), convoked and presided over a synod at St. Peter's basilica, which deposed that unfortunate pope and appointed a successor. Around the same time, and without consulting the pope, Otto inserted into the agreement previously negotiated with John XII (the so-called *Ottonianium*) a stipulation that prior to his consecration every newly elected pope should take an oath to the imperial legates whereby he committed himself, in ominously vague and sweeping terms, to discharging all his obligations to the supreme imperial protector. In theory, given the papacy's demonstrated need for protection against the unruly noble families of Rome, this was not altogether a losing proposition. In practice, however, and as Ullmann properly pointed out, "the modified compact served as a handle for the Germans simply to appoint a new pope if the situation at Rome made it necessary."[65]

From time to time it did, indeed, make it necessary. In the years between 955 and 1057 there were twenty-five popes in all, thirteen of whom were, it seems, maneuvered into the papal throne by one or another aristocratic faction at Rome. But no fewer than twelve were appointed by the emperors themselves, who were also responsible for dismissing five of the overall twenty-five.[66] The most dramatic manifestation of imperial domination came quite late in the day, in the middle years of the eleventh century. And it proved also to signal the beginning of a dramatic turn around in the career of the medieval papacy. For it served, ironically, to open the way to a vindication of papal autonomy and freedom from external control, setting a reformed papacy on the route that was to lead it into the first of several direct confrontations with the empire. Those historic conflicts were to punctuate the late eleventh, twelfth, and thirteenth centuries, generating an enormous body of polemical literature and ushering in the new and distinctive phase in the history of Western political thought on which it will be the purpose of the second volume in this series to focus.

In 1046, the Salian emperor Henry III (1039–56), taking to Rome itself his persistent campaign to restore ecclesiastical order and promote moral reform in the church, summarily deposed three rival candidates to the papal throne and went on to appoint in succession three others, all of them German and the last, Leo IX (1048–54), a relative of his and a vigorous collaborator in the work of reform. In pursuit of that reforming effort, Leo assembled at the papal curia a distinguished coterie of fellow reformers and, by himself convoking and presiding over synods in France and Germany as well as Italy, projected papal power across Europe and began once more the process of vindicating the prerogatives long since claimed by his predecessors to pertain to the papal primacy. And he did something more than that. Though in his reforming efforts he enjoyed the enthusiastic collaboration of Henry III, he signaled right at the start of his pontificate a certain renewed papal aspiration to autonomy. He did so when he insisted on the confirmation of his imperial appointment to the papal office through an invocation of the traditional process of canonical election by the clergy and populace of Rome. In any event, his successor Victor II (1055–57) was to be the last pope to ascend to his office by the route of imperial nomination. In 1059, three years after Henry III's death and in the context of an imperial minority and somewhat wavering regency, Pope Nicholas II (1059–61) presided over an historic synod at the Lateran. It was historic because in addition to reaffirming the principle that popes were to be freely elected, that synod, more significantly, moved to ensure that that should be in fact the case by assigning (and restricting) the electoral role to the cardinal-clergy of Rome, thereby leaving to the Roman clergy and people at large nothing more than the ceremonial formality of assenting to the choice the cardinals had already made.

That crucial electoral decree, intended to prevent the intrusion into the choice of popes of outside forces, imperial no less than local, did not turn out to be foolproof, and it was destined to be tinkered with repeatedly, right down into the twenty-first century. But it marked a critical turning point in the history of the papacy and, at least in retrospect, stands out as having brought to a close one era in the tangled relationship between popes and emperors and as having set the terms for the dawning in the extraordinary and historic pontificate of Gregory VII (1073–85) of a new and vastly different one.

Epilogue

IN THE COMPLEX alternation of moments of continuity and discontinuity that characterizes the unfolding course of history, recent years have seen among historians, most especially those of Foucauldian sympathies, a marked tendency to privilege discontinuity, rupture, caesura, break.[1] But however necessary, historiographically speaking, periodization may be, there is of course nothing given or "natural" about the precise way in which we go about the division of the course of history into discrete, clearly demarcated epochs. And we have always to be alert to the fact that, in any given instance, the particular periodization adopted may well tell us as much or more about the convictions, preoccupations, and commitments of the person doing the periodizing and of his or her own era than it does about the stretch of history under scrutiny. That is surely the case with the Renaissance humanist postulation of a dark or middle age separating the celebrated literary and artistic achievements of their own day from the glories they perceived in classical antiquity. As we bring this volume to a close on the eve of the Gregorian reform, we have to ask ourselves, accordingly, whether the Gregorian reformers, too, moved as they clearly were by an acute sense of crisis in the ecclesiastical order of their day and the concomitant need to push for radical change, were themselves guilty of projecting onto the age immediately preceding their own an unduly gloomy appraisal of the conditions of religious and ecclesiastical life then prevailing.

The question is not to be sidestepped. Upon the answer we give to it depends the wisdom of our having chosen to portray the first phase in the history of medieval political thought as having reached its term in the latter part of the eleventh century. And here it has to be acknowledged that there has been of late a tendency among church historians, responding in this to the research findings of the past half century, to detect less novelty in the "new age" of the eleventh-century church and less drama in the ecclesiastical departures we have traditionally been accustomed to associate with the work of the Gregorian reformers. Whether what is in question is concern for a purer priesthood, for the observation of clerical celibacy, for a revived and more systematized canon law, or for the reassertion of papal prerogatives, the interpretative pendulum has been swinging from revolution to evolution, with attention being directed to forerunners and the emphasis being placed on the importance of the work of tenth-century reformers, as well as on the degree to which, turbulence and aristocratic interference at Rome notwithstanding, "pre-Gregorian popes were often active and important figures."[2]

But as was the case with the humanists of the Renaissance in their own instinctive sense that there really *was* something quite novel about their own era, so too with the leading clerical reformers of the Gregorian era. Where "today's historians may [often] see evolution," those leading reformers from Peter Damiani (d. 1072) to Bruno of Segni (d. 1123) "emphatically did not," seeing instead "an unprecedented crisis requiring radical action." "The Lord hath not said 'I am Tradition' but 'I am the Truth,'" or so Gregory VII was reputed to have said. That truth he was determined to vindicate, even if the unfolding consequences of so doing threatened to be revolutionary in their implications.[3] And as we shall see, those consequences did indeed turn out to be revolutionary in their implications. What was involved in the Gregorian reform, then, is properly to be treated not as a mere coda to earlier developments, but as the transition to a new world of ideas that we will be called upon to address in the second volume of this series.

In the present volume our primary concentration has been on an older world of ideas, on the ideology of late antique and early medieval kingship, on its marked continuity with the pre-Christian past, and on the powerful witness it affords to the extraordinary staying power manifested by a pattern of sacral monarchy that dated far back into the archaic era. With the onset of the Gregorian reform, however, that staying power was destined to be sorely tested. By proclaiming that the age of "priest-kings and emperor-pontiffs" was over, the reformers called brusquely into question the whole extraordinary set of accommodations that, from the time of Constantine onward, Christians had somehow contrived to make with the sacred aura attaching to pagan kingship. But if those reformers certainly succeeded in shaking the ideological foundations on which such accommodations rested, in the end they failed, as we shall see, to destroy them. They too, after all, were creatures of their own time and ultimately responsive to the theopolitical ideas that informed it. As a result, and by yet another of the ironies that punctuate the history of ideas, the popes of the twelfth and thirteenth centuries, having first attacked the sacral pretensions of their royal counterparts, went on themselves to assume the role of fully fledged sacral monarchs in their own right. Ultimately unable, it seems, to escape the magnetic field still exerted by the age-old pattern of sacral kingship, they gradually move to center stage as the true (or most convincing) successors of the erstwhile Roman emperors, claiming some of their attributes (that, for example, of being a *lex animata*), deploying some of their titles ("supreme pontiff," "celestial emperor"), garbed in the imperial costume and possessed of the imperial regalia, greeted by comparable imperial acclamations, and ruling with imperial grandeur a highly politicized church via a centralized bureaucracy modeled on that of the Roman empire and informed by a legal mentality that was unquestionably Roman.

In the ninth century, reacting to the bold vindication of papacy primacy by Nicholas I, two bishops who had felt the sting of his condemnation were moved to protest that he was "making himself the emperor of all the world."[4] Doubtless little more at the time than an outburst of wounded hyperbole, but in retrospect, nonetheless, a portent of developments to come. Three centuries later, two canonistic commentaries on Gratian's *Decretum* could refer to the pope as the "true emperor" (*verus imperator*).[5] And four centuries later, the chronicler Francesco Pipino clearly did not feel that he would be straining credulity when he portrayed Pope Boniface VIII (1294–1302) as having received the ambassadors of Albert of Hapsburg, claimant to the imperial throne, in the following dramatic fashion: "Sitting on a throne, wearing on his head the diadem of Constantine, his right hand on the hilt of the sword with which he was girt, he [the pope] cried out: 'Am I not the supreme pontiff? Is this throne not the pulpit of Peter? Is it not my duty to watch over the rights of the Empire? It is I who am Caesar, it is I who am emperor.'"[6]

Years later, when the ideological dust kicked up by several centuries of intermittent papal-imperial conflict had finally begun to settle, the great seventeenth-century English philosopher Thomas Hobbes described the papacy as "no other than the *ghost* of the deceased *Roman empire* sitting crowned on the grave thereof."[7] The development of high papalist aspirations in the twelfth and thirteenth centuries will, I believe, confirm the propriety of acknowledging that that observation was no less accurate in its fundamental perception for being derisive in its conscious intent.

Notes

General Introduction

1. We are already fortunate enough, after all, to have available to us in English an impressive array of histories of medieval political thought, from the classic multivolume work of the Carlyles, 1903–36, via the shorter accounts by McIlwain, 1932; Morrall, 1962; Ullmann, 1965; Monahan, 1987–94; and Canning, 1996, to the lengthy *Cambridge History of Medieval Political Thought,* 1988, an impressively scholarly collective effort.
2. Thus, in order of citation (all italics mine), Sabine, 1937, 176; Dvornik, 1966, 2:488; Morris, 1967, 166; McIlwain, 1932, 146; Morrall, 1962, 10–11. Cf. among more recent works, Canning, 1996, 127–28.
3. Notably Ullmann, 1961, 1965, 1966a, 1969. For an extended analysis of his position, see Oakley, 1973, 3–48; reprinted in Oakley, 1999, 25–72.
4. Affirmed by John Stuart Mill in a classic statement that Gertrude Himmelfarb has described as "the very epigraph of modernity": "Over himself, over his own body and mind, the individual is sovereign" (Mill, 1985, 69). Himmelfarb's characterization is to be found in the introduction to this edition at p. 29.
5. He did so, adding: "It is not surprising that we go back to that period every time we ask ourselves about our origins" (Eco, 1986, 64–65).
6. Thus Bynum, 1987, 31. For the "mythology of prolepsis," see Skinner, 1969, 22–24; reprinted in Tully, 1988, 44–45.
7. Skinner, 1988, 248. Cf. Dunn, 1969, 208, where speaking very much to the point at issue here, he says: "To present a complex argument from the past in terms of its significance for us may often seem mendacious, and to present it with the greatest concern for historical specificity but without exploring its 'significance' is likely to seem trivial."
8. For a further statement of my views on the matter, see Oakley, 2006b, 407–22. There I place a particular emphasis on the importance of the distinction between *meaning* and *significance* which the literary theorist E. D. Hirsch (following in this the promptings of Gottlob Frege and Edmund Husserl) deployed in an attempt to dissipate the confusion that so often surrounds argument concerning the interpretation of texts. For my own evolving stance vis-à-vis the broader metahistorical debate

concerning textual interpretation at large and the interpretative mode appropriate to the pursuit of the history of ideas, I venture to refer to Oakley, 1984, 11–40, and Oakley, 1999, 1–24, 233–41.
9. Skinner, 1969, 44–45.

Prologue

1. Briefly reprising here the thesis developed at much greater length in Oakley, 2006a.
2. Gilbert, 1987, 298.
3. Cerfaux and Tondriau, 1957, 119–20, refer to it accurately as "la paranthèse republicaine des 'poleis.'" But for a recent and much more aggressive affirmation of the point, see Al-Azmeh and Bak, 2004, 10: "Sacral kingship was a constant motif in old royalist and imperialist arrangements that spanned the entire oecumenical expanse of Eurasia from the very dawn of recorded history until modern times, a vast perspective in which *the primitive republican image of Rome or of Athens seems aberrant, paltry and inconsequential*, if indeed this image of republican purity, of the splendid childhood of rational political man, has any credibility apart from Jacobin and proto-Jacobin imaginings" (italics mine).
4. Guthrie, 1960, 3–4.
5. Thus B. Williams, 1993, 111. Williams's book, a brilliant achievement, is marred I believe by a somewhat reductive rendition of the position he is criticizing, as well as by the intrusion of modern philosophical disagreements into what is an essentially historical dispute. Thus his throw-away aside (p. 46) to the effect that if Homer really did not have a notion of the "will," then "he, and we," would be "better off without [it]." Cf. Lloyd-Jones, 1971, 8–10, for a less sweeping dissent from the views of Fränkel and Snell (see below, n8).
6. It was Onians, 1988 (1951), who, in the course of his massive *Origins of European Thought*, 1–78 (at 2), and analyzing Homer's notions of "the main processes of consciousness" and "the words he deploys to describe them," spoke of "the strangeness of his world."
7. Adkins, 1970, 247; cf. 45, where he speaks of the "low degree of unity and cohesion felt by the Homeric man in his psychological experience." Also Adkins, 1960. Both of these are fine studies.
8. Thus Fränkel, 1975; Snell, 1953, ch. 1.
9. Adkins, 1960, esp. 46–49, 154–68.
10. Taylor, 1989; Adkins, 1960, and 1970.
11. For which injunction, see MacIntyre, 1984, 129, where, discussing "The Virtues in Heroic Societies," he argues that in his treatment of the heroic past "Nietzsche replaces the fictions of the Enlightenment individualism, of which he is so contemptuous, with a set of individualist fictions of his own."
12. Hegel, 1967, 84 § 124, 124 § 185; cf. 51 § 62, 133 § 206, 195 § 299, and 267–68, *Add.* 118, where, among other things, he mentions the differing roles ascribed to "the subject's arbitrary will" in the political life of the ancient and modern worlds.

13. Cartledge, 2000, 13, comments that for the Greeks, "society, not the individual was... the primary point of political reference, and individualism did not constitute a serious, let alone a normal, alternative pole of attraction. In fact, there was no ancient Greek word for 'individual' in our anti-social, indeed antipolitical sense."
14. Voegelin, 1956–57, 2:113–25.
15. Ibid., 2:169–20.
16. Peering anxiously into the mists of the classical past, those Hellenists, German as well as English, were often prone to discerning in the intellectual and political life of the classical Greek polis, and in the writings of the Greek political philosophers, the looming outlines of their own cherished ideals. "Across the Western world," Frank Turner has written, "Victorian authors and readers were determined to make the Greeks as much as possible like themselves and to rationalize away fundamental difference" (Turner, 1981, 7–8). Cf. Jenkins, 1980; Butler, 1935; and Goldhill, 2000, 66, where he asserts, "It would be hard to write a history of German political thought that did not recognize 'the tyranny of Greece' over German intellectual practice. *Antigone* is in this sense a text of nineteenth-century political thought."
17. Fustel de Coulanges, 1955 (1874), 355–60 (the words quoted appear at 357–59).
18. In the doctrines espoused by the successive schools of Stoicism, and with the crystallization of the doctrines of natural law and the equality of men, the element that had been occasional and exceptional with Plato and Aristotle did indeed become increasingly central. But here, too, we have again to avoid the danger of seeing ourselves too readily in the thinking of the ancients. Even if one allows for difficulties of interpretation posed by the fragmentary nature and wide chronological spread of the sources and by shifts that occurred from the early to the late Stoa, there remains a certain fuzziness about Stoic thinking. For another version of this caveat (though advanced on grounds different from my own), see Wolin, 1960, 80.
19. *Republic* VII, 514a–521b, IX, 590–92; trans. Paul Shorey, in Huntington and Cairns, 1961, 747–53, 812–19.
20. *Nichomachaean Ethics* X, 7, §§ 1177a–1178a; trans. W. D. Ross in Ross, ed., 1908–52, 9.
21. *Rhetoric* I, 13 and 15, §§ 1373b–1374b, 1375a–1377b; trans. W. Rhys Roberts in Ross, ed., 1908–52, 11. On this point, see the illuminating commentary of Foster, 1941, 175–78, 192–95.
22. Fustel de Coulanges, 1955 (1874), 11.
23. It is not my purpose to suggest here that the two dualities under discussion—"individual vs. collective" and "secular vs. religious"—are somehow identical. But across time, as we shall see, they did come to be complexly intertwined.
24. *Politics* I, ch. 2; trans. Barker, 1948, 5.
25. *Politics* III, ch. 9; trans. Barker, 1948, 118–19.
26. *Politics* VI, ch. 8, § 18; trans. Barker, 1948, 277.
27. See, e.g., Rousseau, *Du contrat social*, bk. 4, ch. 8; ed. Vaughan, 1947, 113–24.
28. *Republic* II, 377a–382c; trans. Paul Shorey, in Huntington and Cairns, 1961, 623–30; *Laws* X, 908a–909b; trans. E. A. Taylor, in Huntington and Cairns, 1961, 1463–64. Cf. Popper, 1950, esp. 86–118.

29. Foster, 1941, 50, where he adds that, for Plato, "Nature has ordained man to be a social animal, and hence has brought it about that the restraints upon the individual's freedom which the requirements of society impose are the very restraints best calculated to develop his individual excellence as a man."
30. Morris, 1972; Gurevich, 1995; and (magisterially) Taylor, 1989, though in differing ways, together make a compelling case for the historically protracted nature of the process whereby that notion emerged.
31. Eliade, 1959, 34.

Chapter 2. Ancient Affections

1. For synoptic treatments of this worldwide phenomenon, see Mousnier, 1989, and Oakley, 2006a, both of which present illustrative case studies drawn from different eras and most parts of the world. For glimpses of the vast body of historical and anthropological data that has been assembled on the subject and for guidance through the dense undergrowth of scholarly literature pertaining to it, see Edsman, 1959, 3–17, and the other articles (English, German, French, and Italian) gathered together helpfully in *The Sacral Kingship,* 1959. Also the articles by Luc de Heusch et al. in *Le pouvoir et le sacré,* 1962; Claessen and Skolnik, eds., 1978; Boureau and Sergio, eds., 1992; Al-Azmeh and Bak, eds., 2004. The classic works on the subject are Fraser, 1905, 1920, and 1925; Hocart, 1927 and 1970. For the Graeco-Roman world, see, e.g., Cerfaux and Tondriau, 1957, with extensive classified bibliography at pp. 10–73.
2. In his fine work, *The Gnostic Religion,* Hans Jonas, 1963, 241–50, skillfully evokes under the label of "cosmic piety" (and with particular reference to Cicero's *De natura deorum* 2:11–14) the late classical, philosophized version of this cosmic religiosity. See also, Eliade, 1978–85, 1:1–161.
3. In this and what immediately follows I draw upon Oakley, 2006a, 10–43.
4. Frankfort, 1948a, 3.
5. Leeuwen, 1965, 168–70.
6. Ibid., 170.
7. Voegelin, 1956–57, 1:1.
8. Frankfort, Wilson, and Jacobsen, 1949, 237.
9. *Timaeus* §§ 29d-30c; trans. Cornford, 1937, 33–34.
10. Cornford, 1937, 6. Cf. Plato, *The Laws,* in Hamilton and Cairns, eds., 1973, 1225–1513.
11. Though the Stoic philosophical views on the same issue that crystallized during the centuries subsequent to Plato evinced the older monistic sensibility. Thus, e.g., Cicero *De natura deorum* 2:11–14, ed. and trans. Rackham, 1933, 150–59: "The world possesses wisdom, and in the element which holds all things in its embrace is preeminently and perfectly rational, and therefore ... the world is god [*deum esse mundum*], and all the forces of the world are held together by the nature.... [T]he world is an animate being.... [T]he world must be deemed to have been wise from the beginning and [also] to be god [*et sapiens a principio mundus et deus habendus est*]."

12. Frankfort, Wilson, and Jacobsen, 1949, 238.
13. Here again one finds in Plato such notions transposed into a more philosophical key. See esp. *Timaeus*, ed. and trans. Cornford, 1937.
14. For the Maya notion, see Schele and Freidel, 1990, 64–95.
15. Eliade, 1978–85, 1:82.
16. Eliade, 1959, 36.
17. The patristic understanding of the Christian Eucharist affords (as Eliade, 1959, 23, 130, suggests) a helpful analogy. For the eucharistic action was not really understood in temporal terms as a repetition by man or a group of men of Christ's historic sacrifice or, alternatively, as merely a memorial of that sacrifice. More mysteriously, the action was itself conceived as transtemporal. As St. John Chrysostom put it toward the end of the fourth century and in a fashion typical of the early commentators: "We do not offer a different sacrifice like the high-priest of old, but we ever offer the same. Or rather we offer the *anamnesis* of the sacrifice." And the word *anamnesis*, it should be noted, conveyed something akin to an actual "reliving" rather than a merely passive remembering. For all of this, see Oakley, 1979, 82–85.
18. Dawson, 1948, 125.
19. Hardy, 1941, 176–216; Güterbock, 1956, 19; Gurney, 1958, 105–32; Engnell, 1967, 52–70. For a brave attempt to delineate the characteristics of the Persian kingship, one made in the teeth of daunting evidentiary challenges, see Widengren, 1959, 242–57.
20. Engnell, 1967, in particular, places great emphasis (52–53) on the formative influence of the Egyptian and (especially) Mesopotamian cultures upon the Hittites, the latter so powerful, he says, that "the 'Hittite' culture ... may almost be called a provincial offshoot of the Sumero-Accadian." He also emphasizes the "considerable influence" exercized by the Hittite civilization upon the culture of Canaan, and consequently, that of Israel, as well as its "great importance" in mediating Sumero-Accadian components westwards.
21. Engnell, 1967, esp. his comments at p. 2; Frankfort, 1948a and 1948b; Frankfort, Wilson, and Jacobsen, 1949. In addition to these works, I rely also on the more recent studies in O'Connor and Silverman, eds., 1995.
22. Mercer, 1952, vol. 1, § 207c-d, 68 and 21.
23. Frankfort, 1948a, and Posener, 1960, mark the two extremes, with the former firmly insisting on the pharaoh's divine status and the latter, by way of skeptical qualification, emphasizing also his humanity. The current tendency is to deny or restrict the attribution of divinity to the king's person and to link it, rather, with the royal office, emphasizing the fact that it was the office "that provided the ruler with that element of the divine that removed him from the sphere of mortal men." Thus Silverman, 1995, 49–87 (at 67). See also Baines, 1995, 3–45, and Posener, 1960, 102–3.
24. Translation from Pritchard, ed., 1955, 431.
25. Cited in Frankfort, 1948b, 42–43.
26. Frankfort, 1948a, 5.
27. I cite this text from Engnell, 1967, 6.
28. Pritchard ed., 1955, 164.

29. Frankfort, 1948a, 51; cf. 277–78. Also Hornung, 1992, 131–45.
30. Frankfort, Wilson, and Jacobsen, 1949, 37–134 (at 89). For what Baines calls the pharaoh's "cosmic responsibilities," see Baines, 1995, esp. xvii-xxvii and 3–87.
31. Frankfort, Wilson, and Jacobsen, 1949, 214–15.
32. Hornung, 1992, 115–29 ("The Temple as Cosmos").
33. Frankfort, 1948a, 150–51.
34. Translation in Pritchard ed., 1955, 60–72.
35. For a good discussion of the *Enûma elish* and its significance, see Frankfort, Wilson, and Jacobsen, 1949, 182–99.
36. O'Connor and Oakley, eds., 1969, "General Introduction," 5–6.
37. *Timaeus* §§ 53b, 49a; cf. 30a: "[T]he god took over all that is visible—not at rest—but in discordant and unordered motion—and brought it from disorder into order." Trans. Cornford, 1937, 198, 177, and 33.
38. Eliade, 1959, 7, 9, 31–32, 34–35, 122–23.
39. For a recent emphasis on the "remarkable openness among Archaic Greeks toward the Near Eastern and Egyptian civilizations," and for a judicious appraisal of the disputed extent of "Near Eastern... and Egyptian influences on Archaic Greek culture," see Raaflaub, 2000, 50–57 (words cited at 51–52).
40. A point effectively argued and illustrated in the illuminating essays gathered together in Brock and Hodkinson, eds., 2000.
41. Ibid., 21.
42. James, 1960, 129–33; Furnmark, 1959, 369–70. Partial dissent in Rose, 1959, 372–78, though it should be noted that Rose is concerned to reject the presence in the Greek world not of sacred or sacerdotal monarchs *tout court* but only of *divine* kings "of the kind made famous by [Fraser's] *The Golden Bough.*"
43. Brock and Hodkinson, eds., 2000, stressing the diversity of political regimes prevailing in classical Greece, conclude that "the implication for modern views of the Greek polis is that we should abandon the angle of vision in which classical Athenian *dēmokratia* appears as the central point of Greek political experience for a perspective which sees it within a much broader context—a context very unlike the present-day ideological dominance of liberal democracy in which a range of political regimes could lay claim to legitimacy both as viable systems in their own right and as potential models for imitation by their neighbours" (21).
44. Dvornik, 1966, 1:155.
45. Ibid., 1:155n40.
46. *Menexenus* 238d; trans. Benjamin Jowett in Hamilton and Cairns, eds., 1973, 190.
47. *The Statesman* 290b; trans. J. B. Skemp in Hamilton and Cairns, eds., 1973, 1059.
48. Thus Dvornik, 1966, 1:155.
49. *The Constitution of Athens* §§ 57 and 3; trans. E. Poste, 1891, 92 and 4. Cf. James, 1960, 133.
50. James, 1960, 133. Cf. Cerfaux and Tondriau, 1957, 101–21.
51. A good sense of the interpretative challenges involved is conveyed both by Cerfaux and Tondriau, 1957, 125–267, and Dvornik, 1966, 1:205–77. See also the related con-

tributions by McEwan, 1934, and Goodenough, 1928, 55–102. Cerfaux and Tondriau, 1957, conclude their lengthy discussion of the whole matter with the comment: "Ou est tenté de conclure que s'il y a tendance à admettre que les souverains sont issus des dieux et que ces dieux se manifestent par eux, et même s'il sont incorporés au rang divine après leur mort, cela ne préjuge pas, en général, de leur essence même: ils jouent le rôle de dieux sans doute, mais il ne sont pas pour cela de nature pleinement divine" (267).

52. Citing here Fishwick, 1987–2005, Introduction, 1:3–93 (at 41, 4, 44–45). This excellent essay he describes (at 1:x), and I would judge, a trifle diffidently, as no more than "a modest supplement" to the remarkably durable fundamental account by Lily Ross Taylor, 1931. Cf. the useful discussion in Cerfaux and Tondriau, 1957, 101–43, where, stressing (at 119) the complexity of the development leading up to the notion of the divine king, they comment that "le polytheisme grec, croyant fernement à l'immanence du divin et délimitant mal la frontière entre les dieux, les héros et les hommes, se trouvant, tout compte fait, pousse à l'extrême non violé."

53. See the discussions in Dvornik, 1966, 1:213–14, and Cerfaux and Tondriau, 1957, 140–43.

54. See the case made, with extensive documentation, by Dvornik, 1966, 1:207–21.

55. Price, 1984, 24–40 (at 32), argues that "the cults of Hellenistic kings were modeled on divine cult"—i.e., rather than heroic cult. But Fishwick, 1987–2005, 1:4, views the distinction as "beside the point" if Heracles, for example, can enjoy "both forms of veneration."

56. Dvornik, 1966, 1:187–204, comments (at 200), "Although basically a democrat, Isocrates had perhaps contributed more than any one of his contemporaries toward the dissemination of the monarchic idea in his own time and in the Hellenistic period."

57. Though still capable of generating harmonics at Rome as late as the Augustan age. For Virgil *Georgics* 1:27; ed. Fairclough, 1999, 100, Caesar Augustus himself was "author of crops and master of the seasons" (*auctorem frugum tempestatumque potentem*).

58. English translation by Goodenough, 1928, 61 and 98.

59. Ibid., esp. 91 and 100–102. For more recent commentary on the views of Ps. Diotogenus, Ps.-Ecphantus, and Plutarch on kingship, see Centrone, 2000, 559–84.

60. Dvornik, 1966, 1:205–27.

61. He did so in a fine book that has stood the test of time—Cochrane, 1957, 110–13.

62. So far, for example, as ritual and symbolic representation go, Andreas Alföldi, 1970, insists that however real the Hellenistic contributions, they "form only a part of the foundation for the development of this external feature of sovereignty," and affirms at the very beginning of his *Die monarchische Repräsentation im römischen Kaiserreiche* that "wir werden daneben starke italisch-römische Wurzeln, wie auch allein durch die innere Entwicklung bedingte Formen, Einflüsse des Barbarentums usw. aufweisen können" (4).

63. Possession of the office conferred on him, as it had on Julius Caesar before him, a

sacred power that had long pertained to the king, making him supreme priest of all the deities as well as the interpreter of the sacred law. See Cerfaux and Tondriau, 1957, 286.

64. For this and what follows, see esp. Taylor, 1931, 58–204; Fishwick, 1987–2005, 1:46–93; Cerfaux and Tondriau, 1957, 286–94; Dvornik, 1966, 2:463–91.
65. Cicero *Ad Quintum Fratrem* 1:9, 26; ed. Williams, 1927–29, 3:414ff.
66. Taylor, 1931, 129, 144.
67. Ibid., 229–30.
68. Noting that "Christian writers sneered that the Senate made gods," Bickerman, 1973, 13, adds, "Yet, they knew that the vote of the Senate was declarative and not constitutive."
69. Price, 1987, 56–105 (at 52 and 103); also Price, 1984, especially his helpful concluding reflections on "Rituals, Politics and Power" (234–48). For an analysis of the *consecratio*, of the iconography associated with it, and of its later transmutation in Christian hands, see MacCormack, 1981, 93–158. Cf. Bickerman, 1973, and Habicht, 1973.
70. Price, 1984, 234–48 (at 234 and 242).
71. Ibid., 235: "The emperor was honoured at ancestral religious festivals; he was placed within the gods' sanctuaries and temples; sacrifices to the gods invoked their protection for the emperor. There were also festivals, temples and sacrifices in honour of the emperor alone which are calqued on the traditional honours of the gods." For a powerful evocation of the continuing vitality of the "traditional religiousness," see Fox, 1986, 11–261.
72. Pleket, 1965; Price, 1987, 56–105.
73. Formidable evidentiary problems confront the scholar who is trying to assess the nature and impact of the imperial cult. Stressing "the fundamental diversity of cults honoring an emperor," Bickerman, 1973, 9, says that "a universal cult of the ruler did not exist in the Roman empire. Each city, each province, each group worshipped this or that sovereign according to its own discretion and ritual. In practice virtually every emperor was worshipped everywhere, but this coincidence does not negate the fundamental diversity of cults honoring an emperor." For the spread of such cults throughout the province, see, for the West, Fishwick, 1982–2005, which brings together a whole series of localized studies, and, for Asia Minor (in some ways the heartland of ruler worship), Price, 1984.
74. Price, 1984, 246–47.
75. Cerfaux and Tondriau, 1957, 377–79, 385, 407–8.

Chapter 3. Abrahamic Departures

1. Rousseau, *Du contrat social*, bk. 4, ch. 8; ed. Vaughan, 1947, 116.
2. Sabine, 1937, 161, "For purposes of historical accuracy," he adds, "there is no reason why the Christian era should be taken as beginning a new period in political thought."
3. Thus Dunning, 1902; Gettell, 1924; Murray, 1930; McIlwain, 1932; Doyle, 1933; Cat-

lin, 1939; Bhandari, 1963; Harmon, 1964; Beneyto Pérez, 1964; Strauss and Cropsey, 1987; Coleman, 2000.
4. Thus, e.g., Morrall, 1962; Ullmann, 1965; Monahan, 1987; Canning, 1996.
5. Janet, 1887, 1:263–319; Carlyle and Carlyle, 1903–36, 1:81–101; *Cambridge History of Greek and Roman Political Thought,* 2000, 637–50; *Cambridge History of Medieval Political Thought,* 1988, 11–21.
6. In this Janet, 1887, which devotes a whole chapter (1:263–319) to "L'Ancien et le Nouveau Testament," stands out as an exception to the rule. Though it is a protracted meditation in the philosophy of history rather than a simple history of political thought, the first volume of Eric Voegelin's monumental *Order and History,* 1956–57, (*Israel and Revolution*), see esp. 1:111–553, deserves to be emphasized, nevertheless, as a truly outstanding departure from the norm. For a basically sympathetic appraisal by a leading Old Testament scholar of the day, see Anderson, 1975.
7. Kantorowicz, 1946, 6. See below, ch. 7.
8. For a helpful introduction to the complex issues to which the latter gives rise, see the entries by George W. Ramsey, James W. Flanagan, and Walter Brueggeman, respectively, s.v. "Samuel" and "Samuel, Book of 1–2" ("Text, Composition, and Content" and "Narrative and Theology") in *Anchor Bible Dictionary,* 1992, 5:954–73.
9. Note the contrast between 1 Samuel 10:1, 12:1–5, and 1 Samuel 8:4–9, 19–22.
10. For the broader background on these schools, see Segal, 1998. Prominent among the scholars involved were M. Engnell, G. Widengren, A. R. Johnson, and S. H. Hooke. For a useful account of the development and unfolding of the "myth and ritual" approach in Hooke's earlier volumes—*Myth and Ritual* (1933) and *The Labyrinth* (1935)—as well as its affinities with the work of scholars like A. M. Hocart and Sigmund Mowinckel, see Hooke, 1958, 1–21. For a critical appraisal of the school, see Brandon, 1958, 261–91.
11. See above, ch. 2.
12. See, e.g., Mowinckel, 1956, 420–37, and the bibliography on 422n2.
13. Isaiah 9:6–7, 11:3–5, 42:1–7; cf. Jeremiah 23:5–6, 33:15–16.
14. Isaiah 42:1–7, 49:1–9, 50:4–9, 52:13–15, 53:1–12. Cf. the discussion in Dvornik, 1966, 1:339–47, and the literature referred to therein, especially Gadd, 1933, 40–67, which summarizes the unfolding of the New Year festival's ritual of atonement. Cf. above, ch. 2.
15. Voegelin, 1956–57, 1:282.
16. Though they disagreed about the number of psalms to be characterized as "royal," the discovery is associated especially with Gunkel, 1914, and the development of its implications with Mowinckel, 1922, esp. vol. 2. There are excellent discussions of the evolution of biblical scholarship on the whole matter in A. R. Johnson, 1958, 204–35, and, more recently, in Eaton, 1976. Cf. the pertinent essays by Mowinckel and others in section 5 of *The Sacral Kingship,* 1959, 283–365; in Voegelin, 1956–57, 1:282–310; and Johnson, 1967. The remarks that follow are dependent largely on the works cited above.
17. Johnson, 1958, 221–22.

18. The words quoted (cited also by Johnson at 222) are those of Mowinckel, 1922, 2:301.
19. Of what we know about the Temple and its furnishings, Voegelin, 1956–57, 1:320, comments that it "looks more like a connoisseur's collection of Near Eastern cosmological symbols than like the sanctuary of Yahweh who led his Chosen People from the Sheol of civilization into the freedom of his realm." Cf. Leeuwen, 1965, 80–81; Eliade, 1959, 12–18; l'Orange, 1959, 481–92.
20. Thus Mowinckel, 1922, 2:301, is quite prepared to describe the Hebrew king as "an incarnation of the national god."
21. North, 1932, 29–30 and 35.
22. Sigmund Mowinckel, 1959, 288–93 (at 286).
23. See above, ch. 2.
24. The words are those of G. von Rad and E. A. Speiser, respectively, and they are cited from the editors' introduction to O'Connor and Oakley, eds. (1969), 6. The essays gathered together in this volume provide an introductory discussion of the philosophical significance of the biblical doctrine of creation, of the underlying conception of God that it both presupposes and entails, and of its central impact over time on Western notions concerning the nature of man and the nature of nature.
25. For a learned and stimulating meditation on this issue and on the degree to which "the biblical account of creation ... is governed by a *historical* intention, even when it uses materials [like the *Enûma elish*] that were formerly mythical in their presuppositions," see B. W. Anderson, 1967. The words quoted occur at p. 40 (italics mine).
26. See above, ch. 2.
27. On the Sinaitic covenant, see the discussion in Buber, 1967, 121–35.
28. Thus James, 1959, 63–70 (at 68), where he adds: "The Hebrew king ruled by divine permission and the will of the people, just as the priesthood was secure only so long as it was faithful in the discharge of its duties. Therefore, both kingship and priesthood lacked stability, being only the instruments and agents of the covenant which was the real unifying force."
29. The most forceful statement to this effect is that made by Frankfort, 1948a, 337–44.
30. James, 1959, 67.
31. Mowinckel, 1959, 290.
32. Buber, 1967, 75.
33. See Crüsemann, 1978, 54–85.
34. Buber, 1967, 117–18.
35. "It is true that the explicit term 'the kingdom of God' is not found in the Old Testament or in Jewish literature outside the New Testament. . . . But the *idea* is there, nevertheless, at least in its major aspects"—thus Grant, 1959, 439–46 (at 440–41). Dvornik, 1966, 1:311–402.
36. Dvornik, 1966, 1:396–402.
37. Ibid., 1:433.
38. See esp. Brandon, 1967, and for a brief critique, Sweet, 1984, 1–9. "Revolutionary" interpretations of Jesus's message have a long history and have risen and fallen across time in harmony with the rise and fall in the contemporary vogue of revolutionary activism. For a fascinating account, see Bammel, 1984a, 11–68.

39. For a clear and concise teasing apart of the positions, respectively, of Hasidim, Scribes, Pharisees, Sadducees, Zealots, Essenes, and members of the Qumran sect, see Ehrlich, 1962, 105–23. Both Pharisees and Sadducees felt that the longed-for restoration of the kingdom would be the result of a divine initiative. In the interim, they were willing to acquiesce, with varying degrees of enthusiasm, in the continuance of Roman domination. Note, however, that the Pharisees themselves were divided between a peace party and those with stronger nationalist inclinations. On which, see Knox, 1949, 23–24.
40. I follow here Dvornik, 1966, 1:228–402; cf. Voegelin, 1956–57, 1:488–515.
41. As Grant, 1959, 445, properly insists: "It is scarcely possible to recognize the main stages in the development of the earliest Christianity, or its varieties of expression, apart from a thorough source-analysis of the gospels, a type of inquiry which involves textual criticism, philological analysis, study of literary style, exact comparison of parallel passages, historical research, and eventually form criticism (i.e., the attempt to recover and reconstruct the underlying oral tradition)."
42. Grant, 1959, 445.
43. For a thoroughgoing canvassing of all the pertinent texts, extra-scriptural as well as scriptural, along with a concise depiction of the current state of scholarly play, see Dennis C. Duling, s.v. "Kingdom of God, Kingdom of Heaven," in *Anchor Bible Dictionary*, 1992, 4:49–69.
44. See, e.g., Perrin, 1963, 58–78, and Perrin, 1976, 1–88, 194–204.
45. Küng, 1967, 87.
46. Cadoux, 1925, 9–10. Cf. Matthew 10:29–31, 16:24–26, 18:10–14. On this point, see the remarks of Dvornik, 1966, 1:426 and 376.
47. On this point, see the remarks of Dvornik, 1966, 1:426 and 376. See above, ch. 2. In relation to the royal title of "savior," Paul's epistles to Timothy and Titus may be read as a direct attack on the Hellenistic divinization of kings. For Christ alone is the Savior, the "one mediator...between God and men" (1 Timothy 2:1–6; Titus 3:1–8). For a more cautiously qualified reading, see Beskow, 1962, 71–73.
48. Which extended even to the point of his paying a Jewish temple tax, which he seems not to have thought legitimate (Matthew 17:24–27). See the helpful discussion by Harbury, 1984, 265–86.
49. The importance of the incident is reflected in the fact that all the synoptic Gospels report it: Matthew 22:17–21; Mark 12:14–17; Luke 20:22–25. Cf. Bruce, 1984, 249–63.
50. See above, "Prologue."
51. Thus Fustel de Coulanges, 1955, 394, having, I believe, placed undue stress on the contribution of the Stoic thinkers, still says of Christianity: "what was only the consolation of a few, it made the common good of humanity."
52. Thus Peter and the apostles, resisting the attempts of the Jewish authorities to prevent their preaching the Gospel, insisted that "we must obey God rather than man" (Acts 5:29; cf. 4:19).
53. Fustel de Coulanges, 1955, 393–94.
54. Cadoux, 1925, 97.

55. John 12:31, 14:30, 16:11; 1 John 5:18–19; and esp. Revelation 13, where Rome is represented as a beast deriving its authority from Satan and demanding worship from its subjects under penalty of death. See Cerfaux, 1959, 459–70.
56. Thus Romans 2:14–15: "When the Gentiles who have not the law do by nature what the law requires, they are a law to themselves.... They show that what the law requires is written in their hearts."
57. On the text in question, see Bammel, 1984b, 365–83 (at 369–70, 314–75).
58. Mark's Gospel is usually dated to the mid-sixties CE.
59. Thus Cullmann, 1957, 56–70. Over the centuries, the text has been read in many different and sometimes less positive ways—see Bammel, 1984b, 365.
60. See vol. 3 of this work, forthcoming.

Chapter 5. Patristic Affirmation

1. Cited from Hambly, 1968–91, 7:285.
2. For the early antipathy to kingship and the shifting but persistently conflicted Muslim views of the institution, see Crone, 2004, 148–64.
3. In their attempt to condemn the rule of the Umayyad caliphs, their Abbāsid rivals had condemned the use of the title *malik* (king) and the term *mulk* (kingship). But *malik* had earlier been viewed as perfectly acceptable and used as a synonym for caliph. See Ringgren, 1959, 738.
4. For the great importance attending to the Persian inheritance see, in addition to Crone, 2004, 148–64, Al-Azmeh, 1997.
5. Al-Azmeh, 1997, 63–65, where he adds (at 63): "It is now anachronistic to presume that the Rightly-Guided Caliphate (632–61), the primitive proto-Muslim polity at Medina and later briefly at Kēfa, had produced statutes and forms of kingship of any determinative or definitive character that informed the later crystallization of Muslim politics. The Muslim religion and the texts and exemplary genealogies that are ascribed to the formative period of Islam were later elaborations created over many generations in the light of conditions prevailing in polities the Arabs set up from Iraq and Syria. Elements derived from the slight Arab tradition of kingship, heavily impregnated by Byzantine and Iranian paradigms, were combined with the enduring heritage of Semitic religion, priesthood, and kingship."
6. Rosenthal, 1958, 25.
7. On the *Shari'a*, see Rosenthal, 1958, 8.
8. Rosenthal, 1958, 26, 8–9; cf. Crone, 2004, 10–16, 389–90, 393–98; Black, 2001, 11–14; cf. Al-Azmeh, 1997, 15. It should be noted, however, that under the de facto rule of sultans, an essentially secular title (sultan = power), there developed in practice (theoretical formulations to the contrary) a quasi-separation between the "political" and the "religious."
9. Crone, 2004, 163–64.
10. Ringgren, 1959, 738, 740, 746; cf. Al-Azmeh, 1997, 78–79, 156–57.
11. Ringgren, 1959, 738.

12. Black, 2001, 39–43.
13. Al-Azmeh, 1997, 158–62.
14. The reference is to the passage from Hobbes, *Leviathan*, pt. 4, ch. 45, which appears as the epigraph to this book.
15. Pohlsander, 1996, 72: "In his presence a respectful silence was expected; hence the ushers were called *silentiarii*. His advisors stood when meeting with him in council; hence they became known as the *consistorium*.
16. See below, ch. 6.
17. For which, see above, chs. 2 and 3. Arguing, however, that apart from the book of Revelation, "there is no evidence in the New Testament of a clear and unambiguous attack on the Roman Empire," Per Beskow, 1962, 71–73, has questioned any polemical intent in such borrowings of Hellenistic royal terminology and treated them rather as a case of simple "borrowing... through contact with the Hellenistic Judaism of the Diaspora."
18. See above, ch. 3.
19. As early as 155, an account of the martyrdom of St. Polycarp betrays a revealing emphasis on the regality of Christ and applies to him the Hellenistic royal titles of *basileus* (king) and shepherd. Beskow, 1962, 178, 59–60.
20. Dvornik, 1966, 2:589; Beskow, 1962, 72.
21. Dvornik, 1966, 2:558–65 (at 565). In addition to Dvornik, I base my remarks here on Goodenough, 1938, 1–120, and Beskow, 1962, 212–16.
22. See above, ch. 2.
23. For Moses, see Beskow, 1962, 188, and for Melchizedek, Goodenough, 1938, 99.
24. This statement occurs in a fragment from one of Philo's last works that is quoted in a twelfth-century source. I cite it from Dvornik, 1966, 2:563.
25. For an extended discussion, see Wolfson, 1948, 1:216–94 (summary statement at 291). Cf. Sandmel, 1979, esp. 96–97.
26. Beskow, 1962, 188.
27. Dvornik, 1966, 2:594–600 (the words quoted appear at 600); cf. Beskow, 1962, 213–19. For a brief introduction to Clement's thinking, see Chadwick, 1966, 31–65.
28. Dvornik, 1966, 2:596–597, 600.
29. For brief introductions to his thinking, see Chadwick, 1966, 66–123; Beskow, 1962, 219–30; Dvornik, 1966, 2:600–606
30. Farina, 1966, 260 and 279, proclaims Eusebius to have been "the first political theologian of the Christian church," and his "the first Christian political theology."
31. See above, ch. 3.
32. Origen, *Contra Celsum* 2:30; translation cited from Dvornik, 1966, 2:604.
33. Thus George Scholarius, a fifteenth-century Byzantine theologian—see Chadwick, 1966, 95. The surviving evidence for the actual fourth-century teaching of Arius (hence "Arianism") is fragmentary in nature and much of it drawn from the reports of his opponents. But what he appears to have taught, in effect, was that Christ the Son was not of the same substance as the Father but a created being (though not nec-

essarily like other creatures). For the development of Trinitarian doctrine and where Origen stood in that complex process, see Pelikan, 1971–89, 1:172–225 (esp. 191).
34. Thus Baynes, 1934, 13–18.
35. Williams, 1951b, i, 3–33 (at 14); ii, 3–26; cf. Cranz, 1952, 47–65.
36. For Eusebius's life and works, see esp. Barnes, 1981 and 1994. For his political theology I am indebted particularly to Baynes, 1934; Peterson, 1935; Berkhof, 1939; Williams, 1951b; Cranz, 1952; Beskow, 1962; Dvornik, 1966; Farina, 1966.
37. Pertinent also, if in more indirect fashion, are Eusebius's two apologetical treatises, *The Preparation for the Gospel* and *The Proof of the Gospel* (both written after the ending in 313 of the great persecution that Diocletian had launched), as well as his *Theophany*, written in 325 after Constantine had succeeded in extending his rule over the eastern provinces, thereby uniting once more the entire empire.
38. Thus, e.g., Robin Lane Fox speculates that in the late third century the old gods were still taken very much for granted, that Christians may still have constituted no more than 4–5 percent of the empire's population, that Constantine ruled over "an overwhelmingly pagan majority," and that a century had to elapse before "the numerical balance of the population [was to] tip decisively in the Christians' favour."—Fox, 1986, 317, 577, 592, 627, 658, 666. Mark Edwards, on the other hand, asserts that "it is probable that by the mid-fourth century Christians made up more than half the entire population of the empire" (Edwards, 2006, 137–58 [at 137]). And Barnes 1981, 196, believes that "in most eastern cities and provinces" during the Constantinian era "Christians were either a majority of the people or an influential minority," so that "a pagan emperor could no longer govern without the acquiescence and goodwill of his Christian subjects."
39. For discussions of the shift in the interpretation of Constantine's conversion, see Barnes, 1981; Barnes, 1994; Odahl, 2004, 280–84; Drake, 2006, 111–36 (at 113–16).
40. Barnes, 1994, 39–57 (at 47–48); cf. Barnes, 1981, 265–67; Maraval, 2001, 19; Drake, 2000, 357–67.
41. Barnes, 1981, 136.
42. I refer to the text of the *Life of Constantine* as *VC* (*Vita Constantini*), to be found in Winkelmann, 1975, 1–151, and that of the *Oration in Praise of Constantine* as *LC* (*Laus Constantini*), to be found in Heikel ed., 1902, 193–259. I have made use of and cite the recent English translations of the *VC* by Cameron and Hall, 1999, and of the *LC* by Drake, 1975. For *The Proof of the Gospel*, I cite from the English translation in Ferrar, 1920; the Greek text is in Heikel, 1913, 1–492.
43. Peterson, 1935, 89ff., 97; Berkhof, 1939,53–58; Drake, 2000,363–67.
44. *LC* 16:2–3; ed. Heikel, 1902, 248–49; trans. Drake, 1975, 119–20. Maraval, 2001, prints at 211–12 a very useful "table de concordances" identifying the multiple parallelisms between what Eusebius had to say in *LC* 11–18 and in his *Theophany*.
45. *LC* 13:15; 16:4 and 6; ed. Heikel, 1902, 240–41, 249; trans. Drake, 1975, 114–15, 120. Also *Proof of the Gospel*, bk. 3, ch. 7; ed. Heikel, 1913, 145; trans. Ferrar, 1920, 1:161.
46. *LC* 16:4; ed. Heikel, 1902, 248–49; trans. Drake, 1975, 120.
47. *Proof of the Gospel*, bk. 8, ch. 3; ed. Heikel, 1913, 394; trans. Ferrar, 1920, 2:140–41.

48. *LC* 11:1, and 18:1–3; ed. Heikel, 1902, 226–27 and 259; trans. Drake, 1975, 103 and 126–27. Thus what is being referred to here is not simply Constantine's vision before the battle of the Milvian Bridge, the account of which in *VC*, bk. 1, chs. 28–32 (ed. Winkelman, 1975, 30–32; trans. Cameron and Hall, 1999, 80–82) some have maintained was not the work of Eusebius.
49. *VC*, bk. 1, ch. 44; ed. Winkelmann, 1975, 38; trans. Cameron and Hall, 1999, 87.
50. Thus *VC*, bk. 1, chs. 12, 20, 38, and 39; ed. Winkelmann, 1975, 21, 26, 34–36; trans. Cameron and Hall, 1999, 73–74, 77, 84–86. For a useful comment on this "sustained comparison of Constantine and Moses," see Cameron and Hall, 1999, Introduction, 35–39.
51. *VC*, bk. 3, ch. 15; ed. Winkelmann, 1975, 88–89; trans. Cameron and Hall, 1999, 127.
52. *LC* 7:12–13; ed. Heikel, 1902, 215; trans. Drake, 1975, 97. Berkhof, 1939, 58, identifies the parallel argument in the *Theophania* 2:83.
53. Thus Beskow, 1962, 318; cf. 261–67, 189–94. Similarly Farina, 1966, 276–78, and Dvornik, 1966, 2:621.
54. Given the fragmentary nature of the evidence and the eclecticism of those who were usually called Arian, it is hard to be confident on this issue. What is clear enough is that Eusebius was often, in his own lifetime, labeled as an Arian and that modern historians have often been content to accept that labeling at face value. It is true that Eusebius himself accepted the Nicene creedal formula, but he seems to have found it possible to interpret it in a subordinationist fashion. See Barnes, 1981, 171, where he notes that in the *Second Theophany* Eusebius described "the substance of the divine Word" as "different from and inferior to the 'first and uncreated' substance of the Father."
55. *LC* 1:1 and 6:7; ed. Heikel, 1902, 196, 208; trans. Drake, 1975, 84 and 92.
56. *LC* 11:12; ed. Heikel, 1902, 227; trans. Drake, 1975, 105.
57. *LC* 13:16, 14:1 and 4; ed. Heikel, 1902, 241–42; trans. Drake, 1975, 115.
58. *LC* 14 and 15; ed. Heikel, 1902, 241–48; trans. Drake, 1975, 115–19. Commenting on these explanations, Maraval, 2001, 45, notes with justice: "En bon origénien, Eusèbe est d'abord sensible de la fonction révélatrice du Verbe incarné, la plus important à ses yeux."
59. In order of citation, *LC* 11:11, 6:7, 2:4; ed. Heikel, 1902, 227, 208, 199; trans. Drake, 1975, 105, 92, 86.
60. *LC* 4–5, 1:6; ed. Heikel, 1902, 202–206, 198; trans. Drake, 1975, 88–90, 85.
61. *LC* 2:4–5; ed. Heikel, 1902, 199; trans. Drake, 1975, 105.
62. *VC*, bk. 4:65; ed. Winkelmann, 1975, 147; trans. Cameron and Hall, 1999, 179. Upon learning of Constantine's death, Eusebius says, "Tribunes and centurions wept aloud for their Saviour, Protector and Benefactor, and the rest of the troops, suitably attired, mourned like flocks for their Good Shepherd."
63. *LC* 2:5; ed. Heikel, 1902, 200; trans. Drake, 1975, 86.
64. Thus Maraval, 2001, 66 (quoting the judgment of G. Padskalky) and 55.
65. Williams, 1951b, (i), 4.
66. Beskow, 1962, 319; cf. Williams, 1951b, (i), 15–16.

67. See *VC*, bk. 3, ch. 15; ed. Winkelmann, 1975, 88–89; trans. Cameron and Hall, 1999, 127. Cf. Cranz, 1952, 47–64, and esp. 56: "the Constantinian Empire ... is an image on earth of the archetypal kingship of the logos in heaven."
68. Peterson, 1935, esp. 94–100. He alludes (158n168) to the earlier work by Schmitt, 1922; 2nd ed. 1934. In his earlier article "Kaiser Augustus," Peterson, 1933, 289–99, made more explicit the fact that his point of departure was Schmitt's notion of "political theology" (289), and he characterized as theologically "weak" or "problematic" the whole "Augustus-theology" or project of aligning the monarchy of Rome with that of God. Cf. Peterson, 1935, 57, where he depicted Philo, by virtue of pursuing that project, as having got himself into a "theologico-political problem."
69. Thus Williams, 1951b; Sansterre, 1972, 189–95. Cf. Berkhof, 1947, 191–218.
70. I refer to Williams, 1951b—the summary at (i), 9–10, and (ii), 21–22, of the case he lays out in the two articles. For "Byzantinismus" see Burckhardt, 1949, 345; Berkhof, 1947, 83–105.
71. Though Maraval, 2001, 62, observes that "on ne peut ... dire que le subordinationisme d'Eusèbe soit à l'origine de sa théologie politique, dont les conceptions sont certainement partageés par beaucoup d'evêques de son êpoque, qu'ils soient ou non partisans du *consubstantiel* de Niceé." Cf. the comments of Sansterre, 1972, 193–95.
72. Asking whether Peterson's theory "is in fact anything more than a construction without historical foundation" and extending his critique of the approach to the version elaborated by Williams, 1951b, Beskow, 1962, 315–19, questions whether "Arianism as such was state-church minded" or whether "the Nicene theology *per se* led to a demand for the independence of the Church." For a further series of appraisals of Peterson's theory, see Schindler et al., 1978.
73. Beskow, 1962, 323 and 319.
74. Following here the detailed account in Dvornik, 1966, 2:626–723.
75. Thus Geanakoplos, 1966, 55–83, after a lucid reconsideration of "the problem of Caesaropapism," concludes that we would be wise to drop that term as "a modern western coinage" with no roots in the Byzantine literature and as one that is "not only inaccurate but extremely misleading." Something similar may be said of Burckhardt's term "Byzantinism," which he used pejoratively, evoking parallels with Islam.
76. I base my observations on Byzantine political thinking primarily on Barker, 1957; Geanakoplos, 1966; Dvornik, 1966, 2:659–723; Runciman, 1977; Anastos, 2001; Nicol, 1988; and Dagron, 2003.
77. See the succinct accounts in Runciman, 1977, 51–76, and Dagron, 2003, 158–91.
78. Geanakoplos, 1966, 55–83; Dagron, 2003.
79. *VC*, bk. 4:8–13; ed. Winckelmann, 1975, 122–25; trans. Cameron and Hall, 1999, 156–68.
80. Geanakoplos, 1966, 23.
81. Dvornik, 1966, 2:698–99, 782–86.
82. Ibid., 2:772–78.

83. For conflicting modern commentaries on Gelasius, see Carlyle and Carlyle, 1903–36, 1:184–93; Caspar, 1930–33, 2:65–81, 753–58; Ziegler, 1942; Ullmann, 1955, 14–28; Dvornik, 1966, 2:802–9.
84. *De anathematis vinculo*, ed. Schwartz, 1934, 7–15 (at 14); trans. Tierney, 1964, 14–15.
85. See, below, ch. 9.
86. *Epistula ad Anastasium*, ed. Schwartz, 1934, 19–24 (at 20); trans. Tierney, 1964, 13–14.
87. Thus Caspar, 1930–33, 2:65–71, 735–55; Ullmann, 1955, 14–28; Nelson, 1967, 154–62.
88. Dagron, 2003, 302, has denied in the use here of the words *auctoritas* and *potestas* the presence of any "coherent distinction." "Western historiography," he adds, "has seen an ideological revolution where perhaps there had been no more than skilful rhetoric."
89. I incline, then, to the interpretations advanced by Caspar, 1930–33; Dvornik, 1951; and Ensslin, 1955.
90. Dvornik, 1966, 2:808–15.
91. Dagron, 2003, 158–66.
92. Ibid., 6–7. After Basil I (d. 886), Leo VI (d. 912), and Constantine Porphyrogenitus (d. 959), he says, "there was no more speculation about Melchizedek; that direct route towards the [imperial] claim to priesthood, if not entirely closed, was definitely prohibited."
93. Dagron, 2003, 116.
94. Thus, unlike ordinary laymen, emperors could (and did) bless the congregation and preach to them, enter the sanctuary of the church, and at the communion, receive both bread and wine in the same way as did ordained priests; Geanakoplos, 1966, 69–73.
95. Cited from Nicol, 1988, 71; cf. Dagron, 2003, 252–55.
96. For this distinction between the *potestas ordinis* and *potestas jurisdictionis* as well as its history and the literature pertaining to it, see *Dictionnaire de droit canonique*, 1935–65, 8:98–100, s.v. "Pouvoirs de l'église."
97. I draw this descriptive phrase from Barker, 1957, 12.
98. Baynes, 1934, 13; cf. Nicol, 1988.
99. *Corpus Juris Civilis*, 1899–1902, 3:53 (*Novellae*, 7, 2, 1); I cite the English translation in Dvornik, 1966, 2:816.
100. This is the claim advanced by G. Ostrogorsky and cited by Geanakoplos, 1966, 63n22.
101. Dvornik, 1966, 2:644–46; Grabar, 1971, 90–96.
102. Citing the words of Dvornik, 1966, 2:643; cf. Barnes, 1984, 26–36; 1981, 258–59. For the text of the letter itself and Eusebius's comment, see *VC*, bk. 4, ch. 8, 9, and 14; ed. Winckelmann, 1975, 122–25; trans. Cameron and Hall, 1999, 156–58.
103. I cite the translation in Barker, 1957, 194–95.
104. Toynbee, 1948, 182–83.

105. Obolensky, 1950, 59; cf. Summers, 1962, 129–31.
106. Hosking, 2001, 85, 99–107, 132.
107. Cherniavsky, 1959, 462–66, 468, 471, 473, 476; cf. Hosking, 2001, 108–9. T. Anderson, 1967, 82, notes the degree to which, after the reign of Ivan IV ("The Terrible," 1533–84), the title *autokrator* came to be understood as connoting not simply "independence from external or foreign powers" but also "independence from internal, domestic restraints, authority, unlimited by laws, institutions, or customs."
108. For the complexity of the notion of the third Rome, its rootage in clerical ideology, and the caution with which Moscow secular officials approached it, see Hosking, 2001, 99–107, 132.
109. T. Anderson, 1967, 28–29; cf. Dvornik, 1956, 71–121.
110. The words cited are those of the nineteenth-century Russian poet Vasili Zhukovsky and of the novelist Nicolai Gogol. See T. Anderson, 1967, 173–88 (quotations on p. 174.).
111. Noting that the Byzantine ideal was to become the Russian ideal, too, T. Anderson, 1967, 36–37, claims that both in institutional terms and in the popular mind "mutual aid linked . . . church and state . . . together irrevocably."

Chapter 6. Patristic Reservation

1. See above, ch. 3.
2. Here I rely mainly on Peterson, 1935; Löwith, 1949, esp. 160–81; Mommsen, "St. Augustine and the Christian Idea of Progress: The Background of the City of God," "Aponius and Orosius on the Significance of the Epiphany," "Orosius and Augustine," all reprinted in Mommsen, 1959, 265–348; Dvornik, 1966, 2:581–610, 672–83, 724–28.
3. Thus Osborn, 1997; cf. Barnes, 1971; Fredouille, 1984.
4. Thus Cochrane, 1957, 213, commenting on Tertullian *Apologeticus* 21:24–25: "Sed et Caesares credidissent super Christo, sicut Caesares non essent necessari saeculo, aut si et Christiani potuissent esse Caesares," ed. and trans. Glover, 1931, 112–13.
5. Tertullian *Apol.* 32:3, 33:1–3; ed. and trans. Glover, 1931, 154–57. Cf. *Liber ad Scapulum,* cap. 2; in *CSEL* 76:10.
6. Tertullian *Apol.* 31:3, 30:4; ed. and trans. Glover, 1931, 154–55, 150–51.
7. See his *De pallio,* cap. 2, § 7; *CSEL* 76:110.
8. O'Donovan and O'Donovan, 1999, 66.
9. I am mainly indebted here to Markus's succinct account in "The Latin Fathers," in *Cambridge History of Medieval Political Thought,* 1988, 92–102, and to Markus, 1970, 22–32, and Dvornik, 1966, 2:673–83.
10. Thus *Epistola* 75a (*Sermon against Auxentius*), §§ 35–36; *CSEL* 82, pars X, tome 3, 106: "Tributum Caesaris est, non negatur, ecclesia dei est, Caesari utique non debet addici, quia just Caesaris non potest dei templum. [§ 36] Quod cum honorificentia imperataris dictum nemo potest negare. Quid enim honorificentius quam ut

imperator ecclesiae filius esse dicatur? Quod cum dicitur sine peccato dicitur, cum gratia dictur. *Imperator enim intra ecclesiam non supra ecclesiam est;* bonus enim imperator quae rit auxilium ecclesiae, non refutat" (italics mine).

11. *Epistola* 18:7–8, 28–30; in *PL* 16:973–74, 980. Markus, 1970, 27, comments that "Ambrose saw the new world of the Christian Empire coming into being, and he wishes to hasten the completion of the process."
12. Markus, 1988, 97.
13. Peterson, 1935, 80–88.
14. *Enarratio in psalmum 45*, 21; in *PL* 14:1143, where, describing the unification of the Roman world, he says: "Didicerunt omnes homines sub uno terrarum imperio viventes, unius Dei omnipotentis imperium fideliо eloquio confiterri." Dvornik, 1996, 2:281, comments: "The monarchic argument of one God, one empire, one emperor is restated.... [T]he Empire ... was God's chosen instrument for the spread of the faith.... No Roman Christian of Ambrose's time could have failed to identify the interests of the Church with those of the Empire."
15. See above ch. 5.
16. Markus, 1970, 29.
17. Prudentius *Contra orationem Symmachi* 2:620–25; ed. and trans. Thomson, 1949–53, 2:56–57.
18. Ibid., 2:619–20, 634–36; ed. and trans. Thomson, 1949–53, 2:56–57.
19. Ibid., 1:587–88, 506–10; ed. and trans. Thomson, 1949–53, 2:394–95, 388–89.
20. *Quaestiones veteris et novi testamenti,* cap. 91 and 35; *CSEL* 50:157 and 63.
21. For the text of the *Historiarum adversum paganos,* see Zangemeister, ed., 1889. English translation in Raymond, 1936. Helpful commentaries in Peterson, 1935, 88–93; Löwith, 1949, 174–81; Mommsen, 1959, 299–348.
22. See Mommsen, 1959, 332.
23. *Historiarum adversum paganos,* bk. 1:1; ed. Zangemeister, 1889, 4; trans. Raymond, 1936, 33.
24. Ibid.
25. *Historiarum adversum paganos,* bks. 1:prologue, 2:19, 3:20, 4:pref., 5:1; ed. Zangemeister, 1889, 2, 60–62, 89, 97, 141; trans. Raymond, 1936, 31, 104, 140, 152, 205. Cf. Löwith, 1949, 178 and 180.
26. *Historiarum adversum paganos,* bk. 7:41; ed. Zangemeister, 1889, 267; trans. Raymond, 1936, 393.
27. *Historiarum adversum paganos,* bk. 2:28, 7:2; ed. Zangemeister, 1889, 3, 235–36; trans. Raymond, 1936, 72, 320–21.
28. *Historiarum adversum paganos,* bk. 6:1; ed. Zangemeister, 1889, 186–87; trans. Raymond, 1936, 263.
29. *Historiarum adversum paganos,* bks. 3:8, 6:1, 6:20, ed. Zangemeister, 1889, 23, 186–87, 226–27; trans. Raymond, 1936, 120, 263, 310–12.
30. Mommsen, 1959, 340–41.
31. Peterson, 1935, 88, cf. 92.
32. Mommsen, 1959, 348.

33. Alfred the Great translated it into Anglo-Saxon for the instruction of his people, and in the East, the caliph of Cordova, having been presented with a copy by the Byzantine emperor, had it translated into Arabic. See Dvornik, 1966, 2:726.
34. Otto of Freising, *Chronicon*, 3:6; in *MGH: Ottonis Epicopi Frisingensis Opera*, 1:131; trans. Mierow 2002, 229. See Mierow's introduction, pp. 23–25, for the use Otto made of Orosius.
35. Löwith, 1949, 139–40, correctly aligns his theology of history rather with Eusebius than with Augustine. See Bossuet, *Discours sur l'histoire universelle*, pt. 1, Dixième époque; ed. Louandre, 1869, 90–91.
36. *Policraticus* 7:18, 788c; ed. Webb, 1909, 2:363.
37. Thus, e.g., Raymond, 1936, Introduction, states that "the basic principles upon which he founded his philosophy of history were those which he held in common with his guide and friend St. Augustine" (10).
38. *Historiarum adversum paganos*, bk. 1:prologue; ed. Zangemeister, 1889, 1–3; trans. Raymond, 1936, 29–31.
39. At the end of the *Historiarum adversum paganos*, bk. 7:43, and addressing Augustine, Orosius had concluded: "If you publish them [the histories], they must be regarded favorably by you; if you destroy them, they must be regarded unfavorably"; ed. Zangemeister, 1889, 301; trans. Raymond, 1936 398. For the dedication, see Zangemeister, ed., 1889, 1–3; trans. Raymond, 1936, 29–31.
40. *Confessiones*, bk. 8; in *CSEL* 33:169–96. Here I am primarily dependent on Brown (2000), where the epilogue analyzes an intriguing collection of hitherto unknown letters and sermons; O'Donnell, 2005; Chadwick, 1986, where, while observing that Augustine often alludes to "the Christian world," he notes that the term "Christian empire" appears but this once in his writings; Markus, 1972. And for Augustine's political thinking, Mommsen, 1959, 263–348; Deane, 1963; Markus, 1970 and 1988. There is a useful listing of Augustine's works with their locations in the several volumes of the *Patrologia Latina* (PL) and (where applicable) of the *Corpus scriptorum ecclesiasticorum Latinorum* in the appendix to Portalié, 1960, 401–6.
41. O'Donnell, 2005, 229; cf. 74–75.
42. Markus, 1970, 31 and 49–50.
43. *De gratia Christi et de peccato originali* 2:18; *CSEL* 42:179. Cf. Chadwick, 1986, 99.
44. The words are those of Augustine, *Enarrationes in Psalmos* 149:7: "Chorus Christi jam totus mundus est," in *CCSL* 39:2182.
45. Thus O'Donnell, 2005, 296, who stresses in general (234, 271) that "the Augustine we know... [was] transformed by Africa and Donatism." Cf. for a similar emphasis, Markus, 1970, 115; Ratzinger, 1954.
46. Markus, 1970, 81.
47. *DCD* (*De civitate dei*) 18:46; in *CSSL* 48:643–45; trans. Bettenson, 1972, 827–28. In what follows, and with no more than a few exceptions, I draw from Bettenson the English translations of texts cited from *The City of God*.
48. The words cited are from Marcus, 2006, 36. I follow here Marcus's account and the distinctions he draws between "the sacred," "the profane," and "the secular"; see

esp. 4–8, 14–17, 36–37, 60–64. In this set of lectures Marcus attempts interestingly to ascertain how Augustine's "political" stance should be positioned in relation to the range of views on modern liberal society articulated by such philosophers as Alasdair MacIntyre, Charles Taylor, and Michael Walzer as well as by such "theopoliticians" as Stanley Hauerwas, Oliver O'Donovan, and John Howard Yoder.

49. Markus, 1970, 32–34, 49–52; cf. Theodor E. Mommsen, "Augustine on Progress," in Mommsen, 1959, 265–98 (esp. 285–95).
50. The words are those of Markus, 1970, 53.
51. Cf. the pertinent comments in Figgis, 1921, 5–7.
52. *DCD* 10:32; in *CCSL* 47:313–34; trans. Bettenson, 1972, 425–26.
53. *DCD* 11:3; in *CCSL* 48:323; trans. Bettenson, 1972, 431.
54. *DCD* 11:1; in *CCSL* 48:321–22; trans. Bettenson, 1972, 430. The division of the work into two parts, "negative" and "positive," was suggested by Augustine himself in a letter sent to a friend but discovered and printed in the twentieth century in Lambot, 1939, 109–21.
55. Norman H. Baynes, "The Political Ideas of St. Augustine's *De civitate dei,*" in Baynes, 1955, 288–306 (at 288).
56. *DCD* 18:2; *CCSL*, 48:593; trans. Bettenson, 1972, 762. Cf. *DCD* 15:4; *CCSL* 48:456–57; trans. Bettenson, 1972, 599, where he speaks of the *civitas terrena* as "generally divided against itself by litigation, by wars, by battles, by the pursuit of victories," and adds that "if *any section of that city* has risen up in war against another part, it seeks to be victorious over other nations . . ." (italics mine).
57. *DCD* 13:16, 19:23, 19:19; *CCSL* 48:396, 694–95, 686; trans. Bettenson, 1972, 524, 889, 879.
58. *DCD* 20:9. "Ergo et nunc ecclesia regnum Christi est regnumque coelorum," and a little later, "ecclesia, quae nunc etiam est regnum Christi"; *CCSL* 48:716–717, cf. 718; trans. Bettenson, 1972, 915–16, cf. 917. For a discussion of Augustine's identification of *civitas dei,* heavenly kingdom and church, see Cranz, 1952.
59. See above ch. 2.
60. Thus McIlwain, 1932, 154–61; Sabine, 1937, 189–93; Wilks, 1967, 489–510.
61. *DCD* 20:9; *CCSL* 48:715–19; trans. Bettenson, 1972, 914–18.
62. *DCD* 15:1: "Superna est enim sanctorum civitas, quamvis hic pariat cives, in quibus peregrinatur, donec regni ejus tempus adveniat"; cf. 14:13; *CCSL* 48:454, 435; trans. Bettenson, 1972, 595–96, 573. Cf. Markus, 1970, 59–62, where, emphasizing the "radical dichotomy" between the two cities, he rejects as invalid any "antecedent presumption that the heavenly city can be equated with the Church and the earthly with the state." Instead, the two cities are, he says, in a sense "eschatological entities."
63. Augustine's teaching on the Fall, grace, free will, and predestination has been the focus, over the centuries, of persistent and wide-ranging disagreement. For a helpful summary statement, see Portalié, 1960, 177–229.
64. For Pelagius and Augustine's role in the Pelagiam controversy, see Pelikan, 1971–89, 1:313–31. The two chapters on the theology and psychology of fallen man in Deane,

1963, 13–77, cite and analyze the relevant texts in Augustine and point up their implications for his political thinking. These chapters together constitute a clear, sober, and well-supported statement of the viewpoint presented here.

65. As Augustine reminds us in the *Confessions* 10:32: in *CSEL* 33:262–63, trans. Pine-Coffin 1961, 232–38, the powers of our inner selves are "veiled in darkness" even to ourselves, so that "no one should be confident that although he has been able to pass from a worse state to a better, he may not also pass from a better state to a worse."
66. *DCD* 10:6 and 7, 11:9, 12:9, 15:1; *CCSL* 47:278–80, 48:328–30, 363–64, 453–54; trans. Bettenson, 1972, 379–81, 438–40, 481–83, 595–96.
67. *DCD* 12:1, 14:13; *CCSL* 48:355–56, 435; trans. Bettenson, 1972, 471, 573.
68. *DCD* 1:35; *CCSL* 47:33–34; trans. Bettenson, 1972, 45–46.
69. *DCD* 15:1 and 2, cf. 15:8: *CCSL* 48:454–55, 462–65; trans. Bettenson, 1972, 596–97, 607–9. See the helpful analysis of *DCD* 15:2 in Cranz, 1950, 215–25; reprinted in Markus, 1972, 404–21. Cranz emphasizes (at 410) that Augustine "refers to the specifically Christian society either as city of God or as heavenly kingdom or as *ecclesia*" and views "the three concepts . . . [as] to some extent interchangeable."
70. *DCD* 1:35; *CCSL* 47:33; trans. Bettenson, 1972, 45: "While the City of God is on pilgrimage in this world, she has in her midst some who are united with her in the participation in the sacraments, but who will not join with her in the eternal destiny of the saints."
71. *Enarrationes in Psalmos* 61:8; in *CCSL* 39:778, Deane (1963), 31 cites this passage from Schaff, 1886–90, 8:253. The words in parentheses are his clarifying additions. For related texts, see *DCD* 1:35, 10:32, 11:1, 15:2 and 3; *CCSL* 47:33–34, 313–14, 321–22, 454–56; trans. Bettenson, 1972, 45–46, 426, 430, 595–98.
72. *DCD* 14:13; *CCSL* 48:435; trans. Bettenson, 1972, 573. Cf. Deane, 1963, 11–12, where he argues that what Augustine did was to transfer "the classical vision of the state . . . to the heavenly city."
73. Thus Paul, Romans 2:14–15: "When Gentiles who have not the law do by nature what the law requires, they are a law to themselves, even though they do not have the law. They show that what the law requires is written in their hearts." References to the natural law abound in Augustine—see Deane, 1963, 85–91 and the texts he cites in nn35–62, pp. 280–87.
74. In all of this, I follow the descriptive analysis in Deane, 1963, ch. 3, 78–115.
75. *DCD* 13:13–15; *CCSL* 48:395–96; trans. Bettenson, 1972, 522–23. Cf. Markus, 1970, 72–104, with his insistence (at 84) that, from the late 390s onward, "Never again did . . . [Augustine] consider the institutions of society and government as agencies concerned with helping men to achieve the right order in the world. Their task was now to minimise disorder."
76. *DCD* 5:19; *CCSL* 47:155; trans. Bettenson, 1972, 213.
77. *DCD* 19:17; *CCSL* 48:684; trans. Bettenson, 1972, 877.
78. *DCD* 19:26; *CCSL* 48:696–97; trans. Bettenson, 1972, 892.
79. *DCD* 19:17; *CCSL* 48:684; trans. Bettenson, 1972, 877.
80. *DCD* 19:17; *CCSL* 48:685; trans. Bettenson, 1972, 878.

81. *DCD* 8:19; *CCSL* 47:236; trans. Bettenson, 1972, 325–26.
82. *DCD* 19:5; *CCSL* 49:669; trans. Bettenson, 1972, 858.
83. See, especially, *DCD* 19:5, 6, and 7; *CCSL,* 48:669–72; trans. Bettenson, 1972, 858–62.
84. See above, ch. 5.
85. Referring in *DCD* 2:21 (*CCSL,* 47:52–55; trans. Bettenson, 1972, 72–75) to the twin definitions of a "people" (*populus*) and a commonwealth (*respublica*), which Cicero attributes to Scipio in his *De Republica,* Augustine notes that Scipio defines a commonwealth as "the weal of the community (*rem populi*)," and defines the community (*populus*) as not any and every association of the populace, but "an association united by a common sense of right and a community of interest (*populum autem non omnem coetum multitudinis, sed coetum juris consensu et utilitatis communione sociatum esse determinat*)." For the general attitude of the fathers to this question, see Carlyle and Carlyle, 1903–36, 1:161–74. They comment (at 161) that "the Fathers sometimes think of coercive government as being a punishment, as well as a remedy, for sin; but, normally, they think of the State as an instrument for securing and preserving justice." They go on, however (1:164–70), to portray Augustine as a startling exception to this generalization.
86. The disagreement in question hinges primarily (though not exclusively) on the interpretation of a series of passages occurring at *DCD* 2:21, 19:21, 23, and 24, 4:4, and 15:8; *CCSL* 47:52–55, 48:687–89, 690–96, 47:101–2, 48:463–65; trans. Bettenson, 1972, 72–75, 881–83, 889–91, 139, and 607. These texts are best read in the order just given.
87. Thus Wilks, 1967, 489–510 (at 491). He concludes (at 510) with the bold assertion that "Augustine's hopes might be said to be a prophetic indication of the future course of development of the papal-hierocratic system." This "clericalist" interpretation is aligned with the common medieval reading of these passages. For earlier versions, see Bernheim, 1896, and Combès, 1927, 46, 91–92; cf. 427–522. In the Anglophone world, and in critique of the interpretations advanced by the Carlyles and John Neville Figgis, McIlwain, 1932, 154–60, gave vigorous expression to this same "clericalist" approach, noting tartly (at 259) that if "no later writer believed a true commonwealth could exist without justice," this was "not, as Dr. Figgis intimates, because the political writers of the Middle Ages either disregarded or rejected the view of St. Augustine on this important point. It was because their interpretation of St. Augustine was not in accordance with that of Dr. Figgis." In this McIlwain was echoed influentially by Sabine, 1937, 192. For versions of the opposed position adopted in this chapter see Arquillière, 1955, 59–71; Carlyle and Carlyle, 1903–36, 1:164–71; Figgis, 1921, 51–67; Deane, 1963, 118–28; Markus, 1988, 106–7. Analyzing the contributions of an array of scholars—German, Italian, French, and Anglophone—and commenting on "the Protean elusiveness" of the way in which the debate on the matter has ramified, Adams, 1977, 123–35, devotes a pertinent appendix to the issue.
88. *DCD* 19:21; cf. 19:4; *CCSL* 48:687–88, 666; trans. Battenson, 1972, 881, 854.
89. *DCD* 19:23; cf. 19:21; *CCSL* 48:695, 687–89; trans. Bettenson, 1972, 890, 881–83.

90. *DCD* 2:21, 19:21; *CCSL* 47:55, 48:687–89; trans. Bettenson 1972, 75, 881–83.
91. *DCD* 19:24; *CCSL* 48:696; trans. Bettenson, 1972, 891.
92. *DCD* 2:21, 19:23; *CCSL* 47:55, 48:695; trans. Bettenson, 1972, 75, 890.
93. *DCD* 19:24; *CCSL* 48:695–96; trans. Bettenson, 1972, 890–91. Augustine refers to the definition as "more probable" at *DCD* 2:21 (*CCSL* 47:55): "Secundum probabiliores autem definitiones pro suo modo quodam respublica fuit, et melius ab antiquioribus Romanis quam a posterioribus administrata est."
94. *DCD* 19:24; *CCSL* 48:695; trans. Bettenson, 1972, 890.
95. *DCD* 5:24; *CCSL* 47:160; trans. Bettenson, 1972, 219–20.
96. Deane, 1963, 132–33.
97. O'Donnell, 2005, 361n390, evoking the more recent work by W. H. C. Frend and R. A. Markus. Cf. p. 211, where he notes that "fifty years ago . . . [Frend] still thought of Catholicism the norm and Donatism as the divergence. The facts now seem to indicate the reverse of that situation." Marcus, 1970, 102, argues that "what gave Donatism its standing was that it would claim to be, quite simply, *the* African Church."
98. On this whole issue, I am indebted to Baynes, 1955, 12–13; Figgis, 1921, 77–80; Markus, 1970, 131–55; and especially the lengthy analysis by Deane, 1963, 172–220.
99. Deane, 1963, 194 and 197, citing the words of Augustine, *Ep.* 93, #16; *CSEL* 32(2), 461.
100. Deane, 1963, 215.
101. Daniel 3:1–30; Augustine, *Ep.* 93, #9; *CSEL* 32(2), 453; trans. Schaff, 1886–90, 1:385.
102. *Contra litteras Petiliani,* 2:92, § 211; *CSEL* 52:136; trans. Schaff, 1886–90, 7:191.
103. *Contra Cresconium,* 3:51, § 56; *CSEL* 52:462, lines 25–29: "in hoc autem reges, sicut eis divinitus praecipitur, deo serviunt in quantum reges sunt, si in suo regno bona jubeant, mala prohibeant, *non solum quae pertinent ad humanam societatem, verum etiam quae ad divinam religionem*" (italics mine).
104. Markus, 1970, 148–49 and 152, where he adds, "The fact that he did not think of this problem in terms of the state, but in terms of individual members of the Church who held secular office, disguised from Augustine the acute tension between his consent to coercion and the implications of his theology of history and society."
105. Though Deane, 1963, 217, notes that Augustine still did not argue that compulsion "in and of itself . . . [could] make the heretic or schismatic a sincere believer or a good man." Even at the end of the line, when he was perfectly willing to invoke imperial power "to compel heretics to return to the fold of the Church, he clearly states that coercion can do no more than compel the heretic to abandon his open resistance and force him back into the visible Church."
106. Figgis, 1921, 77.
107. Pelikan, 1971–89, 1:309–13, provides a good, succinct analysis of the issues at stake. The words cited appear at p. 309.
108. Troeltsch, 1960, 1:334, 340–41, 2:994.
109. Optatus *Donat.* 2:1; *CSEL* 26:32; cited in Pelikan, 1971–89, 1:311.

110. Pelikan, 1971–89, 1:312:13, where, noting that "it was the recipient...who...took the initiative in presenting himself for the administration of the sacrament and for the dispensation of its grace," he adds that "as medieval theology was to demonstrate repeatedly, the doctrine of ex opere operato could become the basis for assigning to the human initiative [and not, certainly, to the working of divine grace] the decisive role in the determination of the relation between God and man."
111. Pelikan, 1971–89, 1:350–51: "It is perhaps too much to say of Gregory that 'almost everything in him has its roots in Augustine, and yet almost nothing is genuinely Augustinian'; but to understand Gregory as a theologian and to relate the seventh, eighth, and ninth centuries to him it is necessary to see his formulations of doctrine as Augustinian traditionalism." For the importance of Gregory's thinking and the policies he pursued vis-à-vis both the Byzantine emperors and the Germanic kings of western Europe, see Arquillière, 1955, 121–41.
112. Arquillière, 1955, 54–55, and, for the views of the ninth-century churchmen, 142–98.
113. Einhard, *Vita Karoli Magni*, cap. 24; ed. Firchow and Zeydel, 1972, 91.
114. Thus Dvornik, 1966, 2:849; Ullmann, 1969, 3.

Chapter 7. The Early Medieval West (i)

1. Binchy, 1970, 14. Here and in what follows I rely on Binchy as well as on Draak, 1959; MacCana, 1983; and MacCullough, 1911.
2. See above, ch. 1.
3. MacCana, 1983, 117.
4. Similarly, the failure of his powers in any of these areas, or the impairment of his body, might necessitate his abdication or deposition. Thus Draak, 1959, 660–63.
5. Binchy, 1970, 24; cf. MacCullough, 1911, 157–60.
6. Baetke, 1964, 181. For a somewhat critical appraisal of Baetke's approach, see Wolfram, 1968, 2:473–90.
7. Baetke, 1964, 9, 51, 67–68, 175.
8. Ström, 1959, 702–15 (at 714–15), where he adds that "Without blót there would be no future at all." Cf. Turville-Petre, 1964, esp. ch. 9, pp. 190–95; Dumézil, 1939.
9. Höfler, 1956, 75–104 (at 88).
10. Ström, 1959, 702.
11. Baetke, 1964, 6, claims indeed that the whole question concerning Germanic sacral kingship "can...only be answered on the ground of the Nordic material."
12. Thus Baetke, 1964; Graus, 1965; Höfler, 1956; Hauck, 1950, 187–240. In addition to Höfler and Hauck, with whom my sympathies lie (despite Graus's dismissal [314] of Höfler's work as "exceedingly tangled"), I have found particularly instructive H. M. Chadwick, 1926; de Vries, 1950; Chaney, 1920; Wallace-Hadrill, 1971; Schlesinger, 1956; and Kern, 1954, this last the revised version of the original 1914 edition with full, updated footnote apparatus.
13. Thus Wolfram, 1970 and 1990, esp. ch. 1, pp. 14–34. Similarly, Wallace-Hadrill,

1971, esp. 1–20, where (16n56) he concedes to being willing now to give "more weight to 'sacral' background" than he had been prepared to do earlier on in Wallace-Hadrill, 1962a.
14. Thus, e.g., Graus, 1965, 316, 334; cf. 14–25. Referring to the Nazi exploitation of ancient German mythology, Wolfram, 2006, 74–78, comments that "it is only too understandable that scholars such as the late František Graus," who had himself "experienced the crimes of the new pagan cult and ideology of the Nazis, should categorically reject the image of the sacred kingship and *königsheil* [royal sacrality] of Germanic kings and tribes."
15. Stubbs, 1880, 1:2, 231, 233.
16. Güterbock, 1956, 19; Sturtevant and Bechtel, 1935, 191n30; Gurney, 1958, 115, 121.
17. DeVries, 1956, 298; Höfler, 1956, 97–102; Wallace-Hadrill, 1971, 14: "That assembly [i.e., the *Thing*] was without question sacral in character."
18. Schlesinger, 1956, 140; cf. Chadwick, 1926, 365; Höfler, 1956, 695–96.
19. Ammianus Marcellinus, *Res gestae*, xxviii, 5, 14; ed. and trans. Rolfe, 1935–39, 3:168–69; cf. Schlesinger, 1956, 140; Chadwick, 1926, 344; Dumézil, 1939, 51–53; Wolfram, 1990, 43; de Vries, 1950, 293.
20. Höfler, 1956, 104.
21. For the Anglo-Saxon royal genealogies, see Chaney, 1970, 7–43; Wolfram, 2006, 70–90.
22. Procopius *De bello gothico* II, 14:34–42, and 15:27–36; ed. and trans. Dewing, 1919, 3:413, 420, 424. Cf. De Vries, 1950, 293; Schlesinger, 1956, 137; Kern, 1954, 19; Bloch, 1924, 31–32.
23. Wolfram, 1970, 17; 2006, 70–90.
24. In relation to what immediately follows, I have found particularly instructive Markus, 1990; Brown, 1995 and 1997; McKitterick, ed., 2001a—especially the essays on "Politics" and "Religion" by McKitterick and Mayke de Jong, at 23–56 and 131–64, respectively; Wolfram, 2006, 70–90; Wallace-Hadrill, 1971.
25. Brown, 1997, 218.
26. Ibid., 202–6.
27. Wallace-Hadrill, 1971, 53–55.
28. Itself a complicated topic which has been subjected of late to a good deal of rethinking and reinterpretation. On which see Markus, 1990; Brown, 1995, esp. 1–26; 1997.
29. Brown, 1997, 273 and 267–68.
30. Bede, *Historia ecclesiastica gentis Anglorum* 1:30; ed. Mynors, 1968, 106–8; trans. Shirley-Price, 1965, 85–87.
31. Thus December 25, the winter solstice, "birthday of the Unconquered Sun" was reinterpreted as the day of Christ's birth and "absorbed into the cycle of Christian sacred time" (Markus, 1990, 103, 106). See also pp. 107–23 for the problem posed for Christians by the "heavy charge of diffused religiosity" attaching to the traditional round of pagan civic celebrations embedded in Roman public life. Cf. Brown, 1971, 142–43.
32. As Brown, 1997, 267, points out, "It was not to convert a pagan population but,

rather, to end an age of [compromising] coexistence," that Boniface took that dramatic step.
33. *Confessiones* 6:2; *CSEL* 33:114–16; trans. Pine-Coffin, 1961, 112–13.
34. More revealingly, and at a level that eluded prohibition, is the type of curious phenomena to which Brown, 1997, 172, alludes in passing, the "sixth-century Nestorian Cross—a distinctive quasi-cosmic symbol, half a Cross and half an ancient Mesopotamian Tree of Life—... discovered as far east as Travancore." The more striking in that, a thousand years later and dating to the Spanish evangelization of Mesoamerica, one finds in the work of Maya craftsmen a parallel blending of Christian crucifix and pagan cosmic tree. See Edgerton, 2001, 65–71, esp. fig. 2.30, with Jesus as "the World Tree, the symbolic center of the quincunx universe" (at 67).
35. Brown, 1997, 99.
36. See, e.g., the studies by Toussaert, 1963, of Catholic maritime Flanders at the end of the Middle Ages (esp. 361–71), and by Strauss, 1975, of Lutheran Wiesbaden at the end of the sixteenth century.
37. Wolfram, 2006, 81–84; 1990, 204–22. Emphasizing this same fact, Brown, 1997, 306, adds: "As long as power based on genealogies was taken seriously, the gods were taken seriously."
38. So well domesticated in England, ecclesiastically speaking, was the royal practice of touching to cure scrofula that it survived the Protestant Reformation and even found official expression in an order of service incorporated from 1633 to 1715 in the *Book of Common Prayer*. The classic study of this strange practice is that of Bloch, 1924 (trans. 1973).
39. Bede, *Historia ecclesiastica gentis Anglorum*, 3:2, 6, and 12; ed. Mynors, 1968, 214–16, 230–31, 250–53; trans. Shirley-Price, 1965, 217, 231 and 251. Brown, 1997, 213–14, comments that "a raw sacrality—the product of fiercely maintained local memories—flickers around the figure" of Oswald.
40. Cited in Leyser, 1989, 80 and n23.
41. For the pros and cons of the debate, reference may be made to Hauck, 1950, 187–240, and Graus, 1965. And for a powerful version of the case to be made for pagan-Christian continuity in one (perhaps exceptional) region, see Chaney, 1970. There is an excellent analysis of the state of scholarly play in this and related matters in Klaniczay, 2002, esp. 1–113.
42. See above, ch. 3.
43. Brown, 1997, 92. For the subsequent illustrations I am also indebted to Brown, 1997, 206–7, 239–40, 256. For the seventh-century accommodation of Old Testament history to contemporary concerns, see de Jong, 2001, 142–43, and Wallace-Hadrill, 1971, 48–50, 53–57.
44. See above, ch. 3.
45. Wallace-Hadrill, 1971, 48–80; Ewig, 1956, 7–73 (at 21–24).
46. King, 1988, 123–53 (at 128). For other examples (Lombard and Anglo-Saxon) of the use of the *rex dei gratia* title or its equivalents, see Ullmann, 1966a, 118–19.
47. Kern, 1954, 20–22, 28, 66–67. Cf. Kern, 1939, 34–37.

48. For the events of 751 and their significance, see e.g., Wallace-Hadrill, 1962a, 86–98; Kern, 1954, 35, 51–52; Ullmann, 1969, 77–78; Nelson, 1988, 2313–16; 1987, 142–150. Collins, 1998, 31–37, describing the available evidence concerning the events of 751 as "thin and contradictory," speculates that it was the desire to enhance his own status in the context of his ongoing struggle in Bavaria with his half-brother and nephew that led Pippin to take the risky step of deposing the last Merovingian and seizing the throne for himself.
49. See Oakley, 2006a, 10–23.
50. Bloch, 1973, 33: "The *reges criniti* were so many Samsons." Cf. 300n18. Tacitus, *Germania*, ch. 40; in Mattingly, 1948, 133–34.
51. *MGH: Annales Regni Francorum*, 6:8–9, ann. 749: "Et Zacherius papa mandavit Pippino, ut melius esse illum regem vocari, qui potestatem haberet, quam illum, qui sine regali potestate manebat." Cf. 6:8–10, ann. 749 and 750. This account, it should be noted, postdated the actual event by several decades.
52. Thus the contemporary account by Pippin's uncle simply indicates that Pippin, having consulted the pope and received a reply, was in accordance with ancient practice elected king by the Franks and consecrated by the bishop. See the continuator of Fredegar's Chronicle, ch. 33, ed. Wallace-Hadrill, 1969, 102.
53. The term used by Wallace-Hadrill, 1965, 28, where he adds that Charles the Bald, later on, "believed, by having his queen Irmintrud crowned and anointed in 866, she would again become fruitful and give him better children than the bad lot he already had." Cf. Wallace-Hadrill, 1971, 133–35; 1983, 162–68. For a different "take" on this important transition, see Nelson, 1987, 142, and Canning, 1996, 96, who dissents from what he calls the "older historical interpretation."
54. Kern, 1954, 65; 1939, 35–36. Cf. Bloch, 1973, 35–41: "The examples of David and Solomon provided a way of restoring to kings in a Christian setting the sacred character that belonged to them."
55. See above, ch. 2.
56. Bloch, 1973, 36.
57. See Enright, 1985.
58. For the pioneering work of Percy Schramm, Carl Erdmann, and Reinhard Elze on the complex interrelationships among the various national coronation *ordines*, see Bak, 1973, 41–43.
59. For which, see below, ch. 8.
60. For this and what follows, see Kantorowicz, 1946, 53–64 (the words cited appear at 56). Ewig, 1956, 7–73 (at 44–47); Wallace-Hadrill, 1971, 98–103; Nelson, 1987, 151–53.
61. Genesis 14:18: "And Melchizedek, king of Salem, brought out bread and wine; he was priest of God Most High." Psalm 110 (109):4: "The Lord has sworn and will not change his mind, 'You are a priest for ever after the order of Melchizedek.'" This a "royal psalm" addressed to the Israelite king—see above, ch. 2.
62. Kantorowicz, 1946, 57n148; Bloch, 1973, 41.
63. Kantorowicz, 1946, 61–62.

64. Ullmann, 1969, 98–99, 135.
65. De Jong, 2001, 138–40.
66. De Jong, 2005, 107, where, echoing the recent and more positive appraisal of the level of Carolingian literacy, she emphasizes the importance of the role played by the lay aristocracy in matters religious as well as political, and insists that "the ideology of Christian kingship [accordingly] was not merely a matter of an alliance between rulers and a restricted group of clerics." Arquillère, 1955, 166.
67. See above, ch. 5.
68. For developments in East Frankia, I rely on Leyser, 1989; Reuter, 1991; and Goldberg, 2006.
69. See esp. Nelson, 1987, 137–80.
70. "Prospice omnipotens deus hunc gloriosissimum regem serenis obtutibus, sicut benedixisti Abraham, Isaac et Jacob," etc. I follow here Janet Nelson's judicious account in her "Kingship and Empire," 1988, 211–51 (at 217–22). She reprints the text of *Prospice* at 218n36.
71. Deshman, 1980, 417, emphasizes "the later Carolingian foundations for basic features of Ottonian Christ-centered ruler portraits and ruler theology."
72. Wallace-Hadrill, 1971, 102–3.
73. Bloch, 1973, 41; Kantorowicz, 1946, 5n148.
74. For the *potestas ordinis / jurisdictionis* distinction, see above, ch. 6. It should be noted that in medieval (though not in modern) canonistic usage the *potestas jurisdictionis in foro exteriori* was taken to include the magisterial or doctrinal teaching authority.
75. Cited from Kern, 1939, 38; cf. Kern, 1954, 72–74; Wido's words are cited from Bloch, 1973, 110.
76. For which, see Oakley, 2006a, 133–34; cf. Shils and Young, 1953, 63–81. It was from that same Edgar *ordo* that we shall see the Anglo-Norman Anonymous to have drawn so much of his inspiration.
77. *MGH: Epistolae variorum Carolo Magno regnante,* 4:7. Cf. Carlyle and Carlyle, 1903–36, 1:149, 214–15.
78. Smaragdus, *Via regia,* cap. 18; in *PL* 102:958. Cf. Wallace-Hadrill, 1971, 136.
79. Kantorowicz, 1957, 61–78 (at 61); Nelson, 1988, 235, 240.
80. *MGH: Gesta Chuonradi imperatoris,* ch. 3, in *Die Werke Wipos,* 22–24, where he is described as anointing the king, assuring him that all power is of God, and as saying to him: "Ad summam dignitatem pervenisti, vicarius es Christi. Nemo nisi illius imitator verus est dominator" (22–23).
81. Kantorowicz, 1957, 61–78 (at 64–65). *Pace* Kantorowicz, the miniature in question appears to date to c. 996 not c. 975 and the emperor in question to be Otto III not Otto II.
82. Corpus Christi College, Cambridge, MS 415.
83. For the complete set of *Tractates,* see Pellens, ed., 1966. H. Boehmer edited six of the most important of them in *MGH: Libelli de Lite,* 3:642–87. Wherever possible, my references will be given to both editions. Whereas Philipp Funk, 1935, argued for multiple authorship, Boehmer (*MGH: Libelli de Lite,* 3:642–45) had argued that all the

Tractates were the work of a single author, whom he identified as Gerard of York. Cantor, 1958, 172–90, 193–95, 246–48, while not dismissing out of hand the possibility of "varied provenance" aligned himself more or less with Boehmer's view. Williams, 1951a, and Nineham, 1963 (a judicious appraisal), both make a clear and persuasive case for the authorship of a single, Norman writer, working probably at Rouen. Cf. Scherrinsky, 1939, 123, and Woody, 1973, 273–88.

84. Kantorowicz, 1957, 60.
85. See, e.g., Williams, 1951a, 235; Nelson, 1988, 243. For the older view, see Southern, 1961, 22–94; Kantorowicz, 1957, 60–61; Nineham, 1963, 43; Cantor, 1958, 191, 230.
86. For Ambrosiaster, Cathwulf, and Hugh of St. Fleury, see Carlyle and Carlyle, 1903–36, 1:149, 179, 215–16; 2:14, 134. For a classic later echo of such views, see John Wyclif's citation of what he thought to be Augustine but was in fact Ambrosiaster in *The King's Office*, in O'Donovan and O'Donovan, ed. and trans., 1999, 509.
87. See above, ch. 5.
88. Pellens ed., 1966, introduction to the second version of the text of the *De consecratione*, pp. 197–98; = Boehmer, ed., *MGH: Libelli de Lite*, 3:663:5–10.
89. *De consecratione*, ed. Pellens, 1966, 134 and (introduction to the second version of the tract) 198; = Boemer, ed., *MGH: Libelli de Lite*, 3:667:10–16.
90. *De consecratione*, ed. Pellens, 1966, 131; = Boehmer, ed., *MGH: Libelli de Lite*, 3:665:21–30.
91. Following here the interpretation of Williams, 1951a, 128–32.
92. Williams, 1951a, 132; cf. 190.
93. For which, see above, ch. 5.
94. As Canning, 1996, 105, rightly observes. This tendency makes it easier, of course, for the Anonymous to ascribe a priestly status to the king.
95. *De consecratione*, J24.c; in Pellens ed., 1966, 201. Pertinent to this passage is a comment that Williams, 1951a, 149, makes in relation to one of the other *Tractates*, namely, that the Anonymous was "intent upon effacing the barrier which the Gregorian Reform would set up between the clergy and the laity, to the disparagement of the latter."
96. For the Anonymous's emphasis on the truly sacramental nature of unction which, he says, transforms the consecrated person into another man, a *christus* of the Lord, see *De consecratione*, ed. Pellens, 1966, 130; = Boehmer, ed., *MGH: Libelli de Lite*, 3:677, where, quoting the Edgar *ordo*, he speaks of unction as if it were another baptism.
97. *De consecratione*, ed. Pellens, 1966, 167–73. Cf. Williams, 1951a, 36–46; Schramm, 1938, 314, 325f. The latter was the first to identify the royal *ordo* as the Edgar one. Cf. Schramm, 1968–71, 4:169–208 (esp. 180–92, 201–7).
98. *De consecratione*, ed. Pellens, 1966, 134; = Boehmer, ed., *MGH: Libelli de Lite*, 3:667.
99. Ibid. Cf. Pellens, ed., 1966, "Einleitung zu J24 in Fassung II," 199; = Boehmer, ed., *MGH: Libelli de Lite*, 3:663: "Que cum ita sunt, manifestum est; quod rex habet principatum reqendi eos, qui sacerdotali dignitate potiuntur. Non ergo debet excludi rex a regimine sancte ecclesie, id est: populi christiani; quia ita divideretur regnum ecclesie et fieret desolatum." Similarly, Pellens, ed., 1966, 133; = Boehmer, ed., *MGH:*

Libelli de Lite, 3:666. Cf. Pellens, ed., 1966, 161 (Boehmer, ed., *MGH: Libelli de Lite*, 3:679), where, insisting that the king is not to be called a layman (*laicus*), he goes on, "quia christus Domini est, quia per gratiam deus est, qui sum[m]us rector est, quia pastor et magister et defensor et instructor sancte ecclesie, sum[m]us est."

100. *De consecratione*, ed. Pellens, 1966, 132 and 161; = Boehmer, ed., *MGH: Libelli de Lite*, 3:665, 679. Cf. Williams, 1951a, 173.

101. "Quare et peccata remittere, et panem et vinum in sacrificum potest offere, quod utique facit in die quo coronatur, precipue videlicet solemnitas" (*De consecratione*, ed. Pellens, 1966, 159; = Boehmer, ed., *MGH: Libelli de Lite,* 3:678). Cf. Pellens, ed., 1966, 157 (Boehmer, ed., *MGH: Libelli de Lite*, 3:677): "Fit ergo summus rector, et quo superior nullus est, et pacificus propitiator populi christiani, qui est ecclesia sancta et templum Dei vivi; per quod vices Christi potest exequi in remittendis peccatis et reconciliatione peccatoris."

102. *De consecratione*, ed. Pellens, 1966, 118; cf. 140; = Boehmer, ed., *MGH: Libelli de Lite*, 3:377; cf. 3:669. See the extended commentary on these and related texts in Williams, 1951a, 169–74, especially (at 173) his conclusion that "it may be said without exaggeration that the anointed king is thought of by the Anonymous as a real propitiator and savior of his people by virtue of his sanctified headship of the *regale sacerdotium.*"

103. *De consecratione*, ed. Pellens, 1966, 137; = Boehmer, ed., *MGH: Libelli de Lite*, 3:669.

104. See above, ch. 5.

105. *De consecratione*, ed. Pellens, 1966, "Einleitung zu J24 in der Fassung II," 136–37 and 196–200 (esp. 136 and 198); = Boehmer, ed., *MGH: Libelli de Lite*, 3:663–68 (esp. 663 and 668). For the notion of the kings "co-ruling" (*conregnat*) with Christ, see also the *De Romano Pontifice* (J28), ed. Pellens, 1966, *Romanus pontifex gravat ecclesiam . . .*, 216–28 (at 223); = Boehmer, ed., *MGH: Libelli de Lite,* 3:679–86 (at 685).

106. Williams, 1951a, 187–88. For the Anonymous's deployment of such terms as *apotheosis* and *deificatio,* see *De consecratione*, ed. Pellens, 1966, 131; = Boehmer, ed., *MGH: Libelli de Lite*, 3:665.

107. For the pertinent texts and helpful commentary on them, see Williams, 1951a, 170–73, 191–98, 156–57.

108. See Kantorowicz, 1957, 49–52.

109. Williams, 1951a, 77.

110. Bloch, 1973, 195–96, where, speaking now of the seventeenth century, he adds: "In order to have true knowledge of even the most famous doctors of the monarchy, it is as well to be acquainted with the collective ideas handed down from preceding ages.... [T]hese men, like all theologians, were principally engaged in giving intellectual form to the very powerful sentiments that were widespread in their environment, and which they themselves more or less unconsciously shared."

111. Kantorowicz, 1957, 61–62.

112. McKitterick, 2001b, 23–54 (at 34–36); Goldberg, 2006, 187–200; Leyser, 1979, 75–107, esp. 93–95 and 88–89 where, in relation to "the enhanced sacrality and charisma" of the later Ottonians, he notes that "already as a six-year old boy, Otto III

was made to take the field against the Slavs of Lusatia. He could hardly have led his host but his presence gave it cohesion as only that of a king could."

113. Nineteenth-century German neologisms like "feudalism" and "humanism" are currently not very popular. For the wave of historical agnosticism that has broken during the past quarter century over the term "feudalism," see below, ch. 8.

114. Thus Williams, 1951a, 199–200: so that "The king as vicar of the Celestial Melchizedek and antitype of the Pope provides the religio-political unity upon which the Anonymous insists." See also pp. 67, 133, 137–45. The comments that the Anonymous makes on the papal office are complex, marked occasionally by a certain indirection, and broadcast in fragmentary fashion across several of the *Tractates*. Some of his most forceful statements, however, may be found in his *De Romano pontifice*, ed. Pellens, 1966, with the title *Romanus pontifex gravat ecclesiam* (J38), 214–25; = Boehmer, ed., *MGH: Libelli de Lite*, 3:679–86.

115. It is no accident, I believe, that his reflections on the Norman Anonymous frequently led George Williams to look ahead to the divine-right monarchy of late sixteenth and early seventeenth century England and to evoke the thinking of such Anglican divines as Lancelot Andrewes and Archbishops Cranmer and Laud—see Williams, 1951a, 128n419, 134n437, 192n650, 197–98, 200.

Chapter 8. The Early Medieval West (ii)

1. Jonas of Orléans, *De institutione regia*, ch. 3; ed. Reviron, 1930, 139–41; English translation from O'Donovan and O'Donovan, 1999, 711. Cf. Delaruelle, 1955. For the *speculum principum* genre of political writing in general, see Berges, 1938.
2. Sedulius Scottus, *De rectoribus christianis*, 1; trans. Doyle, 1983, 52.
3. Nelson, 1988, 224. Cf. Fried, 1982, 29–33, to which she refers.
4. Kantorowicz, 1961, 97. Cf. Beumann, 1956, 185–224.
5. Thus, e.g., van Caenegem, 1988, 174–210 (at 185–95); cf. Strayer, 1970, where he says that it was "in the centuries between 1100 and 1300 [that] some of the essential elements of the modern state began to appear" (34). Similarly, Canning, 1996, 83. In its specifically modern form the state is usually seen to have come into existence between the fifteenth and seventeenth centuries. In the narrow definition proffered by German legal scholars it is viewed as being constituted "by a homogeneous population inhabiting a contiguous territory under a single government which is characterized by complete independence from any outside authority (sovereignty) and holding a monopoly of jurisdiction and of the legitimate use of violence internally." Thus W. Reinhard, s.v. "State, History of" in the *International Encyclopedia of the Social and Behavioral Sciences*, 2001, 22:14972–78 (at 14972). This is one of an important series of pertinent articles dealing also with "State and Society," "State, Anthropological Aspects," "State Formation," "State, Sociology of," and "State and Civilizations, Archaeology of" to be found in the same encyclopedia at 22:14961–88. Extensive bibliographies are appended to all of these articles.
6. Van Caenegem, 1988, 174–75.

7. Bede, *Historia ecclesiastica*, 2:5; ed. Mynors, 1991, 148–50. Alcuin, 1982, 42–43. In what follows, I draw on Nelson, 1988, 230–46, and Beumann, 1956, 185–224.
8. *MGH: Gesta Chuonradi imperatoris*, cap. 7, in *Die Werke Wipos*, 30, where Conrad added with reference to the imperial buildings that the Pavian mob had looted and destroyed after hearing the news of Henry's death: "Aedes publicae fuerant, non privatae; juris erant aieni, non vestri."
9. I draw the term from Dhondt, 1957. Cheyette 1968, 256–290, has made conveniently available an English translation of this article along with a collection of other essays pertinent to the role of community in medieval life. See also Ullmann, 1961, 215–30.
10. In the course of a distinguished, highly productive, and influential career at Cambridge University, Ullmann occupied the positions of professor of ecclesiastical history and Regius Professor of History. He elaborated his approach from 1960 onward in a notable series of studies. In what follows I rely especially on the succinct statements given in Ullmann, 1961, 19–26; 1965, 11–18; 1966a, 3–6; 1966b, 13–36; 1966c, 49–55. For a full description (and critique), see Oakley, 1973, 3–48; reprinted in Oakley, 1999, 25–72.
11. It is significant that when Ullmann first elaborated the scheme he was concerned specifically with legal thinking rather than political—see his "Law and the Medieval Historian," in the *Rapports of the XIe Congrès International des Sciences Historiques*, 1960–62, 3:34–74. Cf. Oakley, 1999, 69–70.
12. For the notion of the supernatural and the late date at which the word itself emerged during the Christian era, see Lubac, 1946, 325–428.
13. For a fuller statement of this point, see Oakley, 1999, 50–52, 66–68.
14. For these contrasts, see Ullmann, 1969, 8–10, 53–55, 94–96, 163.
15. E.g., Ullmann, 1961, 22–24, 137; 1965, 53–54; 1969, 52–53.
16. See above, ch. 7.
17. Kern, 1939, 43; 1954, 79–80. Cf. Schlesinger, 1953, 225–75 (at 251–52) along with the literature he cites in n1. English translation (though without the complete apparatus of notes) in Cheyette, ed., 1968, 64–99.
18. Kern, 1939, 10; 1954, 11. See the similar sentiment expressed by Bloch, 1964, 2:383–84.
19. *Capitularia Regum Francorum*, in *MGH: Leges. Sectio II*, 2:364, No. 283A: "Ego Hlodowicus, misericordia domini Dei nostri et electione populi rex constitutus, promitto," etc. He added: "Polliceor etiam ne servaturum leges et statuta popolo qui mihi ad regendum misericordia Dei committitur." Ullmann, 1969, 96–97, characterizes it also as "an emergency solution." See to the contrary, Nelson, 1987, 164.
20. Carlyle and Carlyle, 1903–36, 1:240–41. Similarly, Kern, 1939, 47: "Government seemed to result from a combination of election, hereditary right, and consecration," with "the elective element in this triad . . . usually paramount"—at least in the early Middle Ages.
21. *Capitularia Regum Francorum*, in *MGH: Leges. Sectio II*, 1:270–71, No. 136, *Ordinatio Imperii*, July, 817.
22. On these matters the chapters by Luscombe, Van Caenegem, and Nelson in the *Cam-*

bridge *History of Medieval Political Thought*, 1988, 157–251, are particularly helpful. Similarly, the judicious and succinct account in Canning, 1996, 44–81.

23. In his *De ordine palatii*, caps. 29, 30, 35, in *MGH: Leges. Sectio II*, 2:527 and 529, Hincmar of Rheims describes the workings of these assemblies, which, under Charles the Bald, met twice a year. Nelson, 1992, conveys a lively impression of their importance and the role they played in his imperial government.

24. *De ordine palatii*, cap. 8, in *MGH: Leges. Sectio II*, 2:520: "quae [leges] generali consensu fidelium suorum tenere legaliter *promulgaverunt.*" And *Edictum Pistense*, June 864, ibid., 2:313: "quoniam lex consensu populi et constitutione regis fit." On the latter assembly, see Nelson, 1992, esp. 207–9; cf. Carlyle and Carlyle, 1903–36, 1:229–39.

25. Nelson, 1988, 222–23.

26. As was the case with Charles the Bald at Quierzy in 858—see Nelson, 1992, 186. Cf. the comment in Goldberg, 2006, 257.

27. Goldberg, 2006, 220–22, where he adds: "Louis and his brothers saw fidelity and lordship as the glue that held their kingdoms together. They decreed that every freeman was to choose a lord, either the king himself or one of his *fideles.*" For a judicious older account targeted on the Carolingian realms at large, see Odegaard, 1945. Reynolds, 1994, comments extensively on *fideles* and oaths of fidelity in all parts of western Europe.

28. Thus Pollock and Maitland, 1923, 1:66–67, and van Caenegem, 1988, 199–200, both seeing the union of vassalage and fief holding rather than the fief alone as lying at the heart of feudalism. The term *feudum*, from which we derive our word "fief," did not attain general currency as a synonym for *beneficium* (benefice) until the end of the eleventh century.

29. Kelley, 1964, 216. For a further brief comment on the contending uses of the term across time, see Boutrouche, 1959, 1:11–24.

30. Bloch, 1964; Boutrouche, 1959.

31. Thus Strayer, 1965, 14: "A definition which can include societies as disparate as those of the Ancient Middle East, the late Roman Empire, medieval Europe, the southern part of the United States in the nineteenth century, and the Soviet Union in the 1930s is not much use in historical analysis."

32. Thus, classically, Ganshof, 1961, xx: "Feudalism may be regarded as a body of institutions creating and regulating the obligations of obedience and service—mainly military service—on the part of a free man (the vassal) towards another free man (the lord), and the obligations of protection and maintenance on the part of the lord with regard to his vassals. The obligation of maintenance had usually as one of its effects the grant by the lord to his vassal of a unit of real property known as a fief."

33. Strayer, 1965, 12–13.

34. Thus, e.g., Bloch, 1964, 1:59–71, stressing the impact on feudal institutions of the revival in the twelfth century of a commercial and money economy.

35. Thus Joseph R. Strayer, "The Development of Feudal Institutions," in Strayer, 1971,

77–89, stressing (at 81) "the 'realization,' the systemizing, and the bureaucratizing of feudalism" that made it "far more effective as an organizing principle in politics."
36. Thus Strayer, "The Two Levels of Feudalism," in Strayer, 1971, 63–89. The words quoted appear at p. 65.
37. Thus, classically, E. A. R. Brown, 1974, 1063–88, which resonates sympathetically to the "purity" with which Southern, 1961, and Duby, 1957, eschewed "the medieval 'isms'" and concerned themselves "with the individuals rather than abstractions." Also Reynolds, 1994, a remarkable book that amounts to a veritable *summa* of discontent with the very notion itself of feudalism. See also the fine and lengthy review, carefully nuanced but properly admiring of Reynolds's achievement, by Frederic Cheyette in *Speculum* 71, no. 4 (1996): 998–1006.
38. See Max Weber, "Zwischenbetrachtung," in Weber, 1922–23, 1:436–73. I cite the translation in Gerth and Mills, 1946, 323. This notion the critics simply brush to one side with a measure of breeziness and without extended argument. See E. A. R. Brown, 1974, 1070, 1079–80; Reynolds, 1994, 10, 73, 479.
39. The words are Weber's drawn from his "Die Wirtschaftsethik der Weltreligionen," in Weber, 1922–23, 1:237–75; cited from Gerth and Mills, 1946, 294; cf. ibid., 59–60, and Roth and Wittich, eds., 1968, 1:20–22, 57–58.
40. See esp. Max Weber in Roth and Wittich, eds., 1968, 3:1070–1110. Cf. Poggi, 1988; Hintze, 1929; translated excerpt in Cheyette, 1968, 22–31.
41. For these changes and their gradual nature, see Fouracre, 2000, 147–50. Stressing how slowly it was adopted, he leans strongly against the dramatic claims for the importance of the introduction of the stirrup advanced earlier by White, 1962, 1–38. Cf. Halsall, 2003, 71, 173, 185–86.
42. Whereas the Roman lawyers had used the word solely to denote proprietary right and we ourselves use its derivative "dominion" to denote authority of a governmental nature.
43. *Capitulare Carisiacense,* June 1877, in *MGH: Leges. Sectio II,* 2:358, § 9. And Nelson, 1992, 248–51, notes that the "real significance" of the pertinent clause in the decree "lay in what it revealed of one particular father-son relationship: namely that between Charles and Louis the Stammerer." Reynolds, 1994, 112 and 402, insists that "in the circumstances of its promulgation, it [the capitulary] does not seem to be a royal surrender to a new principle of inheritance."
44. In his *Chronicon Anglicanum,* in Stevenson ed., 1975, 135–36, the English chronicler, Ralph of Coggeshall, gives an interesting account of the case and of what Philip II's court judged to be King John's delinquency.
45. Thus J. R. Strayer, "The Tokugawa Period and Japanese Feudalism," in Strayer, 1971, 90–104 (at 96–97). Cf. Reischauer, 1956, 26–48 (at 32–33).
46. Hall, 1962–63, 33–34.
47. Oakley, 2006a, 22–23: "This tradition whereby the emperor (theoretically) delegated executive authority to the shogun alone made credible the way in which the Meiji restoration of 1868 was represented by the oligarchs who had engineered it, namely,

as the moment when the emperor took back into his own hands the power he and his predecessors had previously condescended to confer on the shogunate." Cf. Bloch, 1964, 2:282, 446–47, 451–52.

48. See Asakawa, ed. and trans., 1955, doc. 115A, pp. 373–76, for a memorandum prepared by the shogun's court probably in 1867 and intended to acquaint the foreign diplomats who had been admitted to Japan with the nature of Japanese "feudal" government. Among other things it notes: "The emperors have not concerned themselves in government already for more than six hundred and eighty years. However, as they have been, since the formation of the state, the supreme sovereigns following in a single line of divine succession and forever unalterable, and as they are revered by the nation as heavenly deities likewise the successive *tai-kun* [shogun] on occasion lead *dai-myō* [barons] to pay them court. The emperor entrusts to the *tai-kun* all political powers, and awaits his decisions in silence, the *tai-kun*, holding all political powers of the country, maintains the virtue of humility, and upholds the emperor with the utmost respect. This is the foundation of the profound peace of the country." Cf. Fujitani, 1996, 107–8 and 232–38, for the concomitant representation of the Meiji constitution of 1889 and (more surprisingly) that of 1947 as one "granted" by the emperor to the nation ("a gift of the emperor and his one line of ancestors"), thereby suggesting or affirming that he himself transcended it.

49. See below, ch. 9.

50. Van Caenegem, 1988, 210 and n118, identifies as an "often neglected truth" the fact that the reciprocal, contractual nature of the feudal relationship was "the historic starting point of the limitation of the monarchy and the constitutional form of government whose fundamental idea is that government as well as individuals ought to act under the law." Cf. Ullmann, 1966a, 63–68, though he tends to overstate the case.

51. Holt, 1992, conveys a good sense of the voluminous earlier literature on the Charter and provides conveniently in the appendices Latin and English versions of the original 1215 charter, along with texts of the 1225 revision and of other pertinent documents. For a series of other charters "from one end of the Western world to the other" affirming analogous limitations on the power of kings, see Bloch, 1964, 2:451–57; Holt, ed., 1982, 117–46.

52. *Magna Carta*, ch. 39 (in Holt, 1992, app. 6, pp. 460–61): "No free man shall be taken or imprisoned or disseised, or outlawed or exiled, or in any way ruined, nor will we go or send against him except by the lawful judgment of his peers or (*vel*)—by the law of the land." Holt argues (327–30) against Ullmann's (1961, 165–66) conjunctive rather than disjunctive understanding of *vel*.

Chapter 9. The Early Medieval West (iii)

1. For the invention of the Middle Ages and our current way of periodizing Western history, see Ferguson, 1948.
2. On which see Oakley, 2003, 1–19, 250–63; cf. Schatz, 1996, ix, who comments with specific reference to the papacy: "Whether the papacy is seen . . . as the rock of the

Church or 'a stone of stumbling,' it remains a reality present at the heart of almost every ecclesiastical problem and constantly provoking controversy."
3. See above, ch. 7.
4. Hugh of St. Victor, *De Sacramentis Christianae fidei*, II, pars 2, cap. 4; in *PL* 176:418; *Decretum Gratiani*, C. 12, qu. 1, c. 7; in *Corpus Juris Cononici*, ed. Friedberg, 1879–81, 1:678.
5. Faivre, 1977, 411–13.
6. Testa, 2005, 87–103. MacMullen, 1984, 115 and 168n2, notes the worldly appeal of tax exemptions to would-be clerics and, accordingly, "the recurrent charges [at the time] of bribery to become a priest." Cf. Ullmann, 1972, 8.
7. For the four classic clerical privileges, *privilegium canonis, fori, immunitas*, and *competentiae*, see F. Claeys-Bonnaert, s.v. "Cleric," in *Dictionnaire de droit canonique*, 1935–65, 3:8.
8. De Jong, 2001, 161–62; Robinson, 1988, 261–66.
9. Thus Cardinal Humbert of Silva Candida, *Adversus simoniacos*, lib. 3, cap. 7 and 9; in *MGH: Libelli de Lite*, 1891–97, 1:206, 208.
10. Alcuin, *Epistola* 148; in *MGH: Epistolae variorum Carolo Magno regnante*, 241, where, having addressed Charlemagne as "dilectissime et dulcissime David," he adds, "Surge, vir a Deo electe ... et defende sponsam domini Dei tui. Cognita de sponsa tua."
11. Agobard, *De privilegio*, § 7; in *PL* 104:133; Charles the Bald, *Allocutio missi cujusdam divionensis*; in *MGH: Leges. Sectio II*, 1883–97, 2:292, No. 267, cap. 1. Cf. Robinson, 1988, 244–46.
12. Robinson, 1988, 263–66; Duby, 1978.
13. Oakley, 2003, 3.
14. Cappellari, 1832. During the thirty and more years since its original appearance and the publication of the edition referred to, the book had been read as little as it is read today. But with Cappellari's ascent to the papal throne as Gregory XVI (1831–46), it was republished in Italian and translated into four other languages. Cf. Oakley, 2003, 194, 206–7.
15. Schatz, 1996, 144. In addition to relying on Schatz, I base my account of the rise of the papal monarchy largely on Richards, 1979; Morrison, 1969; Ullmann, 1972; Robinson, 1988; 252–305; Horn, 1998, 193–213; and Henn, 1998, 222–73.
16. For brief commentary on the dire straits in which the papacy found itself, see Oakley, 2003, 182–207.
17. O. Chadwick, 1981, 494–98.
18. Thus Schneider, 1976, 90.
19. Oakley, 2003, 195–98, and the works referred to therein.
20. Hence the insistence of Richards, 1979, 1–5, on the degree to which an overemphasis on ideological factors has resulted in "a one-sided view of papal history in which certain periods [including the sixth to eighth centuries] ... have been downgraded because they are not eras of significant ideological advance."
21. I.e., the churches of real or purported apostolic foundation: Jerusalem, Antioch, Alexandria, Rome, and (more questionably) Constantinople.

22. Morrison, 1969, 37.
23. *Ubique, semper, ab omnibus*—this the celebrated formula of Vincent of Lérins (d. c. 450); see Pelikan, 1971–89, 1:333.
24. Morrison, 1969, 78, 109–10, and 353, in which latter place he comments that "by and large, the emphasis of western thought moved away from tradition, the idea of anciently transmitted authority, and toward a concept of administrative power."
25. Noting the complexity of Siricius's position, Morrison, 1969, 80, argues that what that pope was doing was "using conventional terms to veil a new doctrine of spontaneous administrative power," and that "his new concept of an imperishable and immediate, rather than inherited, apostolicity" could be taken to render "the idea of tradition logically irrelevant."
26. Morrison, 1969, 81.
27. Thus Minnerath, 1998, 129–30; Ullmann, 1972, 19.
28. Ullmann, 1972, 18.
29. Morrison, 1969, 61.
30. In the Latin Vulgate version: "Et ego dico tibi, quia tu es Petrus, et super hanc petram aedificabo ecclesiam meam, et portae inferi non praevalebunt adversus eam. Et tibi dabo claves regni caelorum. Et quodcumque *ligaveris* super terram, erit *ligatum* et in caelis; et quodcumque *solveris* super terram erit *solutum* et in caelis" (italics mine).
31. Ullmann, 1972, 12–14. Cf. above, n30.
32. Ullmann, 1972, 22–23; cf. Morrison, 1969, 96.
33. See below, the section titled "The Rise of the Papal Monarchy (ii): Contextual Factors."
34. Morrison, 1969, 126–40 (words cited at 132).
35. Faivre, 1977, 172–73. In an *Excursus* entitled "La Hiérarchies chez le Pseudo-Denys" (172–80), Faivre gives a useful summary of the notion of hierarchy which Pseudo-Dionysius elaborates in his *De ecclesiastica hierarchica*. The Greek text is in *PG* 3: 370–584, French translation in Gandillac, 1943.
36. Though, as Faivre points out (175), the symmetry between Pseudo-Denys's celestial and ecclesiastical hierarchies is not, in fact, absolute. Cf. *Excursus* (172–80). Cf. Roques, 1954.
37. *Decretum Gratiani*, D. 40, c. 6: "[Papa] a nemine est judicandus, *nisi deprehendatur a fide devius*" (itaics mine), in *Corpus Juris Cononici*, ed. Friedberg, 1879–81, 1:146; *Codex Juris canonici*, 1917, can. 1556. Similarly, in the 1983 Code, can. 1404. For this last canon along with useful commentary, see Beal et al., 2000, 1608.
38. For the Latin text, see above, n37. For the conclusions drawn from this qualification in the later Middle Ages, see Oakley, 2003, 99–110. We will be returning to this issue in the third volume of this series.
39. See the excellent articles by John van Engen, the "Donation of Constantine" and the "Decretals, False," in the *Dictionary of the Middle Ages*, 1982–89, 4:257–59, and 124–27, respectively. For the text of the *Donation* itself, see Fuhrmann, ed., 1968. English translation of its central statements conveniently available in Tierney, 1964, 21–22.
40. Popes were later on to be formally "enmantled" with the crimson imperial cloak; the *phrygium* later evolved, on the one hand, into the mitre worn eventually by all bish-

ops and, on the other (at last, by the fourteenth century), into the triple crown (or *Triregnum*) worn as a symbol of their sovereign power by all popes down into the 1960s.
41. Folz, 1969, 64.
42. The False Decretals were edited by Paul Hinschins, 1863.
43. Schatz, 1996, 69.
44. He did so in the encyclical letter *Eger Cui Levia* (c. 1246), in *Acta Imperii Inedita*, 1885, 2: No. 1035, 696–701; partial English translation in Tierney, 1964, 147–49.
45. *Decretum Gratiani*, D. 96, cc. 13–14; in *Corpus Juris Canonici*, ed. Friedberg, 1879–81, 1:342–45.
46. Ullmann, 1972, 102–3.
47. A point of view shared by his contemporaries. See Morrison, 1964, 35–63. He notes (at 35) that Hincmar of Rheims described the canons as "the tribal law of the priesthood."
48. Morrison, 1969, 218. In what follows I am indebted to Morrison's excellent analysis of Nicolas's position (214–23).
49. Ibid., 216–217.
50. Cited from Morrison, 1969, 218–19.
51. Though no official papal registers survive from pontificates prior to that of Gregory I (590–64). On which, see Ullmann, 1972, 8, 12, 52–53.
52. See above, ch. 5.
53. Ullmann, 1972, 49–50. After the break with Byzantium in the eighth century the role in the making of popes formerly discharged by the imperial government was taken up by the Frankish kings.
54. Schatz, 1996, 52–53. It is startling to note that for the whole latter half of the sixth century the great church of Milan was out of communion with Rome, and the church of Aquileia for another century after that.
55. Schatz, 1996, 52–53.
56. Ullmann, 1972, 50.
57. Thus Einhard, *Vita Caroli Magni*, cap. 33; ed. Firchow and Zeydel, 1972, 110–16.
58. Morrison, 1969, 214–22, 230–31, 364–66.
59. In a later version, episcopalism found eloquent expression as late as 1869 in the *Du concile général et de la paix religieuse* of Henry Maret (1805–84), titular bishop of Sura and last dean of the Sorbonne faculty of theology. See Maret, 1969. Cf. Bressolette, 1984; Oakley, 2003, 207–16.
60. Thus Matthew 18:18–20: "Truly I say to you whatever you bind on earth shall be bound in heaven, and whatever you loose on earth shall be loosed in heaven. Again I say to you, if two of you agree on earth about anything, it will be done for them in heaven. For where two or three are gathered in my name, there am I in the midst of them."
61. For the "episcopalist" strand in the thinking of the ninth-century Frankish bishops, see Ullmann, 1955; 1970, 132–35; Morrison, 1964, 55–100; 1969, 230–33.
62. Cyprian, *Ep.* 68; in *CSEL* 3(2), 746, lines 3–5.

63. See above, n59.
64. Minnerath, 1998, 141.
65. Ullmann, 1972, 119; cf. Ullmann, 1955; 1970, 229–38.
66. Ullmann, 1972, 128.

Epilogue

1. Referring here to Michel Foucault's attempt to map in synchronic fashion the networks or grids of relationship that confer unity on the four great epistemes (or "epochs of epistemic coherence") into which he believed the years since the later Middle Ages to have fallen, and to identify (though certainly not to explain) the stark ruptures that he claimed separated them from one another. See Foucault, 1966. I draw the descriptive phrase quoted from White, 1973, 27.
2. Good summation by Howe, 2005, 22–35 (words cited at 31).
3. Ibid., 32–34.
4. Morrison, 1964, 102.
5. And one of them, going further, adds that "the emperor is his vicar." Cited in Carlyle and Carlyle, 1903–36, 2:224n1.
6. Cited from Folz, 1969, 207.
7. Hobbes, *Leviathan*, pt. 4, ch. 47; ed. Oakeshott, 1946, 457.

Bibliography

Bibliographies

For Greek and Roman, early Christian and Byzantine, and early medieval political thought, extensive bibliographical data and affiliated commentary may readily be found in Christopher Rowe and Malcolm Schofield, eds., *The Cambridge History of Greek and Roman Political Thought* (Cambridge: Cambridge University Press, 2000), 672–728; Francis Dvornik, *Early Christian and Byzantine Political Philosophy: Origins and Background*, 2 vols. (Washington, DC: Dumbarton Oaks Center for Byzantine Studies, 1966), 2:851–939; and J. H. Burns, ed., *The Cambridge History of Medieval Political Thought, c. 350-c. 1450* (Cambridge: Cambridge University Press, 1988), 694–746. For particular topics, and in addition to the above, reference may profitably be made to the helpful selective bibliographies in such works as Gábor Klaniczay, *Holy Rulers and Blessed Princesses: Dynastic Cults in Medieval Central Europe* (Cambridge: Cambridge University Press, 2000), 445–80 (helpful also for sacral kingship in general); Peter Brown, *Augustine of Hippo: A Biography*, new ed. (Berkeley and Los Angeles: University of California Press, 2000), 521–38; Jaroslav Pelikan, *The Emergence of the Catholic Tradition, 100–600* (Chicago: University of Chicago Press, 1971), 358–76; Karl F. Morrison, *Tradition and Authority in the Western Church, 300–1140* (Princeton: Princeton University Press, 1969), 409–43; Klaus Schatz, *Papal Primacy from Its Origins to the Present*, trans. J. A. Otto and L. M. Maloney (Collegeville, MN: Liturgical Press, 1996); Susan Reynolds, *Fiefs and Vassals: The Medieval Evidence Reinterpreted* (Oxford: Oxford University Press, 1994), 487–526.

General Accounts

Until the mid-twelfth century is reached, the historian of political thought will look in vain for the familiar type of primary source devoted specifically (and maybe exclusively) to *political* thinking. Because of that, the political thinking of the late antique and early medieval centuries has not proved easy of access and has been rather less well served by the general histories of the subject than have the later medieval centuries. In the longer histories, the sections devoted to the earlier period have tended to be comparatively brief—thus, for example, Arthur P. Monahan, *Consent, Coercion and Limit: The Medieval Origins of Parliamentary Democracy* (Kingston and Montreal: McGill-Queen's University

Press, 1987), or Janet Coleman, *A History of Political Thought*, 2 vols. (Oxford: Blackwell Publishing, 2000), vol. 2. Of the shorter histories, it is true, Walter Ullmann's *A History of Political Thought: The Middle Ages* (Baltimore: Penguin Books, 1965) is unusual in devoting around 40 percent of its pages to the period before the eleventh century, but that notwithstanding, the church fathers receive no more than a handful of scattered references and Augustine's political thinking is (oddly) not the focus of any sustained attention. Of the longer histories, the old classic account by R. W. and A. J. Carlyle, *A History of Medieval Political Theory in the West*, 6 vols. (London and Edinburgh: William Blackwood and Sons, 1903–36), stands out by virtue of the fact that it devotes a full volume to the period before the tenth century, and that volume is the more valuable because of its generous citation of crucial texts from sources that are frequently not readily accessible. Of the shorter histories, Joseph P. Canning, *A History of Medieval Political Thought, 300–1450* (London: Routledge, 1996), devotes a valuable and balanced, if succinct, section to the earlier period. But for a fuller and more or less up-to-date account, one would do best to turn to the lengthy and meaty chapters contributed to *The Cambridge History of Medieval Political Thought* by such distinguished scholars as Henry Chadwick, D. M. Nicol, R. A. Markus, P. D. King, D. E. Luscombe, R. van Caenegem, and Janet Nelson. Useful collections of translated excerpts from the pertinent late antique and early medieval texts may be found in Oliver O'Donovan and Joan Lockwood O'Donovan, eds., *From Irenaeus to Grotius: A Sourcebook in Christian Political Thought* (Grand Rapids: William B. Eerdmann, 1999), and Brian Tierney, *The Crisis of Church and State: 1050–1300* (Englewood Cliffs, NJ: Prentice-Hall, 1964).

Works Cited

Acta Imperii Inedita. 1880–85. Ed. Eduard Winkelmann, 2 vols. (Innsbruck: Verlag der Wagner'schen Universitäts-Buchhandlung, 1880–85).

Adams, Jeremy du Quesnay. 1971. *The Populus of Augustine and Jerome* (New Haven: Yale University Press, 1971).

Adkins, A. W. H. 1960. *Merit and Responsibility: A Study in Greek Values* (Oxford: Oxford University Press, 1960).

———. 1970. *From the Many to the One: A Study of Personality and Views of Human Nature in the Context of Ancient Greek Society, Values and Beliefs* (Ithaca: Cornell University Press, 1970).

Agobard of Lyons. *De privilegio*, in *PL* 104, 133.

Al-Azmeh, Aziz. 1997. *Muslim Kingship: Power and the Sacred in Muslim, Christian and Pagan Politics* (London: I. B. Tauris, 1997).

Al-Azmeh, Aziz, and James M. Bak, eds. 2004. *Monotheistic Kingship: The Medieval Variants* (Budapest: Central European University Press, 2004).

Alcuin. 1895. *Epistolae*, in *MGH: Epistolae variorum Carolo Magno regnante* (Berlin, 1895).

———. 1982. *The Bishops, Kings and Saints of York*, ed. and trans. Peter Godman (Oxford: Clarendon Press, 1982).

Alföldi, Andreas. (1970), *Die monarchische Repräsentation in römischen Kaiserreiche* (Darmstadt: Wissenschaftliche Buchgesellschaft, 1970).

Ambrose of Milan. 1982. *Epistolae, CSEL* 82.
———. 1898. *Enarrationes in Psalmis,* in *PL* 14.
Ambrosiaster (Pseudo-Augustine). 1898. *Quaestiones Veteris et Novi Testamenti CXXVII,* in *CSEL* 50.
Ammianus Marcellinus. 1935–39. *Res gestae,* ed. and trans. John C. Rolfe, 3 vols. (Cambridge: Harvard University Press, 1935–39).
Anastos, Milton V. 2001. "Byzantine Political Theory: Its Classical Precedents and Legal Embodiment," in Milton V. Anastos, *Aspects of the Mind of Byzantium,* ed. Speros Vryonis, Jr., and Nicolas Goodhue (Aldershot, Hants.: Ashgate Variorum, 2001), 13–53.
Anchor Bible Dictionary, The. 1992. Ed. David Neal Freedman et al., 6 vols. (New York: Doubleday, 1992).
Anderson, Bernhard W. 1967. *Creation versus Chaos: The Reinterpretation of Mythical Symbolism in the Bible* (New York: Association Press, 1967).
———. 1975. "Politics and the Transcendent," *Political Science Reviewer* 1 (1975): 1–29.
Anderson, Thornton. 1967. *Russian Political Thought: An Introduction* (Ithaca: Cornell University Press, 1967).
Anglo-Norman Anonymous. 1966. *Tractates,* ed. Karl Pellens, *Die Texte des Normanische Anonymus* (Wiesbaden: Franz Steiner Verlag, 1966).
Aristotle. 1891. *On the Constitution of Athens,* ed. and trans. E. Poste (London: Macmillan, 1891).
———. 1908–52. *The Works of Aristotle Translated into English,* ed. W. D. Ross, 12 vols. (Oxford: Clarendon Press, 1908–52).
———. 1948. *The Politics of Aristotle,* trans. Ernest Barker (Oxford: Clarendon Press, 1948).
Arquillière, H.-X. 1955. *L'Augustinisme politique: Essai sur la formation des théories politiques du Moyen Age,* rev. ed. (Paris: Librairie philosophique J. Vrin, 1955).
Asakawa, Kan-ichi, ed. and trans. 1955. *The Documents of Iriki,* 2nd ed. (Tokyo: Japan Society for the Promotion of Science, 1955).
Augustine of Hippo. 1896. *Confessiones, CSEL* 33.
———. 1902. *De gratia Christi et de peccato originali, CSEL* 3:123–206.
———. 1909. *Contra Cresconium, CSEL* 52:323–582.
———. 1909. *Contra literras Petiliani, CSEL* 52:1–227.
———. 1955. *De civitate dei, CSSL* 47–48.
———. 1956. *Enarrationes in Psalmis, CSSL* 38–40.
———. 1895. *Epistolae, CSEL* 34.
Baetke, Walter. 1964. *Yngvi und die Ynglinger: Eine quellenkritische Untersuchung über das nordische Sakralkönigtum* (Berlin: Akademie-Verlag, 1964).
Baines, John. 1995. "Kingship, Definition of Culture, and Legitimation," in O'Connor and Silverman, eds., 1995, 3–47.
Bak, J. M. 1973. "Medieval Symbology of the State: Percy Schramm's Contribution, *Viator* 4 (1973): 33–63.
Bammel, Ernest. 1984a. "The Revolution Theory from Reimarus to Brandon," in Bammel and Moule, eds. (1984), 11–68.

———. 1984b. "Romans 13," in Bammel and Moule, eds. (1984), 365–83.
Bammel, Ernst, and C. F. D. Moule, eds. 1984. *Jesus and the Politics of His Day* (Cambridge: Cambridge University Press, 1984).
Barker, Ernest, 1957. *Social and Political Thought in Byzantium from Justinian I to the Last Palaeologus* (Oxford: Clarendon Press, 1957).
Barnes, Timothy D. 1971. *Tertullian: A Historical and Literary Study* (Oxford: Clarendon Press, 1971).
———. 1981. *Constantine and Eusebius* (Cambridge: Harvard University Press, 1981).
———. 1984. *Early Christianity and the Roman Empire* (London: Variorum, 1984).
———. 1994. *From Eusebius to Augustine: Selected Papers, 1982–1993* (Aldershot, Hants.: Variorum, 1994).
Baynes, Norman H. 1934. "Eusebius and the Christian Empire," in *Mélanges Biderz, Annuaire de l'Institute de Philologie et d'Histoire Orientale*, vol. 2 (Brussels: 1934), 13–18.
———. 1955. *Byzantine Studies and Other Essays* (London: Athlone Press, 1955).
Beal, John P., James A. Coriden, and Thomas J. Green, eds. 2000. *New Commentary on the Code of Canon Law* (New York: Paulist Press, 2000).
Bede, the Venerable. 1965. *A History of the English Church and People*, trans. Leo Shirley-Price (Baltimore: Penguin Books, 1965).
———. 1969. *Historia ecclesiastica gentis Anglorum*, ed. R. A. B. Mynors (Oxford: Clarendon Press, 1969).
Bellitto, Christopher M., and Louis I. Hamilton, eds. 2005. *Reforming the Church before Modernity: Patterns and Approaches* (Aldershot, Hants.: Ashgate Publishing, 2005).
Beneyto Péres, Juan. 1964. *Historia de las doctrinas politicas*, 4th ed. (Madrid: M. Aguilar, 1964).
Berges, Wilhelm. 1938. *Die Fürstenspiegel des hohen und späten Mittelalters* (Leipzig: Verlag Karl W. Hiersemann, 1938).
Berkhof, H. 1939. *Die Theologie des Eusebius von Caesarea* (Amsterdam: Uitgevers-maatschappij Holland, 1939).
———. 1947. *Kirche und Kaiser: Eine Untersuchung des Entstehung der byzantinischen und der theokratischen Staatsanfassung im vierten Jahrhundert*, trans. from the Dutch by G. W. Locher (Zurich: Evangelischer Verlag A. G. Zollskorn, 1947).
Bernheim, Ernst. 1896. "Politische Begriffe des Mittelalters im Lichte der Anschauungen Augustins," *Deutsche Zeitschrift für Geschichtswissenschaft* 13 (1896): 1–23.
Beskow, Per. 1962. *Rex Gloriae: The Kingship of Christ in the Early Church*, trans. Eric J. Sharpe (Stockholm: Almquist and Wiksell, 1962).
Bettenson, Henry, trans. 1972. Augustine, *Concerning the City of God against the Pagans* (Harmondsworth, Middlx.: Pelican Books, 1972).
Beumann, H. 1956. "Zur Entwicklung transpersonaler Staatsvorstehungen, in *Das Königtum* (1956), 185–224.
Bhandari, D. R. 1963. *History of European Political Philosophy* (Bangalore: Bangalore Print and Publishing, 1963).
Bickerman, Elias. 1973. "Consecratio," in Bickerman et al. (1973), 1–25.

Bickerman, Elias, et al. 1973. *Le culte des Souverains dans l'Empire Romaine* (Geneva: Foundation Hardt, 1973).
Binchy, D. A. 1970. *Celtic and Anglo-Saxon Kingship* (Oxford: Clarendon Press, 1970).
Black, Antony. 2001. *The History of Islamic Political Thought: From the Prophet to the Present* (New York: Routledge, 2001).
Bloch, Marc. 1924. *Les rois thaumaturges: Étude sur le caractère surnaturel attribué à la puissance royale particulièrement en France et en Angleterre* (Strasbourg: Librairie Ista, 1924).
———. 1964. *Feudal Society,* trans. H. H. Manyon, 2 vols. (Chicago: University of Chicago Press, 1964).
———. 1973. *The Royal Touch: Sacred Monarchy and Scrofula in England and France,* trans. J. E. Anderson (London: Routledge and Kegan Paul, 1973),
Bossuet, J.-B. 1869. *Discours sur l'histoire universelle,* ed. Charles Louandre (Paris: Charpentier, 1869).
Boureau, Alain, and Claudio Sergio, eds. 1992. *Le royauté sacré dans le monde chrétien* (Paris: Éditions de l'EHESS, 1992).
Boutrouche, R. 1959. *Seigneurie et féodalité* (Paris: Aubier, 1959).
Brandon, S. G. F. 1958. "The Myth and Ritual Position Critically Considered," in Hooke, ed. (1958), 261–91.
———. 1967. *Jesus and the Zealots: A Study of the Political Factor in Primitive Christianity* (Manchester: Manchester University Press, 1967).
Bressolette, Claude. 1984. *Le Pouvoir dans la société et dans l'église: L'Ecclésiologie politique du Monseigneur Maret* (Paris: Éditions du Cerf, 1984).
Brock, Roger, and Stephen Hodkinson, eds. 2000. *Alternatives to Athens: Varieties of Political Organization in Classical Greece* (Oxford: Oxford University Press, 2000).
Brown, E. A. R. 1974. "The Tyranny of a Construct: Feudalism and Historians of Medieval Europe," *American Historical Review* 79, no. 4 (1974): 1073–88.
Brown, Peter. 1971. *The World of Late Antiquity, A.D. 150–750* (London: Thames and Hudson, 1971).
———. 1995. *Authority and the Sacred: Aspects of the Christianization of the Roman World* (Cambridge: Cambridge University Press, 1995).
———. 1997. *The Rise of Western Christendom: Triumph and Adversity, A.D. 200–1000* (Oxford: Blackwell, 1997).
———. 2000. *Augustine of Hippo: A Biography,* rev. ed. (Berkeley and Los Angeles: University of California Press, 2000).
Bruce, F. F. 1984. "Render to Caesar," in Bammel and Moule, eds. (1984), 249–63.
Buber, Martin. 1967. *Kingship of God,* 3rd ed., trans. Richard Scheimann (New York: Harper and Row, 1967).
Burckhardt, Jacob. 1949. *The Age of Constantine the Great,* trans. Moses Hadas (New York: Pantheon Books, 1949).
Butler, Eliza Marion. 1935. *The Tyranny of Greece over Germany* (Cambridge: Cambridge University Press, 1935).
Bynum, Caroline Walker. 1987. *Holy Feast, Holy Fast: The Religious Significance of Food for Medieval Women* (Berkeley and Los Angeles: University of California Press, 1987).

Cadoux, C. J. 1925. *The Early Church and the World* (Edinburgh: T. and T. Clark, 1925).
Cambridge Companion to the Age of Constantine, The. 2006. Ed. Noel Lanski (Cambridge: Cambridge University Press, 2006).
Cambridge History of Greek and Roman Political Thought, The. 2000. Ed. Christopher Rowe and Malcolm Schofield (Cambridge: Cambridge University Press, 2000).
Cambridge History of Iran, The. 1968–91. Ed. Peter Avery et al., 7 vols. (Cambridge: Cambridge University Press, 1968–91).
Cambridge History of Medieval Political Thought, c. 350-c. 1450, The. 1988. Ed. J. H. Burns (Cambridge: Cambridge University Press, 1988).
Cameron, Averil, and Stuart G. Hall, eds. and trans. 1999. Eusebius, *Life of Constantine* (Oxford: Clarendon Press, 1999).
Cannadine, David, and Simon Price, eds. 1987. *Rituals of Royalty: Power and Ceremonial in Traditional Societies* (Cambridge: Cambridge University Press, 1987).
Canning, Joseph P. 1996. *A History of Medieval Political Thought 300–1450* (London: Routledge, 1996).
Cantor, Norman F. 1958. *Church, Kingship, and Lay Investiture in England, 1089–1135* (Princeton: Princeton University Press, 1958).
Cappellari, Fra Mauro. 1832. *Il Trionfo della Santa Sede e della Chiesa contro gli assalti degli inovatori* (Venice: Giuseppe Baltaggia, 1832).
Carlyle, R. W., and A. J. Carlyle. 1903–36. *A History of Medieval Political Theory in the West*, 6 vols. (London and Edinburgh: William Blackwood and Sons, 1903–36).
Cartledge, Paul. 2000. "Greek Political Thought: The Historical Context," in *Cambridge History of Greek and Roman Political Thought* (2000), 11–22.
Caspar, E. 1930–33. *Geschichte des Papsttums von den Anfängen bis zur Höhe des Weltherrschaft*, 2 vols. (Tübingen: J. C. B. Mohr, 1930–33).
Catlin, George. 1939. *The Story of Political Philosophy* (New York: McGraw-Hill, 1939).
Centrone, Bruno. 2000. "Platonism and Pythagoreanism in the Early Empire," in *Cambridge History of Greek and Roman Political Thought* (2000), 559–84.
Cerfaux, L. 1959. "Le conflit entre Dieu et le Souverain divinisée dans l'Apocalypse de Jean," in *The Sacral Kingship* (1959), 459–70.
Cerfaux, L., and J. Tondriau. 1957. *Un concurrent du Christianisme: Le culte des souverains dans la civilisation Gréco-Romain* (Tournai: Desclée, 1957).
Chadwick, H. Munro. 1926. *The Heroic Age* (Cambridge: Cambridge University Press, 1926).
Chadwick, Henry. 1966. *Early Christian Thought and the Classical Tradition* (New York: Oxford University Press, 1966).
———. 1986. *Augustine*. (Oxford: Oxford University Press, 1986).
Chadwick, Owen. 1981. *The Popes and European Revolution* (Oxford: Clarendon Press, 1981).
Chaney, William A. 1970. *The Cult of Kingship in Anglo-Saxon England* (Manchester: Manchester University Press, 1970).
Cherniavsky, Michael. 1959. "Khan or Basileus: An Aspect of Russian Medieval Political Theory," *Journal of the History of Ideas* 20, no. 4 (1959): 456–76.

Cheyette, Frederic, ed. 1968. *Lordship and Community in Medieval Europe: Selected Readings* (New York: Holt, Rinehart, and Winston, 1968).
———. 1996. Review of Susan Reynolds, *Fiefs and Vassals* (1994), in *Speculum* 71, no. 4 (1996): 998–1006.
Cicero. 1927–29. *Ad Quintum Fratrem*, ed. and trans. W. G. Williams in *Cicero: Letters to His Friends*, 3 vols. (London: Heinemann, 1927–29).
———. 1993. *De natura deorum*, ed. and trans. H. Rackham (London: Heinemann, 1933).
Claessen, Henri J. M., and Peter Skalnik, eds. (1978), *The Early State* (The Hague: Mouton Publishers, 1978).
Clagett, M., G. Post, and R. Reynolds. 1961. *Twelfth-Century Europe and the Foundations of Modern Society* (Madison: University of Wisconsin Press, 1961).
Cochrane, Charles Norris. 1957. *Christianity and Classical Culture: A Study of Thought and Action from Augustus to Augustine* (New York: Oxford University Press, 1957).
Coleman, Janet. 2000. *A History of Political Thought*, 2 vols. (Oxford: Blackwell, 2000).
Collins, Roger. 1998. *Charlemagne* (Toronto: University of Toronto Press, 1998).
Combès, Gustave. 1927. *La doctrine politique de saint Augustin* (Paris: Librairie Plon, 1927).
Cornford, F. M. 1937. *Plato's Cosmology* (text of the *Timaeus* accompanied by an extended commentary) (Indianapolis: Bobbs-Merrill, 1937).
Corpus Juris Canonici. 1879–81. Ed. A. Friedberg, 2 vols. (Leipzig: B. Tauchnitz, 1879–81).
Corpus Juris Civilis. 1899–1902. Ed. P. Krueger, Th. Mommsen, and R. Schoell, 3 vols. (Berlin: Weidman, 1899–1902).
Coulborn, Rushton, ed. 1956. *Feudalism in History* (Princeton: Princeton University Press, 1956).
Cranz, F. Edward. 1950. "*De civitate dei*, XV, 2, and Augustine's Idea of the Christian Society," *Speculum* 25 (1950): 215–25. Reprinted in Marcus, ed. (1972), 404–21.
———. 1952. "Kingdom and Polity in Eusebius of Caesarea," *Harvard Theological Review* 45, no. 1 (1952): 47–65.
Crone, Patricia. 2004. *God's Rule: Government and Islam* (New York: Columbia University Press, 2004).
Crüsemann, F. 1978. *Der Widerstand gegen das Königtum: Die antiköniglichen Texte des Alten Testamentes und der Kampfe um den frühen israelitischen Staat* (Neukirchen-Vluyn: Neukirchener Verlag, 1978).
CSEL = *Corpus Scriptorum Ecclesiasticorum Latinorum*, 96 vols. (Vienna: G. Geroldi Filium Bibliopolam Academiae, 1866-).
CSSL = *Corpus Scriptorum Christianorum. Series Latina*, 96 vols. (Townholti: Typographie Brepols Editores Pontifici, 1954-).
Cullmann, O. 1957. *The State in the New Testament* (New York: Charles Scribner's Sons, 1957).
Dagron, Gilbert. 2003. *Emperor and Priest: The Imperial Office in Byzantium*, trans. Joan Birrell (Cambridge: Cambridge University Press, 2003).
Das Königtum: Seine geistigen und rechtlichen Grundlagen. 1956. (Lindau and Konstanz: Jan Thorbeke Verlag, 1956).
Dawson, Christopher. 1948. *Religion and Culture* (London: Sheed and Ward, 1948).

DCD = Augustine, *De Civitate Dei,* in *CSSL* 47–48.
Deane, Herbert A. 1963. *The Political and Social Ideas of St. Augustine* (New York: Columbia University Press, 1963).
De Jong, Mayke. 2001. "Religion," in McKitterick, ed., *Early Middle Ages* (2001), 431–64.
——. 2005. "Charlemagne's Church," in Story, ed., 2005, 103–35.
Delaruelle, E. 1955. "Jonas d'Orléans et le moralisme carolingien," *Bulletin de la littérature ecclésiastique* 55 (1955): 129–43.
Deshman, Robert. 1980. "The Exalted Servant: The Ruler Ideology of the Prayerbook of Charles the Bald," *Viator* 11 (1980): 385–417.
De Vries, Jan. 1950. "Das Königtum bei den Germanen," *Saeculum* 6 (1950): 289–309.
Dhondt, Jean. 1957. "Les 'solidarités' médiévales. Une societé en transition: la Flandre en 1127–28," *Annales—Economies—Sociétés—Civilisations* 12 (1957): 529–60.
Dictionary of the Middle Ages. 1982–89. Ed. Joseph R. Strayer, 13 vols. (New York: Charles Scribner and Sons, 1982–89).
Dictionnaire de droit canonique. 1935–65. 7 vols. (Paris: Letourzey et Ané., 1935–65).
Doyle, Phyllis. 1933. *History of Political Thought* (London: Jonathan Cape, 1933).
Draak, Maartje. 1959. "Some Aspects of Kingship in Pagan Ireland," in *The Sacral Kingship* (1959), 651–63.
Drake, H. A., trans. 1975. *In Praise of Constantine: A Historical Study and New Translation of Eusebius' Tricennial Orations* (Berkeley and Los Angeles: University of California Press, 1975).
——. 2000. *Constantine and the Bishops: The Politics of Intolerance* (Baltimore: Johns Hopkins University Press, 2000).
——. 2006. "The Impact of Constantine on Christianity," in *Cambridge Companion to the Age of Constantine* (2006), 111–36.
Duby, G. 1978. *Les trois ordres ou l'imaginaire du feudalisme* (Paris: Gallimard, 1978).
Dumézil, Georges. 1939. *Mythes et Dieux des Germains* (Paris: E. Leroux, 1939).
Dunn, John. 1969. *The Political Thought of John Locke* (Cambridge: Cambridge University Press, 1969).
Dunning, William A. 1902. *A History of Political Theories: Ancient and Modern* (New York: Macmillan, 1902).
Dvornik, Francis. 1951. "Pope Gelasius and Emperor Anastasius I," *Byzantinische Zeitschrift* 4 (1951): 111–16.
——. 1956. "Byzantine Political Ideas in Kievan Russia," *Dumbarton Oaks Papers 9 and 10* (Cambridge: Harvard University Press, 1956), 71–121.
——. 1966. *Early Christian and Byzantine Political Philosophy: Origins and Background,* 2 vols. (Washington, DC: Dumbarton Oaks Center for Byzantine Studies, 1966).
Eaton, John H. 1976. *Kingship and the Psalms* (Naperville, IL: Alec R. Allenson, 1976).
Eco, Umberto. 1986. *Travels in Hyperreality: Essays,* trans. William Weaver (San Diego: Harcourt, Brace and Janovich, 1986).
Edgerton, Samuel. 2001. *Theaters of Conversion: Religious Architecture and Indian Artisans in Colonial Mexico* (Albuquerque: University of New Mexico Press, 2001).
Edsman, C. M. 1959. "Zum sakralen Königtum in der Forschung der letzten hundert Jahre," in *The Sacral Kingship* (1959), 1–17.

Edwards, Mark. 2006. "The Beginnings of Christianization," in *Cambridge Companion to the Age of Constantine* (2006), 137–58.
Ehrlich, Ernst Ludwig. 1962. *A Concise History of Israel*, trans. James Barr (New York: Harper and Row, 1962).
Einhard. 1972. *Vita Caroli Magni*, ed. and trans. E. S. Firchow and E. H. Zeydel (Coral Gables, FL: University of Miami Press, 1972).
Eliade, Mircea. 1959. *Cosmos and History: The Myth of the Eternal Return* (New York: Harper and Row, 1959).
——. 1978–85. *History of Religious Ideas*, trans. Alf Hilfebatel and Diane Apostolos-Cappadone, 3 vols. (Chicago: University of Chicago Press, 1978–85).
Engnell, Ivan. 1967. *Studies in Divine Kingship in the Ancient Near East*, 2nd ed. (Oxford: Basil Blackwell, 1967).
Enright, Michael J. 1985. *Iona, Tara and Soissons: The Origin of the Royal Anointing Ritual* (Berlin: 1985).
Ensslin, W. 1955. "Auctoritas und Potestas. Zur Zweigewaltenlehre des Papstes Gelasius I," *Historisches Jahrbuch* 74 (1955): 661–68.
Eusebius of Caesarea. 1902. *Laus Constantini*, in *Eusebius Werke. Erster Band*, ed. Ivar A. Heikel (Leipzig: J. C. Hinschius 'sche Buchhandlung, 1902).
——. 1913. *Die Demonstratio Evangelica*, ed. Ivar A. Heikel (Leipzig: J. C. Hinrichs, 1913).
——. 1975. *Vita Constantini*, ed. Friedhelm Winkelmann, *Über das Leben des Kaisers Konstantin* (Berlin: Akademie Verlag, 1975).
Ewig, Eugen. 1956. "Zum christlichen Königsgedanken in Frühmittelalter," in *Das Königtum* (1956), 7–73.
Faivre, Alexandre. 1977. *Naissance d'une Hiérarchie: Les premières étapes du cursus clericus* (Paris: Éditions Beauchesne, 1977).
Farina, F. 1966. *L'Impero e l'Imperatore Cristiano in Eusebio di Cesarea: La prima teologia politica de Cristianesimo* (Zurich: Pas Verlag, 1966).
Ferguson, Wallace. 1948. *The Renaissance in Historical Thought: Five Centuries of Interpretation* (Cambridge: Harvard University Press, 1948).
Ferrar, W. J., trans. 1920. *The Proof of the Gospel: Being the Demonstratio Evangelica of Eusebius of Caesarea*, 2 vols. (London: Society for Promoting Christian Knowledge, 1920).
Festschrift für Otto Höfler. 1968. 2 vols. (Vienna: Verlag Notring, 1968).
Figgis, John Neville. 1921. *The Political Aspects of St. Augustine's "City of God"* (London: Longman's, Green, 1921).
Fischwick, Duncan. 1987–2005. *The Imperial Cult in the Latin West: Studies in the Ruler Cult of the Western Provinces of the Roman Empire*, 3 vols. (Leiden: E. J. Brill, 1987–2005).
Folz, Robert. 1969. *The Concept of Empire in Western Europe from the Fifth to the Fourteenth Century*, trans. Sheila Ann Ogilvie (New York: Harper and Row, 1969).
Foster, Michael. 1941. *Plato to Machiavelli* (London: George G. Harrap, 1941).
Foucault, Michel. 1966. *Le mots et les choses* (Paris: Gallimard, 1966).
Fouracre, Paul. 2000. *The Age of Charles Martel* (Harlow, Essex: Pearson Education).
Fox, Robin Lane. 1986. *Pagans and Christians* (San Francisco: Harper and Row, 1986).
Fränkel, Hermann. (1975), *Early Greek Poetry and Philosophy*, trans. M. Hadas and J. Willis (Oxford: Oxford University Press, 1975).

Frankfort, Henri. 1948a. *Kingship and the Gods: A Study in Near Eastern Religion as the Integration of Society and Nature* (Chicago: University of Chicago Press, 1948).
———. 1948b. *Egyptian Religion* (New York: Harper and Row, 1948).
Frankfort, Henri, John A. Wilson, and Thorkild Jacobsen. 1949. *Before Philosophy: The Intellectual Adventure of Ancient Man* (Baltimore: Penguin, 1949).
Fraser, Sir James George. 1905. *Lectures in the Early History of Kingship* (London: Macmillan, 1905).
———. 1920. *The Magical Origins of Kings* (London: Macmillan, 1920).
———. 1925. *The Golden Bough: A Study in Magic and Religion*, abr. ed. (London: Macmillan, 1925).
Fredouille, J.-C. 1984. "Tertullien et l'empire," *Revue des études augustiniennes* 29 (1984):197–206.
Fried, J. 1982. "Der Karolingische Herrschaftsverband in 9 Jh. zwischen 'Kirche' und 'Konighaus,'" *Historische Zeitschrift* 23 (1982): 1–43.
Friedberg, A., ed. 1879–81. *Corpus Juris Canonici*, 2 vols. (Leipzig: B. Tauchnitz, 1879–80).
Fuhrmann, Horst, ed. 1968. *Das Constitutum Constantini* (Hannover: Hahnsche Buchhandlung, 1968).
Fujitani, T. 1996. *Splendid Monarchy Power and Pageantry in Modern Japan* (Berkeley and Los Angeles: University of California Press, 1996).
Funk, Philipp. 1935. "Der fragliche Anonymus von York," *Historisches Jahrbuch* 55 (1935): 251–76.
Furnmark, Arne. 1959. "Was There a Sacred Kingship in Minoan Crete?" in *The Sacral Kingship* (1959), 369–70.
Fustel de Coulanges, Numa Denis. 1955. *The Ancient City,* trans. Willard Small (Garden City, NY: Doubleday Anchor Books, 1955).
Gadd, C. J. 1933. "Babylonian Myth and Ritual," in Hooke, ed., *Myth and Ritual* (1933), 40–67.
Gandillac, M. de. 1943. *Oeuvres complètes de Pseudo-Denys l'Aréopagite* (Paris: Aubier, 1943).
Ganshof, F. L. 1961. *Feudalism,* trans. Philip Greason, 2nd ed. (New York: Harper Torchbook, 1961).
Geanakoplos, Deano J. 1966. *Byzantine East and Latin West: Two Worlds of Christendom in the Middle Ages and Renaissance* (Oxford: Basil Blackwell, 1966).
Gerth, H. H., and C. Wright Mills, eds. and trans. 1946. *From Max Weber: Essays in Sociology* (New York: Oxford University Press, 1946).
Gettel, Raymond G. 1924. *History of Political Thought* (New York: Century Company, 1924).
Gilbert, Michelle. 1987. "The Person of the King: Ritual and Power in a Ghanaian State," in Cannadine and Price, eds. (1987), 298–330.
Goldberg, Eric. 2006. *Struggle for Empire: Kingship and Conflict under Louis the German, 812–871* (Ithaca: Cornell University Press, 2006).
Goldhill, Simon. 2000. "Greek Drama and Political Theory," in *Cambridge History of Greek and Roman Political Thought* (2000), 60–88.
Goodenough, E. R. 1928. "The Political Philosophy of Hellenistic Kingship," *Yale Classical Studies* 1 (1928): 55–102.

———. 1938. *The Politics of Philo Judaeus. Practice and Theory* (New Haven: Yale University Press, 1938).
Grabar, André. 1971. *L'Empereur dans l'art byzantin* (London: Variorum, 1971), 90–96.
Grant, F. C. 1959. "The Idea of the Kingdom of God in the New Testament," in *The Sacral Kingship* (1959), 439–46.
Graus, Frantisék. 1965. *Volk, Herrscher und Heiliger im Reich der Merowinger: Studium zur Hagiographie der Merowinger Zeit* (Prague: Nakladatelstvi Československé akademie věd, 1965).
Gunkel, Hermann. 1914. "Die Königspsalmen," *Prussische Jahrbuch* 158 (1914): 42–68.
Gurevich, Aaron. 1995. *The Origins of European Individualism* (Oxford: Blackwell, 1995).
Gurney, O. R. 1958. "Hittite Kingship," in Hooke, ed. (1958), 105–21.
Güterbock, H. G. 1954. "Authority and Law in the Hittite Kingdom," *Supplement to the Journal of the American Oriental Society*, no. 17 (July-Sept. 1954): 16–21.
Guthrie, W. K. C. 1960. *The Greek Philosophers: From Thales to Plato* (New York: Harper and Row, 1960).
Habicht, Christian. 1973. "Die augustinische Zeit und das erste Jahrhundert nach Christi Geburt," in Bickerman et al. (1973), 39–98.
Hall, John W. 1962–63. "Feudalism in Japan: A Reassessment," *Comparative Studies in Society and History* 5, no. 1 (1962–63): 15–51.
Halsall, Guy. 2003. *Warfare and Society in the Barbarian West 450–900* (London: Routledge, 2003).
Hambly, Gavin R. G. 1968–91. "The Pahlavi Autocracy: Muhammad Riza, Shah," in *Cambridge History of Iran* (1968–91), 7:285.
Hamilton, Edith, and Huntington Cairns, eds. 1973. *The Collected Dialogues of Plato, Including the Letters* (Princeton: Princeton University Press, 1973).
Harbury, W. 1984. "The Temple Tax," in Bammel and Moule, eds. (1984), 265–86.
Hardy, R. S. 1941. "The Old Hittite Kingdom," *American Journal of Semitic Languages and Literatures* 58 (1941): 176–216.
Harmon, M. J. 1964. *Political Thought from Plato to the Present* (New York: McGraw-Hill, 1964).
Hauck, Karl. 1950. "Geblütsheiligkeit," in *Liber Floridus* (1950), 187–240.
Hegel, G. W. F. 1953. *Reason in History: A General Introduction to the Philosophy of History*, trans. Robert S. Hartman (New York: Liberal Arts Press, 1953).
———. 1967. *Hegel's Philosophy of Right*, trans. T. M. Knox (New York: Oxford University Press, 1967).
Heikel, Ivar A., ed. 1902. *Eusebius Werke. Erster Band* (Leipzig: J. C. Hinschius 'sche Buchhandlung, 1902).
———, ed. 1913. *Die Demonstratio Evangelica* (Leipzig: J. C. Hinrichs, 1913).
Henn, William. 1998. "Historical-Theological Synthesis of the Relation between Primacy and Episcopacy during the Second Millennium," in *Il Primato del Successore di Pietro* (1998), 222–73.
Hincmar of Rheims. 1883–97. *De ordine palatii*, in *MGH: Leges. Sectio II*, vol. 2 (Hannover, 1883–97).
Hinschius, P., ed. 1863. *Decretales Pseudo-Isidoreanae* (Leipzig: B. Tauchnitz, 1863.)

Hintze, Otto H. 1929. "Wesen und Verbreitung des Feudalismus," *Sitzungberichte der Preussischen Akademie der Wissenschaften, phil.—hist. Klasse* 20 (1929): 321–30.

Hobbes, Thomas. 1946. *Leviathan*, ed. Michael Oakeshott (Oxford: Basil Blackwell, 1946).

Hocart, A. M. 1927. *Kingship* (London: Oxford University Press, 1927).

———. 1970. *Kings and Councillors: An Essay in the Comparative Anatomy of Human Society*, ed. Rodney Needham (Chicago: University of Chicago Press, 1970).

Höfler, Otto. 1956. "Der Sakralcharakter des germanischen Königtums," in *Das Königtum* (1956), 75–104.

Holt, James C., ed. 1982. *Magna Carta and the Idea of Liberty* (Malabar, FL: Robert E. Krieger, 1982).

———. 1992. *Magna Carta*, 2nd ed. (Cambridge: Cambridge University Press, 1992).

Hooke, S. H., ed. 1933. *Myth and Ritual* (Oxford: Oxford University Press, 1933).

———, ed. 1958. *Myth, Ritual and Kingship: Essays on the Theory and Practice of Kingship in the Ancient Near East and Israel* (Oxford: Clarendon Press, 1958).

———. 1958. "Myth and Ritual: Past and Present," in Hooke, ed. (1958), 1–21.

Horn, Stephen Otto. 1998. "Das Verhältnis von Primat und Episkopat in ersten Jahrtausand: Eine Geschichtlich—Theologische Synthesis," in *Il Primato del Successore di Pietro* (1998), 194–213.

Hornung, Erik. 1992. *Idea into Image: Essays in Ancient Egyptian Thought*, trans. Elizabeth Bredeck (New York: Timken, 1992).

Hosking, Geoffrey. 2001. *Russia and the Russians: A History* (Cambridge: Harvard University Press, 2001).

Howe, John. 2005. "*Gaudium et Spes:* Ecclesiastical Reformers at the Start of a 'New Age,'" in Bellitto and Hamilton, eds. (2005), 22–35.

Hugh of St. Victor. *De sacramentis Christianae fidei*, in PL 176.

Hughes, K. 1996. *The Church in Early Irish Society* (Ithaca: Cornell University Press, 1966).

Humbert of Silva Candida. 1891–97. *Adversus simoniacos*, in *MGH: Libelli de Lite*, vol. 1 (Hannover, 1891–97).

Il primato del Successore di Pietro: Atti de Simposio Teologico, Roma, dicembre 1996. 1998. (Vatican City: Libreria Editrice Vaticanum, 1998).

International Encyclopedia of the Social and Behavioral Sciences. 2001. 26 vols. (New York: Elsevier Science, 2001).

James, E. O. 1959. "The Sacred Kingship and the Priesthood," in *The Sacral Kingship* (1959), 63–70.

———. 1960. *The Ancient Gods: The History and Diffusion of Religion in the Ancient Near East and the Eastern Mediterranean* (London: Weidenfeld and Nicolson, 1960).

Janet, P. 1887. *Histoire de la science politique dans ses rapports avec la morale*, 2 vols. (Paris: Ançienne Librairie Germer Baillière, 1887).

Jenkins, Richard. 1980. *The Victorians and Ancient Greece* (Cambridge: Harvard University Press, 1980).

John of Salisbury. 1909. *Policraticus sive De nugis curialium*, ed. C. C. J. Webb (Oxford: Clarendon Press, 1909).

Johnson, A. R. 1958. "Hebrew Conceptions of Kingship," in Hooke, ed. (1958), 204–35.
——. 1967. *Sacral Kingship in Ancient Israel,* 2nd ed. (Cardiff: Wales University Press, 1967).
Jonas, Hans. 1963. *The Gnostic Religion: The Message of the Alien God and the Beginnings of Christianity,* 2nd ed. (Boston: Beacon Press, 1963).
Jonas of Orléans. 1930. *De institutione regia,* in J. Reviron, ed., *Les ideés politiques d'un evèque du ix siècle: Jonas d'Orléans et son De institutione regia* (Paris: J. Vrin, 1930).
Kantorowicz, Ernst. 1946. *Laudes Regiae: A Study in Liturgical Acclamations and Medieval Ruler Worship* (Berkeley and Los Angeles: University of California Press, 1946).
——. 1957. *The King's Two Bodies: A Study in Medieval Political Theology* (Princeton: Princeton University Press, 1957).
——. 1961. "Kingship under the Impact of Scientific Jurisprudence," in Clagett, Post, and Reynolds, eds. (1961).
Kelley, Donald R. 1964. "*De origine feodorum:* The Beginnings of an Historical Problem," *Speculum* 39, no. 2 (1964): 207–28.
Kern, Fritz. 1939. *Kingship and Law in the Middle Ages,* trans. S. B. Chrimes from the 1st (1914) ed. (Oxford: Basil Blackwell, 1939).
——. 1954. *Gottesguadentum und Widerstandsrecht im frühen Mittelalter,* ed. R. Büchner (Münster-Cologne: Böhlan Verlag, 1954).
King, P. D. 1988. "The Barbarian Kingdoms," in *Cambridge History of Medieval Political Thought* (1988), 123–53.
Klaniczay, Gábor. 2002. *Holy Rulers and Blessed Princesses: Dynastic Cults in Medieval Central Europe* (Cambridge: Cambridge University Press, 2002).
Knox, Wilfred L. 1949. "Church and State in the New Testament," *Journal of Roman Studies* 39 (1949): 23–30.
Küng, Hans. 1967. *The Church,* trans. Ray and Rosaleen Ockenden (New York: Sheed and Ward, 1967).
Lambot, C. 1939. "Lettre inédite de saint Augustin relative an *De Civitate Dei,*" *Revue benedictine* 51 (1939): 109–21.
LC = *Laus Constantini,* in Heikel, ed., 1902.
Leeuwen, Arend T. van. 1965. *Christianity in World History: The Meeting of the Faiths of East and West,* trans. H. H. Hoskins (New York: Charles Scribner's Sons, 1965).
Le pouvoir et le sacré. 1982. (Brussels: Université Libre de Bruxelles, 1982).
Leyser, K. J. 1989. *Rule and Conflict in an Early Medieval Society: Ottonian Saxony* (Oxford: Basil Blackwell, 1989).
Liber Floridus. 1950. *Liber Floridus: Mittellateinischen Studien. Paul Lehmann zum 65. Gebürtstag...gewidmet* (Sankt Ottilien: Eos Verlag der Erzabtei, 1950).
Lloyd-Jones, Hugh. 1971. *The Justice of Zeus* (Berkeley and Los Angeles: University of California Press, 1971).
L'Orange, H. P. 1959. "Expressions of Cosmic Kingship in the Ancient World," in *The Sacral Kingship* (1959), 481–82.
Louandre, Charles, ed. 1869. J.-B. Bossuet, *Discours sur l'histoire universelle* (Paris: Charpentier, 1869).

Löwith, Karl. 1949. *Meaning and History* (Chicago: University of Chicago Press, 1949).
Lubac, Henry de. 1946. *Surnaturel: Études historiques* (Paris: Aubier, Éditions Montaigne, 1946).
Luscombe, D. E. 1988. "Introduction: The Formation of Political Thought in the West," in *Cambridge History of Political Thought* (1988), 157–73.
MacCana, Prionsias. 1983. *Celtic Mythology*, rev. ed. (New York: Peter Bendrick Books, 1983).
MacCormack, Sabine G. 1981. *Art and Ceremony in Late Antiquity* (Berkeley and Los Angeles: University of California Press, 1981).
MacCulloch, J. A. 1911. *The Religion of the Ancient Celts* (Edinburgh: T. and T. Clark, 1911).
MacIntyre, Alasdair. 1984. *After Virtue: A Study in Moral Theory*, 2nd ed. (Notre Dame, IN: University of Notre Dame Press, 1984).
MacMullen, Ramsey. 1984. *Christianizing the Roman Empire, A.D. 100–400* (New Haven: Yale University Press, 1984).
Maraval, Pierre. 2001. *La théologie politique de l'Empire Chrétien: Louanges de Constantin* (Paris: Éditions du Cerf, 2001).
Maret, Henri. 1869. *Du concile général et de la paix religieuse*, 2 vols. (Paris: Henri Plon, 1869).
Markus, R. A. 1970. *Saeculum: History and Society in the Theology of St. Augustine* (Cambridge: Cambridge University Press, 1970).
——, ed. 1972. *Augustine: A Collection of Critical Essays* (Garden City, NY: Doubleday Anchor, 1972).
——. 1988. "The Latin Fathers," in *Cambridge History of Medieval Political Thought* (1988), 92–122.
——. 1990. *The End of Ancient Christianity* (Cambridge: Cambridge University Press, 1990).
——. 2006. *Christianity and the Secular* (Notre Dame, IN: University of Notre Dame Press, 2006).
Mattingly, H., trans. 1948. *Tacitus on Britain and Germany* (West Drayton, Middlx: Penguin Books, 1948).
McEwan, Calvin W. 1934. *The Oriental Origin of Hellenistic Kingship* (Chicago: University of Chicago Studies in Ancient Oriental Civilization, 1934).
McIlwain, Charles H. 1932. *The Growth of Political Thought in the West* (New York: Macmillan, 1932).
McKitterick, Rosamund, ed. 2001a. *The Early Middle Ages: Europe, 400–1000* (Oxford: Oxford University Press, 2001).
——. 2001b. "Politics," in McKitterick, ed. (2001a), 21–56.
Mercer, Samuel A. B. 1952. *The Pyramid Texts in translation and commentary*, 4 vols. (New York: Longman, Green, 1952).
MGH: Monumenta Germaniae Historica:
  —*Annales Regni Francorum inde ab a. 741 usque ad a. 829* (Hannover, 1895), vol. 6.
  —*Die Werke Wipos*, 3rd ed. (Leipzig, 1915).
  —*Epistolae variorum Carolo Magno regnante* (Berlin, 1895).

—*Leges. Sectio II,* 2 vols. (Hannover, 1883–97).
—*Libelli de Lite imperatorum et pontificum,* 3 vols. (Hannover, 1891–97).
—*Ottonis episcopi Frisingensis Chronicon* (Hannover, 1912).
Mierow, Charles Christopher, trans. 2002. Otto of Freising, *The Two Cities: A Chronicle of Universal History to the Year 1140 A.D.,* rev. ed. (New York: Columbia University Press, 2002).
Migne, J.-P., ed. 1857–87. *Patrologiae cursus completus. Series Graeca,* 161 vols. (Paris: Migne, 1857–87).
——, ed. 1884–1904. *Patrologiae cursus completus. Series Latina,* 221 vols. (Paris: Migne, 1884–1904).
Mill, John Stuart. 1985. *On Liberty,* ed. Gertrude Himmelfarb (London: Penguin Classics, 1985).
Minnerath, Roland. 1998. "La tradition doctrinale de la primauté Pétrienne au premier Millénaire," in *Il Primato del Successore di Pietro* (1998), 115–43.
Mommsen, Theodor E. 1959. *Medieval and Renaissance Studies,* ed. Eugene F. Rice, Jr. (Ithaca: Cornell University Press, 1959).
Monahan, Arthur P. 1987. *Consent, Coercion, and Limit: The Medieval Origins of Parliamentary Democracy* (Kingston and Montreal: McGill-Queen's University Press, 1987).
——. 1994. *From Personal Duties towards Personal Rights: Late Medieval and Early Modern Political Thought, 1300–1600* (Montreal and Kingston: McGill-Queen's University Press, 1994).
Morrall, John B. 1962. *Political Thought in Medieval Times* (New York: Harper Torchbooks, 1962).
Morris, Christopher. 1967. *Western Political Thought. I Plato to Aristotle* (New York: Basic Books, 1967).
Morris, Colin. 1972. *The Discovery of the Individual, 1050–1200* (London: S.P.C.K., 1972).
Morrison, Karl. 1964. *The Two Kingdoms: Ecclesiology in Carolingian Political Thought* (Princeton: Princeton University Press, 1964).
——. 1969. *Tradition and Authority in the Western Church 300–1140* (Princeton: Princeton University Press, 1969).
Mousnier, Roger. 1989. *Monarchies et royautés de la préhistoire à nos jours* (Paris: Librairie Académique Perrin, 1989).
Mowinckel, Sigmund. 1922. *Psalmenstudien,* 6 vols. (Kristiana: J. Dybwad, 1922).
——. 1956. *He That Cometh,* trans. G. W. Anderson (Oxford: Oxford University Press, 1956).
——. 1959. "General Oriental and Specific Israelite Elements in the Israelite Conception of the Sacral Kingdom," in *The Sacral Kingship* (1959), 283–93.
Murray, R. H. 1930. *History of Political Science,* 2nd ed. (New York: Appleton, 1930).
Nelson, Janet L. 1967. "Gelasius I's Doctrine of Responsibility: A Note," *Journal of Theological Studies,* n.s., 18, no. 1 (1967): 154–62.
——. 1987. "The Lord's Anointed and the People's Choice: Carolingian Royal Ritual," in Cannadine and Price, eds, (1987), 137–80.
——. 1988. "Kingship and Empire," in *Cambridge History of Medieval Political Thought* (1988), 211–51.

———. 1992. *Charles the Bold* (London: Longman, 1992).
Nicol, D. M. 1988. "Byzantine Political Thought," in *Cambridge History of Medieval Political Thought* (1988), 51–79.
Nineham, Ruth. 1963. "The So-called Anonymous of York," *Journal of Ecclesiastical History* 14 (1963): 31–45.
Noble, Thomas F. X., ed. 2006. *From Roman Provinces to Medieval Kingdoms* (London and New York: Routledge, 2006).
North, C. R. 1932. "The Religious Aspects of Hebrew Kingship," *Zeitschrift für die altestamentisch Wissenschaft* 1 (1932): 8–38.
Oakley, Francis. 1973. "Celestial Hierarchies Revisited: Walter Ullmann's Vision of Medieval Politics," *Past and Present* 60 (August 1973): 3–48.
———. 1979. *The Western Church in the Later Middle Ages* (Ithaca: Cornell University Press, 1979).
———. 1984. *Omnipotence, Covenant, and Order: An Excursion in the History of Ideas from Abelard to Leibniz* (Ithaca: Cornell University Press, 1984).
———. 1999. *Politics and Eternity: Studies in the History of Medieval and Early-Modern Political Thought* (Leiden: E. J. Brill, 1999).
———. 2003. *The Conciliarist Tradition: Constitutionalism in the Catholic Church, 1300–1870* (Oxford: Oxford University Press, 2003).
———. 2006a. *Kingship: The Politics of Enchantment* (Oxford: Blackwell Publishing, 2006).
———. 2006b. "In Praise of Prolepsis: Meaning, Significance, and the Medieval Contribution to Political Thought," *History of Political Thought* 27, no. 3 (2006): 407–22.
Obolensky, Dmitri. 1950. "Russia's Byzantine Heritage," in *Oxford Slavonic Papers* 1 (1950): 37–63.
O'Connor, Daniel, and Francis Oakley. 1969. *Creation: The Impact of an Idea* (New York: Charles Scribner's Sons, 1969).
O'Connor, David, and David P. Silverman, eds. 1995. *Ancient Egyptian Kingship* (Leiden: E. J. Brill, 1995).
Odahl, Charles M. 2004. *Constantine and the Christian Empire* (London: Routledge, 2004).
Odegaard, Charles Edwin. 1945. *Vassi and Fideles in the Carolingian Empire* (Cambridge: Harvard University Press, 1945).
O'Donnell, James J. 2005. *Augustine: A New Biography* (New York: Harper-Collins, 2005).
O'Donovan, Oliver, and Joan Lockwood O'Donovan, eds. 1999. *From Irenaeus to Grotius: A Sourcebook in Christian Political Thought, 100–1625* (Grand Rapids: William B. Eerdman, 1999).
Onians, R. R. 1988. *The Origins of European Thought about the Body, the Mind, the Soul, the World, Time and Fate* (Cambridge: Cambridge University Press, 1988).
Orosius, Paulus. 1889. *Historiarum adversum paganos: Libri VII*, ed. C. Zangemeister (Leipzig: B. G. Teubner, 1889).
Osborn, E. F. 1997. *Tertullian: First Theologian of the West* (Cambridge: Cambridge University Press, 1997).
Pelikan, Jaroslav. 1971–89. *The Christian Tradition: A History of the Development of Doctrine*, 5 vols. (Chicago: University of Chicago Press, 1971–89).

Pellens, Karl, ed. 1966. *Die Texte des Normannischen Anonymus* (Wiesbaden: Franz Steiner Verlag, 1966).

Perez, Juan Beneyto, *Historia de las doctrinas politicas,* 4th ed. (Madrid: M. Aguilar, 1964).

Perrin, Norman. 1963. *The Kingdom of God in the Teaching of Jesus* (Philadelphia: Westminster, 1963).

———. 1976. *Jesus and the Language of the Kingdom: Symbol and Metaphor in the New Testament* (Philadelphia: Fortress Press, 1976).

Peterson, Erik. 1933. "Kaiser Augustus im Urteil des antiken Christentums," *Hochland* 30, no. 2 (1933): 289–99.

———. 1935. *Der Monotheismus als Politisches Problem: Ein Beitrag zur Geschichte der politischen Theologie im Imperium Romanum* (Leipzig: Hegner, 1935).

PG = *Patrologiae cursus completus, Series Graeca,* ed. J.-P. Migne, 161 vols. (Paris: Migne, 1857–87).

Pine-Coffin, R. S., trans. 1961. Saint Augustine, *Confessions* (Baltimore: Penguin Books, 1961).

PL = *Patrologiae cursus completus: Series Latina,* ed. J.-P. Migne, 221 vols. (Paris: Migne, 1884–1904).

Plato. 1937. *Timaeus,* trans. F. M. Conford in *Plato's Cosmology* (Indianapolis: Bobbs-Merrill, 1937).

———. 1973. *The Collected Dialogues Including the Letters,* ed. Edith Hamilton and Huntington Cairns (Princeton: Princeton University Press, 1973).

Pleket, H. W. 1965. "An Aspect of the Emperor Cult: Imperial Mysteries," *Harvard Theological Review* 58 (December 1965): 331–47.

Poggi, Gianfranco. 1988. "Max Weber's Conceptual Portrait of Feudalism," *British Journal of Sociology* 39, no. 2 (1988): 211–27.

Pohlsander, Hans. 1996. *The Emperor Constantine* (London and New York: Routledge, 1996).

Pollock, F., and F. W. Maitland. 1923. *History of English Law,* 2nd ed. (Cambridge: Cambridge University Press, 1923).

Popper, Karl. 1950. *The Open Society and Its Enemies,* rev. ed. (Princeton: Princeton University Press, 1950).

Portalié, Eugene. 1960. *A Guide to the Thought of St. Augustine,* trans. Ralph A. Bastian (Chicago: H. Regnery, 1960).

Posener, Georges. 1960. *De la divinité du Pharaon* (Paris: Imprimerie Nationale, 1960).

Price, S. R. F. 1984. *Rituals and Power: The Roman Imperial Cult in Asia Minor* (Cambridge: Cambridge University Press, 1984).

———. 1987. "From Noble Funerals to Divine Cult: The Consecration of the Roman Emperors," in Cannadine and Price, eds. (1987), 56–105.

Pritchard, James B., ed. 1955. *Ancient Near Eastern Texts Relating to the Old Testament* (Princeton: Princeton University Press, 1955).

Procopius. 1914–40. *The History of the Wars,* ed. and trans. H. B. Dewing, 3 vols. (London: Heinemann, 1914–40).

Prudentius. 1949–53. *Prudentius,* ed. and trans. H. J. Thomson, 2 vols. (Cambridge: Harvard University Press, 1949–53).
Pseudo-Dionysius. *De ecclesiastica hierarchica,* in *PG* 3:376–574.
Ralph of Coggleshall. 1875. *Chronicon Anglicanum,* ed. J. Stevenson (London: Longmans, 1875).
Ratzinger, J. 1954. *Volk und Haus Gottes in Augustinus Lehre von der Kirche* (Munich: Karl Zink Verlag, 1954).
Rauflaub, Kurt A. 2000. "Poets, Lawgivers, and the Beginnings of Political Reflection in Archaic Greece," in *Cambridge History of Greek and Roman Political Thought* (2000), 50–57
Raymond, I. W., trans. 1936. Orosius, *The Seven Books of History against the Pagans* (New York: Columbia University Press, 1936).
Reischauer, Edwin. 1956. "Japanese Feudalism," in Coulborn, ed. (1956), 26–48.
Reuter, Timothy. 1991. *Germany in the Early Middle Ages, 800–1056* (London: Longman, 1991).
Reviron, J. 1930. *Les ideés politiques d'un evèque du ix siècle: Jonas d'Orléans et son De institutione regia* (Paris: J. Vrin, 1930).
Reynolds, Susan. 1994. *Fiefs and Vassals: The Medieval Evidence Reinterpreted* (Oxford: Oxford University Press, 1994).
Richards, Jeffrey. 1979. *The Popes and the Papacy in the Early Middle Ages, 476–752* (London: Routledge and Kegan Paul, 1979).
Ringgren, H. 1959. "Some Religious Aspects of the Caliphate," in *The Sacral Kingship* (1959), 737–48.
Robinson, I. S. 1988. "Church and Papacy," in *Cambridge History of Medieval Political Thought* (1988), 252–305.
Roques, R. 1954. "*L'univers dionysien: Structure hiérarchique du monde selon le pseudo-Denys* (Paris: Aubier, 1954).
Rose, H. S. 1959. "The Evidence for Divine Kings in Greece," in *The Sacral Kingship* (1959), 372–78.
Rosenthal, Irwin I. J. 1958. *Political Thought in Medieval Islam: An Introductory Outline* (Cambridge: Cambridge University Press, 1958).
Ross, W. D., ed. 1908–52. *The Works of Aristotle Translated into English,* 12 vols. (Oxford: Clarendon Press, 1908–52).
Rousseau, Jean-Jacques. 1947. *Du contrat social ou principles du droit politique,* ed. C. E. Vaughan (Manchester: Manchester University Press, 1947).
Runciman, Steven. 1977. *The Byzantine Theocracy* (Cambridge: Cambridge University Press, 1977).
Sabine, George H. 1937. *A History of Political Thought* (New York: Henry Holt, 1937).
Sacral Kingship: Contributions to the Central Theme of the VIIIth International Congress for the History of Religions, Rome, April, 1955, The. 1959. (Leiden: E. J. Brill, 1959).
Sandmel, Samuel. 1979. *Philo of Alexandria: An Introduction* (New York and Oxford: Oxford University Press, 1979).

Sansterre, J. M. 1972. "Eusèbe de Césarée et la naissance de la théorie 'césaropapiste,'" *Byzantion* 42 (1972): 131–95, 532–94.

Schaff, Philip, ed. and trans. 1886–90. *A Select Library of the Nicene and Post-Nicene Fathers*, 1st series, 14 vols. (New York: Christian Literature, 1886–90).

Schatz, Klaus. 1996. *Papal Primacy: From Its Origins to the Present*, trans. John A. Otto and Linda M. Mahoney (Collegeville, MN: Liturgical Press, 1996).

Schele, Linda, and David Freidel. 1990. *A Forest of Kings: The Untold Story of the Ancient Maya* (New York: William Morrow, 1990).

Scherrinsky, Harold. 1940. *Untersuchungen zum sogennanten Anonymus von York* (Würzburg: Anmülde, 1940).

Schindler, Alfred, et al. 1978. *Monotheismus als politischer Problem? Erik Peterson und die Kritik der politischen Theologie* (Gütersloh: Verlagshaus Mohn, 1978).

Schlesinger, Walter. 1953. "Herrschaft und Gefolgschaft in der germanisch-deutschen Verfassungsgeschichte," *Historische Zeitschrift* 126, no. 2 (1953): 225–75.

———. 1956. "Über germanisches Heerkönigtum," in *Das Königtum* (1956), 104–41.

Schmitt, Carl. 1934. *Politische Theologie: Vier Kapiteln zur Lehre von der Souveränitat*, 2nd ed. (Berlin: Drucker and Humblot, 1934).

Schneider, Hans. 1976. *Das Konziliarismus als Problem der neuren Katholischen Theologie* (Berlin: de Gruyter, 1976).

Schramm, Percy. 1938. *History of the English Coronation*, trans. L. G. Wickham-Legg (Oxford: Clarendon Press, 1938).

———. 1968–71. *Kaiser, Könige und Papste: Gesammelte Aufsätze zur Geschichte des Mittelalters*, 4 vols. (Stuttgart: Hiersemann, 1968–71).

Schwartz, E., ed. 1934. *Publizistische Sammlungen zum Acacienischen Schisma* (Munich: Verlag de Bayerischen Akademie der Wissenshaften, 1934).

Sedulius Scottus. 1983. *De rectoribus christianis*, trans. E. G. Doyle (Binghamton, NY: Medieval and Renaissance Texts and Studies, 1983).

Segal, Richard, ed. 1998. *Myth and Ritual Theory: An Anthology* (Oxford: Blackwell, 1998).

Shils, E., and M. Young. 1953. "The Meaning of the Coronation," *Sociological Review*, n.s., 1 (1953): 63–81.

Silverman, David. 1995. "The Nature of Egyptian Kingship," in O'Connor and Silverman, eds. (1995), 49–87.

Skinner, Quentin. 1969. "Meaning and Understanding in the History of Ideas," *History and Theory* 8 (1969): 3–53; reprinted in Tully, 1988, 29–67.

———. 1988. "A Reply to My Critics," in Tully (1988), 231–88.

Smalley, Beryl, ed. 1965. *Trends in Medieval Political Thought* (Oxford: Basil Blackwell, 1965).

Smaragdus of St. Mihiel. *Via regia*, in *PL* 102.

Snell, Bruno. 1953. *The Discovery of Mind*, trans. T. G. Rosenmeyer (Cambridge: Harvard University Press, 1953).

Story, Joanna, ed. 2005. *Charlemagne: Empire and Society* (Manchester: Manchester University Press, 2005).

Southern, Richard. 1961. *The Making of the Middle Ages* (New Haven: Yale University Press, 1961).

Strauss, Gerard. 1975. "Success and Failure in the German Reformation," *Past and Present* 67 (May 1975): 30–63.

Strauss, Leo, and Joseph Cropsey, eds. 1987. *History of Political Philosophy*, 3rd ed. (Chicago: University of Chicago Press, 1987).

Strayer, Joseph R. 1965. *Feudalism* (Princeton, NJ: D. Van Nostrand, 1965).

———. 1970. *On the Medieval Origins of the Modern State* (Princeton: Princeton University Press, 1970).

———. 1971. *Medieval Statecraft and the Perspectives of History* (Princeton: Princeton University Press, 1971).

Ström, Ake V. 1959. "The King God and His Connection with Sacrifice in the Old Norse Religion," in *The Sacral Kingship* (1959), 702–15.

Stubbs, William. 1880. *The Constitutional History of England*, 3rd ed., 3 vols. (Oxford: Clarendon Pres, 1880).

Sturtevant, E. H., and G. Bechtel. 1935. *A Hittite Chrestomathy* (Philadelphia: Linguistic Society of America, University of Pennsylvania, 1935).

Summers, B. H. 1962. *Peter the Great* (New York: Collier Books, 1962).

Sweet, J. P. M. 1984. "The Zealots and Jesus," in Bammel and Moule, eds. (1984), 1–9.

Tacitus, Germania. 1948. *Tacitus on Britain and Germany*, trans. H. Mattingly (1948).

Taylor, Charles. 1989. *Sources of the Self: The Making of the Modern Identity* (Cambridge: Cambridge University Press, 1989).

Taylor, Lily Ross. 1931. *The Divinity of the Roman Emperor* (Middletown, CT: American Philosophical Association, 1931).

Tertullian. 1931. *Apology and De Spectaculis*, ed. and trans. T. R. Glover (London: Heinemann, 1931).

———. 1957a. *Liber ad Scapulam, CSEL* 76:7–16.

———. 1957b. *De Pallio. CSEL* 76:104–25.

Testa, Rita Lizzi. 2005. "Clerical Hierarchy and Imperial Legislation in Late Antiquity: The Reformed Reformers," in Bellitto and Hamilton, eds. (2005), 57–103.

Tierney, Brian, ed. 1964. *The Crisis of Church and State, 1050–1300* (Englewood Cliffs, NJ: Prentice-Hall, 1964).

Toussaert, Jacques. 1963. *Le sentiment religieux en Flandre à la fin du Moyen Age* (Paris: Librairie Plon, 1963).

Toynbee, Arnold J. 1948. *Civilization on Trial* (New York: Oxford University Press, 1948).

Troeltsch, Ernst. 1960. *The Social Teaching of the Christian Church*, trans. Olive Wyon, 2 vols. (New York: Harper Torchbooks, 1960).

Tully, James, ed. 1988. *Meaning and Context: Quentin Skinner and His Critics* (Cambridge: Polity Press, 1988).

Turner, Frank M. 1981. *The Greek Heritage in Victorian Britain* (New Haven: Yale University Press, 1981).

Turville-Petrie, E. O. G. 1964. *Myth and Religion of the North: The Religion of Ancient Scandinavia* (New York: Holt, Rinehart and Winston, 1964).

Ullmann, Walter. 1949. *Medieval Papalism: The Political Theories of the Medieval Canonists* (London: Methuen 1949).
———. 1955. *The Growth of Papal Government in the Middle Ages* (London: Methuen, 1955).
———. 1960–62. "Law and the Medieval Historian," in *XIe* Congrès *International des Sciences Historiques: Rapports,* 7 vols. (Göteborg: Almqvist & Wiksell, 1960–62), 3:34–74.
———. 1961. *Principles of Government and Politics in the Middle Ages* (London: Methuen, 1961).
———. 1965. *A History of Political Thought: The Middle Ages* (Baltimore: Penguin Books, 1965).
———. 1966a. *The Individual and Society in the Middle Ages* (Baltimore: Johns Hopkins University Press, 1966).
———. 1966b. *The Relevance of Medieval Ecclesiastical History* (Cambridge: Cambridge University Press, 1966).
———. 1966c. *Papst und König: Grundlagen des Papsttums und der englischen Verfassung im Mittelalter* (Salzburg and Munich: Pustet, 1966).
———. 1969. *The Carolingian Renaissance and the Idea of Kingship* (London: Methuen, 1969).
———. 1970. *The Growth of Papal Government in the Middle Ages,* 3rd ed. (London: Methuen, 1970).
———. 1972. *A Short History of the Papacy in the Middle Ages* (London: Methuen, 1972).
Van Caenegem, R. C. 1988. "Government, Law and Society," in *Cambridge History of Medieval Political Thought* (1988), 174–210.
VC = *Vita Constantini*, in Winkelmann, ed. 1975. *Über das Leben des Kaisers Konstantin.*
Virgil. 1999. *Georgics,* in *Eclogues, Georgics, Aeneid 1–6,* ed. H. Rushton Fairclough (Cambridge: Harvard University Press, 1999).
Voegelin, Eric. 1956–57. *Order and History,* vols. 1–3 (Baton Rouge: Louisiana State University Press, 1956–57).
Wallace-Hadrill, J. M. 1962a. *The Long-Haired Kings and Other Studies in Frankish History* (London: Methuen, 1962).
———. 1962b. *The Barbarian West, A.D. 400–1000* (New York: Harper Torchbooks, 1962).
———. 1965. "*The Via Regia* of the Carolingian Age," in Smalley, ed. (1965), 22–41.
———. 1969. Fredegar, *Chronicle* (London: Nelson, 1969).
———. 1971. *Early Germanic Kingship in England and the Continent* (Oxford: Clarendon Press, 1971).
———. 1983. *The Frankish Church* (Oxford: Clarendon Press, 1983).
Webb, C. C. J., ed. 1909. John of Salisbury, *Policraticus sive De Nugis curialium* (Oxford: Clarendon Press, 1909).
Weber, Max. 1922–23. *Gesammelte Aufsaetze zur Religionssoziologie,* 3 vols. (Tübingen: Mohr, 1922–23).
———. 1968. Max Weber, *Economy and Society: An Outline of Interpretive Sociology,* ed. and trans. G. Roth and G. Wittich, 3 vols. (New York: Bedminster Press, 1968).
White, Hayden. 1973. "Foucault Decoded: Notes from the Underground," *History and Theory* 12 (1973): 23–54.

White, Lynn, Jr. 1962. *Medieval Technology and Social Change* (Oxford: Oxford University Press, 1962).

Widengren, Geo. 1959. "The Sacral Kingship of Iran," in *The Sacral Kingship* (1959), 242–57.

Wilks, M. J. 1967. "Roman Empire and Christian State in the *De civitate dei*," *Augustinus* 12 (1967): 489–510.

Williams, Bernard. 1993. *Shame and Necessity* (Berkeley and Los Angeles: University of California Press, 1993).

Williams, George H. 1951a. *The Norman Anonymous of 1100 A.D.* (Cambridge: Harvard University Press, 1951).

———. 1951b. "Christology and Church-State Relations in the Fourth Century," *Church History* 3 (1951), (i) 3–33, and 4 (1951), (ii) 3–26.

Williams, W. G., ed. 1927–29. Cicero, *Letters to His Friends*, 3 vols. (London: Heinemann, 1927–29).

Winkelmann, Friedhelm, ed. 1975. *Über das Leben des Kaisers Konstantin (Eusebius Werke, Erste Band, erster Teil)* (Berlin: Akademie-Verlag, 1975).

Wipo. 1915. *Gesta Chuonradi imperateris*, in *MGH: Die Werke Wipos*, 3rd ed. (Leipzig, 1915).

Wolfram, Herwig. 1970. "The Shaping of the Early Medieval Kingdom," *Viator* 1 (1970): 1–20.

———. 1968. "Methodische Frage zur Kritick am 'Sacralen' Königtum Germanische Stämme," in *Festschrift für Otto Höfler* (1968), 2:473.

———. 1990. *The Roman Empire and its Germanic Peoples*, trans. Timothy Dunlap (Berkeley and Los Angeles: University of California Press, 1990).

———. 2006. "*Origo et religio:* Ethnic Traditions and Literature in Early Medieval Europe," in Thomas Noble, ed., *From Roman Provinces to Medieval Kingdoms* (London: Routledge, 2006).

Wolfson, Henry Austryn. 1948. *Philo: Foundations of religious philosophy in Judaism, Christianity, and Islam*, 2 vols. (Cambridge: Harvard University Press, 1948).

Wolin, Sheldon. 1960. *Politics and Vision: Continuity and Innovation in Western Political Thought* (Boston: Little, Brown, 1960).

Woody, Kennerly M. 1973. "Marginalia on the Norman Anonymous," *Harvard Theological Review* 66 (1973): 273–88.

Zangemeister, C., ed. 1889. Paulus Orosius, *Historiarum adversus paganos: Libri VII* (Leipzig: B. G. Teubner, 1889).

Ziegler, Aloysius K. 1942. "Pope Gelasius I and His Teaching on the Relation of Church and State," *Catholic Historical Review* 27, no. 4 (1942): 412–37.

Index

Aaron, 54, 103, 106
Abbasid caliphate, 80
Abbey of Reichenau, 167
Abel, 122
Abimelech, 45, 50
Abraham, 49, 87
Abrahamic tradition, 82, 87
absolutism, 39, 107–8, 176; descending political structure and, 181; divine-right monarchs and, 176, 185; Plato's ideal commonwealth as, 9
Achaeans, 13–14
Acropolis, 31
Acts of the Apostles, 61, 62
Adam, 123, 124, 125, 128
Aegean islands, 14
Aegean Sea, 14
Aeolia, 14
Aethelred, king of Northumbria, 156
Africa. *See* North Africa; sub-Saharan Africa
afterlife, 52
Agobard of Lyons: *De privilegio et jure sacerdotii*, 202
agrarianism, 1–2, 27, 34, 155, 188
Akkadians, 23, 28
Albert of Hapsburg, 222
Alcuin, 72, 141, 156, 179, 202
Alemanni, 68
Alexander the Great, king of Macedonia, 15, 29, 32, 33
Alexandrian church fathers, 85–86, 87–89, 90, 92, 94
Altar of Victory, 113, 114
Amaterasu-ō-mikami, 196
Ambrose of Milan, St., 98, 99, 113–14, 117, 118, 130, 155
Ambrosiaster (Pseudo-Augustine), 97–98, 114, 163–64, 166, 168, 173
Amen-em-het III, pharaoh of Egypt, 24
Amenhotep III, pharaoh of Egypt, 26–27
Ammianus Marcellinus, 149
Ammonites, 51

Amos, 51
Anastasius I, Byzantine emperor, 101, 102
ancestor cult, 5, 19, 33
ancient past. *See* archaic past
angels, 121, 125; hierarchical choirs of, 203, 208–9; imperial entourage parallel with, 114
Anglo-Norman Anonymous (Anonymous of York), 165–66, 167–73, 174, 175, 200–201; Christology of, 168–70, 171; on *laicus*, 175, 201; *Tractates*, 167–68, 170, 173, 175
Anglo-Saxons, 68, 72, 149, 157, 158, 167, 170; kingship and, 76, 179, 183–84
Anna, tsarina of Russia, 110
Annointed One. *See* Messiah
anointing. *See* unction
Anonymous. *See* Ambrosiaster
Anonymous of York. *See* Anglo-Norman Anonymous
Anthesteria, 31
anthropogony, 10
anthropology, 4, 6, 144, 147
antipopes, 217
antiquity. *See* archaic past
Antonius IV, patriarch of Constantinople, 107–8
Antony, Mark, 36, 37
Anum (god), 26
apocalypse, 53, 55, 56
Apocalypse of John, 61
apocalyptic literature, 43, 61, 123, 130–31
Apologeticus (Tertullian), 112
Apologists, 85–86, 121
apostasy, 138
Apostolic age, 55–56, 135
apostolic church, 137, 205
Apostolic See, 207, 211, 214
apostolic succession, 205, 207, 214, 216–17
Arabs, 70, 81. *See also* Islamic empire
archaic past, xi, 1–10, 18–39, 146, 147, 221; barbarian waves and, 67; classical Greek inheritances and, 29–31; cosmic religiosity and, 18, 19–21, 26–27, 37–38, 39, 49, 81; creation myths and, 28–29, 48;

287

archaic past (*continued*),
  divine continuum belief and, 48–49; Homeric epics and, 30; natural world and, 21, 48. *See also* classical world; Near East, ancient; paganism; sacral monarch
archetypes, 22, 29
archon, 31, 50
Arianism, 68, 71, 88, 96, 99, 113, 143, 210; as heresy, 97; Visigoth conversion from, 152
aristocracy. *See* nobility
Aristotle, 3–4, 6, 7, 10, 181; church and state and, 8–9; kingship and, 31; works of: *Constitution of Athens*, 31; *Nichomachean Ethics*, 7; *Politics*, 7, 8–9; *Rhetoric*, 7
armed forces. *See* warriors
Arquillière, H.-X., 141, 164
arts censorship, 9
Aryans, 13
ascending political structure, 180–81, 182, 183
Asia Minor, 13, 14, 30, 36, 70
Asmeh, Aziz al-, 80–81
assemblies: anachronistic view of, 148–49, 182; Carolingian era and, 184; consent of governed and, 199; Germanic peoples and, 148, 182, 195
Assyrian empire, 13, 14, 16, 17, 23, 122
Athanasius, St., 97
Athens: Hellenization and, 33; king-archon and, 31, 50; Macedonian conquest of, 15; monarchical forms and, 31, 34, 36; polis and, 15, 29; political society of, 3–4, 5, 6, 31
atonement, 28, 43
auctoritas, meaning of, 101
Augustan peace, birth of Jesus correlated with, 62–63, 84–85, 88, 91, 113–14, 116–17, 119
Augustine of Hippo, St., 40, 111, 116, 117–42, 162; Catholic orthodoxy norm and, 137, 138; conflicting positions of, 139–42; conversion experience of, 117–18; Donatist schismatics and, 120, 131, 134–42; early Christian ideology of, 112, 117–18, 139; fundamental shift in thinking of, 118–19; on heresy penalties, 135, 137; on ideal Christian emperor, 131, 134, 136, 141; interpretations of, 132, 142, 144, 163; mature political thinking of, 83, 111, 119–31, 133–37, 139, 141–42, 143, 174; originality of, 111; political theology of the Anonymous and Eusebius contrasted with, 174; predestination belief of, 119, 124–25, 139, 140; works of: *Confessions*, 124, 154–55; *The City of God*, 116, 119–34, 137, 139, 140, 141, 142, 143, 163; *De gratia Christi et de peccato originali*, 118; *Retractationes*, 118
Augustinian tradition, 111
Augustus (Octavian). *See* Caesar Augustus
augustus (Roman title), 37

Austria, 68
autonomous individual, xi, 8, 181
Avars, 67, 69, 70
Axum, kingdom of, 159
Aztec monarchy, 3

Baal (god), 51
Babylon: Jerusalem contrasted with, 122, 127; meaning of name, 22
Babylonia, 23, 43, 45; creation myth of, 10, 28, 47, 48; dominance of, 116; kingship and, 23, 43, 45; New Year's festivals and, 28, 45, 46
Babylonian exile, 17, 53, 54, 87
Bactria, 33
Baetke, Walter, 146, 147, 148–49
Balkans, 69, 70
banais righi (inauguration rite), 146
baptism, 137, 160; as fundamental sacrament, 170, 175, 201; priesthood and, 171
barbarian invasions, 13, 14, 16, 83, 120, 147, 150, 189; fall of Rome and, 115; papacy and, 100; royal power restrictions and, 186; Russia and, 108–9; waves of, 67–68, 69, 71, 74, 77, 115, 176, 186
baronial grievances (England), 197–98, 199
basileus, 104, 106, 109
Baynes, Norman H., 105
Bede, St. (Venerable Bede), 156, 179; *Ecclesiastical History of the English Nation*, 156
Bellius, Michael, 186–87
Benedictines, 154
benefactor: Christ as, 89, 95; God as, 85; king as, 58, 84, 95
benefice (*beneficium*), 190, 192
Benin, 3
Beskow, Per, 87, 97
biblical texts: Augustine's study of, 118–19, 121, 135–36; divine continuum undercut by, 48–49; early Christian political thought and, 55–63; Hebrew kingship and, 45–47, 50–52; Kingdom of God meaning and, 45–68; Latin translation of, 208; Messiah teachings and, 53–54; two interpretative schools of, 42–43, 45, 51. *See also* New Testament; Old Testament; *specific books and gospels*
Binchy, D. A., 145, 146
binding and loosing, 207–8, 217
bishop of Rome. *See* papacy
bishops, 77, 114, 160–62, 202; apostolic succession and, 205, 208, 217; consecration of, 165; emperor as bishop of, 96–97, 99, 166, 175; hierarchy and, 206, 207, 212; as image of Christ, 166, 168; papacy and, 175, 212; parity among, 175, 216–17; power in early Christian church of, 151–53, 212; sacraments and, 104

Black Sea, 14–15
blasphemy, 9, 50, 51, 54, 61, 80, 82, 158
Bloch, Marc, 161, 173, 187
Boniface, St., 154, 160
Boniface I, Pope, 207
Boniface VIII, Pope, 222
Bossuet, Jacques Bénigne, bishop of Meaux, 117; *Discours sur l'histoire universelle*, 117
Boukolion (Athens), 31
Boutrouche, Robert, 187
Britain, 42, 69, 72, 74, 76, 146, 158, 164, 175; anointing of kings and, 161, 166, 170, 171; church and state and, 78, 199; constitutional roots in, 148, 197–98, 199; Germanic institutions and, 148; liturgical kingship and, 166; Old Testament parallel and, 157; royal lawgivers and, 183–84; royal touch healing power and, 156. *See also* Anglo-Saxons
bronze, 14
Brown, Peter, 152
Bruno of Segni, 221
Brythonic Celts, 146
Buber, Martin, 50, 51
Buddhism, 19
Bulgars, 159
Burckhardt, Jacob, 97
Burgundians, 68, 149
Burgundy, 76, 77
Byzantine empire, 15–16, 18, 69–74, 98–110, 157, 211; barbarian invasions and, 68, 69, 70, 74; church's public functions and, 152; coronation ritual and, 171; demise of, 109; duration of, 16; Eusebian political theology and, 98, 142, 173, 174; expansion of, 69–71; Germanic kingdoms and, 150; iconoclastic controversy and, 72–73, 98, 99, 100, 102–3, 157, 216; iconography of, 106; imperial sacrality and, 103–4, 106, 110, 142, 173; Latin West's political thought contrasted with, 174–75; Roman imperial legacy and, 71; Roman papacy and, 72–73, 214, 215, 216; Russian links with, 109–10; stability of political thinking of, 105; threats to, 70, 72–73, 74, 157; as totalitarian, 108
"Byzantism," 97, 98
Byzantium. *See* Constantinople

Cadoux, C. J., 60
Caesar, Julius, 36; *De bello gallico*, 148
Caesar Augustus (Octavian), 36–37, 208; divinizing of, 37. *See also* Augustan peace
Caesarea, 89
"Caesaropapism," 97, 98
Cain, 122
calendric events, 19–20

caliphate, 80, 81–82
Cambridge History of Greek and Roman Political Thought, 41
Cambridge History of Medieval Political Thought, 41
Canaanites, 2, 13, 16, 42, 45, 48, 50; Hebrew kingship and, 51
canon law, 104, 221; on clerical distinctions, 201; Orthodox Church and, 110; papal decretals and, 206–7; papal judicial supremacy and, 210, 213, 217; twentieth-century codifications of, 210; Visigothic kingdom and, 173, 178
Cappellari, Fra Mauro: *The Triumph of the Holy See and the Church over the Attacks of the Innovators*, 203–4
Carlyle, R. W. and A. J., 41, 183
Carolingian empire, 71–75, 153–55, 170, 214; crowning of Charlemagne and, 71, 163, 164; end of, 75, 76; fidelity oaths and, 192, 198; law and, 183–84; mayor of the palace and, 159, 196–97; nature of kingship of, 158–63, 164, 165, 166, 178, 179, 182, 183, 196–97; nobility's central role in, 161, 175, 183–84; papal alliance with, 216; political writers of, 177–78, 179; scholarship and, 141; vassalage and, 185, 192. *See also* Charlemagne
Carolingian renaissance, 72, 74
Carthage, 112, 116, 138
Carthage, Council of (411), 139
catholic, 137, 138, 139. *See also* Roman Catholic Church
Cathwulf, 166, 168
cavalry, 188, 191–92
Celestial Christ, 172
celestial emperor, 222
celestial hierarchy, 203, 209–10
celibacy, 77, 221
Celsus, 88
Celts, x, 2, 68, 71, 115, 118, 143–47, 154, 174; Christian churches and, 152; Roman papacy and, 72; sacral kingship and, 145–46, 149. *See also* Ireland
Central Asia, 2, 109
Cerfaux, L., 32
Chaldean empire, 17, 23
chaos, creation from, 28, 29, 45, 47, 48
Charlemagne, king of the Franks and emperor of the West, 72, 73, 76, 153, 154, 156; crowning (800) of, 71, 163, 164; ecclesiastical powers of, 163, 165, 166, 202; fidelity oath and, 184; as ideal Christian ruler, 141, 142; imperial title of, 179; papacy and, 216
Charles Martel, 160
Charles the Bald, king of the Franks and Holy Roman emperor, 183, 184, 192–93, 202

Cherniavsky, Michael, 109
Childerich III, king of the Franks, 71–72, 158, 160
Ch'in dynasty, 2
Chinese empire, 2, 19–20, 22
Chios, 30–31
Chlothar II, king of the Franks, 158
choirs of angels, 203, 208–9
chosen people: Frankish self-identification as, 41, 157, 158, 161–62, 165; Israelites as, 47, 49, 52–53, 54, 57, 59, 103, 157
chrism, anointing with, 160, 165, 170
Christ. *See* Christology; Jesus Christ; Trinitarianism
Christianity, ix–x, 2, 55–63, 82, 83–110, 143; Augustine's theological importance to, 120, 140–42; barbarian invasions and, 115, 176, 186; bishops' power and, 151–53, 212; changed status of, 151–57; conversions to, 39, 62, 68, 72, 75, 83, 89, 90, 117, 144, 149, 159 (*see also* Christian Roman empire); descending political thesis and, 181, 182–83; doctrinal differences and, 68; Eusebius's writings on, 89–98, 111, 112; first coherent political theology of, 88, 89–98, 105; first general history of, 115; fourth-century theopolitical thinking and, 86, 96–110; Hellenism and, 29, 57–58, 61–62, 85–88, 92, 94, 102, 105, 106, 113–14, 117, 127, 173; heresy and, 97, 135, 210–11; ideal commonwealth of, x; ideal emperor and, 131, 134, 136, 141; Latin church fathers and, 111–42; legacy of Jewish Bible to, 17; *logos* doctrine and, 86–89, 91, 92–95, 97; messianic motif and, 53–54; micro-Christendoms and, 152–53; pagan syncretism and, 154–56, 160, 221; papal monarchy foundations and, 203; persecution of, 60, 61, 83–84, 90, 112, 137–38; political thought and, 40–41, 55–63, 88–98 (*see also* church and state); prevailing ideology of, 112–17; providential optimism of, 114–15, 116–18, 130, 132, 136, 141; regionalization of churches and, 152; as Roman established religion, 95–96, 131, 151, 206; Roman persecutions and, 60, 61, 83–84, 90, 112; rulership ideal and, 134, 141; synodal governance and, 206; unction rite and, 160–61. *See also* Orthodox Church; papacy; Roman Catholic Church
Christian Roman empire, 39, 60, 61–63, 72, 83–110, 151–57; Augustinian political theology and, 119–20, 134–36; belief in providential destiny of, 113–14, 117–18, 119–21; Byzantine emperors and, 98–110, 111; chain of disasters (406–410) and, 115, 118–19, 120–21; Constantine as first emperor of, 39, 89–92, 94–96, 107, 151; established religion of, 95–96, 131, 151, 206; European evangelization and, 68, 72, 75, 144; Eusebian political theology and, 87, 89–98, 99, 102, 106–7, 110, 111; evangelized western provinces of, 151–57; Germanic successor kingdoms and, 143, 148–51; Nicene-Catholic vs. Arian view of, 96–97; Orosius's view of, 116; paganism and, 114, 150–51, 152; papal primacy claims and, 215–19; Russia and, 107–10, 111
Christmas, dating of, 154
Christocentric kingship, 165, 166–68, 169, 170–71, 172, 173, 174, 175
Christology, 86, 87, 93–94, 106, 174; Anglo-Norman Anonymous and, 168–70, 171; church and state and, 96–97; Eusebius and, 89, 97, 168, 169; Nicene-Catholic, 96, 97, 168; subordinationists and, 88–89, 92, 94, 96, 97, 168
Chromatianos, Demetrios, 103–4
Chronicle (Otto of Freising), 116–17
Chrysostom, John, St., 98, 99
church and state, x, 19; Ambrose of Milan and, 114; Arian vs. Nicene-Catholic view of, 96–97; Aristotle and, 8–9; Augustine and, 127, 135–37, 141, 163; Byzantine emperors and, 98–110; Christology and, 96–97; classical world and, 38–39; desacralization of human society and, 48–49; distinction between, 19; Frankish kingdom and, 153–54, 158, 162–63, 214; German emperors and, 76, 77–78; heresy punishment and, 135–36; imperial power and, 217–19; Islamic *umma* and, 81; Jesus' separation of, 40, 58, 61, 62; Kingdom of God and, 59–60, 62–63; medieval Christian Europe and, 159–76, 182; papal primacy claims and, 99–102, 213, 214, 215; papal reforms and, 77–78, 219; papal-royal clashes and, xii–xiii, 199, 214, 219; Roman Christianization and, 95–96, 151, 152–53. *See also* theocracy
church councils. *See* councils, church
church fathers. *See* patristic writers
Church of St. John Lateran, 211
Cicero, 4, 36, 40, 132
Cilicia, 36
cities, 22
citizenship: Athenian basis of, 5; of individual, 181; Roman Christians and, 61; virtue training and, 8
city of God. *See civitas dei/civitas terrena*
City of God, The (Augustine), 116, 119–34, 137, 139, 140, 143, 163; central point of, 130; on ideal "happy" Christian emperor, 131, 134, 136, 141; understanding and misunderstanding of, 122–23
city-state. *See* polis
civil society. *See* state
civitas dei/civitas terrena, 121–28, 132, 142; asymmetry between, 126; invisible demarcation line between, 127, 129; medieval political theory breakdown of, 140–41

Index

classical world, 3–16, 29–39, 220; conception of nature and, 21; continuity of political thought and, ix, x, 1, 4; kingship and, 29–32; political-religious fusion and, 38–39; politically anachronistic view of, 4, 9–10; religious-political merger and, 8–9, 59; representative vs. monarchical government and, 3–4; striving for good life and, 118

Clement of Alexandria, 87–88, 92, 106

Cleopatra, queen of Egypt, 36

clerical order, 175, 199, 200–203; abuses by, 77; Byzantine imperial conflict with, 98–104; celibacy and, 77, 221; Christology and, 169; Diocletian persecutions and, 137–38; economic system and, 188, 201; hierarchy and, 175, 199, 202, 203, 207, 210; order vs. jurisdiction powers and, 169–70; ordination rite and, 160–61; privileges of, 201; regional early Christian churches and, 152; sacral kingship and, 155–56, 165, 197; sacrament of holy orders and, 104; tonsure and, 160, 201. *See also* bishops; priesthood

clerus. See clerical order

Clovis, king of the Franks, 68

Cluny monastery, 77

Cochrane, Charles Norris, 35

Code of Canon Law (1983), 210

Code of Hammurabi, 26

Codex Juris Canonici (1917), 210

Coelestius, 124

Cologne, archbishop of, 204–5

commonwealth: Christian ideal of, x; definition of, 132–33; Platonic ideal of, 9. *See also* state

communities, 2, 180–82; as independent jurisdictions, 188; personal loyalty oaths and, 190

comparative religion, 5, 144, 147

Concerning the Consecration of Pontiffs and Kings and Their Rule in the Holy Church (Anonymous), 167–68

Concord of Discordant Canons (Gratian), 210–11, 213

concubinage, clerical, 77

Confessions (Augustine), 124, 154–55

confirmation, 160

Confucian thought, 19

Congress of Vienna (1815), 204

Conrad II, king of Germany and Holy Roman emperor, 166, 179

conscience, 6–7, 9, 134; sacrament of penance and, 104

consecration, 162–63, 165, 166, 169, 170, 171–72; divinity of kings by, 172

consent of governed, x, 2, 148, 181, 182, 184; taxation and, 195, 199

Constantine, Pope, 216

Constantine, emperor of Rome, 15, 221; as Christian Caesar, 107, 142; Christian conversion of, 39, 62, 83, 89, 90, 119, 151, 211; Christian re-sacralization of, 95–96, 107; clerical privileges and, 201; Donation of Constantine forgery and, 73, 211; Eusebian portrayal of, 89–90, 91–92, 94, 95, 99, 118; imperial legacy of, 39; letter (324/6) to Persians by, 106–7

Constantine V, Byzantine emperor, 99

Constantine XI, Byzantine emperor, 16, 109

Constantinople, 15, 69, 70, 71, 211; as new Rome, 109, 110; Ottoman conquest of, 16, 109

Constantius II, Byzantine emperor, 97

constitutionalism, 176; roots of, 148, 197–98; feudal institutions and, 185, 194, 196, 197–98

Constitution of Athens (Aristotle), 31

consuls, Roman, 35

contract, feudal, 184, 194–95, 196, 197

Contrat social, Du (Rousseau), 40

Coptic Christians, 154

Corinthian League, 33

Corinthians, Epistles to the, 208

Cornford, F. M., 20

coronation ceremonies, 110, 145–46, 160–61, 165, 171, 172–73; liturgies for, 164, 167, 170; papacy and, 179; pharaoh and, 28. *See also* unction

Corsica, 74

cosmic order, 27; king as representative of, 45, 47, 51, 84; omnipotence of God and, 48; state as embodiment of, 19

cosmic religiosity, 18, 19–21, 39, 81; biblical undercutting of, 49; emperor as center of, 19–20, 26–27, 37–38; Hebrew kingship and, 45, 52; Hellenistic echoes of, 34; king as *logos* manifestation and, 34; mountain symbolism and, 28; natural-supernatural distinction and, 181–82; pagan kingship and, 174; sacral kingship's roots in, 19; Scandinavian kings and, 146–47; survival in rural western Europe of, 155. *See also* sacral monarch

cosmogony, 10, 25, 28, 45; kingship analogy with, 26, 34; order-out-of-chaos struggle and, 28, 29, 47, 48. *See also* creation myths

councils, church, 92, 99, 103, 104, 155, 206, 216; principle decisions of, 212. *See also* specific councils by key word

counsel, 194

counts, (nobles)192, 193

covenant, 49, 52, 53, 54

Cranz, F. Edward, 120

Creation, 47–58, 79, 119, 123, 124; Augustine's Christian vision of, 121; human suffering and, 115

creation myths, 10, 28; biblical account contrasted with, 47–48, 49, 52, 79; kingship and, 22, 25, 28, 45; parallelism among, 28, 29, 47

cremation, 155
Crete, 2, 13, 14, 29, 30
Crucifixion, 93–94
cult of the dead, 155
customs (*nomoi*), 7
Cynics, 6
Cyprian of Carthage, 217
Cyrene, 30

Dagobert, king of the Franks, 158
Damasus, Pope, 206, 212
Damiani, Peter, 166, 221
damned, 126
Daniel, 55, 87, 116, 135
Danube frontier, 67
Dark Age (Greece), 14–15, 30
David, king of Judah and Israel, 16, 41, 45, 49, 53, 57, 103, 106, 158, 162; royal morality and, 178. *See also* House of David
De bello gallico (Caesar), 148
De consecratione pontificum et regum et de regimine eorum in ecclesia sancta (Anonymous), 167–68, 170
decretals, papal, 206–7, 211–12
Decretum (Gratian), 210–11, 213
De excidio et conquestu Britanniae (Gildas), 157
De gratia Christi et de peccato originali (Augustine), 118
deification, 36, 85
De institutione regia (Jonas of Orléans), 177, 178
de Jong, Mayke, 163
democracies, 3, 30
demos (territorial grouping), 5, 10
Denmark, 75
De ordine palatii (Hincmar of Rheims), 177, 184
De privilegio et jure sacerdotii (Agobard), 202
De rectoribus christianis (Sedulius Scottus), 177, 178
De regis persona (Hincmar of Rheims), 177
descending political structure, 181, 182, 183, 209–10
despotism, 15, 17
Deutero-Isaiah (Second Isaiah), 43, 44, 47, 48, 55; Kingdom of God meaning and, 57
Deuteronomy, 178
diakonia, 57
Diocletian, emperor of Rome, 15, 39, 83, 137
Diogenes, 85
Dionysian festival, 31
Dionysian universe, 209
Dionysius the Areopagite, 209, 213
Dionysus (god), 31
Diotogenes, 34
Discours sur l'histoire universelle (Bossuet), 117
divine continuum, 48–49
divine grace: Augustinian doctrine of, 124, 125, 127, 128, 137, 138, 139, 140; human cooperation with, 140; kingship and, 182; modified Augustinianism and, 140; sacraments as channels of, 140, 171
divine immanence, 20, 21, 48, 49, 52, 181–82
divine judgment, 115; elect and, 125
divine law, 85
divine *logos*, 93–94
divine monarch. *See* sacral monarch
divine ordination, 158, 210
divine-right monarchs, 176, 185
Domitian, emperor of Rome, 61
Donation of Constantine, 73, 211, 212–13
Donatists, 120, 131, 134–35, 136, 137, 138, 139, 140–41, 142
Doria, 14, 15
double predestination, 125 (*see also* elect)
drought, 46
druids, 152
Druzes, 82
dual kingship, 30
due process, 198
dukes, 192, 193
Dumuzi Tammuz (god), 27
Dvornik, Francis, 85

early medieval Europe. *See* Middle Ages
early modern period, xi, 9
earthly city, 121, 126–29, 130, 133; ambiguity in usage of, 126; Augustinian meaning of, 125
Easter, 154
Eastern church. *See* Orthodox Church
eastern Mediterranean. *See* Mediterranean civilizations
Eastern Roman Empire. *See* Byzantine Empire
East Frankia. *See* Germany
Ecclesiastical History (Eusebius), 89
Ecclesiastical History of the English Nation (Bede), 156
ecclesiastical power, 169–70, 171
ecclesiastical reform movement, 176, 201–2, 212, 219, 220, 221–22
ecclesiology, 200
Eco, Umberto, xi
economic system, 187, 188–89, 201
ecumenical councils. *See* councils, church
Edgar coronation *ordo* of 973, 166, 171, 173
Egypt, 2, 13, 14, 18, 19, 22–28, 43; Alexander the Great and, 15; Christian syncretism and, 154; continuity of beliefs and, 24; creation myth of, 10, 28; definition of kingship and, 25; divinity of pharaoh and, 22, 25; Fatimid caliphate and, 82; Israelite deliverance from, 49, 92; kingship history in, 22–28, 33, 42, 149; Mesopotamia kingship vs., 23, 25–26; Muslim expansion and,

70; Old Kingdom pharaohs and, 23–24; Old Testament style and, 44; Roman empire and, 36–37; symbolism of pyramids of, 22; temples of, 27–28
Einhard, 142, 216
Elbe River, 76
elect, 123, 125, 127, 128, 129; invisible church of, 126, 139, 140
Eleusian Eumolpidas, 31
Eleusian Kerukes, 31
Eleusian mysteries, 31
Eliade, Mircea, 10, 22, 29
Elijah, 51
Elizabeth II, queen of Great Britain, 166
emperor. *See* kingship; sacral monarch
empire, idea of, 179. *See also specific empires*
end of time. *See* eschatology
England. *See* Britain
Engnell, Ivan, 24, 42
Enil (god), 26
Enoch, 55, 57
Enùma elish (Babylonian creation myth), 10, 28, 47, 48
Eostre (goddess), 154
Ephraim. *See* Israel/Ephraim, kingdom of
epics, 30, 145
Epicureans, 6
episcopal collegiality, 206, 212, 216–17
episcopalism, 216–17
epistemonarches (Byzantine imperial title), 103–4
Epistles of Paul. *See* Pauline Epistles
eschatology, 43–44, 56; Augustine and, 119–20, 121, 123, 126, 127; Kingdom of God and, 56, 127–28; Last Judgment and, 121, 123, 139
Ethiopia, 157, 159
ethnos-states, 29
Eucharist, 171
Eusebius, bishop of Caesarea, 87, 89–98, 99, 102, 106–7, 110, 114, 116, 132, 142, 164; Anonymous compared with, 168, 172, 173, 174; Augustine contrasted with, 111–12, 119, 130, 131; Christology of, 89, 97, 168, 169; Latin West and, 112, 174; Origen's influence on, 89; works of: *Ecclesiastical History*, 89; *In Praise of Constsantine* (*Oration*), 89–90, 92, 93, 94–95, 105, 118; *Life of Constantine*, 89–90, 95
evangelization. *See* missionaries
exceptionalism, Germanic, 144, 147
excommunication of kings, 199, 214
Exodus, 49, 92

faith, 207, 211; consent of the governed vs., 181; rule of, 206
Fall, 121; Augustinian centrality of, 123, 124, 128, 133. *See also* sin
fallen angels, 125

False Decretals, 211–12, 213
fathers of the church. *See* patristic writers
Fatimid caliphate, 82
Feast of the Tabernacles, 45, 46
Feis Temhra (feast of Tara), 145–46
feodum. *See* fief
fertility rites, 27, 28, 31, 34, 45, 51, 52, 146, 147, 155
festivals and feasts: ancient Near East parallelisms and, 45, 46; archaic world and, 21, 22, 27; Christian substitutes for pagan, 154; classical Greek religion and, 31
feudalism, 75–76, 185–99; contractual nature of, 185, 194–95, 196, 197; as controversial construct, 186–87, 189–90; definitional profile of, 188–89; first and second stages of, 189; fundamental characteristics of, 188, 194–95; hierarchy of, 193, 194, 195, 196; historical roots of, 184–85, 190–91; ideal-typical approach to, 190; institutional variations in, 189; Japanese system of, 196; Magna Carta and, 198; two levels of, 189
fidelity (*fidelitas*), 180; personal oaths of, 184, 186, 190, 192, 194, 198
fief (*feodum*), 190–95; forfeiture of, 195
Figgis, John Neville, 137
First Vatican Council (1870), 204, 210, 218
folk assemblies, 148, 182, 195
folklore, 155
forgeries, 73, 209, 210–11, 212, 213
Forms (Platonic), 29
Foucault, Michel, 220
France, 68, 69, 70, 75, 78, 117; barbarian raiders and, 74; biblical kingship and, 164; feudalism and, 76; kingship and, 179; Roman Catholic Church and, 204, 205; royal touch healing power and, 156. *See also* Carolingian empire; Franks
Frankfort, Henri, 19, 24, 25, 28
Frankfurt, Council of (794), 162, 165
Franks, 71–74, 150, 156, 157–59, 161–63, 214; anointing of kings by, 161; cavalry use by, 191; Christian conversion of, 68, 159; defeat of Muslim invaders by, 161, 191; extent of kingdom of, 68; leadership in West of, 71, 153–54; as new Israel, 41, 157, 158, 161–62, 165; papal relations with, 216–17; Roman legacy to, 71–72, 73. *See also* Carolingian empire; Germany; Merovingian kingdom
Fredegar, 160
freedom, 5, 6–7
free will, 124
French Revolution, 204, 205
Frisians, 68
Fustel de Coulanges, Numa Denis, 6, 7, 59–60

Gaul, 161, 190
Gaza Strip, 16
Geblütsheiligkeit (royal mana), 150, 160

Gelasius I, Pope, 99–102, 106, 172, 215
Genesis, 28, 47–48, 49, 100; *Enùma elish* parallel with, 28
Genghis Khan, 108–9
Gentiles, 57, 61, 63, 82
Gerard, bishop of Hereford, 167
German emperors. *See* Holy Roman empire
Germania (Tacitus), 148
Germanic peoples: barbarian waves of, 67–68, 147; Christian conversion of, 68, 149; fidelity oaths and, 190; kingship and, 2, 68–69, 70–71, 76, 143, 144, 147, 148–51, 182, 195, 198; natural-supernatural distinction and, 182; paganism and, 10, 16, 30, 144, 146–49, 182; royal genealogies of, 149–50, 155–56. *See also* Franks; Visigothic kingdom
Germany, 74, 75, 76, 158, 164–65; biblical kingship and, 164; Christian syncretism and, 154; Christocentric kingship and, 165; coronation liturgies and, 170, 171; expansion of, 76; imperial title and, 76–78, 164; liturgical kingship and, 165–67; nobility's central role in, 175; oaths of fidelity and vassalage and, 184–85; revived Roman empire of (*see* Holy Roman empire); Roman Catholic Church in, 204–5; Roman papacy and, 72
Gibbon, Edward, 112, 179
Gideon, 45
Gildas: *De excidio et conquestu Britanniae (On the Ruin of Britain)*, 157
God: archetypal kingship of, 85, 88, 90–91; covenant with chosen people of, 47, 49, 52–53, 54, 57, 59; descending political structure and, 181, 182, 209–10; emperor as image of, 110, 168; grace of (*see* divine grace); Hebrew kingdoms and (*see* Yahweh); imperial parallels with, 114; kingship as gift from, 105, 112, 153, 158, 182; *logos* distinguished from, 86; as loving Father, 57; Messiah and, 53–54; miraculous interventions by, 87; as one, transcendent, and omnipotent, 48, 49, 50, 53, 57, 79, 81, 87, 106; predestination and, 125, 139, 140. *See also* Jesus Christ; Kingdom of God
gods: Christian syncretism and, 154; creation myths and, 28; dual royal partners and, 30; human separation from, 33; as kingship model, 90; king's relationship with, 26–27, 28, 30, 31, 33, 44, 45, 49, 51, 145–46; pharaoh as incarnation of, 24, 25; Roman emperor and, 37; royal genealogies and, 149–50, 155–56, 196; royal sacred mating with, 27, 28, 31, 145–46
"golden cap" of Monomachus, 109
Goodenough, E. R., 34
Gospel Book of Aachen, 167
Gospels, 55–63, 87; church hierarchy and, 207;

208; Kingdom of God conception of, 58, 127–28; *logos* and, 86; Roman history linked with, 62–63, 84. *See also specific gospels*
Goths. *See* Ostrogothic kingdom; Visigothic kingdom
government authority. *See* state
grace. *See* divine grace
Grant, F. C., 55–56
Gratian, 201, 210; *Decretum (Concord of Discordant Canona)*, 210–11, 213
Graus, František, 147
"Great House" (pharaoh), 25
Greece, 13–16; as Byzantine legacy, 16; colonies of, 14–15, 29–30; Dark Age of, 14–15, 30; Hellenic era and, 9, 29–32; kingship and, 15, 26, 29–31, 33, 34; Mycenaean Age and, 2, 14, 15, 29, 30; polis and, 3–4, 5, 7, 8, 9, 10, 14–15, 30–34, 38; political legacy of, 3–8, 9–10, 15.*See also* Hellenistic era
Greek canon law, 110
Greek church fathers, 86, 98, 99. *See also* Eusebius
Greek philosophy, 3–4, 5–7, 7, 10, 34, 87–88; Christian inheritance of, 117, 127
Greenland, 74
Gregory I (he Great), Pope, 72, 152, 154, 177, 209, 212, 214; modified Augustinian teachings and, 140; *Regula pastoralis (Pastoral Care)*, 177
Gregory II, Pope, 102, 212
Gregory IV, Pope, 141, 213
Gregory VII, Pope, xiii, 78, 214, 219; reform and, 201–2, 212, 220, 221–22
Gregory of Nyssa, St., 98
Gunthram, king of the Merovingians, 156
Gustavus Wasa, king of Sweden, 147
Guthrie, W. K. C., 4

hadith, 80
Hadrian II, Pope, 217
Hakim bin Amr Allah, al-, Fatimid caliph, 82
Hammurabi's code, 26
Han dynasty, 2
Hasmonean kings, 62
Hauck, Karl, 147
heavenly city (Augustinian), 121, 126, 127, 129–30
Hebrew kingdoms, 14, 16–17, 41–55, 157, 158; as chosen people, 47, 49, 52–53, 54, 57, 59, 103, 157; desacralization and, 58; disparate traditions of, 42; exilic and post-exilic hostility toward, 52; Franks' identification with, 161–62, 163, 165; king's divine status and, 46; Messiah and, 53–54, 55, 58; monarchical style of, 45; moral development and, 178; non-Davidic, 52; political legacy of, 16, 17, 41, 103, 106, 157–58, 168; political positions of, 54–55, 79, 157; priesthood and, 17,

45, 46, 50, 54, 100, 103, 106; religious syncretism and, 51–53; theocracy of, 53, 162; unction rite and, 160, 161
Hebrews, Epistles to the, 168
Hegel, Georg Wilhelm Friedrich, 5–6
Hellenic era, 29–32; definition of, 29; political vocabulary of, 9, 30, 128; Roman imperial sacrality and, 34, 35–39
Hellenistic era, ix, 29, 32–39, 209; Christian thought and, 29, 57–58, 61–62, 85–88, 92, 94, 102, 105, 106, 113–14, 117, 127, 173; definition of, 29; hero-god dividing line and, 33; kingship and, 15, 34–35, 57–58, 61, 62, 83, 84–85, 87–88, 94, 102, 105, 106, 168, 173, 174; royal titles and, 84–85, 88, 94, 95
Hellenists, 5, 6
Henry II, king of Germany and Holy Roman emperor, 179
Henry III, king of Germany and Holy Roman emperor, xiii, 77–78, 213
Heracles (god), 33
Heraclius, Byzantine emperor, 70
heredity: of kingship, 30, 31, 149–50, 155–56, 182; of public office, 193
heresy, 97, 210–11; Augustine on, 135–36, 137, 139, 141
hero cult, 5, 33
Heruli kingdom, 150
hieros gamos (sacred coupling), 27
High Middle Ages, 74, 201
high priest, 50
Hilary, St., 97
Hincmar of Rheims, 183, 184, 212, 213, 214; *De ordine palatii (On the Government of the Palace)*, 177, 184; *De regis persona (On the Person of the King)*, 177
Hintze, Otto, 190
Historiarum adversum paganos. Libri VII (Orosius), 115, 117
historical periodization, xi, 200, 220
History of Political Theory (Sabine), 40
Hittites, 2, 13, 15, 23; kingship form of, 148
Hobbes, Thomas, xiii, 63, 82, 222–23
Höfler, Otto, 147, 149
holiness, 137, 138–39
holy orders, sacrament of, 104
Holy Roman empire, 76–78, 183, 217–19; Christocentric rulers and, 166–67; coronation of Otto I and, 164; dissolution of, 204; papacy and, xiii, 76–77, 179, 217–18
Homer, 4, 30
Horus (god), 25, 154
Hosea, 51, 52
household knights, 191, 194

House of David, 45, 59; Messiah and, 53, 54
Hugh of Fleury, 168
Hugh of St. Victor, 201
humanism, 200, 220, 221
humankind: corrupted nature of, 124, 128; desacralization of, 48–49; free will and, 124; individual rights and, xi, 181, 195; individual will and, 5, 8; natural justice and, 61; nature's integration with, 21, 22, 52; pessimistic view of, 115–16, 124, 130; predestination, 119, 124–25; relationship with God of, 52, 142; sacraments and, 137. *See also* individual identity
Hungary, 75
Huns, 67
Hurrians, 23

Iceland, 144
iconoclasm, 72–73, 98, 102–3, 157, 216
ideal commonwealth (Platonic), 9
Ideas, Platonic doctrine of, 29
idolatry, 155, 157
Ife, priest-king of, 22–23
Iliad (Homer), 30
imam, 81, 82
imperial sacrality. *See* sacral monarch
impiety, 9
inalienable rights, 181
Inanna-Ishtar (goddess), 27, 28
Inca monarchy, 3
Incarnation, 93–94, 121
India, 30, 70
individual identity, xi, 4–5, 6–7, 52; bilateral ties and, 180–85; direct contact with God and, 57, 60; state vs. 6, 7, 8, 9, 10, 181; subjective righteousness and, 138
individual rights, xi, 181, 195
individual will, 5, 8
Industrial Revolution, 2
Indus Valley civilization, 13
Ine, king of Wessex, 158, 183–84
innocence, 128
Innocent III, Pope, 199
Innocent IV, Pope, 213
In Praise of Constantine (Eusebius), 89–90, 92, 93, 94–95, 105, 118
invisible church, 123, 126, 139, 140
Iolians, 15
Ios, 30–31
Iran. *See* Persian empire
Iran, shah of, 79–80
Iraq, 70. *See also* Mesopotamia
Ireland: evangelization and, 68, 72, 144; as micro-Christendom, 152; Old Testament parallel and, 157; sacral kingship and, 145–46, 149, 161

Irminsul (giant tree), 154
iron weaponry, 10
Isaac, 87
Isaiah, 43, 44, 51, 52, 173
Isidore Mercator, 211–12
Isidore of Seville, 153, 158, 211
Isis (goddess), 154
Islamic empire, 18, 67, 70–71, 76, 79–82, 215; as Byzantine empire threat from, 70, 72, 157; expansion of, 70–71, 74, 153; Frankish victory over, 161, 191; inherited ancient Near Eastern practices and, 80–81; kingly rulers and, 2–3, 79–81; medieval European threat from, 74, 161, 186, 191; monotheism of, 79, 81; religious-political unity and, 81–82; Roman imperial legacy and, 71; Spain and, 70, 74, 173
Isocrates, 34
Israel/Ephraim, kingdom of, 2, 17, 41, 42, 44, 178; destruction of, 52. *See also* Hebrew kingdoms
Israelites. *See* Hebrew kingdoms; Judaism
Italy, 33, 164; barbarian waves and, 68, 69, 73, 74, 100; Byzantine provinces in, 152; German expansion and, 76, 215; Norman conquests in, 76; papal claims to, 73, 212, 216. *See also* Roman empire; Rome
Ivan III, tsar of Russia, 109
Ivan IV (the Terrible), tsar of Russia, 107

Jacob, 43, 87
James, E. O., 31, 32
Janet, Paul, 41
Japan, 2, 22, 159, 196, 197
Jeremiah, 53, 54
Jericho, 13
Jerome, St., 208
Jerusalem, 17, 44, 45, 46, 178; Babylon contrasted with, 122, 127; fall of, 53; Solomon's Temple at, 17, 45
Jesus Christ: birth correlated with Augustan peace, 62–63, 84–85, 88, 91, 113–14, 116–17, 119; church hierarchy and, 207–8, 209, 213, 217; as eternal royal Christ, 171; Eusebian political theology and, 87, 93–94; Gospel accounts of, 55–63; as King of Glory, 167; as *logos*, 86, 87, 88, 89, 92, 93–94, 95; as Messiah, 54, 57, 106; monarchical manifestation of, 165–75; New Testament attributes of, 55–63, 84–85, 86, 89; patristic writings and, 86–87, 93–94; political thought and, 40, 58, 61, 62; as rock of church, 209, 217; as Savior, 89, 91; as Son of God, 87, 97, 116, 207; superseding of emperor by, 100; universal Kingdom of, 55, 57, 58, 60, 62, 123, 127, 172, 201; Zealots and, 54, 58. *See also* Christology; Trinitarianism
Jewish Bible/Christian Old Testament. *See* Old Testament

John, St.: First Epistle of, 61; Gospel according to, 57, 61, 62; identification of Jesus with *logos* by, 86; Revelation of, 119, 123
John VII, Pope, 73
John VIII, Pope, 217
John XII, Pope, 217–18
John, king of England, 195, 197–98, 199
John of Salisbury, 178; *Policraticus*, 117
Jonas of Orléans, 178; *De institutione regia (On the Institution of the King)*, 177, 178
Josephus, Flavius, 53
Jotham, fable of, 50, 51
Judah, kingdom of, 2, 17, 41, 42, 44; destruction/revival of, 52, 53. *See also* Hebrew kingdoms
Judaism, 17, 39, 53, 57, 85; one, omnipotent, omniscient God of, 87, 106; questioned compatibility of kingship with, 51. *See also* Hebrew kingdoms; Old Testament
Judges, 45, 50, 51
justice, 61, 84, 125, 132–34, 141; Augustinian definition of, 132–33; kingship and, 134, 178, 197
Justinian I, Byzantine emperor, 76, 102, 150; ecclesiastical concerns of, 105; reconquests by, 69, 70, 71, 215
Justin Martyr, 87

Kamikura shogunate, 159
Kantorowicz, Ernst, 161, 166, 167, 178
Kassites, 23
Kelley, Donald, 186–87
Kern, Fritz, 158, 160, 182–83
khanate, 108–9
khilafa. *See* caliphate
Khomeini, Ayatollah Ruholla Mussaui, 79–80
Kierkegaard, Søren, 48
Kiev, principality of, 109, 110
king-archon, 31, 50
Kingdom of Christ, 123, 172, 201
Kingdom of God, 53, 116, 127, 172; Christianized Roman Empire and, 96, 105, 106; Christian rulers and, 134; Christocentric kingship and, 173, 174; as eschatological kingdom, 56, 127–28; as future vs. present, 56–59, 127–28; modified Augustinian thought and, 141; universality of, 57, 59, 60, 62–63, 91; worldly conflict with, 61
Kingdom of Heaven, 53, 55, 123; Augustinian view of, 129; Peter's keys of, 207–8
King of Glory, 167
Kings, 51
kingship: ancient notion of, 19, 30; assembly election of, 148–49, 182, 183; do-nothing kings and, 159–60, 196; fundamental sacred character of, xiii, 19, 22, 49; hereditability of, 30, 31, 149–50, 155–56, 182; Homeric epics and, 30; individual royal personage vs. office of, 178–79; institu-

tions of, 26; limitations on power of, 185; as living law, 34; nobility's relationship with, 184; personal moral deportment and, 177–79; popular sanctions on, 183; regalia of, 15, 109, 211; ritual responsibilities of, 26–27, 28; titles of, 26, 34, 58, 84, 85; transpersonality of, 179–80; ubiquity and longevity of, 1–3; warrior role and, 26, 30, 52. *See also* sacral monarch

Kleisthenes, 5
knights, 188, 189, 191–92, 193, 194–95
Korea, 2
Kuba monarchy, 3
Kyrios (Lord), 85

laity 175, 201, 202
landholders, 191, 192
Langton, Stephen, archbishop of Canterbury, 199
Last Judgment, 121, 123, 139
Lateran, 214
Latin Catholic Church. *See* Roman Catholic Church
Latin church fathers, 111–42; importance of Augustinian political theology and, 117–42
Latin Middle Ages. *See* Middle Ages
Latin West, 18, 111, 215; archaic sacral patterns and, 150–51; barbarian waves and, 74, 176; Byzantine political thought contrasted with, 174–76; canonistic distinctions and, 104; Christianity's dominance in, 144; divine and human parallelism and, 97; first theologian of, 112; Frankish leadership in, 71, 153–54; imperial sacrality and, 99–100, 142; kingship ideology of, 114–15, 157–76; micro-Christendoms and, 152, 153; nobility and, 175, 183–84; popularization of modified Augustinian in, 140, 142; rebound in late tenth and eleventh century of, 175–76. *See also* Middle Ages
Laudes regiae, 162
law: as basis of justice, 6; Byzantine empire and, 106; Carolingian era and, 183–84; Code of Hammurabi and, 26; competing conceptions of, 180–82; feudal relationships and, 189, 193–94, 195, 196, 197–98; heresy penalties and, 135; human fallen condition and, 128; Islamic religious-secular unity under, 81; medieval communities and, 180; monarch as embodiment of, 84, 85; natural law and, 7, 128, 133; papacy and, 208, 210; profane vs. sacred, 141. *See also* canon law
Laws (Plato), 9
legends, 155. *See also* creation myths
Leo I (the Great), Pope, 99, 206, 207, 208, 209, 210, 215
Leo IV, Pope, 214
Leo IX, Pope, xiii, 77–78, 214, 218–19
Leo III, Byzantine emperor, 99, 102, 216
Leo IV, Byzantine emperor, 99

Léon, kingdom of, 179
Levi priesthood lineage, 54, 103
liberties, 195, 198
Libri Carolini (document), 163
Life of Constantine (Eusebius), 89–90, 95
liturgical kingship, ideology of, 165–76
Locke, John, 8, 9; *Second Treatise of Government*, 8
logos: Christian adoption of, 86–89, 91, 92–95, 97; king as manifestation of, 34, 84, 85; Philo Judaeus on, 86, 92–93; salvation and, 95; twin denotations of, 86
Lombards, 69, 70, 73
Lord, Christ as, 85
lord-vassal relationship, 191, 192, 193; reciprocity of, 194–95, 196
Lorraine, 77–78
Lothair I, Holy Roman emperor, 183
Lothar II, king of Lotharingia, 214
Louis I (the Pious), king of the Franks and emperor of the West, 141, 179, 183
Louis II (the Stammerer), king of the Franks, 183
Louis II (the German), king of Germany, 184
loyalty. *See* fidelity
lugal (Mesopotamian ruler), 25–26
Lukan tradition, 88, 112, 113–14, 116; expressions of, 90
Luke, Gospel according to, 56, 57, 58, 61, 84; correlation of birth of Christ with Augustan peace, 62–63, 84–85, 88, 113–14, 116
Lutheranism, 155
Lycia/Caria, 30

maat, 26–27
Macedonian empire, 29, 32–39, 116; monarchical legacy of, 15
Magna Carta (1215), 198, 199
Magna Graecia, 29–30
Magyars, 67, 74, 75, 76, 176, 186
Mainz, archbishop of, 166, 204–5
Maistre, Joseph de, 204
Manassah, 51
manorial system, 188, 192
Maraval, Pierre, 94
Marduk (king-god), 28, 47
margraves, 193
Mark, Gospel according to, 56, 57, 61
Markus, R. A., 20, 113, 118–19, 136
martyrdom, 72, 90, 112, 130
Marxist thought, 187
Matthew, Gospel according to, 56, 57, 87; church hierarchy and, 207, 208, 217
Maxentius, emperor of Rome, 92
Maximian, emperor of Rome, 38
Maya monarchy, 3, 22
Medb (earth goddess), 145–46

mediator: Christ as, 87; king as, 84, 85, 172
medieval Europe. *See* Middle Ages
Medina, 81
Mediterranean civilizations, 2, 13–39; Byzantine empire and, 69, 71; creation myths and, 28; Hebrews and, 16–17; Hellenistic empire and, 15, 32; Islamic expansion and, 70, 71, 74; Roman unity and, 67, 68; traditional pagan religiosity of, 13, 38. *See also* Near East, ancient
Melchizedek, 44, 85, 100, 103, 106, 162, 165, 168; as priest and king, 171, 172
Memphis Theology (Egyptian creation myth), 10
Menexenus (Plato), 31
Mernephtah, pharaoh of Egypt, 25
Merovingian kingdom, 71–72, 156, 183, 184; do-nothing kings and, 159–60, 196–97; end of, 158, 159, 160, 197; vassalage and, 190
Mesoamerica, 3, 19, 22, 28
Mesopotamia, 2, 13, 14, 16, 17, 18, 19, 22, 23, 25–29; Assyrians and, 13, 14, 16, 17, 23, 122; Egyptian kingship vs., 23, 25–26, 27; kingship rituals and, 27, 28, 42; non-divine nature of king and, 25–26; Sumerians and, 2, 23, 24, 26, 28, 43
Messiah, 43, 44; concept of, 53–54, 55; Jesus as, 54, 57, 106. *See also* Kingdom of God
messianic prophecies, 43–44, 53–54, 55, 57, 58, 86–87, 106; Christian Roman empire and, 117; monarch's coronation feast and, 172–73, 174
metropolitans, 207, 210, 212, 214
Michael III, Byzantine emperor, 214
micro-Christendoms, 152, 153
Middle Ages: barbarian waves and, 67–68, 69, 71, 74, 77; calamities of fifth century and, 115–16, 118, 120–21; calamities of late ninth and tenth century and, 175–76, 217; Christian evangelization and, 68, 72, 75; church and state and, 159–76, 182; classical Greece and, 3, 4, 10, 14; clerical orders and, 201–2; collapse of Christian commonwealth ideal and, x; cultural mergers and, 74; development of communities and, 180; early Christian kings and, 2, 155–56; feudal institutions and, 75–76, 185–99; Germanic successor kingdoms and, 143–76; historians of, 116, 117, 123, 147–48, 180–82, 186–87, 189–90, 221; Islam political life and, 80–81; kingdom development and, 71–72, 75–76; "mirror of princes" genre and, 134; Old Testament influence and, 157–59; papal election disputes and, 210; papal ideology and, 209–10; political Augustinianism of, 137, 139–42, 143, 144; political stage for, 15–16; political thought and, x, 9, 41, 42, 47, 157–76, 177; regionalized churches and, 152–53; religious motifs dominating, ix; religious orthodoxy basis and, 139, 140; Roman inheritance claimants and, 70–71; theocratic Christian kingship and, 159–76; traditional historical periodization of, xi, 200, 220

Middle Kingdom (Egypt), 24
Milan, 113, 117, 118, 155
Miletus, 30–31
military forces. *See* warriors
Milvian Bridge, battle of (312), 92
Minoan civilization, 2, 13, 29, 30
miracles, royal, 156
"mirror of princes" genre, 134, 177–78
missionaries, 68, 72, 75, 144; syncretism and, 154–55
Mommsen, Theodor E., 120
monarchy. *See* kingship; sacral monarch
monasticism, 77, 103, 152, 176, 202
money economy, 188
Mongols, 67, 108–9
Monica, St., 155
Monomachus, golden cap of, 109
monotheism, 47–49, 50, 53, 57, 82; Islam and, 79, 81; Judaism and, 87, 106; monarchy correlated with, 85, 90–91
morality: holiness and, 138, 139; individual conscience and, 6–7, 9, 134; individual rulers and, 177–79; objective standard of, 7; original sin and, 128; political community and, 7, 8, 9; Roman Christians and, 124; social expediency vs., 9
Morrison, Karl, 206, 207, 214
mosaics, 106
Moscow, duchy of, 108; as third Rome, 109, 110
Moses, 49, 54, 85, 87–88, 92, 162; priesthood and, 54, 103, 106
mountain dwellers, 10
Mowinckel, Sigmund, 45, 46–47
Muhammad, prophet, 70, 80, 81, 82
Muslims. *See* Islamic empire
Mycenae, 14, 15, 16; sacral kingship of, 2, 29, 30, 31
Mycenaean Age, 30
myth and ritual school (biblical interpretation), 42, 43, 45, 51
mythology, 10, 22, 43, 149. *See also* creation myths; gods

Napoleon I, emperor of the French, 204, 205
national covenant, 52
nation-state. *See* state
natural disasters, 21, 155; king's wrongdoing linked with, 46
natural justice, 61
natural law, 7, 128, 133
natural vs. supernatural, 181–82
nature, 19, 20–21, 155, 174; divine immanence in,

20, 21, 48, 49, 52, 181–82; monotheistic belief and, 48–49; Muslim caliphate and, 82; ritual and taboos and, 21–22. *See also* cosmic religiosity
Naxos, 30–31
Near East, ancient: anointing with chrism and, 160; Hebrew kingship differences with, 47–48, 49–50; Hebrew kingship religious syncretism and, 51; Hebrew kingship similarities with, 43, 44, 45, 46–47, 48, 51, 54, 157; monarchical style and status in, 2–10, 18–39, 43, 45, 80; myth of primordial man and, 43; shared cultic patterns in, 42–43, 46–47. *See also* Babylonia; Egypt; Mesopotamia
Nebuchadnezzar, king of Babylon, 87, 135–36
Nelson, Janet, 178
Neolithic era, 1–2
Neoplatonism, 117, 120, 209
Nero, emperor of Rome, 61, 129
Nerthus (goddess), 159
Netherlands, 68
New Kingdom (Egypt), 24
New Testament, 55–63, 122; attributes of Jesus and, 55–63, 84–85, 86; as Augustinian influence, 118–19, 121, 123, 127, 128, 130–31, 132, 137, 163, 174; church hierarchy and, 207–8; nature of Christ and, 86; political ideas and, 40–41, 53, 59–63, 84, 92, 100, 130–31, 137, 141, 162. *See also* Gospels; Pauline Epistles
New Year's festivals, 21, 22, 28, 43, 45, 147; Hebrews' parallel with, 45, 46
Nicaea, Council of (325), 92, 96–97; theopolitical thinking and, 106
Nicene Creed, 137, 139
Nicene orthodoxy, 97, 137, 138–39; Christology and, 96, 97, 168
Nicholas I, Pope, 73, 141, 209; importance of, 214–15, 216, 217
Nicholas II, Pope, 219
Nichomachean Ethics (Aristotle), 7
Nigeria, 22–23
Nile River, 27
Nile Valley, 2
Ni-maat-Re, pharaoh of Egypt, 24–36
nobility, 30, 77, 173; bishops as, 151–52; Carolingian monarchs and, 161, 175, 183–84; collaboration and consensus of, 183–84; factional rivalry and, 217; feudal institutions and, 189, 191, 197–98; fidelity oaths and, 184, 190; independent jurisdictions of, 188; pagan assemblies of, 148; restrictions on royal power by, 186; as royal vassals, 192, 193
nomadic tribes, 67
nomoi (customs), 7
Nordic culture. *See* Scandinavia; Vikings

Normandy, 74, 75
Normans, 167, 191
North, C. R., 46
North Africa: Augustine and, 118, 120, 124, 134–35, 154–55; Byzantine rule in, 69, 215; Christian syncretism and, 154–55; Donatist schismatics and, 120, 131, 134–35, 137, 138; Greek colony in, 30; Islamic expansion in, 70, 74; as Latin West, 111, 215
North America, 4, 74
Northumbria, 155, 156
Norway, 75, 144, 159

Oakeshott, Michael, 4
Oak of Thunor (Geismar), 154
obligation. *See* fidelity
Octavian. *See* Caesar Augustus
Odyssey (Homer), 30
Olbia, 30–31
Old Kingdom (Egypt), 23, 24, 25
Old Testament, 14, 17, 41–55, 160; apocalyptic literature and, 43; Byzantine influences from, 103, 106; desacralization of kingship and, 48–49, 58; Frankish identification with, 157–59, 161–62, 165; Greek philosophers and, 87–88; iconoclastic controversy and, 102–3; kingship ideology and, 41–44, 58, 135–36, 157–59, 161, 168, 173, 178; messianic prophecies and, 43–44, 53–54, 55, 57, 58, 86–87; monotheistic Creation account and, 47–48, 79; omnipotence of God and, 47–48, 50, 87; parallelisms and, 28, 47, 103, 143, 161, 162, 165; priesthood lineage and, 54, 103, 106; schools of interpretation of, 42–43
oligarchy, 30
Olmec monarchy, 3
On Christian Rulers (Sedulius Scottus), 177, 178
Oné (Ife priest-king), 22–23
1 Kings, 51
1 Samuel, 50–51
oneness, 137, 139
On the Celestial Hierarchy (Pseudo-Dionysius), 209
On the Ecclesiastical Hierarchy (Pseudo-Dionysius), 209
On the Government of the Palace (Hincmar of Rheims), 177, 184
On the Institution of the King (Jonas of Orléans), 177, 178
On the Person of the King (Hincmar of Rheims), 177
On the Ruin of Britain (Gildas), 157
ontocratic state, 19
Optatus, 138
optimism. *See* providential optimism
oral tradition, 144
Oration (Eusebius). *See In Praise of Constantine*

Origen, 87, 88–89, 90, 106, 114
original sin, 115, 124, 125; Augustinian emphasis on, 127
Orosius, Paulus, 98, 114–16, 117, 130, 132, 141, 174; *Seven Books of History against the Pagans (Historiarum adversum paganos. Libri VII,* 115, 117
Orthodox Church, 86, 98–110; emperor's relationship with, 103–4, 106–10; iconoclasm and, 72–73, 98, 99, 102–3, 157, 216; papal power and, 208
Osiris (god), 25
Ostrogothic kingdom, 68, 69, 149, 215
Oswald, St., king of Northumbria, 156
Otto I (the Great), king of Germany and Holy Roman emperor, 164, 217–18
Otto III, king of Germany and Holy Roman emperor, 179, 212
Otto, bishop of Freising: *Chronicle,* 116–17
Ottoman empire, 16, 80, 109, 175
Ottonian dynasty, 158, 166, 170, 183, 217
Ottonianium, 218
Outer Mongolia, 67

paganism: Augustinian political theology and, 131–32, 133, 134, 136; Celtic Christian successors to, 152, 161; Celts and, x, 115, 118, 144, 145–46, 154, 174; Christian adaptations of, 150–51, 154–56, 160, 221; Christian desecrations of sites of, 154; Germanic and Scandinavian kingship and, 10, 144, 146–49, 182; monotheism vs. polytheism of, 48; Roman and Mediterranean world and, 38, 113; Roman proscription of, 114, 151, 152; Rome's decline and, 121; royal inaugural rites and, 161; survival of cultic practices of, 155–56. *See also* archaic past; creation myths; gods
palaces, 22, 31, 45
Palestine, 2, 13, 70
Pamphilus, 89, 90
papacy, 72–73, 74, 77–78, 169, 179; abuses and, 77, 217–18; apostolic succesion and, 205, 207, 208; archives of, 214–15; Byzantine emperor and, 72–73, 214, 215, 216; clerical caste and, 175; crowning of Charlemagne by, 71, 163, 179; decretals of, 206–7, 211–12; disputed elections of, 210; electoral decree and, 219; Frankish kingship and, 160, 161, 163, 197; as heir to St. Peter, 208; Holy Roman emperors and, xiii, 76–77, 217–18; imperial domination of, 217–19; monarchical independence and, xii–xiii, 199; as monarchy, 199, 200, 203–19, 222; peak of power and prestige (twentieth century) of, 203, 204; primacy claim by, 99–102, 175, 203, 205–19; reform movements and, 176, 201–2, 212, 219, 220, 221–22;

regalia of, 211, 222; restraints on, 216–19; turmoil and scandal and, 217–18
papal infallibility, 204
Papal States, 73, 212
Parthians, 32, 34
Pascha, 154
Pastoral Care (Gregory the Great), 177
pater patriae (father of the fatherland), 37
patriarchs, 103, 106, 107, 108, 210
patristic writers, 82, 83–98, 111–42, 143, 168; Alexandrian fathers, 85–86, 87–89, 90, 92, 94; Eusebian political theology, 89–98, 99, 102, 106–7, 110; Latin fathers, 111–42; mainstreaming of Hellenistic thought by, 85–86, 87–89, 106
Paul, St., 61–62, 72, 112, 128, 129, 205, 209; papal claims and, 207–8
Pauline Epistles, 61–62; as Augustinian influence, 118–19, 124; Corinthians, 208; Hebrews, 168; Romans, 61–62; Timothy, 62, 112, 129
pax Augusti. See Augustan peace
peace, 130
peasantry, 155, 188, 192
Pelagianism, 117, 136, 139, 140
Pelagius, 123–24
Peloponnese, 29
penance, 104, 137; by emperor, 113
Pépin. *See* Pippin
Persepolis, 79
Persian empire, 2, 15, 17, 23, 33, 70; Alexander the Great and, 32, 33; Christianity and, 107; Islamic expansion and, 81; royal titles and, 26, 80; sacral kingship and, 79–80, 83
personal humility, 177
Peter, St., 62, 72, 205; apostolic succession and, 205, 207, 208, 209, 214, 217; episcopalism and, 216–17; keys of, 207–8
Peter I (the Great), tsar of Russia, 107, 108
Peterson, Erik, 96, 116, 120
Petrarch, 115
pharaoh, 24–28, 36, 44
Pharisees, 55, 58
Philip, king of Macedonia, 15
Philip II, king of France, 195
Philistines, 16
Philo Judaeus, 85–86, 87, 89, 90, 92–93
Phoenicians, 45
phrygium, 211
Pilate, Pontius, 57, 58, 62
pilgrimage, 126, 128, 129, 130, 211
Pipino, Francesco, 222
Pippin III (the Short), king of the Franks, 71, 158, 160, 197
piracy, 74
Pitres, Edict of (864), 184

Pius VII, Pope, 205
Pius XII, Pope, 203
plague, 46, 83
Plato, 3–4, 6, 7, 9, 10, 29; kingship and, 31, 34; *Laws*, 9; *Menexenus*, 31; *Republic*, 6, 9, 20, 127; *Timaeus*, 10, 20, 29
Platonism, 88, 128
plentitudo potestatis, 208
Plutarch, 3, 30
Policraticus (John of Salisbury), 117
polis, 3–4, 5, 7, 10, 38; conformity and, 5; foundations for, 14; heyday and end of, 15; New Testament teachings and, 59; original meaning of, 8, 9; as politically unrepresentative, 29; survival of monarchical forms and, 30–31, 32, 33–34, 36; universe as, 85
political Augustinianism, 136–37, 141, 142, 143, 163
political thought, ix–xx, 89–98, 143; ancient Greece and, 3–8, 30, 127; Anonymous and, 168–73, 174; Aristotelian vs. Lockean views and, 8, 9; Augustine and, 111, 120–42, 143, 163, 174; Byzantine empire and, 98–110; Carolingian era and, 177–78; Celtic and Germanic successor kingdoms and, 144–54; Christian-pagan distinction and, 134; Christocentric theory of kingship and, 167–68; Christological considerations and, 169; distinction between religion and politics and, 19; divine-right absolutism and, 176, 185; dominant characteristics of, x–xx; early Christians and, 40–41, 55–63, 88–98; Eusebius and, 89–98, 114, 174; formation of feudal institutions and, 185–99; Hellenistic writings and, 34, 85, 87–89, 127; individual identity and, xi, 4–5, 6, 8; Isidore of Seville and, 153; Islamic world and, 81–82; Israelite ideal and, 53; Latin West vs. Byzantine East and, 174–76; medieval Europe and, ix, x, 75–76, 177, 179; medieval Islamic world and, 80–81; modern characteristics of, x–xx, 4, 8; natural law and, 7, 128, 133; New Testament and, 40–41, 53, 59–63, 84, 92, 100, 130–31, 137, 141, 162; orthodox Trinitarianism and, 96; preservation of cosmic order and, 20; Roman early medieval simplification of, 150. *See also* church and state
Politics (Aristotle), 7, 8
Polybius, 3
Polynesia, 2
polytheism, 48, 91
pontifex inditus, 102
pontifex maximus, 36, 37, 83, 100, 102
popes. *See* papacy; *specific popes*
Portugal, 61, 70
potestas, meaning of, 101
potestas ordinis/jurisdictionis, 106, 169–70

predestination, 119, 124–25; unknowing elect and, 123, 126, 129, 139, 140
prehistory. *See* archaic past
priesthood, 5, 85; of all believers, 170; Aristotelian view of, 8–9; Byzantine emperor and, 99, 102, 105, 110; Carolingian monarchs and, 165; celibacy and, 221; early medieval status of, 202; Hebrew kings and, 17, 45, 46, 50, 100; Homeric kings and, 30; jurisdictional power vs. power of order of, 104, 169–70; kingdom coupled with, 172; kingship as higher than, 170, 171, 175; Levi lineage of, 54, 103; Mesopotamia and, 27; Mycenaean priest-king and, 31; ordination rite and, 161; Roman Catholic hierarchy and, 140, 202, 210; Roman royal function with, 34–35, 37; sacraments and, 140, 170, 171; temporal supremacy of, 100–101; unction and, 170. *See also* clerical order
primordial man, myth of, 43
primordial chaos, 28
princeps (first citizen), 15, 37
principatus, 208
principatus divinae potestatis, 213–14
private property. *See* property rights
Procopius, 150
profane space, 21–22
property rights, 128, 188, 191, 198–99; public office as, 192
prophets, 43, 44, 47, 50, 51, 53, 54, 91, 113; Augustinian eschatological interpretation of, 119–20; Christian imperial Rome and, 117, 118; desacralization of kingship and, 58. *See also* messianic prophecies
proskynesis, 33
prostitution, sacred, 51
Protestantism, 120
Protestant Reformation, 62, 153
providential optimism, 114–18, 132, 136, 141; Augustinian salvation dichotomy vs., 119, 120, 130, 131
Prudentius, 114, 130
Psalms, 118, 168; chosen people and, 47; royal, 44, 45, 46
Ps.-Ecphantus the Pythogorean, 34
Pseudo-Augustine. *See* Ambrosiaster
Pseudo-Dionysius, 209; *On the Celestial Hierarchy*, 209; *On the Ecclesiastical Hierarchy*, 209
Pseudo-Isidorean (False) Decretals, 211–12, 213
Ptolemaic kingdom, 32, 34
public power, 178–79; private control of, 188, 192–94
punishment, sin and, 115
pyramids, 22, 27, 28
Pyramid Texts, 24
Pythagoras, 34

quality of life, 8
Quiercy, Capitulary of (877), 192–93
quietists, 55
Qumran documents, 57
Qumran sect, 55
Quran, 80, 81, 82

Ravenna, 69, 215, 216; mosaics of, 106
Ravenna, archbishop of, 214
Ré (sun god), 27, 28, 36; pharaoh as son of, 25
reason, 6, 34, 86
reciprocal obligation, 194–95, 196, 198
Reformation. *See* Protestant Reformation
regalia: monarchical, 15, 109, 211; papal, 211, 222
regal sacrality. *See* sacral monarch
reges criniti, 160
Regula pastoralis (Gregory the Great), 177
Rekhmire (Egyptian vizier), 25
religio-political thought. *See* political thought
religious–religious–secular flow of ideas, 10
Renaissance: classical Greece and, 3; humanist "Middle Age" notion and, 200, 220, 221
renovatio imperii Romanorum, 179
representative government, 2, 3, 148, 181, 199
Republic (Plato), 5, 9, 20, 127
republica. *See* commonwealth
republican government, 2, 3, 15, 32, 33, 38, 148
Resurrection, 93–94
Retractationes (Augustine), 118
Revelation of John, 119, 123
rex dei gratia, 158, 182
rex sacrorum, 36
Rheims, 212
Rhetoric (Aristotle), 7
Rhineland, 67, 68, 76
righteousness, 57, 138
rights. *See* individual rights
rituals, 19–20, 21, 22; king's sacred role in, 28, 31, 34, 45, 146–47; unction and, 160–61. *See also* coronation ceremonies; fertility rites; festivals and feasts
Roman Catholic Church, 71, 113, 143; apostolic foundation of, 205; Augustinian theology and, 120, 139, 140; changed status of, 143, 151–57, 206; church fathers and, 111–42; clerical abuses and, 77; clerical order and, 175, 199, 200–203; coronation of monarchs and, 164, 167, 170; Donation of Constantine and, 73, 211; ecclesiastical administration and, 152, 153; Frankish kingdom and, 68, 71, 153, 163; German emperors and, 76–77; heresy and, 135, 210–11; hierarchy and, 139, 140, 175, 199, 200, 206, 207–8, 209, 212–13, 214; monarchical head of (*see* papacy); monarchs' religious powers and, 136–37; national churches

and, 204–5; Nicene Christology and, 96–97; Nicene four marks of, 137, 139; reformers and, 202, 220–22; tradition-discretion tension and, 206, 207; as universal church, 205–6; as visible church, 139, 140. *See also* Latin West; papacy
Roman empire, 2, 17, 67–78, 116; barbarian invasions and, 67–69, 71, 74, 83, 115, 118, 120–21; Carolingian revival of, 71–74, 153–54, 162; Christianization of (*see* Christian Roman empire); claimants to inheritance of, 70–71; classical Greek thought and, 3–4, 16; disintegration of, 186; division of, 16, 69; Eastern imperial authority of (*see* Byzantine empire); fidelity oaths and, 190; imperial deification and, 37–38, 61; imperial power and, 15, 32–39, 61, 72, 83–84, 208; imperial regalia and, 211; Jesus and, 58, 62–63, 84–85, 88, 91, 116–17; paganism and, 38, 113, 114, 121, 131; as papal bureaucratic model, 222–23; persecutions of Christians and, 60, 61, 83–84, 90, 112; reconstitution in West of, 71–72, 92, 179 (*see also* Holy Roman empire); sacral monarch and, 15, 32, 33, 34, 35–39, 61, 83, 174; Zealot opposition to, 54, 58
Romania, 152
Roman law, 208
Roman republic, 3, 15, 32; sacral kingship remnants in, 34–35
Romans, Epistle to the, 61–62
Rome, 69–70, 109, 110, 132, 215; as Apostolic See, 207, 211, 214; Donation of Constantine and, 211; revitalized inheritance of, 153; Visigoths' sack (410) of, 115, 118, 120–21. *See also* papacy
Rome, bishops of. *See* papacy
Rousseau, Jean-Jacques, 40, 58; *Du contrat social*, 40
royal psalms, 44, 45, 46, 49
royal sacredness. *See* sacral monarch
royal saints, cult of, 156
royal titles, 26, 34, 58, 84, 85
royal touch, 156
royal unction. *See* unction, of monarchs
Royal Way (Smaragdus), 177
Russia, 18, 74, 107–10
Russian Orthodox Church, 108, 109–10

Sabine, George H., 40; *History of Political Theory*, 40
sacral monarch, xiii, 19, 32–39; absolutism and, 39, 107, 176, 181, 185; archaic roots of, 1–10, 19, 30, 48, 128, 141, 148, 174, 221; Arian vs. Nicene-Catholic view of, 96–97, 99; Augustinian ideal Christian emperor and, 131, 134, 136, 141; Augustinian political theology and, 141–42; Byzantine empire and, 98–110; Carolingian writers on,

177–78, 182; Celts and, 145–46, 149; Christianized version of, 60–63, 106, 141–42, 153–76; Christian theocratic powers of, 136–37, 141; as Christocentric, 165, 166–68, 169, 170–71, 172, 173, 174, 175; Christocentric theory of, 167–68; classical Greece and, 30–31; clericalization of, 164, 165–66, 167, 202; as cosmic center, 19–20, 26–27; cosmic creation and, 28, 47; as defender of the faith, 104; deification after death of, 24, 33, 37–38, 147, 148; divine and popular sanctions of, 182–83; divine forms of, 22–25, 30; divine genealogies of, 149–50, 155–56, 196, 197; as divinely ordained, 141, 182–83; divine model for, 90; divine ordination of, 153, 158, 182; divinization of, 22, 24–25, 30, 33, 46, 60, 82, 83–89, 109, 147, 149, 172; early Christians and, 60–61, 84, 89, 92, 94, 95–96, 99, 112–13, 153, 155–56, 206; Egypt and Mesopotamia and, 23–29; Eusebian vision of, 89–98, 99, 102, 106–7, 110, 142; feudal network and, 75–76, 185–86, 192, 193, 194, 195–99, 196–97; fidelity oaths to, 180, 184, 186; Frankish kingdom and, 157–62; fundamental character of, xiii, 19, 22, 49; German emperor and, 76–77; Germanic successor kingdoms and, 144, 146–51, 182; Gregorian reform and, 221–22; healing power of, 156; Hebrews and, 16–17, 41–42, 45–55, 58, 157, 158, 161; Hellenistic revival of, 15, 29, 32–39, 57–58, 61, 62, 83, 84–85, 87–88, 94, 102, 105, 106, 168, 173, 174; heresy punishment and, 135–36; Hittites and, 148; idea of empire and, 179; inaugural rites for (*see* coronation ceremonies); Islamic world and, 80–81; Japanese feudal system and, 196; Latin West and, 99–100, 114–15, 142, 157–76; liturgical ideology of, 165–76; meanings attached to, 32–33; as mediator between divine and subjects of, 49; messiah motif and, 44, 53–54, 172–73; "mirror of princes" genre and, 134, 177–78; Mongol khan and, 108–9; monotheism as challenge to, 48, 49, 50, 53, 57, 79–80, 81; monotheism correlated with, 85, 90–91; New Testament preclusion of, 84, 141, 162; New Year's festivals and, 22, 45; Old Testament desacralization of, 48–49, 58; papal anointment of, 160; papal challenge to, 78, 99–102; papal domination by, 217–19; Philo Judaeus on, 85–86, 92; political Augustinianism and, 141; pope as, 199, 200, 203–19, 222; regalia of, 15, 109, 211; religiosity pattern behind, 22–23; Roman Christianization and, 95–96, 102; Roman imperial cult and, 15, 32–39, 61, 72, 83–84, 208, 211; Russian tsars and, 109; sainthood and, 156; Scandinavian pagans and, 146–49, 182; staying power of, 221; titles assumed by, 26, 34, 58, 84, 85, 88, 95, 108, 166, 167, 172, 182, 222; unction and, 160–61, 164, 165, 170, 171, 172, 173, 197

sacraments: baptism's importance as, 170, 175; divine grace and, 140; kingship and, 171; Nicene orthodoxy and, 137, 138–39; power of order and, 104, 170; priesthood and, 103, 104, 170; visible church and, 139. *See also* unction

sacrifices, ritual, 19–20, 22, 31, 146, 154, 155

Sadducees, 55, 58

Safavid dynasty, 80

St. Peter's Basilica, 211, 217–18

saints, 123, 125; royal, 156

Salian dynasty, 76, 158, 164, 166, 170, 173, 175, 183, 219

salvation, 49, 95, 96, 113, 115, 134, 161; Augustinian dichotomy in, 119, 125, 139, 140; Charlemagne and, 163; Christocentric kingship and, 168, 173, 174; divine grace and, 124, 140; free will and, 124; modified Augustinianism and, 140; one true Catholic church and, 139; Roman empire and, 118

Samaria, 17, 57

Samuel, 45–46, 49, 50, 51, 158

sanctuaries, 2

San Vitale (Ravenna), 106

Sardinia, 74

Satan, 61, 125, 126, 131, 138

Saul, king of Israel, 16, 50–51

savior: Christ as, 89, 91, 95; God as, 85; king as, 34, 58, 84, 85, 95, 172

Saxons, 68, 76, 154, 157, 163, 164, 173. *See also* Anglo-Saxons

Scandinavia, 42; Christian conversions and, 68, 75, 144; pagan sacral kingship and, 146–47, 148–49, 182; Vikings and, 67, 74, 75, 76, 176, 186

scepter, 15

Schiller, Johann Christoph Friedrich, 48

schismatic churches, 137. *See also* Donatists

Schlesinger, Walter, 149

Schmitt, Carl, 96

Scholasticism, 201

Scotland, 144, 152

seasonal festivals, 21, 147

Second Isaiah. *See* Deutero-Isaiah

Second Treatise of Government (Locke), 8

Second Vatican Council (1962–65), 217

secularity, 10, 119, 126; boundaries between sacred and, 202; Hebrew kingship and, 49–50; status of state and, 59, 130. *See also* church and state

Sedulius Scottus: *De rectoribus christianis (On Christian Rulers)*, 177, 178

seignorial economy. *See* manorial system

Seleucid kingdom, 32, 34

Senate, Roman, 37, 113

Senchas Már (Irish legal collection), 157
Seneca, 40
Servant of God, 43, 178
Seth (god), 44
Seven Books of Histories against the Pagans (Orosius), 115, 116, 117
shame culture, 5
Shang dynasty, 2
Shari'a (Islamic law), 81
shepherd: Christ as, 89, 95; king as, 26, 34, 58, 84, 85, 88, 95, 158, 172
Shiite Islam, 79, 82
Shilluk kingdom, 3
shogunate, 159, 196, 197
Sicily, 74, 76
Sidonians, 51
simony, 77, 210
sin, 43, 121, 123–25, 127, 128, 129, 133; free will and, 124; kingship mediation of, 171, 172; Last Judgment and, 123; punishment and, 115; sacraments and, 137
Sinai, 49
Siphnos, 30–31
Siricius, Pope, 207
Skinner, Quentin, xii
Slavs, 68, 71, 76
Smaragdus of St. Mihiel, 166; *Via regia (Royal Way)*, 177
social mores, 5
social status, 181, 202
Socrates, 6
Solomon, king of Israel, 16, 17, 41, 45, 51, 106, 158, 162; royal morality and, 178
Solomon's Temple (Jerusalem), 17, 45
Son of God, 87, 97, 116, 207
Son of Heaven, 108
"Son of Man," source of, 43
Sophia Palaeologa, 109
Sophists, 6
Soviet Union, 107–8
Spain, 114–17, 164, 179; Byzantine reconquest of, 98, 215; Islamic expansion into, 70, 74, 173; Vikings and, 74; Visigothic kingdom of, 68, 69, 152–53, 161, 173
Sparta, 15, 30
speculum principum ("mirror of princes"), 134, 177–78
spirituality, 8
state, x; ascending vs. descending structure of, 180–81, 182, 183, 209–10; Augustine's political theology on, 126, 128–30, 132–33, 134, 141; Christian accommodations to, 59–60, 61–62, 130; Christian thought and, 87; church's public functions in, 152; competing conceptions of, 180–82; as cosmic totality embodiment, 19; feudal institutions and, 188–99; fragmented political power in, 187; individual identity vs., xi, 6, 7, 8, 9, 10, 181; Islamic religious union with, 81; justice and, 132–33, 134; Kingdom of God as transcending, 57, 59–63; king's relationship with, 34; Lockean vs. Aristotelian concept of, 8, 9; as public entity, 178–79. *See also* church and state; polis; theocracy
Stephen II, Pope, 160
Stephen III, Pope, 165
Stobaeus, Joannes, 34
Stoics, 6, 7, 85, 86
Strayer, J. R., 188
Stubbs, William, 148
subjective freedom, principle of, 5
sub-Saharan Africa, 3, 19, 22, 30
Suevi, 68
suffering, human, 115
suffering Servant of God, 43
sultans, 80
Sumerian kingship, 2, 23, 24, 26, 28, 43
sun god, 25, 27, 28
Sunni Islam, 79, 81, 82
sun symbolism, 94
supernatural, ix; natural contrasted with, 181–82
supreme pontiff (papacy), 222
supreme pontiff (Roman republic), 34–35
Swaziland, 3
Sweden, 75, 144, 147, 149
Switzerland, 68
Sylvester I, Pope, 211
symbolism, 20, 28, 45
Symmachus, Pope, 210, 213
Symmachus (Roman prefect), petition of, 113, 114
syncretism: Christian evangelization and, 154–56; Druzes and, 82; Hebrew kingship and, 51–52
synods, 206, 212, 214, 217–18; freely elected popes and, 219
synoptic Gospels, 56
Syria, 2, 70; kingship, 2. *See also* Canaanites; Mesopotamia

taboo, 21
Tacitus: *Germania*, 148
Tanzania, 3
Taoism, 19
Tara, 145–46
Tatars, 108, 109
Tatian, 87
taxation: clerical exemption from, 201; without consent, 195, 199

Taylor, Charles, 5, 6
Temple at Jerusalem, 17, 45
temples, 2, 22, 27–28, 36; ancient Near East and, 45; Greek poleis and, 31
tenancies, 191, 192, 199
Tertullian, Quintus Septimus, 112, 124; *Apologeticus*, 112
Themistius, 90
theocracy: Augustine and, 136–37, 141, 142, 143, 163; Carolingians and, 159–63, 164, 165, 166, 178, 179, 182, 183; early Roman Christianity and, 152, 159; Islam and, 81; Israelites and, 53, 162; medieval Christian Europe and, 159, 163–76, 182; Ottonian and Salian kingships and, 183
Theodoric, king of the Ostrogoths, 69, 210
Theodosius I, emperor of Rome, 15–16, 97, 113, 114, 117, 118
theogony, 10
Theophrastus, 34
Thessalonica massacre, 113
Thing (German assembly), 148, 149
Third Reich, 96
Thirteenth Council of Toledo (783), 212
thought control, 9
Thuringians, 68
Thutmose, pharaoh of Egypt, 44
Thutmose III, pharaoh of Egypt, 25
Tiamat (sea monster), 28, 47
T'ien-tze (Son of Heaven), 108
Tigris and Euphrates basin, 2
Timaeus (Plato), 10, 20, 29
Timothy, 62, 112, 129
Titus, 62
Tokugawa shogunate, 159, 196
Toledo, 153, 155, 173, 212, 216
Toltec monarchy, 3
Tondriau, J., 32
Tonga, 30, 159
tonsure, 160, 201
totalitarianism. See absolutism
Toynbee, Arnold, 107–8
Tractates (Anonymous), 167–68, 170, 173, 175
trial by peers, 195
tribal relationships, 4; decline of, 190
tribute money, 58
Trier, archbishop of, 204–5
Trinitarianism, 68, 82, 86, 88; orthodoxy and, 96
Triumph of the Holy See and the Church over the Attacks of the Innovators, The (Cappellari), 203–4
Troeltsch, Ernst, 138
true justice (*vera justitia*), 132–33
tsar, 109–10
Turks. *See* Ottoman empire

two cities, 121–22, 126, 133; Augustinian theology of elect and, 125. *See also* civitas dei/civitas terrena
2 Corinthians, 208
2 Kings, 51
2 Samuel, 45–46, 49, 50
tyrants, 129

Uganda, 3
Ullmann, Walter, x, 180–82, 183, 208, 218
ultramontanism, 204
Umayyad caliphate, 80
umma (Muslim community), 81
unction: of bishops, 175; of monarchs, 160–61, 164, 165–66, 169, 170, 171, 172, 173, 182, 197
Uppsala school (biblical interpretation), 42, 43, 51, 56
urbanization, 2

Valentinian II, emperor of Rome, 113
Vandals, 68, 115, 159
Varican, 211
vassalage, 184–85, 190–96; bilateral contractual obligation of, 194–95, 196
vera justitia (true justice), 132–33
Via regia (Smaragdus), 177
vicar of Christ, 76, 166, 167, 208
vicar of St. Peter. *See* papacy
vicars of God, 217
Victor II, Pope, 219
Victorian scholarship, 4
Vikings, 67, 74, 75, 76, 176, 186
Virgil, 120
Virgin Mary, 154
virtue, 8
visible church: earthly city and, 126, 133; invisible church vs., 123, 125, 126, 139, 140; Kingdom of God and, 56; Roman Catholic Church as, 139, 140
Visigothic kingdom, 68, 69, 70, 71, 152–53, 155, 158; canon law and, 173, 178; Muslim destruction of, 153; Roman Catholic Church and, 215; royal anointing and, 161
Visigoths, sack of Rome by, 115, 118, 120–21
Vladimir I, prince of Kiev, 109–10
Vladimir II, tsar of Russia, 110
Voegelin, Eric, 6, 44
Volk assemblies, 148, 182, 195
Vulgate, 208

warriors: early medieval, 188, 191–92; as feudal aristocracy, 193; fidelity oaths of, 190, 194; kings as, 26, 30, 52
Weber, Max, 190

western Church. *See* Roman Catholic Church
West Frankia. *See* Franks
Wido of Osnabrück, 166
Williams, George H., 96, 169, 171, 172–73
Wipo (court chaplain), 166, 179
Woden (god), 149, 150, 155
Wolfram, Herwig, 150, 155–56
writing, invention of, 2

Xenephon, 34

Yahweh, 45, 46, 49, 50–51, 52, 158; supreme kingship of, 53–54. *See also* God
Yggdrasill (cosmic tree), 146
York, archbishop of, 167
Yorubaland monarchy, 3

Zealots, 54, 55, 58
Zeno, Byzantine emperor, 100
Zeus (god), 30, 33, 90
ziggurats, 22, 28